D1432748

American Money and the Weimar Republic

The Political Economy of International Change
John Gerard Ruggie, General Editor

Columbia University Press
New York   Guildford, Surrey
Copyright © 1986 Columbia University Press

Printed in the United States of America

Library of Congress Cataloging-in-Publication Data

McNeil, William C.
  American money and the Weimar Republic.

  (The Political economy of international
change)
  Bibliography: p.
  Includes index.
  1. Loans, American—Germany—History—20th century.
2. Germany—Economic conditions—1918–1945.
3. World War, 1914–1918—Reparations. 4. United
States—Foreign economic relations—Germany.
5. Germany—Foreign economic relations—United
States I. Title. II. Series: Political economy of
international change series.
HG3949.M38 1986   336.3′4′0943   85-29962

Library of Congress Cataloging-in-Publication Data

ISBN 0-231-06236-2

This book is Smyth-sewn.

to Vicki, Emily, and Nathan

Contents

Acknowledgments

In researching and writing any work of history, one is forced to call upon many archives for aid and assistance. I would like especially to thank the archivists at the Politisches Archiv des Auswartiges Amtes in Bonn, the Bundesarchiv in Koblenz, the Federal Reserve Bank in New York and the Gutehoffnungshutte in Oberhausen for generous and friendly assistance during my use of their sources.

The Fullbright-Hays/DAAD provided financial support for the initial research for my dissertation and the Volkswagen Foundation and the Institut fur Europaische Geschichte in Mainz provided a grant that allowed the further research that helped turn the dissertation into a book. A fellowship from the American Council of Learned Societies permitted the time off from teaching required to rewrite the manuscript and Barnard College paid for retyping and indexing of the book. To all of these organizations I want to express my grateful appreciation.

I am also pleased to acknowledge my debt to the many friends and colleagues who read and commented on all or parts of the manuscript in its many incarnations. Richard Abrams, David Bailey, Theodore Balderston, Henry Fetter, Robert Hath-

Introduction

On the 10th of October 1924 the New York money market bid so enthusiastically for the American share of the Dawes Loan that the bonds were nearly sold out by the end of the day. They were soon ten times over subscribed, and a new era in international finance had begun.[1] The United States had emerged from the First World War as the major source of investment capital in the world and European states that had once made loans to America were now reduced to supplicants for that American money. But Europe's political and economic instability kept prudent American investors from lending their money abroad until 1924. With the Dawes Plan's promise of an end to Europe's problems, Americans rushed to gain the big profits offered by overseas investments. Outside of Canada, Germany became the greatest single recipient of American money. This is a study of how Germans and Americans attempted to use this money between 1925 and 1929.

By 1924, a decade of war, revolution, and hyper-inflation had destroyed Germany's once strong capital market.[2] What little money was available commanded real interest rates in the range of 50 percent per year. Germans looked to New York to relieve this financial pressure. Between 1925 and 1930,

American private bankers lent nearly three billion dollars to German borrowers—over twice the $1.3 billion Germany received from the United States under the Marshal Plan after World War II. In both Germany and the United States, the loans became critical tools in efforts to define a broad range of international and domestic policy options.

Within Germany the channels cut by the new capital imports reveal the lines of political power in the "Golden Years" of the Weimar Republic. Since Germany had little experience in borrowing abroad, the anticipation of capital imports at rates cheap by German standards set in motion a flurry of political jockeying to determine which groups would have access to the money. Conservatives, industrialists, and agrarians insisted that the foreign manna must be used to increase the nation's productive capacity. In other words, it must be reserved for their own use. Social reformers in municipal governments, labor unions, and left-liberal political parties countered with the argument that investments in public works such as housing, roads, utilities, and an expansion of the nation's welfare system were more pressing needs of a German society suffering from ten years of social, economic, and political upheaval. Since the foreign loans were vital to financing these alternate visions of Germany's future, an examination of how they were used helps us understand the complex politics of Weimar's middle years.

The American loans to Germany not only raised fundamental domestic issues for Germany, they also became entangled in German foreign policy planning. The loans created strong ties between the United States and Germany. German policymakers understood that these ties might be exploited to create a kind of financial partnership between the United States and Germany or they might become a dangerous international liability that could reduce Germany to financial subordination to American bankers.

As German government spending increased in the late twenties, and as the spending became more dependent on the capital imports, German foreign and domestic policies came into conflict. Attempts to stabilize the internal economy made Germany more dependent on foreign loans, and this restricted the policy options open to the German Foreign Office. At the same time, attempts to use the loans to achieve foreign policy goals restricted the options available to stabilize the domestic economy. The policy choices made between 1925 and 1929 shaped Germany's response to the Great Depression. Examination of these links between foreign and domestic implications of the American loans and their impact on German policies form the core of this study.

For the United States, the foreign lending that emerged in the 1920s represented America's first use of the financial power it had won in the First World War. But how would the new world power use its wealth? Revisionist historians writing in the 1950s and 60s concluded that America used its power to dominate the world economy in the service of narrow business self-interests.[3] More recently, a more sympathetic consensus has formed among American historians who agree that the United States was indeed active in European affairs but argue that American policy was formulated to help stabilize European economies, not exploit them.[4]

American economic power in the 1920s was a product of its rich capital markets. Examination of how the United States controlled and used its capital exports gets to the core of American foreign economic policy. How did the United States determine where its money would be used and how consciously did the American government or banks regulate the loans with a view toward specific long-range goals? What do the loans tell us about the reality of American isolationism or interventionism in the 1920s? How much influence did the American lender have over the economic and social policies of the German borrower? The answers to these questions have broad implications for understanding one of the fundamental international phenomena of the modern world. The relationship between borrowers and lenders and the obligations assumed by each will either help stabilize the world economy, or, as the reality of the 1920s demonstrated, will make a major contribution toward destabilizing the world economy. In examining how the United States set its international financial policy in the twenties and how those policies influenced German options, we can construct a picture of the traditions which set the framework for future American policy.

Efforts to control the foreign loans and direct them toward either privately or publicly owned enterprise also became part of a broader effort to define the role of the state in modern, capitalist societies. Would state spending help stabilize the national economy and promote public welfare, or would it actually lead to greater instability? The social and economic dislocations suffered by Germany during and after the First World War brought these issues into focus sooner and more violently than in other industrialized countries. Yet the efforts to find an acceptable level and range of government influence in the national economy had to be faced by all capitalist states, and echoes of the debates aired in Germany in the nineteen twenties can still be heard in industrial countries in the nineteen eighties.

Chapter 1
Power and Politics in the Weimar Republic

The First World War and the crisis following German defeat in 1918 altered many of the basic structures of the German economy and German society. When revolution broke out in November 1918, it appeared that capitalism would be destroyed and a socialist society erected in its place. But the socialists proved too timid to consolidate their gains, and the capitalists proved more resilient than they had initially appeared. By 1924, conservative industrial-agrarian elites regained a degree of power which in 1918–19 had seemed to be forever lost.

In late 1923 and early 1924, businessmen won major concessions as Germany ended nearly a decade of inflation and struggled to stabilize its currency and economy. Industries that had feared nationalization in 1918 now were being courted and protected by a state that was more concerned with increasing productivity than income redistribution. Important social reforms which had been antithetic to industry, especially the government guaranteed eight-hour day, were suspended and owners were given greater discretion over factory operations. The industrialist could once again begin to feel master of his own house.

The combination of this rollback of social reform on the one side and emphasis on industrial production on the other demonstrates the degree to which "bourgeois" society was saved and reformed in Weimar Germany.[1] Yet the demonstration of this "conservative" victory in 1923–25 is far from the end of the story for the Weimar Republic. Excessive fascination with this victory can obscure the drama of later years. The captains of industry might appear to have been safe and secure in the view of modern historians, but in their own view they remained locked in mortal combat with the forces of the Left which so recently had appeared ready to destroy them. If they had briefly gained from the flood tide of political fortunes, they were soon to feel the ebb as well.

To understand the forces that shaped German policy in the second half of the 1920s, we need to bring together three divergent strands in German political evolution. In looking at German political institutions in the first section of this chapter, it becomes apparent that German capital shortages played a central role in setting the stage for the social conflicts that dominated the Weimar Republic. The second section examines the origins and impact of this capital shortage. The final section explores the role of the Dawes Plan in resolving the conflicts between German foreign and domestic policies.

Institutions in Stalemate: Germany
Between Inflation and Depression, 1924–1929

In Germany, as in the United States, government is divided into three tiers: federal, state, and local. Under the Bismarckian empire, state governments had retained near sovereignty in almost all areas except foreign policy. The Reich government was even dependent on the states for income, since the states retained control over most direct taxes. At the same time, municipal governments enjoyed a great deal of independence from state control since they collected a large share of their own tax revenues.

Under the Weimar constitution the federal government assumed far more power and responsibility than it had under the Empire. These gains were made largely at the expense of the state governments. The financial reforms introduced in 1919 by Matthias Erzberger granted the major taxing authority to the federal government and effectively destroyed local financial autonomy. Under the new arrangements, the Reich collected most taxes, including the income tax. It then granted the state governments a certain percentage of the tax revenues—a sum that varied from year to year. The states, in turn, passed on a specified share of the centrally collected taxes to the city governments.

Despite the decline in state power, the states retained enough influence to exercise a veto over some federal policies inimical to their interests. The state of Prussia, with over half the German population within its borders, was by far the most powerful of the state governments. Its ruling coalition remained oriented toward the left even after the Great Coalition collapsed at the Reich level in the fall of 1923. This had been an uncomfortable ruling block stretching from the conservative, industrial oriented German People's Party on the right to the Social Democratic Party on the left. From 1924 to 1928, the Social Democrats were excluded from participation in the national government, and Germany was ruled by shifting coalitions of the right. In Prussia, however, the Social Democrats continued to play a vital and even dominant role in the state government. From this vantage point, moderating pressure was persistently applied to Reich policies—as often as not through offers of cooperation in return for reformist modifications of federal laws. Beyond Prussia, Bavaria led the smaller states in a losing battle to impede the centralization of power in Berlin. Often attacking Prussia along with the Reich, the Bavarians offered enough resistance to Reich policies to delay important decisions or postpone reforms.

In contrast to the declining power of the states, the prerogatives of the city governments actually increased as they were charged with greater responsibility for unemployment compensation, welfare relief, and social overhead investment.

Their political influence also increased as they strengthened their national organization to lobby for their special interests. The *deutsche Städtetag* and the city governments it represented played a central part in determining Germany's social policies in the years between the inflation and the great depression.

Traditionally dominated by local business leaders, city governments in the 1920s tended to respond sympathetically to the welfare needs of their citizens. In the larger cities, coalitions of small businessmen, civic leaders, and Social Democrats formed alliances striving to promote municipal enterprise and civic improvement. Under the leadership of strong mayors such as Konrad Adenauer in Cologne, Gustav Böss in Berlin, and Ludwig Landmann in Frankfurt a.M., the *Städtetag* and the cities became a major force for a more generous social policy.[2]

In the process of reforming the relationships between the various levels of government, an unfortunate paradox emerged. Local governments were not responsible for collecting taxes, but they were responsible for an expanded range of welfare programs. In meeting their responsibilities, city governments may have been overly generous in their spending decisions because they no longer had to raise the taxes themselves to cover their expenses. Instead, they could demand that the Reich transfer a larger share of the national tax receipts to them to cover the mounting municipal spending.[3] The potential for trouble in the financial relations between municipalities and the Reich was made even greater by the disastrous state of municipal finance in the wake of the inflation. High rates of urban unemployment and a massive immigration from rural areas (Berlin's population grew by 100,000 persons per year throughout the twenties) created ever mounting pressures on an already inadequate housing supply and outdated city services.[4]

In one way, the inflation itself had actually been beneficial to public finances. Public debts, both national and municipal, had been nearly wiped out as old bonds became all but worthless. The cities were particularly helped by this, since as "debt free" public administrations, they became a very attractive investment for foreign money lenders. They were also desperately eager for foreign capital, since years of neglect in public investment and increased population created a backlog of demands for improvements in electric, water, and gas supplies, roads, street cars, public housing, and less essential projects such as theaters, museums, and sports facilities. The financial needs of municipal governments were made all the worse by the fact that during the final phase of the inflation municipal income had fallen to almost nothing, nearly bankrupting many city governments. After the stabilization, their position was further hurt when the municipal share of the income tax was reduced.[5] When state incomes were also cut by the central government, they could respond, as Prussia did, by taking the receipts from the sales tax away from the cities and adding it to state income.[6] Thus city governments had growing responsibilities thrust on them throughout the twenties, while their capacity to pay for their spending was steadily eroded.

The combination of municipal financial need and the fact that the inflation had eliminated their debts made cities a natural recipient of loans once the German market was reopened to foreign capital in 1925. The resultant borrowing of German cities on the foreign and especially the American market soon became the center of bitter political controversy. German industrialists resented the use of scarce and cheap foreign capital for what they regarded as socialist purposes. In the fight to regulate public borrowing abroad, the bitter social struggles which in other areas remained quiet during the mid-twenties raged on without interruption. But this time the issue also took on important international repercussions. By increasing its foreign debt, some international financial experts feared that Germany was also reducing its ability to meet its reparations payments. Thus, the domestic social struggle surrounding the public loans soon became embroiled in the complex reparations debates which often dominated international relations in the 1920s.

In the same way that German decision making was complicated by disagreements and competition among the Reich, the states, and the cities, so too was it made more difficult by

ernment spending increase in order to stimulate the economy and save industry from the full effects of the business cycle.

The Economics Ministry was led by men who tended to be less conservative than those in the Finance Ministry. The extremely influential ministerial director, Hans Schäffer, even expressed Socialist sympathies while working for the capitalist order. Julius Curtius, who served as Economics Minister from 1925 to 1929 maintained close ties to leaders in all branches of industry, but tended to identify ideologically with the pragmatists in the finishing and electrical industries.[8] From this position he struggled to moderate the demands of heavy industry while promoting industrial growth and profits. Furthermore, Curtius persistently fought to avoid any threat of a new economic crisis in Germany, and this stand forced him steadily to extend the range of government policy in the areas of economic stimulation and stabilization. More than any other agency, the Economics Ministry under Curtius saw and understood the links between foreign and domestic policies. This placed the ministry in the middle of the social conflict between right and left and led it to resolutely urge moderation, caution, and patience in formulating German reparations policies in order to avoid any disruption of the internal economic order.

The Labor Ministry provided the most active demand within the Cabinet for expanded government aid to the economy, and it acted as the left-wing balance to the Finance Ministry's inherent conservatism. Even under the "bourgeois" governments after the stabilization, the Labor Ministry remained a strong advocate of union rights and social welfare legislation. During the long tenure of Heinrich Brauns as Labor Minister, the Reich government consistently cast its weight in support of wage settlements and state support for the economy, which enraged German industrialists.

Brauns' power was based on the bizarre position and constituency of his Catholic Center Party. A confessional party containing representatives of all social groups, the Center Party was steadily strained to hold its diverse elements together. It had to find policies that could satisfy its business supporters without alienating Catholic workers. Throughout the middle twenties, Brauns was able to win concessions for the left, because without those concessions the party would lose its large labor vote and break apart. At the same time, Brauns was able to use this leverage within the Center Party to move even conservative governments toward the left because the Center Party was vital to every government in the Weimar era. It could and did form alliances with parties either to the left or right, and its basic needs had to be met by every government that wished to preserve a parliamentary majority. Even under the bourgeois governments, conservatives had to bite their tongues and permit the Labor Ministry its concessions to the left.

In formulating and advocating certain domestic, social, and economic policies, each of these three ministries—Finance, Economics, and Labor—took positions that directly influenced German foreign policy. Time after time, German reparations policy was confounded or promoted by domestic social and economic decisions. Time after time, these three ministries and the Foreign Office engaged in disputes that inexorably tied foreign to domestic policy.

It soon became clear that the critical element linking reparations policy and domestic policy was the flow of foreign capital into the German economy. By stimulating the economy, the foreign capital promised to ease the strains that agitated the Economics and Labor Ministries. At the same time, the inflow of capital gave Germany the foreign currency it needed to fulfill the Dawes Plan without putting excessive pressure on the Finance Ministry to balance the budget. But the loans carried dangers with them as well. By permitting deficit spending, the loans frustrated allied demands that Germany balance its budget as proof of its commitment to a fulfillment policy. They also created the fear that if taken in excessive measure they might destroy Germany's ability to formulate an independent foreign policy by making it dependent on foreign bankers. Finally, in the aftermath of the inflation, Germans worried that the loans might so expand the money supply that a new inflation would result. This fear of inflation and the antagonism felt by the international banking community to government deficits drew a final actor into the formation of German foreign and domestic policymaking.

During the inflation period, the German central bank, the Reichsbank, received most of the blame for the destruction of the German currency. By running the printing presses non-stop, the Reichsbank made the inflation possible by supplying unlimited credit to the government and to private industry. With stabilization came the conviction that the Reichsbank had to be completely freed from government control so that it could never again be forced to condone such an irresponsible credit expansion. The obvious fact that monetary policy is an essential part of economic and social policy meant that the new and independent central bank would become a major political force. When longtime Reichsbank president Rudolf Havenstein suddenly died just as the mark was being stabilized in November 1923, it was clear that his successor would have important political influence in determining how the burdens of stabilization would be distributed.

The directors of the Reichsbank immediately seized the initiative and urged the appointment of Karl Helfferich, former Secretary of the Treasury in the old imperial government, to the post of Reichsbank president. A brilliant economist and financier, Helfferich was also one of the most outspoken nationalists in Germany. His violent and vicious denunciation of Walter Rathenau came only days before Rathenau's assassination and is considered by many to have been an important factor leading to his murder. In spite of Helfferich's politics, or more probably because of them, the Reichsbank directors wrote Reich president Ebert that Helfferich was "the only man" who was qualified to become Reichsbank president. They were so confident that he would be selected that they had already talked to Helfferich about taking the job and were pleased to report that he had agreed to do it.[9]

The only serious alternative to Helfferich was the recently appointed currency commissioner Hjalmar Schacht, who was being vigorously promoted by Foreign Minister Gustav Stresemann. British leaders aided Schacht's candidacy when they warned German officials that selection of Helfferich would be suicidal for Germany. If appointed, Helfferich's reputation as an Anglophobic reactionary would ensure that no Briton would loan so much as a penny to Germany. As for Schacht, the

British were not thrilled but felt that at least it would be possible for him to work with the Bank of England. Schacht, the British felt, "even if not a Social Democrat, is at least known to have good banking experience and a pleasant personality."[10] The Social Democrats themselves jumped on the Schacht bandwagon in the assumption that anyone would be better than Helfferich.[11] The state governments, represented in the Council of States (Reichsrat), also supported Schacht and in fact even approved his appointment before the Cabinet could reach a decision. Under this pressure, when the Cabinet could find no majority for Helfferich, it felt compelled to accept Prussia's proposal that Schacht be named the new Reichsbank president.[12]

Even as the Cabinet prepared to accept Schacht as Reichsbank president, the Reichsbank directors wrote Chancellor Marx insisting that Schacht was completely unqualified to hold the office. His theoretical understanding, they argued, was nonexistent; he was unreliable, and he was so vain that he took credit for the successful stabilization policies which he had in reality opposed when they were being considered. To top off their opposition, the bank directors accused Schacht of dishonesty. They charged that while working for the government in occupied Belgium during the war, Schacht had used his official position to help the Dresdener Bank in currency speculation.[13] The charges were repeated by the newspaper *Kreuz-Zeitung,* the mouthpiece of the conservative German Nationalist Party, indicating that at least at this time Schacht was no friend of German conservatives.[14] The moving force behind the attack on Schacht was none other than Karl Helfferich himself.[15] The government investigated the currency manipulation charges against Schacht and reported that it found nothing to impeach his honor.[16] With little apparent alternative, the government stuck to its decision to name Schacht Reichsbank president. In time it was to learn that if the charge of his illegal activities was unfounded, the charges that he was pathologically ambitious and vain were all too true.

As Reichsbank president, Hjalmar Schacht soon became one of the most powerful political figures in Germany. When initially appointed, Schacht was closer to the left than to the right. While acting as Currency Commissioner, prior to his appointment to the Reichsbank, he had thoroughly alienated German businessmen. His first official act had been to order the Reichsbank not to accept the emergency paper currency issued by many large industries and cities during the inflation. As he later wrote, "This first measure was quite sufficient to make me very unpopular both with the municipalities and with the large scale industrial undertakings. For the latter, the fact that the blow was delivered by a man whom they regarded as one of themselves, the director of a big bank, added insult to injury."[17] As Reichsbank president, his tight money policies after April 1924 further contributed to his difficulties with conservatives and industry. But, in time, Schacht not only became closer to German industrialists and conservatives, he became a leader of their cause. This transformation was only a gradual process and Schacht always maintained some distance between himself and business leaders. In 1924 and 1925 he was still resented for his tight money policies, but by 1926 his policies, including the credit stop, were being defended by industrialists such as Paul Silverberg, who insisted that the "oppressive" unemployment caused by Reichsbank policy had been necessary to rationalize the economy.[18]

Schacht's drift to the right became official when he resigned from the Democratic Party in 1926 over its stand on the property settlement with the German princes.[19] Schacht refused to join those who wanted to confiscate property held by the princes, and declared that even though the party urged compensation for the confiscated estates, its stand was insufficiently supportive of private property. His increasingly vicious attacks on public spending and foreign borrowing cemented Schacht's alliance with the right. A complex man whose motives and policies are taken up in some detail in following chapters, Schacht was driven by determination to preserve the value of the currency, enhance his own reputation and power, and strengthen Germany's economy and international position. That his vision of what these goals should be was often eclectic and fluctuated widely from moment to moment makes any simple classification of Schacht on the political spectrum exceedingly difficult. During the mid-twenties, Schacht tied his policies and demands to the vision of orthodox fiscal policies supported by the international banking community. His power in German politics was greatly strengthened by these international connections and especially by his close personal friendship with Bank of England governor Montagu Norman. Yet his increasingly nationalistic and even unbalanced behavior in the late twenties and his economic manipulations for the Nazi regime in the thirties demonstrate that he was not bound by the rules of gold standard orthodoxy and instead employed economic doctrine as a tool of his political demands.

Although Schacht's policies were often helpful to private business, he never really became fully tied to the industrial elites. As late as October 1928, directors of the Reich Association of Industrialists needed reassurance that Schacht was sympathetic to their needs. Association Director Ludwig Kastl felt compelled, after a conversation with Schacht, to assure the other directors that there was a wide range of agreement between industry and Schacht. In particular, Kastl was pleased to report that the Reichsbank president recognized that the primary goal of economic and financial policy was the rebuilding of industrial capital within Germany.[20] Yet, in 1930 when Schacht was removed as Reichsbank president, few business leaders mourned his loss.

In the mid twenties, the emerging power of the Reichsbank over German monetary policy, added a new element to Germany's political process. Whereas the various government ministries and their social constituents fought for control over the national product, the monetary authority began to set limits on the size of that product. Germany's capital weakness restricted the policy options open to the government and increased the influence of the Central bank and the foreign lenders who could provide the funds needed to fuel the economy. From 1924 to 1929, German leaders would learn that international and monetary restraints provided a final and vital influence over Germany's domestic political struggles.[21]

German Capital and the Economy
after the Inflation

By late 1923, nearly a decade of war, revolution, and inflation had virtually destroyed Germany's reserves of liquid capital. One historian has estimated that a century of savings had been wiped out and that Germany's capital reserves in 1923 had been reduced to the level found at the beginning of the nineteenth century.[22] The vast majority of what little money remained was loaned out for seven days or less at annual interest rates running from 45 percent to 87 percent.[23] Unable and unwilling to commit funds to long-term investment, Germans found themselves looking longingly to foreign sources of capital. Exactly how much Germany borrowed abroad in the next five years will never be known. Some loans were issued publicly and many banks were forced to reveal their private loans. But large volumes were also lent between strictly private parties, and no small amount of German capital was sent abroad against the grain of the predominant capital inflow.

By the middle of 1930, Germans had floated long-term bond issues abroad worth about 10.8 billion RM, or $2.6 billion at the exchange rate of 4.2 RM to the dollar. Of this amount, $1.25 billion or nearly 50 percent came from the United States, while British and Dutch markets each took about 12 percent of the German bonds.[24]

German short-term borrowing abroad is much more difficult to calculate since money was moved among businesses and banks with no public accountability. The best current guess is that by mid-1930, Germans had taken short-term loans abroad of 15.5–16 billion RM. America's share of these loans is open to speculation, but the international committee of experts called to assess German banking conditions after the financial collapse in the summer of 1931 estimated that Americans held 37 percent of the short-term loans the committee was able to uncover.[25] If this share held true for the funds they could not identify, it would mean that Americans held nearly 6 billion RM ($1.4 billion) in German paper.

The importance of this capital movement may be lost on modern readers used to international debts ranging into the hundreds of billions of dollars. But when we consider that Germany had accumulated a foreign debt by 1930 of 26 billion RM at a time when Germany's net national income was 75 billion RM per year, the importance of the foreign loans becomes more clear. Between 1925 and 1928 as much as one third of Germany's total investment may have been financed by capital imports, of which by far the largest share came from the United States.[26] At the same time, the German loans were an important share of the American capital market where they represented 20 percent of the foreign bonds sold in the United States in the five years following the Dawes Plan.[27] Clearly Germany's capital weakness had wide-ranging consequences.

The process by which Germany fell from one of the world's great capital markets in 1913 to a virtual financial pauper by 1924 is part of a complex web involving war, inflation, monetary stabilization, and reparations. The very process of wartime consumption and finance from 1914 to 1918 set the stage for Germany's future financial weakness. Determined to pay for the war without inordinate tax increases, the Reich government began a systematic monetary expansion which quickly undercut the value of the mark. At the same time, huge investments in war industries diverted resources from more "normal" investment. Over the course of the war, this led to deterioration in agricultural productivity, a backlog in demand for public utilities and housing, and a paucity of investment in nonwar related industries. By 1918, German investment needs far exceeded prewar levels just to make up for the lack of investment during the war. Losing the war compounded these weaknesses, since Germany had hoped to base its postwar economic recovery on profitable economic treaties which would exploit the resources of conquered countries. Instead, Germany lost its foreign investments, most of its revenue-earning merchant marine, and had to begin paying reparations for damage done to the Allies. All these factors created an overstrained capital market which was totally destroyed by the postwar inflation.

The German inflation was inaugurated by the financial and fiscal policies pursued during the war, but did not reach its dramatic conclusion until 1922–23. By the time the mark was stablized in October 1923, it took 4.2 trillion marks to buy one dollar. In more normal cases, economists would argue that the process of inflation alone cannot harm the total supply of capital available to an economy. For every middle-class investor whose savings were wiped out by the inflation, there had to be a borrower whose debts were reduced by the same amount. Thus, if one man lost because the money he lent to a home buyer was repaid at a tiny fraction of its original value, the man whose debt was so dramatically reduced gained and presumably now had fewer debts and more savings. At exactly what point this simple equilibrium breaks down is not obvious, but that it failed in the German inflation cannot be doubted.

The explanation for the capital shortage may lie in two sectors of the economy, which suffered the most severe losses in the course of the inflation, and which were crucial to the maintenance of Germany's monetary liquidity. On the one hand, German banks were dealt a smashing blow by the inflation, and on the other, the rentier class of moderately wealthy savers saw its paper assets virtually wiped out.[28]

German banks, in a process that became familiar in the 1970s, were slow to adjust to the reality of a long and erratic inflation. With surprising uniformity, German private banks lost nearly two thirds of their reserves and 70 percent of their joint stock values between 1913 and 1924.[29] Of particular interest, a study of one South German bank reveals just when these losses were suffered. The bank in question had, like other German banks, lost 70 percent of its stock capital by 1925. Given the total loss as 100 percent, it lost 27.5 percent by the end of 1917. During 1918, the last year of the war and the time of the early revolution, it lost 16.5 percent more. In 1919, the period of instability after the revolution, it suffered the most severe losses—39.9 percent of its total loss. And finally, from 1920 to 1923, which includes the period of the hyper-inflation, it lost 16.1 percent more. Thus, the most severe banking losses came, not in the hyperinflation, but during the earlier period of inflation combined with violent social upheaval and revolution.[30]

Although all banks suffered during the inflation, the greatest losses were in savings deposited with the publicly owned savings banks. The savings banks played a central role in providing credit for home construction and small industry, so when their deposits collapsed from 18,970 million RM in 1913 to only 25 million in 1923, it meant that credit was simply unavailable to these important sectors of the German economy.[31]

The loss of reserves suffered by German banks eliminated the most readily available source of liquid capital. In addition, after the stabilization, the bankers compounded the illiquidity as they attempted to rebuild their lost reserves. By artificially holding interest rates high and extracting large profits from a small volume of loans, the private bankers rebuilt their reserves but did further harm to the economy. In pursuing these policies, the banks were aided by the Reichsbank's refusal to expand the money supply.[32]

When we add to this loss of bank reserves, the losses suffered by the traditional German class of savers, the rentier, the picture of the capital scarcity begins to be completed. With liquid assets gone and German savers wary of committing themselves to long-term investments for fear of a renewed inflation, Germany was slow to rebuild the assets lost during the inflation.[33]

Beyond the loss of monetary assets, real capital was also lost in the so-called "flight into real values." As the inflation picked up momentum, and as Germans began to realize that it would not be reversed, they searched for material goods to hold which would retain some value. Savers rushed to buy material goods that had no appeal except as a hedge against inflation. Perhaps an even more insidious result was the inflation's influence on the investment decisions of businessmen. Under normal conditions, a rational businessman will base his rate and area of investment primarily on his anticipation of future sales and profits. Under a rapid inflation, the rational businessman is likely to find that other considerations are more important. Long-range planning becomes impossible and greater emphasis must be placed on immediate purchases of goods which will hold their values better than currency (almost anything). The result, as often discussed by historians of the period, will be massive "misinvestment." Investment which makes

great. The British government refused to see the issue in such narrow terms. Instead, it argued that the real problem was to find a means of balancing the German budget, restoring Germany's credit, and ensuring the stability of the mark. When it became apparent that the Franco-British disagreement might abort the conference before it had even begun, the two sides agreed to form two committees: one charged to investigate the flight of capital, the other to set out conditions for stabilizing the German budget and credit.[47] From the beginning, British, German, and American officials assumed that the committee investigating how to balance the budget would be the most important, and it was the chairman of that committee, the Chicago banker Charles G. Dawes who would give his name to the entire plan emerging from the conference.

Although the American government encouraged the new conference of experts and provided State and Commerce Department officials to help the American representatives, the government itself refused to accept any responsibility for negotiating a financial settlement. Specifically, the United States refused to admit any links between the war debts owed the United States by its former allies and the reparations that the allies were demanding from Germany.

When the United States agreed to have American citizens participate in the reparations discussions, Germany's ambassador to the United States, Otto Wiedfeldt, tried to explain the motives behind this new policy. American intervention, he wrote, would find its origins in America's idealism, its own self-interest, and in no small degree in the efforts of the Republican Party to achieve a major foreign policy success before the 1924 presidential election. In dealing with the Americans, he warned, one had always to be careful to play to their concept of honor and legality, while also making use of the Americans' self-image as hard-nosed, practical men. This had to be done by emphasizing how much the United States stood to gain by a stable, prosperous Europe. Above all, Germans should remember that "it must be something grand, yes, even colossal which the American government undertakes. Just as earlier they wanted to save the world for democracy, so now Europe must be saved from collapse."[48] Although Ambassador

Wiedfeldt overestimated how directly involved the American government would become, his analysis of American motives and self-conception seems squarely on the mark.

The Dawes Committee met from January to April 1924. Under the tactical leadership of Owen Young, the head of the General Electric Company, months of hard negotiating led to a compromise that all representatives could support.[49] Under the Dawes Plan, German reparations payments would begin at a very low level and Germany would be given a large international loan to stabilize its currency and pay for some of the initial reparations. Over a four-year period, the reparations payments would rise to an annual sum of 2.5 billion RM by 1928, and be maintained at that level for an undetermined time into the future.

Even as the plan was being accepted, officials in the British Treasury, German government, and American banking circles did not believe that Germany could actually ever pay the sums set out by the Dawes Plan. In recognition of this fear and believing that no one could foresee how much Germany would be able to pay, the experts tried to create a system flexible enough to respond to any eventuality. If Germany proved extremely prosperous, an escalator clause called for payments above the 2.5 billion mark limit. In the event that any complications arose in the system, an Agent General for Reparations was charged with the responsibility of overseeing the plan's operation. The Agent General was to ensure that Germany paid the maximum amount possible without threatening the stability of the German currency. Occupying a key position, his primary responsibility was to ensure that the allied powers received every cent possible from Germany. But he was also charged with protecting Germany from the danger of a new inflation inaugurated by excessive reparations payments. As the balance wheel between the two sides, the Agent General would be the mediator of European affairs under the Dawes Plan.

The experts understood that in order to pay reparations without creating a new inflation, Germany would have to create a budget surplus large enough to cover the costs of reparations. In fact, Germany's primary responsibility under the Dawes Plan was to raise its taxes high enough to provide a budget surplus. It would use this surplus to deposit German marks with the Reparations Agent, who would actually transfer the funds to the allied governments. As a guarantee that the German government could not finance deficits by forcing the Reichsbank to issue paper currency, the bank was reconstructed and made independent of the government. With the Reichsbank free to determine monetary policy and the Reparations Agent charged with ensuring that Germany paid as much as possible, the German government's freedom to determine its fiscal policy would be severely restricted.

The power and delicate position of the Reparations Agent as "King" of the Dawes Plan meant that it was essential to find the right man to fill the job. To guarantee that Germany loyally did its part to meet the terms of the plan, he would have to review German tax and spending policies. Yet, since these policies would be determined by Germany's domestic social-political needs and by its foreign policy goals, this could and would lead to bitter disputes between the Agent General and German officials. As German Economic Minister Edward Hamm advised the Reich Chancellor, "There is no legal security against a disloyal transfer policy." The success of the plan, he stressed, rested on the moral authority of the Reparations Agent.[50]

Since continued American involvement in the Dawes Plan was essential to Europe's stability, it was assumed from the beginning that an American would be given the job as Agent General. From the German perspective, the best candidate must not only have a strong personality and international reputation, he also had to have close ties to American bankers and government leaders. Since German officials were sure that the Dawes Plan would soon fail, it would be up to the Agent General to convince the world that Germany had done its best to fulfill the plan but could not do so.[51]

To find a leader with the authority to bring the Dawes Plan to life, Bank of England governor Montagu Norman turned to the most powerful banker in America to name a candidate.[52] J. P. Morgan had financed the allied cause during the Great War, had worked to stabilize the international monetary system after the war, and now was called upon to support this last attempt to bring the financial catastrophes of the war to a satisfactory conclusion. Jack Morgan himself and the principle partners in the firm, Dwight Morrow, Thomas Lamont, and Russell Leffingwell, all had serious reservations about the plan.[53] Despite these doubts, Morrow, perhaps the most brilliant of the partners and who would later go on to serve as American ambassador to Mexico and United States Senator from New Jersey, agreed to take the position as Agent General. The nomination foundered on erroneous reports that the Germans would not accept a Morgan partner as the overseer of their economy and the Coolidge administration's fear of alienating German-American voters.[54] With Morrow out of the running, the administration and Morgan partners nearly found themselves unable to agree on a candidate. In the end, the selection fell on a young banker and financial expert named Seymour Parker Gilbert. Only thirty-two years old in 1924, Gilbert's youth was his major liability.[55] Germans worried that he lacked the international stature they were counting on to protect their interests. Furthermore, the government feared that "the German public will find it hard to put up with such a young man" having a large say in German affairs.[56] The realization that only a hard compromise had resulted in Gilbert's selection and that a real protest could upset the whole delicate structure of the reparations agreement led the government to drop its protest.[57]

A protégé of former Assistant Secretary of the Treasury and current partner in J. P. Morgan, Russell Leffingwell, Parker Gilbert had begun his career in the Treasury when Woodrow Wilson was President and stayed on to become an intimate of Andrew Mellon under the Coolidge administration. As Leffingwell would write, "The fact that he was able to render brilliant service under two administrations, democratic and republican, is a demonstration of his ability to subordinate political to financial and economic considerations."[58] As a financial expert with an overriding belief that world financial stability depended on fiscal responsibility and a balanced budget, Gilbert was the perfect man to make the "experts" plan work.

Brilliant, determined, and strong willed, Parker Gilbert would aggressively pursue his duty during his five years as Agent General. Yet German officials, especially those in the Finance Ministry, often found it difficult to work with Gilbert. Finance Minister Heinrich Köhler, who engaged in bitter disagreements with Gilbert described him: "Reserved and taciturn, the tall lanky man with the impenetrable features appeared considerably older than he really was and . . . made an eery impression." "Here," in Germany, Köhler went on, "he did nothing but work without interruption. No theater, no concert, no other cultural events intruded into his life. . . . The 'Plan' must function. To this everything else was subordinated."[59]

Since Gilbert apparently did not learn German in his five years in Berlin, all business between him and German officials had to be conducted in English or through translators. This left Gilbert isolated within German society and created awkward confrontations when English and German transcripts of conferences did not match.[60] Conducting business in English was also not always easy. Another Finance Minister, and one who did not have a personal axe to grind, found Gilbert only a little more agreeable than Köhler had. Describing his first meetings with Gilbert, Paul Moldenhauer wrote, "These, like subsequent [meetings] were never pleasant. Parker Gilbert had a peculiar way of speaking. He spoke with a mixture of awkwardness and arrogance, mumbling the words so that one could hardly understand his English."[61] British officials tended to share this view. British Ambassador Sir Ronald Lindsay believed that Gilbert found verbal exchanges difficult and often "adopts a self-protective attitude of abstract detachment . . . He is really a bad man at verbal discussion and I should think he would be at his worst at a conference."[62] Despite these complaints, German officials knew that Gilbert offered their best hope for proving to the world that reparations would have to be reduced. During the Dawes Plan years, Gilbert would become one of the most powerful actors in world financial affairs, and he would demonstrate that, despite his youth, he could use his banker's view of the world to shape the framework of the continuing reparations debate.

As they contemplated the Dawes Plan, Germans found a little that they liked and much that they did not. The early years of low payments were attractive, and the assumption that the Reparations Agent would protect them from unreasonable allied demands offered some hope. But as for Germany's ability to pay any large volume of reparations, Germans were unanimous in believing it could never happen. Only the desperate condition of the capital market and the economy made acceptance thinkable. Reich Chancellor Wilhelm Marx told a conference of Reich ministers and state officials that "sad as it is, we must nevertheless follow the only path which can lead to our obtaining the absolutely essential foreign credits." In a flight of rhetorical exaggeration, Finance Minister Hans Luther warned the assemblage that without foreign loans he saw "no possibility at all of further existence for the German people." Approval of the Dawes Plan provided the only way to secure the foreign capital vital to the restoration of the German economy. Foreign Minister Gustav Stresemann added his voice in support of the plan, and agreed with Luther that the "overwhelming probability" indicated that the Dawes Plan would never last long enough for Germany to have to pay the full 2.5 billion RM annual payment.[63] Stresemann anticipated that by 1927 it would be clear that reparations had to be reduced. In the meantime, Germany would once again secure its influence in the Rhineland and control the Ruhr. He even speculated that it was possible that if the Dawes Plan opened the market for extensive American loans to Germany, the United States might find itself defending Germany in the next European crisis.[64]

The Foreign Ministry's reparations expert, Karl Ritter, outlined Germany's most optimistic view of the Dawes Plan in a policy paper written in August 1927. Ritter argued that in the short run, the plan offered the best chance for German economic recovery. It would allow the economy room for growth for two to four years. But he believed that this growth would probably not be sufficient to permit transfer of the full 2.5 billion marks. With complete German cooperation and without any act of bad faith on the German side, the plan would fail. Then the allies would realize that the payments

were impossible and a new settlement could be found.[65] This
hope could only come true if the Agent General supported
German claims that it could not pay, and he would only support
Germany if it had made a serious and convincing effort to
meet the "impossible" terms. Stresemann summed it all up as
he so often did with an apocryphal story he told in a speech
to the leaders of his German People's Party. "A competent
French politician who was recently asked if he would be going
to London [to take part in the final Dawes Plan arrangements],
was not so wrong when he said: 'no, I'm more interested in
the next conference that will come after the London Conference.' "[66]

Despite the German anticipation that the Dawes Plan
could not work and the fact that British leaders and Morgan
partners agreed with this evaluation, the plan seemed to offer
the last and only hope for restoration of world financial stability.
With the expectation that the plan itself would permit orderly
revision and assurance that the loans behind the plan were
safe, it was finally accepted by all participants. Within Germany,
even the conservative German National Peoples Party ended
up providing critical support for the plan and its implied acceptance of the detested Versailles Treaty. With the promise
of foreign loans and tariff relief for agriculture, and even the
possibility of entering the Cabinet, enough Nationalists swal-
lowed hard and voted for the laws implementing the plan to
ensure its passage.[67]

After hectic last minute negotiations, the 800 million
RM Dawes loan was issued on October 10, 1924. For Germany,
the loan was the central benefit to be gained from the Dawes
Plan since it would provide the gold needed to back the new
gold mark and would help pay for the next year's reparations.
The United States floated half the total loan, or 400 million
RM, while Britain took 200 million, and France, Belgium, the
Netherlands, Italy, Sweden, and Switzerland divided most of
the rest.

The American money market had been carefully prepared
by circumstances and manipulation to take the Dawes loan.
The Federal Reserve banks had reduced their discount rate in
the spring primarily to combat a domestic recession, but the

move also promoted foreign borrowing in New York by reducing American interest rates and making foreign bonds relatively more attractive.[68] Bankers, government officials, and the
press joined in a massive propaganda campaign to sell the
bonds as both a profitable investment and as a giant step
toward stabilization of the world economy and expansion of
American exports.[69]

More important than this propaganda is the fact that
the bonds were issued at terms that were extremely lucrative
for bankers as well as private investors. American banks bought
the bonds at 87 (Europeans took them at 87½); the bonds were
sold to the public at 92 and were to be redeemed at 105.
Germany, to receive 800 million RM, had to issue bonds with
a face value of 1,027 billion RM.[70] Both American and British
investors jumped at the chance for profits of this size and the
bonds were nearly sold out on the first day. In Britain, the
issue was oversubscribed thirteen times, and in New York nearly
ten times.[71] As German financier Ludwig Bendix was quick to
point out, this excitement did not necessarily reflect such a
great interest in German bonds as one might have guessed. It
was, indeed, a surprise that the bonds had been so greatly
oversubscribed, but at least part of the explanation for this was
that speculators bought heavily, forced the price up, and then
sold their bonds for a profit.[72]

Although some of the initial enthusiasm for the Dawes
loan was artificially inspired, the loan signalled American willingness to lend abroad. High profits for American investors
and securing life-giving liquid capital for German borrowers
were the obvious attractions which stimulated what would soon
become a vast capital migration. Yet, on both sides of the
Atlantic responsible government leaders knew that the loans
carried dangers as well as benefits. Americans worried that
German loans might become entangled in the never-ending
reparations conflict in a way that would draw the United States
into Europe's problems or lead to severe losses by American
investors. German officials hoped that the loans might commit
the power of the United States to protect German interests.
Yet they also feared that Germany could become so dependent
on foreign capital that its economic stability would be endan-

gered or that Germany could even lose its political freedom to maneuver. The difficulty for both Americans and Germans lay in determining how to regulate the flow of loans so as to extract the benefits while avoiding the dangers.

Chapter 2
The Origins of Loan Control

During the First World War and the years immediately following, the United States became the world's primary source of financial capital. But the systematic mobilization of funds for the Allies undertaken by the government during the war years gave way to haphazard private capital movements in the following years of peace. Much of this private capital went into currency speculation in foreign countries, especially in Germany.[1] As early as 1921, in the United States, the new Republican administration became concerned that this often unstable capital flow might carry with it real dangers to the economic and monetary welfare of the United States. By 1925, when the Dawes Plan introduced a more ordered framework for the American loans to Germany, the American government had established patterns in dealing with the loans that would help set policy in the second half of the 1920s. Despite good intentions and nagging worries, the American government was not able to formulate a coherent system for supervising the foreign loans. Yet it was continually concerned about the destabilizing effects of the loans and sought some means of achieving order in the flow of American money abroad.

In 1924, Germany took up the issue of loan regulation which had already become a concern to the Americans. In part, the Germans responded to American pressures to guarantee loan security, but they also acted under the pressure of their own interests, objectives, and restraints.[2] Their efforts would be far from meeting the needs of the American government. In both the United States and Germany, these early efforts to control the flow of capital politicized the loans and introduced issues that would be played out over the course of the 1920s. The first section of this chapter reviews the goals and ambiguities of American policy as it developed up to 1925. The second part presents the German side of loan regulation.

The American Side, 1921–1924

Soon after taking office in March 1921, the Republican administration had to confront the novel problems raised by America's emerging role as the world's greatest financial power. The new Secretary of Commerce, Herbert Hoover, had already given much thought to the role that American capital might play in reconstructing the world's economy. Hoover had entered the Cabinet with the understanding that he and the Commerce Department would have a major influence in formulating economic policy both within the United States and in foreign economic relations.[3] During the next decade and more, Hoover took a central place in determining how the government dealt with American foreign lending. Hoover's complex vision of the role of government in managing an advanced capitalist economy set guiding principles for his approach to formulating policies for dealing with foreign loans. Since Hoover had by far the most fully developed theoretical perspective of any of the Republican leaders, it is worth spending a moment to consider his larger ideas on the role of government.

Hoover's notion of the ideal capitalist society was based on early twentieth-century progressive reform ideology, and the conviction that only competitive, small, even rural societies could preserve what was best in American life. Given this orientation, it would have been easy for Hoover to insist that government must remove itself from any role in regulating this ideal economy. But his strong Quaker background and dedicated service during the war and after combined with an activist strand of progressivism to convince Hoover that government had a legitimate, if limited, place in stabilizing capitalist societies. He believed, for example, that the government should help stabilize the business cycle by providing businessmen accurate statistical information on the economy so that investment plans could be based on realistic long-run growth strategies. Going beyond this, Hoover felt that the government should help private firms work together to improve industrial efficiency, productivity, and planning.

As Secretary of Commerce, Hoover persistently used the Commerce Department as the agency for his "associational" vision. The department would encourage businessmen to work together to increase efficiency while preserving some sense of capitalistic competition. The proper goal was to allow smaller firms to enjoy the advantages of planning and organization while avoiding the twin evils of monopoly and excessive government control. This was the most subtle of Hoover's ambitions. Government was to help stabilize the economy not by directly dominating it, but by helping private industry organize while preserving a competitive market. Thus, Hoover wanted government to play a role and indeed an important one, but he always sought to keep that role limited to advising and organizing private firms. In regulating foreign lending as in all other spheres, this limited objective was difficult to achieve and gave rise to ambiguous and often hesitant policies. Sometimes pushing for greater government involvement and sometimes insisting that the government was too powerful, Hoover managed to find allies and enemies across the political spectrum.[4] Although Hoover's encouragement of business cooperation may be seen as the forerunner of the New Deal, he was horrified by the lack of balance and excessive governmental role in the economy of the New Deal. In the same way, Hoover's program for controlling foreign loans would see him encourage responsible, conservative lending, but always refuse to insert the government too actively into a business that he felt had to remain in the hands of private enterprise.

In dealing with America's foreign lending, Hoover consistently voiced the dual beliefs that world economic prosperity depended on growth in the American private economy and on the establishment of stable economies abroad. He wrote that as early as 1920, "I insisted that private credit was needed [to rebuild Europe's economy] but that our government should not mix with the affair, and that our system for extending private credit should be better organized to prevent fraud, waste and loss."[5] Government's constructive role lay in coordinating the organization of private lenders, and in ensuring that the private loans served the best interests of the American economy.

In May 1921 Hoover began to lobby for a statement by President Harding "warning the country against further foreign loans unless the proceeds are to be used to pay for purchases in this country."[6] Although Hoover would soon be convinced that this effort to force foreign borrowers to "buy American" was unnecessary and unwise, he, along with many others, hoped to stimulate American industry and agriculture through increased exports financed by foreign loans.

At Hoover's request, President Harding, Secretary of State Hughes, Secretary of the Treasury Mellon, J. P. Morgan partner Thomas Lamont, and Hoover met on May 25, 1921, to discuss how the United States should deal with its new power as a major world capital market.[7] Hoover's desire to use the government to oversee the loans and ensure that their proceeds were spent in the United States was rejected by his more cautious colleagues. Instead of taking up Hoover's plan to tie foreign loans to the purchase of American products, the cabinet officials agreed only informally to request bankers to keep the government advised on their foreign loans.[8] It is symbolic of Republican foreign policy that notification of the bankers was not undertaken by the government, but by J. P. Morgan. By early June, Morgan informed President Harding that all the major banks involved in lending to foreign governments would keep the administration advised of any negotiations.[9]

President Harding and Treasury Secretary Mellon had been the principal opponents of Hoover's attempt to introduce a limited control over America's foreign lending. They in turn had been influenced by the opposition to any government regulation by New York Federal Reserve Bank Governor Benjamin Strong. The most powerful government banker in the United States, Strong had been advised of Hoover's plans by the young Assistant Secretary of the Treasury and future Reparations Agent, S. Parker Gilbert.[10] From his earliest government service, Gilbert's correspondence shows that he was close to Strong, and they exchanged ideas frequently during the 1920s. As a result of Gilbert's warning in May 1921, Strong wrote a letter opposing any attempt by the American government to force foreign borrowers to spend the proceeds of their loans in the United States. Strong's protest was influential in mobilizing a rejection of Hoover's plan. Gilbert wrote back to Strong, "Confidentially, I know that both the President and Secretary were much impressed and I think that you may count on plenty of cooperation in Washington."[11]

As the most powerful banker within the most powerful country in the world, Benjamin Strong would exercise a major influence on world financial relations until his death in 1928. Strong constantly strove to balance his two principle aims. On the one hand, unlike his peers Montagu Norman in England and Hjalmar Schacht in Germany, Strong believed that the Central Bank had an important responsibility for preserving national prosperity. By expanding the money supply he could reduce interest rates and stimulate the American economy. At the same time, Strong was dedicated to international financial cooperation and always struggled to help European central bankers preserve stable monetary systems and sound economic growth. Strong was especially inclined to believe that the export of American capital was essential to both American and European prosperity. He opposed the regulation of American lending abroad since, as he wrote Parker Gilbert, "The maintenance of our export trade generally depends upon foreign credits, and if they are restricted in any way, in the long run it will come out of our exports." He added, "This class of business should be encouraged and not discouraged, especially at a time when America has a surplus of products for export, and when most of the world owes us money anyway."[12] To this emphasis on the importance of foreign lending for the United States, Strong always added that stabilization of European economies depended on the willingness of Americans to lend.[13] Thus for Strong, preservation of an unrestricted American market for foreign bonds was a crucial step toward both foreign and domestic prosperity. In opposition to Hoover who wanted the government to help ensure that the foreign loans were sound investments, Strong consistently took the side of the New York bankers and fought to keep politicians from interfering in the foreign loan business.

Strong's argument that American prosperity rested on promoting exports through increased foreign lending was the same argument used ten years later to justify the loans after they began to fail under the pressure of the great depression. American bankers could quite rightly argue that only their foreign loans kept the international system functioning in the 1920s.[14] But the primary motive for making the loans was surely the spectacular profits to be made and throughout the 1920s both bankers and public officials refused to accept the responsibility for a well-planned stabilization policy which America's monetary predominance demanded.[15]

America's foreign loans not only had the potential to stimulate economic growth, they also provided at least a temporary solution to the intractable monetary problems created by the First World War and its aftermath. By 1920, the allies, principally Britain and France, owed nearly 10 billion dollars to the United States. They in turn expected Germany to pay reparations of even a larger sum or, in the case of Britain, hoped to renounce any claim to reparations in return for being released from their debt to the United States. In the absence of any such mutual cancellation of debts—and the United States made it clear that it would never simply cancel the war debts— a vast chain of indebtedness tied the European states and the United States together. German reparations and the allied war debts could be paid only if each debtor nation could develop an export surplus to earn the gold required to meet its obligations. The United States, as the final recipient of this entire debt structure, would have to run a large import surplus in order to provide Europe with the money needed to keep the system alive. But the Republican Party was firmly devoted to high tariff protection for its industrial and agricultural supporters. Hoover insisted that American purchases of services from foreigners—primarily dollars spent abroad by American tourists—meant that the high tariffs would not prevent the allies from repaying their debts, but there can be no doubt that the high tariffs would make repayment more difficult.

Throughout the twenties, the Republican administration tried to play both sides of the foreign debt issue. It insisted on debt repayment in order to pay off the American public debt while still reducing taxes. At the same time it could not open the doors to world trade because its political supporters demanded high tariffs. By promoting American foreign lending, the circle could be squared, and the entire complex system made to function. European economies could be stabilized; Germany could pay its reparations; the allies could pay their debts; the United States could keep its tariffs; and the Republicans could lower their taxes. Given all these virtues, one might well expect an unrestrained promotion of American foreign lending. Yet the loans often appeared so risky and insecure that Hoover, State Department officials, and finally the Reparations Agent would try to restrain them or, at the very least, try to ensure that the government could not be blamed for encouraging bad investments. The problem was how to find a policy agreeable to all parties.

The initial effort of May 1921 to have bankers informally advise the government of impending foreign loans soon proved unworkable. By December 1921, rising volumes of loans to Europe which were not viewed by the government as productive, and the failure of bankers to keep the State Department informed of negotiations led Secretary of State Hughes to seek a stronger policy.[16] Hughes wanted to coerce the bankers into cooperation by making a public statement revealing their agreement to keep him informed. This would also ensure that all bankers, not just those involved in the summer conference, knew that they were obligated to report their loan plans to the State Department.[17]

Secretary of the Treasury Mellon concurred in the plan for a public notice but emphasized that the government must in no way "assume responsibility in connection with these transactions." But Hoover vigorously opposed any public statement. He was concerned that all loans might be stopped and was also unwilling to see the State Department gain a leading role in controlling America's foreign lending. Most critical for Hoover, however, was the fear expressed by Mellon that if the government publicly announced that it was reviewing loan requests, it could lead investors to believe that the government was guaranteeing that the loans were a sound investment.[18]

Having staked out his turf, Hoover opened the way to a limited government influence over America's foreign loans. He arranged a second conference with the bankers and President Harding and Secretaries Hughes, Mellon, and himself in February 1922. The bankers agreed to submit all prospective loans to the State Department for an opinion as to the political desirability of the loan. Proposals would then be passed on to the Commerce Department for advice on their "security and reproductive character" and finally to the Treasury for an opinion on their financial implications. The agreement was made public in a notice issued March 3, 1922.[19]

The agreement appears to have been a compromise between the positions of the State and Commerce Departments. By resolving the issue at a private meeting which included government officials and leading bankers, Hoover had prevented a belligerent, unilateral public announcement by the State Department which would have threatened all foreign lending and undercut the Commerce Department's influence. At the same time, the State Department's concern that only a public statement could compel bankers to keep it informed had also been taken into account. For Hoover, however, this agreement seems to have been more the starting point for a thorough reconsideration of government's role in loan regulation rather than a final statement of its policy.

Soon after the public notice that banks would keep the government informed of their loan plans, one of the leaders of the Commerce Department began to press for further clarification of American policy. In a series of wide-ranging memos to Hoover, Grosvenor Jones, Chief of the Finance and Investment Division, argued for an expanded policy. He wrote Hoover,

There appears to be an urgent need for the formulation of a definite, consistent and constructive policy on the part of the State and Commerce Departments with reference to the issue of foreign loans in the United States—a policy that takes into consideration the general political and economic aspects and implications of such loans and is reasonably conservative and far-sighted. The government has a responsibility in this matter which it cannot avoid by assuming a noncommittal attitude.[20]

Jones argued that "as the world's best source of credit . . . it is our duty to dispose of the credit wisely and farsightedly . . . Because of the alluring underwriting commissions offered, there is danger that bankers may be tempted in certain instances to disregard or minimize the undesirable features of certain loans." But Jones drew back from proposing a formal policy and instead suggested a "gentlemen's agreement," with the bankers promising to consult the government before agreeing to place any loan. Jones did not, however, assume that the informal nature of this agreement would mean that the government could refuse to accept responsibility. Instead, he felt the government had to accept its task and set out tests which acceptable loans must meet. He prescribed some standard conditions for acceptability including useful purpose, good credit risk, reasonable terms, and, when the loan was to a government, that government must be taking steps to balance its budget. He recognized that "this involves the assumption of a somewhat paternalistic attitude on our part toward foreign governments but there is little danger that this attitude will do them any harm but rather that it will be as helpful as it is intended to be." Finally, Jones completely broke with American businessmen and others (including Hoover) who had insisted that foreign borrowers be forced to spend their proceeds in the United States. "It is not fair, in my opinion to insist that all or any part of the proceeds of such loans shall be spent in this country regardless of price. . . . That seems to me to be taking an unfair advantage of the borrower."

Jones' memorandum is worth discussing at length because, together with another which he wrote a few days later, it represents the clearest formulation of what was to become Hoover's policy. The winter's debate had forced Hoover to think through his policy goals, and he responded keenly to Jones' suggestions. It may well be, too, that New York bankers were not dealing as openly as he wished and that increasing evidence of financial losses by American investors contributed to his demands for an augmented governmental role. As suggested by Jones, Hoover gave up his earlier insistence that loans be tied to American purchases, and he evidently agreed that since direct government control had been publicly proclaimed as a result of the State Department's initiative, then that interference should be decisive. Jones completed his proposal a few days later when he suggested that a responsible committee of the Investment Bankers' Association working with the State and Commerce Departments "should fix the amount that each foreign country can borrow a year ahead of time" in much the same manner as banks fix credit lines for their clients.[21]

As Hoover took up Jones' proposals and began a campaign for a stronger policy of loan regulation, he once again found himself in conflict with Benjamin Strong of the Federal Reserve Bank. Strong supported foreign lending with the argument that even unproductive loans would promote American exports, and he was willing to ignore Hoover's concern that repayment of unproductive loans might not be possible. He argued instead that "there seems to be no evidence of a reckless plunging into new fields" and called attention "to the evidence . . . of the careful discrimination with which these loans have been sifted out by our bankers before they have been offered for sale."[22] But Strong's basic concern was to prevent the government from accepting responsibilities it could not satisfactorily discharge. "If our government undertakes to pass upon the goodness of a loan, even in a minute degree," he asked Hughes,

does it not inaugurate a system of responsibility to which there may be no termination except by the assumption of full responsibility? . . . my point is that once regulation, supervision, or control is attempted, there is no limit to which it may develop and no limit to the responsibility which our government may ultimately be called upon to assume. It may indeed lead to responsibilities which would involve us in those very disputes and dissensions which I am so eager that this nation should always successfully escape.[23]

Hoover's reply to Strong's criticisms demonstrates the subtlety of Hoover's thinking on the role of the American government in the world economy. He was in absolute agreement that "foreign loans are vital in the present situation of the world and of our commerce." The Republican administration "through practically all its officials insisted that the only method by which American exports can be promoted is through extension of credits abroad."[24] But he was unwilling to agree that exports should take precedence over the development of America's domestic economy. "When we consider that 94% of our activities are domestic, the burden is against the domestic situation." But this defense of the domestic economy was really secondary to another, more basic, disagreement that Hoover had with Strong.

Following the lines set out by Jones, Hoover argued that in the event of future defaults, the government would have to be involved in any attempt to recover the foreign investments. He wrote that "the security and form of these loans should, at the outset, involve a fair hope that the Federal Government will not be required to enter upon intervention." Hoover warned against private loans to nations already heavily in debt to the U.S. government (the wartime Allies). "Our Federal authorities must have some responsibility in not informing our citizens (or the promoters to them) that these nations will probably have to confess inability to meet their creditors. Unless some such action is taken, the citizens from whom such information has been withheld would seem to me to have the moral right to insist that the Federal Government should not press its governmental claims to the prejudice of their investments."[25] Thus Hoover was afraid that if the government did not speak out to warn its citizens against making unsound loans, the government might end up having to give up its claim to repayment of the war-time debt in order to protect private loans made after the war.

In their debate over how to deal with America's foreign lending, Hoover, Strong, and Hughes shared a belief that the loans were risky and, of even greater importance, all three men wanted to ensure that the government could not be held accountable if the loans proved worthless. In their formulation of how to deal with this risk, each of the three men took a position that reflected his attitude toward government and business. Hughes and the State Department, with no ties to business, wanted a simple public statement that would force banks to submit loan proposals to the government for review. Benjamin Strong opposed all regulation with the warning that any government involvement would force the government to accept responsibility for the loans in the case of future default. Hoover recognized this problem but argued that if foreign loans went into default, the government would be pressured to help American lenders regardless of any commitment made or avoided during negotiations for the loans. Given this reality, he argued that the government must try to ensure that only productive and sound loans were made so that chances of future default could be held to a minimum. Hoover's solution was to work quietly with the bankers and give the government the responsibility not of guaranteeing the loans, but of ensuring that the bankers used their own discretion carefully. In pushing his plan, Hoover would find not only that other Cabinet officials opposed the growth in government responsibility which he proposed, but that his own vision of limited government activity prevented him from carrying through a policy of active loan regulation.

While Herbert Hoover and Benjamin Strong debated the role that government should take in regulating America's foreign lending, they both believed that American bankers did not have the experience to be leaders in the world financial system. Both felt that somehow this inexperience had to be supplemented by outside experts. For Hoover, the government, and, of course, particularly the Commerce Department possessed the information which could make American investments safe and productive. As he wrote Secretary of State Hughes:

Our citizens have had but little experience in international investment. They are not possessed of the information with regard to the security of many of these offerings which is possessed by the Government or such offerings would not be entertained. A serious question arises in my mind as to whether the Federal Government has the moral right to withhold this information from its citizens.[26]

As of April 1922, Hoover estimated that Americans had lost nearly $500 million in bad foreign investments since the end of the war.[27] As the German inflation moved into its final catastrophic hyper-inflation, this sum would be multiplied many times over as Americans who had speculated that the mark would rise in value lost their gamble.[28] To avoid these kinds of losses, Hoover wanted the Commerce Department to serve as an active advisor warning bankers and investors about the dangers of a treacherous world.

Benjamin Strong agreed that American inexperience required expert advice. But he would never concede the role to government that Hoover now demanded. Instead, Strong believed that America should provide the capital and Britain the expertise in deciding where and how to use it. As he wrote Montagu Norman in 1924:

I have believed and stated that under present conditions, it is natural to expect that the London money market by reason of its better knowledge of German conditions will be able to do more in the way of credit assistance for Germany than we can expect to do at first. . . . On the other hand, it will be obviously to Germany's advantage to obtain all possible credits in this market.[29]

By late 1922, Hoover had failed in his attempt to involve the Republican administration in an active loan control policy.[30] Although bankers continued to inform the State Department of their pending loans, the government never suggested that a loan was an unwise or risky investment. Such few loans as were opposed were singled out because the government borrowing the money had not yet funded its war debt to the United States or the money was to be used to fund a foreign monopoly that might hurt American consumers.[31] Hoover blamed Secretary of the Treasury Andrew Mellon for influencing President Harding to "retreat from our original standards" of passing on the quality of foreign loans. When Calvin Coolidge became President, the official review of the loans was further reduced to "passing upon the effect which any particular loan might have directly on our foreign political relations."[32]

In the second half of 1922, America's massive speculation in German marks came to a disastrous end, and for the next two years little American capital went to Germany. In 1924, when the United States once again began to make loans to Germany, the old fears of dangerously unsound and overly aggressive American lending reemerged. As in 1922, American leaders agreed on the need for a slow and cautious expansion of American lending. Yet they remained divided and deadlocked on how to achieve this goal. When the German government began to become concerned about possible excessive foreign borrowing, American officials hoped that Germany would provide the loan control that the United Sttes could not provide.

But when Germany took up the problem of loan regulation, it was only natural that it would look at the issue on the basis of its own needs and problems. In the years after the Dawes Plan, the conflicts surrounding loan regulation would be centered on Germany's social, political, and economic conflicts.

Germany 1924

When Germany ended its passive resistance to the Ruhr occupation in September 1923, it hoped that it would quickly secure a revision of its reparations payments and attract the foreign capital it needed to stabilize the mark. These hopes would be frustrated as negotiations for the Dawes Plan and its international loan dragged on for over a year during which time Germany had to survive on its own weakened credit. In April 1924, when the Reichsbank began a tight credit restriction to head off the threat of a renewed inflation, it eliminated the last source of funds within Germany and many businesses and local governments found themselves in a desperate scramble for money. The only alternative seemed to be the nearly mythical American capital market. By the end of July 1924, there were reports of as many as 853 German representatives seeking loans in the United States.[33] The German Foreign Ministry was swamped with petitions asking for help in securing foreign loans, but refused to provide any encouragement. In fact, until the Dawes Plan was formally accepted and the Dawes loan was safely floated, the Foreign Ministry urged restraint on German borrowers and requested that foreign governments discourage their citizens from extending any loans to Germany.[34] In its standard reply to German requests for help, the Foreign Ministry warned that it doubted whether "foreign credit on acceptable terms was to be had at all." In spite of this official discouragement, Germans sought loans through numerous newspaper ads in Switzerland, Britain, and Holland, and they continued to press German consulates abroad for assistance.[35] Although several Ruhr cities received short-term loans on revolving accounts to purchase milk and food products from Holland, few of the applicants were successful.[36] Most of the representatives knew next to nothing about how to secure a loan and were unwilling to provide the full disclosure of municipal and industrial finances demanded by foreign lenders.[37]

As late as October and November 1924, American bankers were openly hesitant to make any German loans. Benjamin Strong suggested that Americans would not lend to Germany until it became clear as to whether reparations or foreign loans would have first claim on Germany's scarce funds available to pay foreign debts. Furthermore, uncertainty about revaluation of German mark loans lost during the inflation made it hard to judge the credit capacity of German borrowers. A high revaluation would vastly increase the debt of German cities and states and hurt their credit position. Strong concluded that "it may be fortunate that these doubts exist, as they may serve to be a check upon overoptimism and excessive borrowing which would be bad for both borrower and lender."[38]

German industrialists as well as municipal and state governments found foreign lenders unwilling to make acceptable loan offers. The Association of German Industrialists was advised by its leaders that it would be "extraordinarily difficult" to secure acceptable terms from American bankers. Association director Haller reported that he "could not escape the impression, that in most of the negotiations up to this point, the Americans have only wanted to sound out the situation, and in most cases a positive conclusion of negotiations was not to be counted on." Americans also were making excessively strin-

gent demands for security, which included solid mortgage obligations and assurances that industrial debts under the Dawes
Plan would not harm industry's ability to repay private loans.
Haller warned that "the Americans do not seem to be satisfied
even with a guarantee of high interest rates." Beyond a high
return, they demanded such extras as adjustable interest rates
which would rise if dividend payments rose and repayment of
the loans above par. Haller's discouragement reflected a widespread sense of frustration in dealing with the Americans.[39]

Although very few if any foreign loans were actually
being secured, concern about the potential dangers from a flood
of foreign capital grew as implementation of the Dawes Plan
drew near. The government warned industry that many of the
offers of foreign support were really designed to gain foreign
influence in German firms.[40] By the end of July, the Foreign
Ministry felt it was necessary to send a circular to the national
organizations of German industry, trade, agriculture, and municipalities urging them to restrain their members from seeking
foreign loans. They were warned that flooding foreign money
markets with loan requests was counterproductive and could
only hurt German credit.[41] If Germany seemed too desperate
for credit, loan prices would be bid up or lenders might become
frightened away from all German loans. Until the Dawes Plan
went into effect and the reparations loan was floated, no one
expected a real flood of loans to begin. Only as the reparations
issues were finally settled did the hypothetical danger become
a real threat.

In early September 1924, still a month before the Dawes
loan was issued, Germany took its first step to implement
control over borrowing abroad. Significantly, it was not the
Reich government that led the way, but the Prussian state
government. Interior Minister Carl Severing called for a conference of the Public Credit Banks, larger cities, the Reichsbank,
the Reich Economics Ministry, and the national associations
of German municipalities to discuss the loan situation with an
emphasis on controlling municipal borrowing. The conference
was held September 8–12 and was chaired by Dr. Oskar Mulert
of the Prussian Interior Ministry. Mulert, it should be noted,
was soon to give up his state position and take over leadership

of the *deutsche Städtetag,* the strongest of the organizations representing German cities. In this post, he became a leader in the fight for municipal autonomy and the right of cities to take foreign loans. He was in many ways a typical representative of the bureaucrats assembled by Severing in the Prussian Interior Ministry, which was a rare stronghold of liberal and Social Democratic thinking.

It is worth emphasizing that this initial move to reduce municipal borrowing did not come from a conservative organization which opposed urban spending on social welfare projects, but rather from one of the few organizations in Weimar Germany which might have viewed such spending with some sympathy.[42] Later, Germany's bitter social conflicts would become a central feature of foreign loan control. But this initial attempt to regulate the loans was based on the fear that excessive borrowing would undermine the German currency and make Germany overly dependent on foreign states.

At this first meeting in September, Mulert urged the cities to form a central organization that would lead negotiations for all municipal loans. The dangers presented by excessively expensive foreign loans and foreign acquisition of mortgages on municipal property prompted the representatives to agree that some central coordination was desirable. They also agreed that loans must only be taken for projects that could repay interest and amortization from their own profits. For the first time, a pattern was set at this conference which was to become characteristic of almost all future agreements. Whenever any group met to discuss foreign loans, everyone could agree that self-restraint was necessary, and they could further agree that self-restraint had to be exercised by someone who was not present. In this case, smaller cities, unrepresented here, were to be forbidden to undertake direct negotiations with foreign lenders.[43]

A month later, Prussia had become so concerned with Germany's wild scramble for foreign loans that it sent another circular to the state governments urging caution in seeking foreign loans.[44] The Prussian government also took the lead in regulating its own affairs. It forbade Prussian and city-run banks from taking foreign loans and urged Prussian cities not to seek any loans until after the Dawes loan was floated. The Prussian officials also warned city leaders that most municipal projects would not improve Germany's export capacity and repayment in foreign currency would become impossible. To avoid this danger, they encouraged cities to do any essential borrowing on the domestic market. If larger cities were determined to borrow abroad, they should be certain that the projects to be financed would be "productive" in that they would directly increase German industrial output and could pay for themselves out of earned revenues. Projects such as natural gas plants and water works were offered as examples of acceptable undertakings. Interest rates must be no more than the Dawes loan. Repayment should be in marks, and under no circumstances should mortages on city property be given as security. More generally, the Prussians warned that most loan offers were apparently not serious and might be intended only to uncover the property and credit situation of German cities. They concluded that "only by unified negotiations can severe economic and foreign policy disadvantages be avoided." Prussia moved further a few days later by forbidding foreign borrowing by Prussian cities. It justified the restrictions with reference to the "sharp competition on the foreign money market . . . thereby hurting loan terms." Both Saxony and Württemburg issued similar orders soon after this.[45]

Even as the states debated possible action, far broader concerns in the Reich government would soon take matters out of their hands. To the Finance Ministry, the rush to foreign borrowing seemed to bring with it a vast array of potential dangers. While it was true that the foreign capital might briefly help pay for greater production and consumption, in the long run, it was feared, the loans could cause an increase in prices and further destabilize the currency by hurting Germany's balance of payments. A further domestic consideration grew out of the fact that the inflation had totally disrupted the division of tax receipts among the Reich, states, and cities, and it was clear that a bitter fight was in store before a permanent settlement could be reached. If the cities and states borrowed heavily abroad now, they would need extra revenue later when the time came to repay the loans. To increase the "legitimate" financial demands of local governments could only make a solution to the tax problem that much more difficult. Internationally, heavy foreign indebtedness of German public corporations (cities and states) could increase the power of foreigners in German affairs and thereby reduce the independence of German foreign policy. Finally, and of more significance for the future, repayment of the loans might hurt Germany's ability to transfer reparations. As a Finance Ministry expert warned, if repayment of the loans causes reparations problems, the transfer committee "will not quietly accept this kind of damage to its task. It will point out that the public loans are inopportune and superfluous. The result will be to increase international tensions."[46]

It is worth pausing at this point to consider the implications of this last statement which expresses a concern that will come up repeatedly in discussions of German policy options. As other historians have noted, and as will also be argued here, many German leaders hoped to exploit loans from the United States to force a reduction in future reparations payments.[47] If American bankers would loan enough to Germany so that repayment of these loans would be endangered by high reparations payments, the Americans could be used to force a reduction in reparations. But, as the Finance Ministry realized, the power of this argument was weakened by the fact that Germany would have to run grave risks before the Americans could be moved to support Germany's reparations position. Increased international tensions and the threat of economic collapse had first to be faced before Germany could make use of this tool. Many Germans were not convinced that these risks were worth the potential benefits. Indeed, pointing to Germany's failure to find any international support during the Ruhr occupation, the commissar of the Prussian Finance Ministry drew out the dangers expressed by the Reich Finance Ministry. He argued that Germany must fully live up to the Dawes Plan or face a total domination of the German economy by the Allies. He told the leaders of the other states that if Germany failed to practice the fiscal frugality required to meet its Dawes Plan commitments, "we will fall into an enslavement from which there will be no escape and which even the words 'absolute financial control' cannot fully describe.''[48]

Despite these concerns, the Finance Ministry could not yet agree on any action to stem the threatening tide of debt. The Reich had recently emerged from a bitter fight with the state governments over tax reform and was not anxious to institute a new battle.[49] Since there were few loans actually being made, the Finance Ministry decided that it could meet its obligations by writing the states a letter calling their attention to the potential dangers of excessive foreign loans.[50]

At the Reichsbank, President Hjalmar Schacht had also been warning about the foreign loans, and he was determined not to drop the matter so easily. As soon as he heard that the Finance Ministry would not take any action to control the loans, Schacht wrote Finance Minister Hans Luther, reminding him that the two of them had already agreed that some control over state and city spending was essential.[51] But Schacht now raised an issue that would be far more politically explosive than the concerns of Severing or the Reich Finance Ministry. Schacht pointed to the high taxes being imposed on industry and argued that they must be reduced as quickly as possible to stimulate the economy. Furthermore, excessive public spending for "party and social-policy" projects hurt the credit market and thwarted Reichsbank control of the money supply.

Schacht's desire to reduce public spending was motivated by at least two rather different concerns. On the one hand, he argued that a stable currency depended on preservation of a balance in international trade. This could only be achieved if German governments (federal, state, and local) balanced their budgets. This argument was also specifically made by the Dawes Committee experts who reported that the German inflation had been a direct product of unrestrained government deficits financed by an expansion of the money supply. Thus, Schacht could argue that balancing government budgets by reducing public spending was an issue of international importance, and he had the weight of international financial experts to back up his position. On the other hand, there were clear questions of social policy involved in the issue. While unwilling yet to actively promote more private industrial loans, Schacht clearly intended to pursue a policy favoring investment in the private industrial sector over the public sector of the economy.

The attitude of President Schacht and the Reichsbank leadership toward public spending had been clearly expressed a month earlier, when a bank director told the Prussian Interior Ministry that public borrowing should be discouraged since it competed with private industry's efforts to find foreign capital. He argued that only industrial loans could increase German productivity and exports to create a positive balance of trade.[52] While publicly careful to tie its demands to a stable currency, the bank's interests in these issues were broader than merely protecting the mark. Its attack on public spending and defense of private industry was justified by drawing on classical economic doctrine. But other, similar policies do not have even this potential justification. The bank's attack on city-controlled savings and loan banks and efforts to close the foreign loan market to them was clearly an attempt to strengthen German private banking. By closing the foreign market to the savings and loan banks, the Reichsbank hoped to stop their rapid growth and restrict them to their limited prewar activities.[53] That this was a major demand of the Association of German Private Bankers can be no accident.

These issues of social policy, first introduced by the Reichsbank, were to become central elements in the debate over loan regulation. The complex ties between foreign and domestic policies are clearly revealed by the Reichsbank's position. When monetary policy took precedence over all other considerations, the powers of bankers and especially central bankers was greatly enhanced. If governments increased their spending, the Reichsbank's control of the money supply would be threatened at the same time that business would have to face higher social costs and higher taxes. Schacht, bankers, and businessmen were happy to employ the power of international economic orthodoxy to protect their personal interests. Yet the issue was not solely one of social policy. The international bankers were not wrong when they argued that unrestricted deficit spending had been instrumental in causing the German inflation. Furthermore, with German economic and political stability dependent on a conciliatory reparations policy, demands for fiscal responsibility did not necessarily serve only the purposes of narrow interest groups. Economic theory, domestic social politics, and international diplomacy were so closely entwined that each action in one area could confuse and destabilize other policies.

Schacht pressed for a conference to organize loan regulation, and with support from Finance Minister Hans Luther, he won his point. In late October, both the Prussian and Reich Finance Ministers issued invitations to the state governments to attend a conference on foreign loans.[54] They both emphasized the benefits that Germany as a whole could gain by a united policy. The Prussians emphasized that interest rates abroad were falling and would continue to fall if Germany would only exercise enough restraint. An unregulated mass of borrowers could only promote excessive competition which would hurt all German borrowers. They called for a "moral guarantee pact" to set out common guidelines and protect Germany's future credit needs. The agreement, they suggested, should be based on voluntary cooperation to solve a common problem. Prussia clearly hoped that state cooperation could circumvent a more rigid Reich control and also make better loan terms available for all Germans.

In his letter, Luther expanded on the arguments made by Prussia and also addressed the concerns of his own ministry. He admitted that indeed few loans had been secured because of the "continued reserve" of foreign lenders. But this should not lead to the mistaken conclusion that there was no danger "because large numbers of negotiations of a damaging nature are in the works." A unified policy was needed to protect the financial interests of the Reich and to support general credit and currency policies. He added that regulation of public loans was more important than regulation of private borrowers, since "the influence of foreign lenders can have even wider ranging political consequences here than in private enterprises." Arguing that the problems had to be dealt with immediately, he called for a meeting with the states on the thirty-first of October to discuss a "unified financial and monetary policy."

Luther came to that conference ready to overpower any opposition. The main thrust of his argument was a carefully prepared attack on American finance capitalism, followed by a clever scheme laying out how Germany could exploit the Americans to her own advantage. He began by pointing out that although the Americans expected Germany to pay at least as high a rate of interest on future loans as they had paid for the Dawes loan, Germany should not give in to this unreasonable demand. Indeed, he argued, Germany could gain a great deal by waiting, since "America has got a surplus of money and therefore needs to make loans." He added with bitter irony, "America has not been authorized to take advantage of us and to impose a sort of second reparations burden on us through high interest rates."[55]

Then, in a subtle blending of foreign and domestic objectives, Luther launched into a warning on the dangers of public loans. The fact that foreigners had lost faith in the reliability of German private industry had led them to seek some sort of public guarantee for loans intended for private industry. A part of private industry had responded to this by calling on the Reich, the Reichsbank, and the states to mediate loan negotiations and guarantee private loans. Luther warned that if Germany had to endure foreign influence in its affairs, it would have to be careful to use that influence to promote its own economic prosperity in opposition to the economic and political demands of other nations. Specifically, if German governments guaranteed loans, then the loans could be repaid through taxes even if the German economy was being ruined. As Luther put it, "the foreign lender will not have the same interest in the prosperity of our economy when his capital is insured by the public purse and the payments are not exclusively dependent on the prosperity of our economy. . . . If the guarantee of the public purse were to become a reality, we would soon become absolutely dependent on the foreign capital market." Private industrial loans could tie the lender to the interests of the German economy, but only if they were free of any state guarantee. American bankers would help protect German interests if repayment of their loans depended on German prosperity. The United States would not only aid Germany in reducing the reparations demands of the Allies, but would become a partner in promoting German welfare and prosperity. If Germany proceeded carefully, it might gain a great deal through the foreign loans. But if it could not control the loans, they threatened economic and political disaster.

The Prussian Finance Minister, Richter, agreed that Germany must exercise restraint and urged a two-month moratorium on loans to force a reduction in interest rates. However, he rejected Luther's call for a centralized control as a violation of state sovereignty. The Bavarian delegate agreed with Richter on the need to go slowly and that a central control was "completely impossible." In addition, Bavaria and several other states were in the midst of negotiations for foreign loans and would not agree to a full stop until they had closed the deals. As Bavaria's representative at the meeting put it, "We need a loan as quickly as possible so we can't agree to any postponement of borrowing."[56] Most of the other states agreed with Bavaria's refusal to be rushed into an agreement. Unable to reach a concensus, the state representatives were asked to consult their home governments and attend another meeting in eight days.

Luther had lost his bid to stop the inflow of loans by cooperative action with the states. The fact that nearly every state agreed in principle that something had to be done, but also insisted that its own interests take precedence over national policy, prompted Luther to pursue the issue further. He was reinforced in this determination as other branches of the Reich government added their concerns about the dangers from foreign loans. The Economics Ministry repeated its warning that the loans might increase the money supply and create a new inflation.[57] The Foreign Ministry argued against "forcing" foreign loans to come to Germany via municipal and state governments. It even prepared a lengthy list of the factors that spoke against public loans. They included "the need to exercise the greatest possible frugality; need to reserve credit possibilities for productive purposes; the relatively good financial position of public bodies; the danger of an economically dangerous abundance on the money and foreign exchange markets [and] an unwarranted increase in Germany's ability to transfer reparations through the Agent General."[58]

Thus the pressures for action as well as the sources of concern were extremely varied. Yet by the end of October, German policy was taking an increasingly ominous path. Initially, for a number of reasons, it had been almost universally agreed that some sort of regulation of public spending was necessary. Second, Prussia led in the effort to get a cooperative, voluntary agreement among the states, which was intended primarily to reduce municipal borrowing. Finally, Schacht and Luther moved beyond this and pushed for a centralized control over all borrowing to be directed by the Reich. They apparently had considerable support for this in both the Economics Ministry and the Foreign Ministry, but found reservations in Luther's own Finance Ministry. Capitalizing on the universal fear of economic and monetary instability which a flood of loans might unleash, Schacht and Luther then went far beyond this and introduced social and reparations policy motives which conformed to their own conservative political viewpoints.

In a Cabinet meeting on the afternoon of October 31, the same day that the states had refused to agree to any compulsory loan control, Luther brought the issue up again. He demanded immediate action to grant the Finance Ministry veto power over state and municipal loans. He reported that at the meeting with the states "he had the impression that if most of the states had not agreed with his proposals, in any event their representatives had promised not to take any decisive action [to close a foreign loan] until at least Thursday of next week."[59] But, he continued, this informal agreement had been upset by the tiny state of Anhalt, which insisted on proceeding immediately to close an immense foreign loan. It planned to take 30 million Reichsmarks which would be passed on to private industry. Unwilling to allow this precedent, Luther demanded that the Cabinet ask Reich President Ebert to use his power of decree to put public borrowing under the control of the Finance Ministry. Foreign Ministry official Karl Ritter warned that he thought Stresemann would oppose Luther's proposal. But the Cabinet, evidently intimidated by Luther's threat of resignation, approved the request.[60]

The next day, November 1, in response to the Cabinet's petition, Reich President Ebert issued a decree under Article

48 of the Constitution requiring all states and cities to obtain approval from the Reich Finance Ministry before taking any foreign loans or credits. The government was pleased to find that the foreign response to the decree was very favorable.[61] The Reparations Agent, S. Parker Gilbert, told the American Chargé d'Affaires in Berlin that he thoroughly approved of the order. But he added that, despite rumors to the contrary, he had nothing to do with its origination.[62] The state governments, however, were not happy.

Bavaria was particularly incensed by the Cabinet's action. The Reich representative in Munich wired Berlin that the order was "received with displeasure in Bavaria where it was viewed as an infringement on the financial sovereignty of the states and a misuse of Article 48, especially since neither the Reichsrat nor the states had been consulted." He noted that Bavaria had been negotiating for an American loan which was now being held in suspension. But he added, "To be sure, even here men are of the same opinion as the Reich government that order must be created and maintained in this field."[63]

This use of Article 48 was especially frustrating to the Bavarians because they, along with the other states, agreed that Anhalt's action had been inexcusable. Bavaria's Justice Minister complained that Berlin was slowly and cleverly trying to bury the independent states. The Reich leaders were careful to be sure they had right on their side every time they moved to destroy some authority of the independent states. "Anhalt's actions, which led to this order, are to be condemned absolutely and every responsible government can perceive that one cannot take up foreign credit in this manner, since where would it lead if the other states and finally the cities carried on so?" But he insisted that the states should have been consulted. They could simply have agreed to Prussia's proposal to give the foreign lenders the "cold shoulder" and soon loan terms would have improved.[64]

While sympathetic to the Reich's need "to do something" to counter Anhalt's irresponsibility, most of the states were prepared to fight to maintain their voice in decision making. Their protests forced the government to agree to reconsider its action and to conduct further negotiations with them. This did not imply that anyone expected that the new negotiations would fail to result in some form of loan control. The National Association of Municipalities was already warning the cities that they could expect some form of control over their foreign borrowing and that they would have to accept this with good grace.[65]

At a meeting between the state Finance Ministers and Luther on November 7, the states bitterly protested the use of Article 48 to give the Reich Finance Minister absolute control of foreign borrowing.[66] Prussia led the attack on Luther's action. It again urged the states to cooperate in order to avoid competing with one another for foreign loans, but insisted that "control by the Reich is wrong and insupportable." Most of the other states agreed,[67] and in the face of this united opposition Luther conceded that the government was not rigidly committed to any one plan and would accept a compromise as long as financial and currency policies were protected. He agreed to lift the emergency decree if the states would agree to abstain from taking any more loans until a new policy could be arranged.[68]

As Germans debated how best to control foreign borrowing in order to protect Germany's national interests, the issue began to take on complex international aspects as well. Long worried about the German market, American bankers were becoming increasingly concerned not only with the general security of all German loans but also with how one could determine which of the hundreds of loans being sought by German agents were sound. Representatives of National City Bank in Berlin had asked Luther if Germany could not do something to organize the loan requests. And in New York, bankers were discussing the possibility of creating some sort of screening board in Germany.[69] This trend of American concern evolved independently of developments within Germany, and reports of American interest came only after the initial presidential decree regulating loans on November 1. This would indicate that American bankers were not being kept fully informed of events within Germany, and that they had little influence over those events.

Of more concern for Germany, the American bankers were being encouraged by the State and Commerce Departments to approach the Reparations Agent and ask him to screen loan requests to determine which loans were acceptable and which might come into conflict with reparations payments. Grosvenor Jones of the Commerce Department argued that "the Transfer Committee should take action now to prevent excessive borrowing abroad. It should support the German government in the steps which the latter is said to be taking toward the restriction of foreign loans by the States and municipalities." He also asked the commercial attaché in Berlin to "encourage" the German government to extend this control to cover private loans. But Jones had to admit that up to that time the Transfer Committee had not been inclined to cooperate in screening the loan requests. He characterized its responses to inquiries as "vague" and "not very helpful."[70] At this early stage of the game, the Transfer Committee and the Reparations Agent held to the view that "private loans were a matter of private concern and that the function of the Transfer Committee was to take care of reparations payments." As for the loans, it was deemed "unthinkable" that the committee would stop the repayment of private loans in order to pay reparations, but the committee would not respond to American pressure, and, as one member expressed it, they believed that "nature should be allowed to take its course."[71]

While the Americans were finding that the Transfer Committee and Parker Gilbert would not be helpful in regulating the loans, the very thought of such interference in German affairs was frightening to Hans Luther. He sent a sharp telegram to Germany's ambassador to the United States emphasizing that neither Gilbert nor the Transfer Committee had any authority to discuss German loans. He warned that if they once got involved, "the danger exists that the Reparations Commission, Transfer Committee or the Agent General will attempt to gain influence over German foreign credit."[72]

Luther was no doubt genuinely concerned about the threat of foreign control over the German economy, but at the same time he was happy to use this threat to bludgeon the state governments into acceptance of his policies. The State

Secretary in his Finance Ministry joined Prussia's Finance Minister in warning the states that excessive foreign borrowing could overstimulate Germany's economy and give it a false image of prosperity as well as lead to intervention by the Reparations Agent in German affairs. American bankers, they were warned, were insisting on consulting with Parker Gilbert despite Germany's protest that he had no authority over Germany's internal affairs. Although Gilbert refused to assure the bankers that their private loans would be repaid prior to reparations, the Reich Economics Ministry urged quick action to ensure that the matter was permanently removed from Gilbert's hands.[73] Prussia's fear that excessive loans might hurt Germany economically and politically was now being exploited by the Reich as a springboard to argue for greater Reich authority over state finances.

In spite of these pressures for a quick settlement, negotiations were complicated by the inability of the states to agree among themselves on many of the key issues. While some felt that loan regulation should be left to the Reichsbank and the Finance Ministry, others insisted that the states must have a larger role. Deciding what types of projects could be considered "productive" and therefore acceptable forced further long negotiations.[74] Only after another month of haggling could all the states be induced to accept a compromise settlement. On January 29, 1925, the Reich president issued a new decree creating an "Advisory Board for Foreign Credit" *(Beratungsstelle für Auslandskredit).* The Reichstag approved the action in March. The only opposition came from the Social Democrats, who protested the use of Article 48 to carry out policy decisions by presidential emergency decree. But even they recognized that the act was a "necessary preventative measure," and supported Reichstag approval.[75]

Operating under the chairmanship of the Finance Ministry, the Advisory Board had representatives from the Reich Economics Ministry, the Reichsbank, the Prussian State Bank (Seehandlung), the Bavarian State Bank, and one from the state requesting action. Technically, the states retained legal control of foreign loans, and the board was to act in an advisory capacity. In reality, the board was clearly intended to have far more power, and it was effective in reducing the size of many municipal loans.

Under the provisions of the new law, municipal foreign loans and any loans that had municipal guarantees had to be submitted to the responsible state government for screening. If the state decided that the loan was "productive" and necessary, it would submit the request to the Advisory Board. Here experts supplied by the Reich Finance Ministry would evaluate each loan and recommend that the board either accept or reject it. If three of the five members of the board voted against a loan, it was rejected. An appeal procedure was set up in case the state refused to accept the board's decision, but in fact it was never used. Although the states retained the legal authority to approve or reject city loans, they were "obliged" to approve only those loans accepted by the Advisory Board.[76] The states were not formally required to submit their own loans for approval. In spite of this, they did in fact submit almost all of them, and the Advisory Board reciprocated this courtesy by approving almost all the state loans.

The Advisory Board was charged primarily with regulating long-term loan taking of German cities. But, since short-term loans which were regularly renewed were in effect long-term loans, some restrictions were also placed on short-term borrowing. Cities could take short-term loans without clearance from the board only if the loan was to cover immediate working expenses and could be repaid on schedule out of regular city tax receipts. Under no circumstances were cities to convert short-term loans into long-term bond issues, or take short-term loans which could not be repaid when they first came due.

In evaluating loans, the board was to ensure that only "productive" projects be financed by foreign loans. Initially, "productive" was defined to mean that the project constructed with the loan proceeds could generate enough revenue to be self-liquidating and to increase German national income. As a final qualification, acceptable loans could not exceed 8 percent interest and had to run for at least ten years.

Technically, these regulations gave the Advisory Board for Foreign Credit impressive influence over the course of German public policy and public finance. In fact, enforcement of the regulations was difficult as cities desperate for money sought and found ways to circumvent the board's control. As hard as it had been to agree on a policy of loan regulation, it would prove even harder to enforce the regulations once they were in effect.

In 1924–25, Germans were in almost universal agreement that public borrowing on the foreign market had to be controlled. Regulation of borrowing by private businesses did not, however, command the same consensus despite similar dangers. If public borrowing threatened to undermine Germany's currency stability, trade balance, or reparations policy, so too did private borrowing. Although it might be argued that in contrast to city governments, private borrowers would automatically use their money for productive purposes, this was hardly true. Vast sums were sunk into profitless agricultural investment and much of the rest went into overcapitalized industries such as iron, steel, and textiles which seemed safe investments but were not profitable enough to repay the expensive foreign loans. The main difference between the public and private loans lay in the political climate in Germany in 1924. Whereas public spending was under attack as conservatives reestablished their authority, private industry was being supported and encouraged.

In the spring of 1924, when it first began to appear that foreign capital markets would be reopened to Germany, the Reich Economics Ministry had viewed private borrowing and public borrowing as equally dangerous to Germany's trade balance and currency stability.[77] Throughout the rest of the year, however, private loans were ignored as the Reich concerned itself with regulating city and state borrowing. In January 1925, when agreement on the Advisory Board for Foreign Credit seemed near, the Economics Ministry once again took up the issue of private loans. It initiated several meetings with industrial leaders in an attempt to secure agreement on a law regulating private loans. But private industry was determined to keep the state from meddling in its affairs. The representatives of the powerful national business organizations unanimously declared that review of private loans was "not possible." And they argued that there was no need for control since "long-term credit to German businesses from abroad so far has been hardly practical." While willing to admit that concern should be taken to ensure that loans were sound, they would not grant the state this task. Instead, the national organizations agreed to form their own advisory committees and to counsel members on sound loan practices.[78] The Association of German Industrialists followed up on this agreement with a lengthy notice to its members urging borrowers to use German banks as intermediaries in any negotiations with foreign lenders. The association also urged smaller firms not to even seek a foreign loan since they would increase demands without any realistic hope of success.[79]

In January 1925, Hans Luther formed a new government and drew the German National Peoples Party (DNVP) into the cabinet. The new Finance Minister, Otto von Schleiben, was unsatisfied with the voluntary regulation of industrial loans which had been accepted prior to his entry into office. He asked for a cabinet meeting to discuss the private loans and the dangers they created for the stability of the currency. But his concerns found no support within the Reich Chancellery where it was argued that if private capital imports could help reduce German interest rates, they should actually be encouraged.[80]

The political realities dictated that in 1925 industry would not allow the state to expand its control over private business. The emotional rejection of the war-time and inflation experience of state economic control—the detested *Zwangswirtschaft*—made it impossible to regulate the private loans. In March a Finance Ministry official would concede that as for controlling private loans "it has . . . been demonstrated that a practical possibility of its achievement cannot be seen, if one doesn't want to come to a sort of forced management *(Zwangsbewirtschaftung)* of the foreign loans."[81] Thus the Advisory Board for Foreign Credit would regulate the borrowing of state and city governments, but German industry would be left to use its own discretion in turning to the foreign capital market.

Although public discussion about the Advisory Board focused on its role in ensuring currency stability,[82] its function was not quite so straightforward. A growing emphasis on the social implications of loan control was spelled out only after the Advisory Board was fully established. In a memorandum submitted to the Reichstag in 1926, the Reich Finance Minister boldly admitted that concern over excessive borrowing by public organizations was the primary consideration in creating the Advisory Board, and ensuring that foreign capital was available to private borrowers was the board's primary function. There were several interrelated justifications for this policy. By reducing the volume of public borrowing, private capitalism could be defended. Loans guaranteed by state or city governments but going to private businesses would be specifically opposed, since this would undercut the position of other private industries seeking foreign loans.[83] In 1924–25, it had been feared that in view of the large demand for capital, the broad tax base of governmental organization would give them a favored position in the competition for long-term foreign loans. This would deprive private industry and agriculture of a chance to secure cheap capital.[84]

From the very beginning, conservatives hoped to use the regulation of the foreign loans as a way to direct capital away from public organizations and toward private business and agriculture. The position of German businessmen was exemplified by the Chamber of Commerce of the city of Altona, which passed a resolution supporting regulation of public loans.[85] These businessmen particularly attacked public loans which might be reloaned to private industry and any public guarantee of private loans. "It is not the task of States and cities to aid individual businesses in this way. In this manner, the entire people have to bear the risk. Public funds should only be used to serve the general public." Private entrepreneurs who sought support and assistance from city and state governments were warned that "businessmen who use states and cities in this way to support their private financial interests must understand that they concede the state or city an ever growing influence in the private economy and countenance socialization of the business." Since many states were seeking loans to help private industry, it is clear that not all businessmen shared Altona's attitude. Yet the issue of private versus public interest which was so bluntly drawn in this resolution became one of the dominant issues raised by Germany's dependence on imported capital. By denying government organizations access to foreign capital, conservatives could hope to reduce their own dependence on the state and strike another blow against what was soon to be called "cold socialization."[86]

When American government officials worried about loans to Germany, they were primarily concerned that Germany should invest the money to make its economy more productive and earn profits to repay the loans. Sound loans, it was hoped, would allow the American government not to become involved in attempts to collect American money. Despite a shared concern in all branches of the government, American officials were unable to agree on how to protect the foreign loans. So, when Germany began to regulate its own borrowing, Americans were greatly relieved. This was especially true when Germany appeared to base its control on the need to ensure that the loans would be repaid, and that the German currency would be protected. Unfortunately for American policymakers, a dangerous political struggle underlay German loan regulation.

In early 1925, German conservatives won a major victory when they were able to institutionalize strong control over city and state borrowing abroad and defeat efforts to extend this regulation to cover private borrowing. The alliance of private industry, the Reichsbank, and leaders of the Reich government had apparently been able to block public access to foreign capital markets. But decisive support for loan regulation had come from the Social Democratic leaders of the Prussian state government. To these men struggling to make the Weimar system work, sound economic policy dictated that excessive and irresponsible foreign borrowing must be restrained. The "right" won its victory in early 1925 because of the conjuncture of fears felt by all Germans about a new inflation, reparations payments, and domination of the German economy by American capitalists. As these dangers began to fade, the "rightist" victory seemed to evaporate into thin air.

Chapter 3
Politics and Foreign Loans, 1925

During the year following implementation of the Dawes Plan, the flow of American capital into Germany began to take on social, economic, and political dimensions which were to play a central role in the remaining years of the Weimar Republic. The very velocity of capital movements itself became an important and destabilizing factor in German economic life. Efforts to formulate coherent and consistent monetary and fiscal policies were constantly thwarted by the twin international constraints of vacillating capital movements and the steady burden of reparations payments. These difficulties, which were to become more serious over the years, found their beginning in 1925. Furthermore, once capital in important amounts did become available to German investors, it was injected into the social struggles which ultimately tore the Republic apart. The apparent victory for private industry which creation of the Advisory Board for Foreign Credit represented soon proved illusory. Efforts to direct money away from city governments and toward private borrowers failed, since the security of German municipal bonds was too appealing to American investors to be long denied. As industry began to realize that it was losing the race for funds, it inaugurated a virulent campaign to stop the flow of money toward the "socialist" municipalities. As this social conflict developed, a political power struggle between the Reichsbank and the German government complicated the picture even further. Finally, in late 1925, the United States for the first time became actively involved in attempts to regulate the flow of loans to Germany. Partially in response to its own interests, and partially under pressure from German special interest groups, American influence became important in German politics. Tracing these developments as they evolve through 1925 reveals the interaction between foreign and domestic affairs brought into play by efforts to control the flow of capital from the United States to Germany.

The Flood of Loans

Having assumed that approval of the Dawes Plan would supply the key to unlocking America's vast wealth, Germans were shocked to discover in early 1925 that the coffers remained closed. German cities, desperately short of cash and anxious to increase social services, had entertained especially high hopes with respect to the American market. In the first months of 1925, city officials flooded the powerful Association of German Cities, the *deutsche Städtetag,* with requests for help in securing foreign loans. Typically, one mayor wrote that he had heard that "other German cities have taken large loans and it should be possible for Gera to secure one, too." But he had suffered nothing but frustration for his efforts.[1] Responding to a barrage of such complaints, the *Städtetag* conducted a poll of city governments asking for reports from cities which actually had been successful in obtaining foreign loans. Oberbürgermeister Konrad Adenauer of Cologne supplied one of the few positive responses, but he counselled other cities not to be misled by Cologne's success. Although it was true that Cologne had taken a loan, he cautioned that it was a short-term credit that had been secured only through "personal connections." American bankers continued to insist on moving very slowly and on being provided full and detailed accounts of municipal finance and security. As late as the end of March 1925 the *Städtetag* reported that "most of the press announcements about cities securing foreign loans are untrue. The negotiations by the central clearing bank *(Girozentrale)* and many German cities with American lenders have shown no success so far."[2]

The rash of negotiations and overgrown hopes which had accompanied the Dawes Plan proved largely unfruitful. Only a few very large industrial firms and cities were able to secure American loans. The Reparations Transfer Committee listed Berlin, Cologne, and Bremen as the only three cities that were successful. At least two of these were only short-term credits.[3] Robert Kuczynski records no long-term city loans until July 1925.[4] Benjamin Strong, in a letter to Dr. Walter W. Stewart of the Federal Reserve Board, noted that "the facts are very little understood and the few loans which have been made have received such widespread publicity that the amount of credit extended to Germany has been exaggerated to the public." He reported that in all of 1924 only $125 million had been borrowed by Germany, which included $115 million taken by the German government, mostly through the Dawes loan. From January through April 1925, an additional $58.5 million was borrowed, of which $50.5 million was taken by private borrowers and $8 million by public corporations. As Strong summed up, these data make it look "as though our bankers were using an unusual degree of caution in handling foreign offerings."[5] Unsure of themselves, and afraid to move too fast, American lenders demanded detailed financial information, hoped that British bankers would join them to provide expertise on German conditions and generally hesitated to commit themselves to firm contracts.

Records and correspondence of the powerful German iron and coal company, August Thyssen-Hütte, offer a rare insight into the confusing and tedious negotiations bogging down German loan endeavors. In 1924, the Thyssen concern was the largest pig iron producer in Germany and also owned and produced nearly 10 percent of Germany's coal. An entirely family-owned operation, it had 50,000 employees and operated within its works a railroad with more traffic per year than the former kingdom of Württemberg. It was not only immense, but its attractiveness as a recipient of foreign capital was increased by the fact that it exported 30 percent of its production so that it had ready access to foreign currency for repaying its debts.[6] Thus, when Thyssen asked Cologne banker Walter Barth to begin searching for an American loan, it might well have expected quick results. Thyssen specified that it wanted a loan of at least $8 million for not less than three years in order to consolidate its short-term debt of 33 million Goldmarks (about $7.8 million).[7]

Initially, Thyssen began negotiations as part of a consortium of German iron and steel firms with the New York banking house of Dillon Read, which was noted for its vigorous leadership and aggressive bond sales techniques.[8] Early negotiations centered around formation of a syndicate led by the German-American Securities Company, which planned to take a $100 million loan in the United States to be used for German industry. For their part in putting the syndicate together and selling the bonds, Dillon Read and the issuing banks expected 3 percent of the gross while offering the German industrialists directly involved a 2 percent share as a net, immediate profit. By selling the bonds at 93 percent of face value but giving the corporation only 88 percent, the consortium would yield an instant profit to the bankers of $3 million while the Germans would get $2 million, of which Thyssen's share was $400,000.[9] Attractive as the plan at first appeared, it was not scheduled to come into effect immediately. Instead, while waiting for the grand scheme to mature, Dillon Read offered the German industrialists a short-term loan to cover their immediate needs. It suggested a one-year loan of $5 million which the Germans could divide six ways with Dillon receiving an option on a larger loan later. Since the loan was totally inadequate for Thyssen's needs alone, the offer shocked the German industrialists. Not only did they consider the small sum and short-term nature of the loan unacceptable, but the Americans' demand that the loan be secured by claims on the goods to be financed was also rejected.[10]

Despite these unpleasant surprises, negotiations for the consolidated loan continued. But a series of delays produced growing frustration and irritation on the part of the Germans.

Barth's diary records his feeling. First, Clarence Dillon, the head of Dillon Read, was reported to be sick, as Barth wrote, "if in reality or only diplomatically we could not determine." Barth's pressure for clarification of continuing uncertainties remained fruitless. When he and his colleagues were finally told that Dillon Read's sales department had approved the loan, they were put off again by being informed that an expert on German loans would have to review the plan and go over the German account books. Most irritatingly, the Americans suddenly added that of course the loan would have to be secured by a mortgage on industrial property as was customary in the United States. As Barth recorded, "Since this wish could have been expressed long before, we saw it as a means to further drag out the decision." When the Germans insisted on a quick decision, Dillon Read responded with the news that its expert on German loans ("this mysterious confidant" as Barth called him) was indisposed.[11]

Even as Dillon Read continued to insist that it wanted to finance the "big-Six" together, it dropped a new bombshell into the negotiations. It announced that the German industrialists would have to improve their credit ratings by commercializing their Dawes Plan debts in order to pay off those debts immediately.[12] German industry had been assessed large shares of Germany's reparation debt, and those debts were backed by a first mortgage on industrial assets. The Americans wanted to back their own loans with a first mortgage on German industry, and to do this, they wanted industry to sell international bonds to buy out their Dawes Plan debt.[13] The Americans viewed their demand as a business proposition aimed at making a sound loan, but the political implications of the demand were monumental. It was generally felt that any part of the Dawes Plan debt taken by international bankers and sold on the world capital market would be safe from German repudiation. Germany might welsh on its reparations payments, but to refuse to pay off a "legitimate" international loan held by private foreign investors would be unthinkable. Thus, France and to a lesser degree Britain hoped to commercialize the reparations bonds in order to firmly commit Germany to paying. When Dillon Read set this as a precondition for its loan, it was, in effect, assuming the role of enforcer of the Dawes Plan. With this demand, the German industrialists and the American bankers stood in direct confrontation; either the Americans had to back down or Germany had to openly accept its reparations debt. The outcome of this confrontation would provide the first test of the ability of American bankers to influence German policy when it involved a matter of vital interest to Germany.

This newest development prompted the Thyssen negotiators, Barth and Rabes, to ask Thyssen's home office for permission to seek a separate loan. With this permission in hand, they immediately confronted Dillon Read. They protested the plan to commercialize the reparations debt and told Dillon Read that "we are no longer willing to tolerate the slow rate of progress on the loan project." They insisted that a firm of Thyssen's stature could easily find another bank with which to do business. Even this threat was not enough to bring Dillon Read to make an acceptable offer. However, when another New York bank did in fact make Thyssen a loan offer, and it was revealed that Krupp had secured a loan on better terms than Dillon Read was offering, the American resistance began to crumble. Advising Dillon of the alternative offer, Barth and Rabes informed the Americans that "we are now contemplating the termination of our mission to Dillon Read." Aware that any further delay or pressure would mean the loss of an immense account, Dillon's resistance completely broke. As Barth recorded, "From this time on, Dillon took giant steps to make up for the earlier lost time."[14] Even Dillon's insistence on a mortgage guarantee was surrendered, and the final loan was secured by a vague claim on the "Assets and Reputation" of the Thyssen concern.

The August Thyssen loan was closed on January 9, 1925, and within hours the bonds were reportedly sold out, although as soon became clear, this was an illusion created by fake purchases of the bonds by the bank syndicate that was selling them. The firm received $11,177,681 from a loan of $12 million. The proceeds were used almost entirely to finance working capital for the firm; $8.4 million was spent to consolidate short-term debts to German and Dutch banks while the remaining $2.4 million was used for working capital and minor capital improvements.[15] This use of the proceeds provides a disturbing picture of the financial condition of heavy industry after the inflation. Industry may have been a relative "winner" from the inflation, but by 1925 it was starved for working capital and its needs in this regard were immense. When we consider that during the inflation and stabilization, a firm with huge export capacity such as Thyssen had been forced into taking over $8 million in high-interest, short-term loans, it is evident that other German industries were in even tighter financial straits.

Barth was exuberant about the benefits to accrue to Germany as a result of his negotiations. He wrote in his diary that when one considers "that we had to carry out pioneering work since precedence for German industrial loans on a mortgage basis did not exist and the burden of the Dawes obligations had to be overcome, it is obvious that a tough job in the interests of wide circles of industry was not bungled."[16] Indeed, it was not!

The loan negotiations reveal that despite American financial power, exploitation of that power was not going to be easy. On some occasions, such as during the Dawes Plan negotiations, a united American financial community (led or whipped into line by a determined J. P. Morgan) might be able to wield effective influence. In smaller negotiations, individual American bankers would not be able to force any crucial concessions from German borrowers. In early 1925, other German firms were able to use Thyssen's tactic of dealing with several different banks to get the best terms.[17] With a little experience, American bankers learned how to reduce the dangers of competition and of being played off against one another. They bluntly informed the Germans that dealing with more than one lender at a time could lead to a termination of all loans. In the fall of 1925, the German government warned its borrowers against the practice, and it was greatly reduced.[18] Through this device, the Americans hoped to reduce competition and secure high returns on their German loans. Yet this attempt at competitive restraint failed, as the large number of American bankers, plus the introduction of Swiss, Dutch, and British competitors, ensured that no monopoly rates could be fixed. No further effort, such as Dillon Read's attempt to commercialize the reparations debt, was made by American bankers. When German national policy was threatened, American capital would be hard-pressed indeed to force any alteration.

The Thyssen negotiations clearly demonstrated that despite the apparent scramble of lenders and borrowers to make a quick deal, the actual negotiations by reputable agents were slow and painful. Even with the most desirable of loans, the Americans hesitated and delayed until finally they were almost blackmailed into granting the credit. Whether one emphasizes their initial reserve or their final rush to close the loan, it is apparent that the Americans were not simply throwing their money at every passing German who might or might not really need it. The "flood" of loans reported by newspapers and even modern historians[19] simply did not exist. While unable to say precisely how many loans were actually made in late 1924 and early 1925, the number is unmistakably small. By April 1925 even this slow rate of German borrowing was declining. The American capital market began to tighten as the Federal Reserve raised discount rates from 3 percent to 3.5 percent, and American speculative funds flowed into England in anticipation of the pound's return to parity. Despite high returns on the German loans, the interest rates were not high enough to convince Americans that their money was safely invested in Germany. Early enthusiasm for the Krupp and Thyssen loan had been an illusion, and by March, banking syndicates were forced to retain large portfolios of unsold bonds out of fear that their release on the market would drive prices drastically downward.[20] When World War I hero General Paul von Hindenburg was elected President of the Weimar Republic that spring, the fear that he represented a return to German monarchical expansionism further dampened American interest in German loans.[21] The anticipated flood, which in reality had been a small stream, now fell to a trickle. The Reichsbank, which within two years was to become a bitter foe of foreign loans, found that in the spring of 1925 they offered no inflationary dangers. In fact, the bank argued that Germany needed more capital imports and defended its high discount rate as a policy which would attract that much needed capital.[22]

In the early months of 1925, the massive and unregulated rush of foreign capital which had so concerned policymakers in late 1924 did not happen. Indeed, it was the very lack of capital that created the gravest problems. Only months later, in the late summer and early fall, would Americans finally begin to find the confidence and inclination to begin large-scale investments in Germany. And, precisely as had been feared earlier, they found German municipal bonds to be the safest and most attractive investments available. The ability of the cities to attract American capital unleashed a multi-sided power struggle within Germany. As the loans flowed into social spending projects of the city governments, conservatives found their victories of 1924 being dangerously eroded. When they launched a new assault on the political left, Germany's dependence on American capital ensured that the German domestic conflict would soon spill over into the international political arena.

Economic Power and Social Conflict: Germany, 1925

In the autumn of 1925, as German cities began to secure more and larger loans in the United States, city leaders found themselves at the center of Germany's resurgent social crisis. During the Weimar era, in Germany as in other industrial societies, a vast struggle was underway to redefine the role of the state in the modern economy. How far should the state go in providing economic security to its citizens? How much aid should the state give to private businesses that found themselves in economic trouble? How much influence could the state actually have in controlling the course of the capitalist business cycle? In the German cities, these issues began to take on political form and exert a national impact in 1925.

Many of Germany's largest cities—Berlin, Cologne, Frankfurt a.M., and Hamburg for example—were dominated by loose coalitions of middle-class progressives and worker

representatives from both the Catholic Center Party and the
Social Democratic Party. Although these allies had vastly differing ideological orientations, they often shared short-range
political goals which created a powerful lobby to expand government's role in society and the economy. The free labor
unions and the SPD fought for an expansion of public enterprise
as a first step toward socialism. They saw public ownership as
an attack on private industry, and thus supported almost all
efforts to expand it. Middle-class progressives, perhaps best
represented by the Association of German city governments
(deutsche Städtetag) remained wedded to a free enterprise,
capitalist ideal. They regarded themselves as pragmatists who
wanted to use public funds to finance specific technical projects
which could not be efficiently developed by private industry.[23]
Despite these ideological differences, the shared day-to-day
agreements ensured that this alliance remained effective at the
municipal level long after the national government's much-
heralded swing to the right in 1924–25.[24]

Even as this progressive alliance responded to increased
demands on the city governments, municipal finances had to
be rebuilt after the near bankruptcy imposed by World War I
and the postwar inflation. Low tax revenues had made maintenance of essential services such as gas and electric works,
hospitals, schools, and transportation facilities impossible. At
the same time, the Reich government forced municipalities to
assume a much wider responsibility for social welfare payments,
especially unemployment compensation.[25] Pumped up by progressive political alliances at the local level and the new legal
responsibilities placed on them by the Reich government, city
budgets ballooned. Although perhaps more a quantitative growth
in spending than an expansion of municipal responsibility into
entirely new fields,[26] the increased expenditure itself was great
enough to make the change important.

From 1924 to 1930 public investment exceeded investment in private industry.[27] A great deal of this investment was
indisputably productive and necessary. At the local level, out-
moded gas and electric works were replaced, while state and
federal governments invested heavily in aluminum manufac-
turing, mining, and electricity. Even opponents of public spend-

ing were forced to agree that German electric capacity was badly underdeveloped as a result of neglect during the war and inflation and that public investment in electricity was both essential and productive.[28] Private industry, however, refused to accept this growth in the public sector passively. Although industrialists most often concentrated their attacks on "non-productive" public spending on projects such as new housing, theaters, and swimming pools, their real aim was often to prevent projects that would incontestably be productive. Public projects such as municipal electric works which competed with private firms often were the most vigorously opposed areas of public spending.[29]

Oddly enough, the most bitter attack on public enterprise was not inaugurated by private industry but by private commercial banks. The commercial banks, facing a long-term trend which reduced their power over private industry, were further weakened by the destruction of many of their paper assets during the inflation. Within the banking field itself, they were being even more dramatically threatened by the growth of publicly owned banks. Led by city-run savings and loan banks, public banking grew with remarkable vigor after 1924. Assets of the over 3,000 savings and loans grew from 1,567 million RM in 1924 to 13,670 million in 1930, and as early as 1926 they controlled nearly 50 percent of the capital held by German banks.[30] Their rapid absorption of domestic savings made them a vital source of capital to liquidity starved small industries, and as they expanded their field of activity they ran into direct conflict with the privately owned banks.

The private bankers were not only threatened by the growth of public banks, but they also found themselves being blamed for Germany's lack of capital and exhorbitant interest rates. During the second half of 1924, the Reich Association of Industrialists (RDI) received so many complaints from businesses about high interest rates that it formed a committee to negotiate with the bankers to try to make more and cheaper credit available to industry.[31] Bank interest rates were so high that within the government, consideration was given to charging the big banks with usury. But when it became apparent that nine-tenths of all the banks would have to be charged, the government drew back from such a confrontation.[32] The industrialists likewise failed to achieve any positive results. As one of them reported, "The negotiations have in most cases not led to any result which corresponds to the interests of industry."[33]

Although industrial distress with bank policy declined along with interest rates in 1925, the bankers moved to ensure that they were not blamed for Germany's continuing capital scarcity. In November 1925, the bankers national organization—the Central Association of German Banks—charged that high interest rates were caused by excessive government spending and took the initiative in organizing German industry to fight the spread of socialism in the German economy.[34] Reichsbank president and banking leader Hjalmar Schacht even coined a term to describe this "creeping socialization." He called it *Kalte Sozialisierung* (cold socialization), and the fight against *Kalte Sozialisierung* became a keynote of the Weimar Era.[35] By focusing on how state enterprise absorbed scarce capital funds, banking interests were well served. Irritation over high interest rates was deflected from them to the common enemy of state socialism. The private bankers' campaign to force the publicly owned banks to restrict their activities could also be tied into the broad attack on the expansion of the state role in the economy. For political and economic reasons, German industrial and commercial groups were more than ready to join this attack on public enterprise, and the bankers' initiative fell on fertile ground.

In the course of 1925 and 1926, leaders of national organizations representing industry, commerce, insurance, wholesale and retail trade, banks, and, to a lesser degree, agriculture and handicrafts worked to formulate a united opposition to public interference in the economy.[36] As municipal borrowing grew in late 1925, industrialists focused their attack on government spending which they believed was absorbing the funds essential to meet their own liquidity needs. The business associations hired a full-time lobbyist to collect evidence of socialization and lead an organized protest. They solicited local chambers of commerce for examples of destructive governmental interference with business. In this endeavor they met with mixed results. While businessmen in many cities supported the business organizations' effort to organize a protest, others, such as the Bremen Chamber of Commerce, found no evidence of municipal government harming private business.[37] And well it might not have, since the Bremen government actively solicited foreign capital which it made available to Bremen's private industry.[38] Here was the Achilles heel of the businessmen's fight. Even they had to admit that a major impetus for expanded public activity was the fact that at least in 1924 and 1925 huge tax yields made government the largest reservoir of liquid funds, and many private firms actively solicited municipal financial largesse and fought for contracts on public construction projects.[39] Some industries, such as the electrical industry, found themselves heavily dependent on construction of public utilities owned by cities or national governments.[40] Yet industrialists seemed to find it easy to separate their own individual demands for public assistance for their own firm from their attacks on the abstract idea of "Kalte Sozialisierung."[41]

As foreign money markets opened to municipal borrowing in late 1925, the campaign against *Kalte Sozialisierung* focused on municipal foreign loans, and on tax advantages granted to public enterprises. During the depression of late 1925–26, the attack on *Kalte Sozialisierung* gained momentum and attracted mass support at several large public demonstrations. Under the combined pressures of the business organizations and the mass demonstrations, the "bourgeois" political parties became increasingly fearful of expanding the public sector.[42] This conservative orientation was far from uniform, however, as the Center Party remained open to public spending and the *deutsche Städtetag,* largely a "bourgeois" organization led by the mayors of Berlin, Cologne, and Frankfurt, vigorously promoted and defended municipal enterprise. As we shall see in the next chapter, even the German Democratic Party and Reich Finance Minister Peter Reinhold, for all their loyalty to private industry, were determined that the federal government should actively help stimulate the economy in the face of the depression of 1925–26.

America Gets Involved:
Autumn, 1925

In the United States, as in Germany, the events of 1925 would bring into the open all the old fears and conflicts surrounding America's foreign lending. Americans would find it no easier to formulate a consistent policy in 1925 than they had in 1922. But this time, the very fact that American leaders were concerned about the German loans fed the growing conflict within Germany over who should have access to American money.

Throughout 1925 concern grew in the United States that loans to Germany might be both politically and economically dangerous, a concern expressed not only in government circles but by some bankers as well. In fact, the most powerful private banking house in the United States, J. P. Morgan and Company, was led by men who openly questioned the wisdom of making loans to Germany. Morgan had maintained close ties to Britain and France during the war and some of these ties remained even after the Dawes Plan conflicts. Jack Morgan himself had the reputation of being "a notorious enemy of Germany" as one German diplomat put it.[43] Soon after the Dawes Plan had been approved, Morgan informed Germany's ambassador to the United States that he believed that leading German businessmen and government officials, especially Foreign Minister Gustav Stresemann, were still monarchists and might recall the Kaiser and promote a war of revenge if given the chance.[44] Exactly a week after floating the Dawes loan, Morgan publicly announced that, having fulfilled its obligation as fiscal agent for England, France, and Belgium, it would take no further part in loans to Germany.[45] This remained the company's policy throughout the twenties. In 1931, Morgan partner Thomas Lamont informed a Senate investigating committee that Morgan had taken part in only two long-term loans to Germany—the Dawes and Young Plan loans—and had made no short-term loans, "because we did not have dealings with German banks."[46]

The opposition of the Morgan partners to the German loans should be kept in mind when trying to determine how "American bankers" wanted loan policies to be determined.

The picture is made even more complex by the fact that despite Morgan's public refusal to participate in German loans, other banks which were closely allied with J. P. Morgan were active in the market. Bankers Trust Company, which was led by two partners from J. P. Morgan, had extensive interests in German loans.[47] In 1929, Bankers Trust Berlin representative, Eric Archdeacon, wrote back to the head office in New York that "Prins told me also that our friends from 28 Nassau Street [Dillon Read] are telling everyone that the Morgan Group is anti-German, which accounts for the fact that this group did up to now no financing in Germany. Well, I proved to Prins the contrary, but gained the impression that the said slogan will be doing its job generally around Germany."[48] Morgan also maintained close ties to Lee Higginson and Company, which was extremely active in the German market. Morgan was even reported to have secretly taken a large part of a loan floated by Lee Higginson in 1930, an action which, if true, was remarkable both because of Morgan's direct participation in a German loan and its secret participation in a consortium led by another bank.[49]

Despite these disclaimers, Morgan's announcement in 1925 that it would not participate in further German loans was undoubtedly sincere. Furthermore, not only Morgan but other American leaders in business and politics took public stands against moving too rapidly into the German bond market. Owen Young, who in principle supported some lending, warned American investors that a flood of unsecured loans might be so damaging that all investments could be lost. What Germany needed, he said, was a moderate but steady stream of capital over a period of years.[50] Leaders of the Democratic Party, such as Norman Davis and Cordell Hull, cast a wider net and attacked the Republican Party's policy of supporting high tariffs and encouraging American bankers to sell foreign government bonds. Davis charged that although the outflow of American capital might temporarily promote American exports, in the long run the high tariff policy would make it impossible for foreigners to earn the revenue required to repay their loans, and the entire debt structure would collapse.[51]

Otto Wiedfeldt, Germany's ambassador to the United States, found this strong current against the German loans very disturbing. When he heard rumors in January 1925 that the Commerce Department intended to inform American bankers that it would be unwise to make further loans to Germany, he sought out his American contacts in order to counter the move. He warned the Americans that "the whole purpose of the Dawes plan was to make Germany and Europe economically viable again and these credits are part of the plan. If you close off further credit, even the best plan could not achieve this goal and the Dawes plan will surely fail." He informed the German Foreign Office that he would wait until a respectable German firm was refused a loan, and then he would formally take up the issue with American officials.[52]

Wiedfeldt's information was correct. Charles Herring, the American commercial attaché in Berlin, had sent the Commerce Department a long memorandum enumerating the dangers to American loans caused by structural weaknesses within the German economy. Carefully and with great insight, Herring warned that loan repayment could be thwarted by a whole series of complications. Not only might repayment come into conflict with reparations transfers, but a high revaluation of old debts wiped out by the inflation might overburden both industrial and public borrowers. Added to these problems was the fact that the government, in need of new sources of tax revenue, might well set off another bitter class struggle to determine who would have to bear the expanded tax burden. All these possibilities could mean economic disruptions with dangerous repercussions for American investors. Under these conditions, he urged that only a minimum of credit be extended to Germany.[53]

Herring's report prompted the Commerce Department to worry that Germany might be taking American loans in order to pressure the United States to take its side in a future reparations crisis. But Herring did not believe that any such political motive lay behind German borrowing. Germans believed they really needed the funds and, while Herring felt this need was exaggerated, he found no sinister motive behind it.[54]

Leaders in the Commerce Department hoped that Herring's report would provide the means for dealing with their long-standing concern about German borrowing. As Grosvenor Jones wrote Herring, the department planned to send a copy of his report to all the "big wigs in high finance . . . Then if anything happens four or five years hence, the Department of Commerce will be on record and no one can blame us for the debacle."[55] Before releasing the report, Secretary Hoover sent an advance copy to the Treasury Department for approval. Hoover supported his proposal with the observation that "we do have an obligation to protect American investors when the problem involves international relations in which we have knowledge and the public generally has not."[56] But the Treasury was not inclined to have the report sent out. Responsible bankers would already be aware of any information that Hoover might send them. But of greater concern, the Treasury hesitated to do anything that might harm the value of loans already made or assume for the government a position as financial advisor on the loans. Hoover shared this fear that government action might imply a guarantee of loans which were not actually discouraged, and the issue was allowed to drop.[57] Fortunately for their peace of mind, the flow of loans to Germany was proving to be more illusion than reality, so at least for the moment, the pressure for a firm policy subsided.[58]

In the late summer and fall of 1925 a new, and this time active, phase in the course of American loans began. The long awaited and dreaded flood of communal and state loans finally began in earnest. In the last six months of the year, sixteen public organizations secured foreign loans, while only four private firms were successful.[59] In Germany, the failure of the Advisory Board for Foreign Credit to prevent these public loans demonstrated that the issues had not been settled as clearly as it had appeared six months earlier, and the debate over loan control once again became heated. The argument which everyone had accepted in December 1924, that loans had to be controlled to preserve a stable currency, now fell into the background, and the issue of public versus private investment came to the fore. In the United States, too, the earlier relief that the threat of excessive lending had not materialized gave way to a growing conviction that some new, forceful policy was required.

Despite mounting concern in the United States, the initiative to reduce loans came from Germany and from Americans living in Germany. As German officials watched their efforts to reduce municipal borrowing begin to collapse, they began to play on American anxieties about the loans to bolster the conservative position within Germany. Charles Herring, the American commercial attache in Berlin, informed Grosvenor Jones that:

the Undersecretary for Economic Affairs in the Foreign Office, who is a friend of mine, asked me recently to do anything I could in the way of additional reports or cables to induce caution in American lenders, particularly those interested in municipal loans or others not directly used for increased production and export.

Jones was pleased to hear that Germans, too, were concerned about excessive German borrowing. He did misinterpret part of Herring's point, however. He assumed that Germany was worried about both "municipalities and corporations borrowing so freely abroad."[60] It is highly unlikely that any German officials opposed industrial loans, and the thrust of Herring's letter certainly aimed to stop municipal and not industrial loans.

The problem for Jones and the Commerce Department was that although they might believe that municipal loans were unsound, their constituency, the American business community, cared little about the city loans, but was deeply resentful of loans to German industry. As Jones noted, there was a serious campaign under way by April 1925 to "kill off interest in German loans." The major attack was against loans to German chemical, dye, and machine tool firms which would use the American money to buy American firms or modernize German plants to compete against American products. Dr. Julius Klein had asked that the Commerce Department prepare a stock reply "to American manufacturers and others who are flooding the Bureau with objections to German industrial loans."[61] Thus, while German conservatives and government officials wanted to stop American capital from going to German cities, American businessmen wanted to stop American capital from going to

German industry. Jones' relief that Germans wanted to reduce the rate of borrowing was therefore based on the erroneous assumption that the two nations shared the same objectives.[62]

Benjamin Anderson, a highly respected economist and editor of the Chase National Bank's *Chase Economic Bulletin*, was much more in tune with the desires of German conservatives. He recalled that during a trip to Germany in the fall of 1925 "I found German financial opinion virtually unanimous [that American loans to cities were unwise] and I was personally asked by a representative of the Reichsbank, a representative of the German Treasury, a representative of Mr. Gilbert's office, and various German bankers, to cable New York that, while loans to German industrialists would be very helpful, loans to the states and municipalities were very harmful and should be discontinued. . . . I sent this cable to New York and I am glad to be able to say that our own securities corporation respected the advice of the German financial authorities, and virtually ceased to underwrite German state and municipal issues in the United States."[63]

Charles Herring, whose earlier warning had so nearly resulted in Commerce Department action against the German loans, wrote an even more scathing report as the loans picked up over the summer. He charged that security for German loans was "lamentably weak, and the whole credit position of the municipalities strongly disapproved."[64]

As these concerns grew, the State Department received a final shove by its ambassador to Germany, Jacob G. Schurman. Schurman had been quietly critical of municipal loans earlier, but in mid-September he inaugurated a personal campaign to end German municipal borrowing in the United States. He informed the State Department:

I have discussed the matter with a number of the higher German officials, and many of the leading industrialists and financiers, and their opinion without exception, has been that, if American capitalists continue granting considerable loans to German municipalities, the result will be disastrous for the future of the German economy and will eventually lead to interference, on the part of the transfer committee, with the transfer out of Germany of the interest charges involved.[65]

He went on to explain that many German businessmen "fully realized" that in order to pay reparations plus interest and amortization on the loans, exports had to be increased. To do this, German agriculture and industry must be built up, but this was very difficult in the face of high interest rates. "These men of business say that the only thing that can save them is the ability to borrow abroad. They feel that they, and not the greedy municipalities, should have first call on all money loaned to Germany." He concluded that "with these factors in mind, I believe that the demands of the municipalities should be relegated to the background; and I have come to the conclusion that we can do no better service to Germany and to ourselves than to discourage further placing of German municipal loans in America." Schurman was not content to express his opinions only once and followed up his report with two more denunciations of municipal borrowing.[66]

Schurman's reports, combined with the Commerce Department's concerns and persistent pressures from the Reparations Agent, German officials, and German business leaders, prompted the State Department to try to resolve the conflict over the loans.[67] However, even now, the State Department was reluctant to go very far in order to protect American lenders. This reserve was expressed most clearly by the department's economic adviser, Arthur N. Young. Young argued persistently that the government should continue to review foreign loans under the 1922 formula. But his concern had nothing to do with protecting American investors. Instead, Young believed and convinced his superiors, that the government needed to review the loans in order to further its own policy. Specifically, the department wanted to have a means to close the American capital market to borrowers from nations that were not repaying their war debts.[68] As for regulating private loans which did not endanger national policy, Young came down strongly against any action. As he informed the Secretary of State, "this Department would have no warrent in law for interfering with loan transactions even should it clearly appear that they tend to be economically injurious."[69]

By the autumn of 1925, both the Treasury and State Departments had become so concerned with the German loans that leading officials felt something had to be done. The reparations payments and war debts made the loans to Germany more complex and political than loans to any other countries. In the Treasury, Under Secretary Garrard Winston shared Young's view that the government's prime concern should be to ensure that the government continued to receive its war debt payments even if private loans went into default. He urged Secretary of State Kellogg to adopt "some form of advice to the bankers which brings home to them warnings that installments due under debt settlements to the United States will not be subordinated to the service of private loans." Kellogg refused openly to declare that government debts would have precedence over private loans for fear that it would have the effect of blocking loans to nations which had begun paying their war debts to the United States.[70]

Kellogg did instruct his unofficial delegate to the Reparations Commission, James Logan, to ask the Transfer Committee if it would favor repayment of private loans or of reparations in the event of a transfer crisis. When the Transfer Committee refused to speculate on its response to a hypothetical crisis,[71] the State Department decided to issue a warning directly to the banks about the dangers of a clash between loan repayment and reparations. The opportunity came when the banking house of Speyer and Company consulted the department in routine fashion about a loan for Franfurt am Main.

Instead of the old bland expression of disinterest in the loan, Secretary Kellogg sent a long and strong warning on the dangers of the German loans. He wrote Speyer that "the Department is advised that the German Federal authorities themselves are not disposed to view with favor the indiscriminate placing of German loans in the American market, particularly when the borrowers are German municipalities and the purposes are not productive." Beyond that, Speyer was advised to determine if the Transfer Committee might interfere with the repayment of the loan. In the event that the reparations entanglements could not be cleared up, Kellogg concluded, "the Department believes that you should consider whether you do not owe a duty to your prospective clients fully to advise them of the situation."[72] As soon as Speyer got the letter, bank head James Speyer and Henry W. Taft ran to see the Secretary of State. Speyer and Taft were, in Arthur Young's words, "greatly wrought up" by the department's letter and insisted that the State Department was "going outside of its proper field in suggesting what the bankers should tell their clients." With firm support from Hoover, the State Department refused to back down, "since the matter is not an ordinary matter of business risk, but is related to negotiations in which this government has had a part."[73]

When James Speyer tried to pin down what exactly the government wanted, he found no room for encouragement. He informed Arthur Young that as a result of their conversation his firm had arranged the Frankfurt loan "subject to the views" of the State Department. As Young reported, "I stated that the Department did not desire that bankers condition their financing upon its action. Mr. Speyer replied that he had not seen any other way to act in the circumstances."[74]

Speyer was not the only one who found the State Department's new policy confusing. Parker Gilbert was besieged by American bankers trying to find out if he would prevent repayment of their loans.[75] Gilbert was irate that the State Department was sending bankers to see him without having informed him of this change in policy. He speculated that the department was attempting to "smoke out the Transfer Committee" and force it to make its position clear. He objected that the State Department's letter "raises questions which nobody can answer, and suggests doubts which no one can settle, except by the test of actual experience." While Gilbert wanted state and city loans restrained, he was afraid that the new American policy would also hurt the market for German industrial and agricultural loans that he believed were desirable. Yet what upset Gilbert the most was the self-rightous moral tone of the State Department's position. He thoroughly agreed with Shepard Morgan's observation that the letter "ought to be set to music, and it is on such a high moral plane that nothing less than a pipe organ would do for the purpose." As he complained to Garrard Winston, the State Department not only had the nerve to give the bankers a lesson in high morals, but it then "proceeds to relieve itself of all responsibility by a closing sentence to the effect that, no question of Government policy being involved, it raises no objection! What a wonderful little tail for all that dog." Gilbert's frustration was based on his clear perception of the State Department's irresponsibility; an irresponsibility which was only confirmed by the other branches of the American government.[76] Having successfully tried to force Gilbert to do their job, they had jumped at the chance to have Germany do it, and when this too failed, they fell back on a policy which "passed the buck" to the bankers in order to avoid being blamed if something went wrong in the future.

While Parker Gilbert fumed over State Department policy, Benjamin Strong set out to curtail the department's tentative step toward foreign loan regulation. He sought out Reichsbank President Hjalmar Schacht, who was traveling in the United States at the time, and the two men agreed to pressure the German government to strengthen its control over Germany's foreign borrowing.[77] If the Americans were frightened of assuming responsibility for any positive action, Hjalmar Schacht certainly was not. Schacht was already in the midst of a drawn-out battle with the German government over control of German interest rates and had launched an aggressive campaign to concentrate control over all monetary policies in his own hands.[78] Before his trip to America, Schacht had also begun what was to become a persistent attack on municipal borrowing through public speeches, warnings to American bankers, and protests to the Reich and state governments.[79]

Immediately upon hearing about the State Department's letter to American bankers, Schacht swung into action. Although his visit to the United States was initially undertaken at least in part to reduce municipal borrowing, he quickly saw that if the State Department's letter became public, all loans to Germany might be endangered, and Germany might be caught in a catastrophic squeeze.[80] He wired the Foreign Ministry reporting the situation in the United States, and observed that the State Department's letter was "apparently perceived as maladroit by the Treasury as well as the Federal Reserve Bank of New York." To avoid endangering desirable loans, Schacht requested permission to negotiate a deal with the

Treasury Department. He suggested that the current situation offered a chance for the Reich government and the Reichsbank to seize the initiative and establish a firm control of German borrowing without the need for further consultation with the state governments. Specifically, he proposed that he tell the American Treasury Department that "negotiations and marketing of loans issued by state governments, municipalities, and political organizations must first receive joint approval of the German Government and Reichsbank."[81]

For the United States, Schacht's proposal to take control of German loans solved an intractable dilemma. Benjamin Strong was particularly pleased that Germany now seemed prepared to reduce its own foreign borrowing. He informed the Treasury that "my recommendation from the beginning has been that the matter be dealt with by direct representations to the German Government, so that some working arrangement or formula may be developed which will have the effect of controlling undesirable loans at the source." He even proposed a diabolical scheme to ensure that American loans would not be endangered by the Transfer Committee. Once an arrangement was made by the German government, the plan should be presented to the Reparations Agent to see if he had any objections. "Failure to express such objections necessarily would leave the operation of the Dawes Plan in such a position that it would be very difficult in later years for the Agent General to interfere with service of loans which had been placed in this country in pursuance of a plan of which he had been fully informed and to which he had not made objection."[82]

Secretaries Mellon and Hoover also found German control appealing since, as Mellon wrote, "a prohibition of all German municipal financing would deprive the American investment public of some of the best foreign loans. England may soon remove her restrictions upon foreign flotations and be an active competitor." Thus continued loans were desirable, but only secure ones, and, as he noted, "without information on and control of the city's budget we would be helpless to decide whether the loan was productive or not." Only an effective agency within Germany could accurately discriminate between safe and risky borrowers. Secretary Kellogg encouraged

Ambassador Schurman to pursue the project in Germany so that, by November of 1925, all interested parties in the United States had finally agreed upon a policy toward German loans.[83] That policy was to hope that Germany would supervise its loan taking, because the United States was unwilling to regulate its lending.

Schacht's scheme to expand the Reichsbank's influence over German borrowing appealed to the Americans precisely because it meant that the United States would not have to take any action to deal with what was universally perceived as a dangerous situation. In Germany, however, the plan met shocked outrage.[84] The state governments had not been consulted about a change that would completely circumvent their power. A crisis like that of November 1924 when the states had forced the government to repeal a presidential order giving the Finance Ministry control of loans seemed to be threatening.[85] To avoid it, the Finance and Economic Ministries suggested that Schacht inform Mellon that the Advisory Board for Foreign Credit was competent to do all that was necessary, and in the future the Reichsbank and the Reich government representatives on the board would cooperate to reduce municipal loans even more.[86]

Secretary Mellon was not convinced that the Advisory Board would wield any really effective control, but along with other American officials had concluded that any regulation from the American side was also impossible.[87] While Benjamin Strong remained optimistic that Germany was instituting significant reforms,[88] other American officials in the State and Commerce Departments shared Mellon's more accurate view that neither the American nor the German government was able or willing to control the international financial markets.[89]

When Schacht returned to Germany, he attempted to use the American concern over the foreign loans to finally ensure that cheap money went to industry and not city governments. He insisted that he was only conveying the wishes of the American government and argued that Germany had to give in to the American pressure.[90] Schacht related how the State Department had attempted to restrict all loans to Germany and how this effort had been foiled by the Treasury's opposition. If Germany failed to take command of its loans, the Treasury, which he stated wanted the Reichsbank to approve all loans, would lose influence and all loans might be stopped. Although a few productive city loans might be permissible, he insisted that the foreign market be largely reserved for private industry.[91] Once again, the power of the Americans was called in to do battle for German private industry, and Schacht played the American and German governments off against each other in an attempt to expand his own authority.

With the support of the Reich Finance Ministry, Schacht was able to impose a modest reform in German foreign loan policy.[92] By redefining "productivity" more narrowly, the Reich government hoped to reduce the total volume of public loans taken abroad, ensure that the loans which were taken would be repayable, and at the same time work within the structure of the Advisory Board so that no new conflict with the states would emerge.[93] Agreement was reached by February 1926, so that a "productive" (and therefore acceptable) loan must not only raise national income, but must also either reduce imports or expand exports.[94] Even this modest reform in defining what would constitute a productive loan proved more illusory than real, and little real change was made. Neither American fears nor Schacht's attempts to exploit those fears were able to substantially change German policy.

Despite the continuing anxiety about the loans in government circles, broader political developments created an atmosphere ever more conducive to German borrowing. In October 1925 Germany and France joined Britain, Italy, and Belgium in accepting the Locarno pact which appeared finally to resolve the political conflicts between the victorious allies and the German Reich. Britain and Italy guaranteed French security, while Germany accepted its western borders and promised only peaceful revision in the east. With Germany's entrance into the League of Nations, Europe found the political peace it needed to match the Dawes Plan's promise of economic order. Over the next years, tensions between France and Germany fell away as Aristide Briand and Gustav Stresemann gave up the politics of confrontation and sought security or treaty revision through cooperation and negotiation.[95]

As the spirit of Locarno spread across Europe, American investors shook off the restraints which had slowed investment in Germany. For a time, American money would underwrite the Locarno pact and submerge the simmering social conflict within Germany under a sea of imported capital.

Chapter 4

1926: Depression, Reparations, and Fiscal Policy

Coming fast on the heels of the inflation and the "stabilization crisis," a new economic depression beginning in late 1925 would force Germany to confront the implications of both its domestic and foreign policies. The violent economic catastrophies that marked the birth and death of the Weimar Republic have lead historians to overlook the importance of the German depression of 1925–26 as a turning point in Weimar history. Yet, like the inflation and Great Depression, the depression of 1925–26 would also exercise a major influence on the structures of Weimar society and politics. The severity of the crisis coming so soon after the hyper-inflation led the German government to give up the extreme fiscal conservatism that had helped end the inflation.

As it began to accept deficit spending policies, Germany soon found itself entangled in a web of international politics and debts which would reveal how closely German domestic economic decision making was tied to the world economic and political order. In responding to the economic crisis, the German government would have to deal with the fiscal restraints imposed upon a sovereign state by heavy international debts and obligations. Germany's severe capital weakness in the aftermath of the inflation made it as dependent upon the importation of foreign capital as many third world nations became in the 1970s and 1980s. Germany, like its latter-day successors, would find that its dependence on the international capital market drastically complicated its domestic economic policymaking.

As unemployment slowly grew in the second half of 1925 and then exploded to near record levels in the winter of 1925–26, pressures on the government to provide some sort of relief became irresistible. Not only the Reich, but state and municipal governments as well began expanding their spending and borrowing in response to the pressing needs of businessmen, farmers, and workers, who demanded government assistance as they faced the newest economic crisis. Hesitantly, yet inexorably, public spending increased and provided a critical stimulus to the faltering German economy. But these fiscal deficits undermined Germany's obligation under the Dawes Plan to maintain a balanced budget. As will be argued in the first section of this chapter, the depression of 1925–26 taught German policymakers the costs that a fulfillment policy would entail. The difficulty of maintaining a deflationary or even a balanced budget policy in the face of the economic crisis is the focus of the second section of the chapter.

Reparations and Fiscal Policy

Could Germany pay the reparations demanded of it after its defeat in the First World War? Over the past fifteen years perhaps no historical issue has seen more extensive revision than this question. During most of the interwar period and the 1950s, scholars generally believed that Germany was incapable of paying what were regarded as outrageously high reparations demanded by the British and French governments. In the past fifteen years, historians and economists interested in the economic problems of the 1920s reversed this consensus and agreed that Germany could have paid had it wanted to. Yet within this new consensus, the debate has moved on to focus on the political implications of the reparations conflict.

Historians now see that much more was at stake than simply German ability to pay reparations. The most intriguing new work has explored the role played by reparations as a medium for inter-allied debates and power struggles. French use of reparations to force British and American leaders to confront the reality of Europe's financial weakness has become a major theme of recent work.[1] Yet, it is not only in its international dimension that reparations became a political issue. Within German and French domestic politics, critical debates and policy decisions also turned on the reparations issue.[2]

During the period of the inflation, Germany was so unstable economically and politically that it is probably un-productive to speculate on the effects of a German policy of fulfillment. But as Germany ended the inflation by massive increases in taxes and drastic reductions in government spending, it also created the conditions for a real fulfillment policy. For a brief time in 1925 and 1926, Germany pursued the monetary and fiscal policies that made it possible for her to make large-scale reparation payments. By reviewing the evolution of contemporary analysis of German capacity to pay, and then looking at the impact of the prescribed policies when they were put into effect in 1925–26, it is possible to provide some clarification of the question, "Could Germany Pay?", but also to indicate some of the economic and political costs of the reparation conflict.

The new consensus on German ability to pay begins with the argument that the huge sums demanded under the London schedule of 1921 were more a face-saving formula for Allied statesmen than a realistic expression of Allied expectations.[3] The much lower and more concrete requirements of the Dawes Plan represented a fairly small share of German national income.[4] The greatest single problem for Germany was transforming the Reichsmarks collected in Germany into gold and foreign currency to be transferred abroad to the victorious Allies. This obstacle, too, is no longer regarded as the barrier it once was. Had the German government cut spending and raised taxes to collect the reparations in Reichsmarks, it could have transferred the payments abroad. Germany's resistance to making any payments at all, especially before the Dawes Plan, but to some degree afterward as well, is now regarded as the principal factor complicating reparation payments. This view, a total reversal of the 1920s consensus that Germany could not pay reparations, is based on parallel developments in economic theory and German social history.

The economic experts who drafted the Dawes Plan insisted that the German government had to maintain a balanced budget to help make the transfer of reparations possible. In spite of this, they believed that raising the necessary funds in Reichsmarks had to be considered a separate process from transferring the money abroad as gold or foreign currency. Only in the course of debates during the twenties did economists, led by Bertil Ohlin, Jacques Rueff, and Fritz Machlup, begin to understand that the very process of raising the funds in Germany by high taxes would be the major factor making transfers abroad possible.[5] Their emphasis on changes in national income as a major determinant of the trade balance, once ignored by economists, is now almost completely accepted.[6] As will be discussed more fully below, this analysis suggests that had Germany generated a large tax surplus, the resultant fall in income would have transferred reparations automatically.

Recent research in German social history has fortified the economic argument that reparations could have been paid by convincingly demonstrating German unwillingness to pay anything at all. As summed up by Stephen Schuker, historians now agree that reparations failed because "the Germans had no intention of making the tangible sacrifice in the form of higher taxes that was necessary to promote effective transfer."[7] Having first expected to win the war and loot a conquered Europe, and then hoping that a Wilsonian peace would be a peace without victors, Germans were totally unprepared to recognize the legitimacy of any claims on themselves.[8] During the postwar inflation, Germany experienced rapid economic growth and enjoyed huge imports of capital which foreign investors lost as the inflation continued. Even as Germany benefited from the inflation, German leaders exploited the inflation by arguing that it signaled German economic bankruptcy and proved that Germany could not pay reparations.[9] After the mark was stabilized, most German leaders continued to believe that ending reparations was among Germany's first priorities.[10] This overwhelming demonstration of German resistance to pay anything has quite naturally led modern historians to regard German pleas of poverty with little sympathy. When combined with the economists' theoretical argument proving that Germany really could have paid had it wanted to, their conviction became even firmer.

The one catch in the economic model of German ability to pay is the nagging possibility that the decline in income needed to make the transfers possible would produce high levels of unemployment. Although given greater emphasis in earlier literature, recent accounts have tended to de-emphasize this possibility. Charles Maier reflects the new view when he observes that a successful reparations policy "meant having Germans work an hour or two a week for the allies. Substituting foreign consumers for Germans should not have led to a contraction of output or employment."[11] Fritz Machlup acknowledged the danger that a deflationary policy might cause high unemployment but failed to consider the costs of this possibility. Writing in 1962, he summed up what seems to be the dominant historical thinking today. "It is hard to understand," he wrote, "why some economists in the late 1920's made such a fuss about the supposed severity of the German transfer problem."[12] Consideration of the process of adjustment in 1926 will confirm German ability to pay reparations, but will also demonstrate that there was good reason to "fuss" about the consequences. Historians who have used Machlup's economic analysis to argue that Germany could pay reparations need to go further than simply assuming this solves the problem and must consider the realities which faced German policymakers.

In order to earn the gold required to pay reparations, Germany had to sell more goods abroad than it bought. Gold or foreign currency could also be earned by providing services to foreigners such as insurance, shipping, and services to tourists in Germany. But the basic functioning of the Dawes Plan depended on development of an export surplus of real products. Several alternative policies might be employed to achieve this.

It has been suggested that the easiest and surest method for Germany to transfer reparations involved delivery of German products directly to the allies ("deliveries in kind").[13] This solution raises a number of complications which makes its value as a realistic alternative suspect. Initially, German insistence on fixing a high price on goods delivered clashed with Allied efforts to set prices much lower. The Dawes Plan seemed to settle this conflict. However, the opposition of French businessmen to German imports grew stronger as the 1920s progressed. During the Young Plan negotiations in 1929, France's representative, Emile Moreau, rejected deliveries in kind as a viable solution. As reported by the German negotiator, Moreau raised the issue repeatedly in order to discredit it. The German government was informed that "Moreau launched another long Philippic against deliveries in kind. He declared that they would be unanimously rejected by agriculture, commerce, and industry." The only large deliveries that France was willing to accept consisted of coal products.[14] This fact raises a second and probably even more important problem for arguments that deliveries in kind could solve the transfer problem. The former Allies demanded as deliveries in kind precisely the products they would have bought from Germany in an open market. Far from solving the transfer problem, these products were simply removed from the "export" side of trade and added in later as direct deliveries.[15] Only if the Allies accepted products which they would not have bought from Germany could these deliveries help solve the transfer problem. This was obviously an unlikely situation. The deliveries in kind were in essence merely exports under another name, and they do not seem to solve any of the potential difficulties inherent in cash payments.

The best, most realistic, and perhaps the only model of how reparations could have been paid remains the basic free market adjustment of the balance of trade. Under this model, a nation which is importing more than it exports and wants to reverse this situation has several policy options. Modern economists would advise it to devalue its currency. This would make its products less expensive relative to other nations' products and should stimulate other nations to purchase more of its goods. It would also make that country import less, since imports would become more expensive. In the 1960s, economists asserted that this would automatically solve the problem. Today, hard experience has raised doubts as to the "automatic" nature of this adjustment. In the 1920s, Keynes stood almost alone in understanding that an adjustment through devaluation was theoretically possible. For German financial leaders so recently burned by the inflation, the gold standard seemed the one remaining safe policy, and devaluation was nearly inconceivable.

Given this background, Germany was forced to hope it would be helped by developments in the world economy. If the rest of the world experienced rapid economic growth with rising incomes and prices, Germany's trade problems might be easily solved. German products would become relatively cheaper and therefore more attractive as world demand for all imports increased. The very process of Germany's transferring gold to the Allies should have stimulated this growth. That it did not do so is one of the truisms of the interwar period. The Allies, including the United States, refused to accept the large trade deficits essential to a successful reparations policy. They were unwilling and perhaps unable to use the money received from Germany to stimulate their own economies. Europeans were forced to pass most of their receipts along to the United States as repayment of war debts. This meant that even under a perfect gold standard, expansion of the money supply would have been small. Even without this constraint, fear of inflation and their own balance of payments concerns prevented any systematic expansionary monetary policies.[16] In spite of these restraints, German exports grew slowly but steadily until the Great Depression destroyed world trade. However, they did not grow enough to yield a painless export surplus. In the face of relative stagnation in the world economy, Germany could achieve its export surplus only by reducing its national income.

As figure 1 indicates, throughout the nineteen twenties, Germany's balance of trade was dominated by fluctuations in imports which were largely determined by the business cycle

within Germany. The recession of 1925–26 reduced both German income and imports so that for the only time in the
1920s, Germany was able to achieve a significant export surplus.[17]

    The catch in this process is that declining national in-
come almost invariably produces a rise in unemployment. Although it might be possible to imagine a policy that could
prevent this by a combination of high taxes and export subsidies
to preserve full employment,[18] it seems a doubtful exercise.
The economic skills and technical information required to
pursue such a policy are not readily apparent today, and it
does not seem very useful to "assume" them for the 1920s.
We need also to remember that Germany needed to develop
this export surplus to pay a debt it did not recognize as
legitimate. The payment of subsidies to create an artificial export
surplus would, in essence, have been an extra reparations
payment for which Germany would receive no credit. Is it

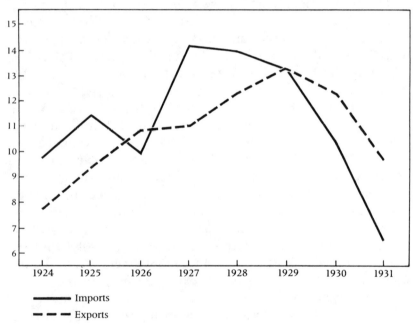

Figure 1. German Exports and Imports, 1924–1930 (in Reichmarks billion)
SOURCE: *The Economist,* 22 August 1931, annex I, and *Statistisches Jahrbuch
für das deutsche Reich,* 1933, p. 185.

reasonable to ask Germany to pursue such a policy? Conversely, would the allied governments have been willing to accept these subsidies as a partial payment of Germany's reparations debt? The answer to both questions is quite obviously no, and until some hypothetical compromise can be framed, this alternative must be shelved.[19] It is possible that after an initial period of adjustment, the stimulation of increased exports would reduce unemployment, but this is at best a slow and uncertain process. In fact, Germany suffered an unemployment rate of over 10 percent for sixteen months in 1925–26 without developing a sustained export surplus.

In turning from these general comments to the specifics of the economy in 1925–26, it should be noted that it is always difficult to establish the precise turning points of economic cycles since timing varies from sector to sector. Germany's highly erratic economic performance even in the "golden years" of the Weimar Republic makes it all the more difficult. Since we are concerned here primarily with the social and political implications of economic fluctuations, rates of unemployment provide the most useful index. However, this does not mean that the underlying pattern of economic development is completely captured by unemployment rates. Consideration of other indexes will be used to try to determine some causes of the economic downturn of 1925–26.

Referring to figure 2, the trend of unemployment among labor union members demonstrates the outline of depression and recovery in 1925–27. Rates of unemployment fell until the summer of 1925, then stabilized over the summer, began a slow rise in the autumn, and shot upward during the last two months of the year. Unemployment reached a peak of 22.6 percent in January 1926, then fell only slowly throughout the year with real recovery not apparent until the spring of 1927.[20] This trend is supported by data on total employment in Germany, which is, however, not available in monthly series.[21]

Following Machlup's model, a budget surplus to reduce national income should provide the stimulus to a positive balance of trade. In both 1924 and 1925, the German federal government as well as most state and local governments enjoyed

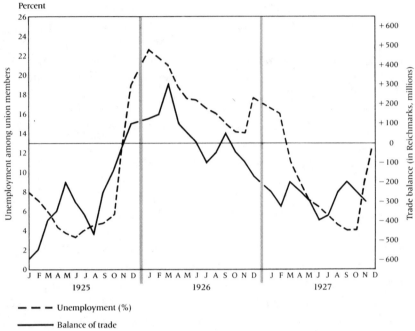

Figure 2. German Unemployment and Trade Balance, 1925–1927

surpluses.[22] This excess of revenue over expenditure exerted a contractionary pressure on the economy which may have been the origin of the recession, but it was not the only factor. In figure 3, three important indexes of economic activity are portrayed. The general index of consumption, compiled by Bresciani-Turroni, demonstrates that rising personal consumption which had stimulated the economy during the second half of 1924 became stagnant and even declined in 1925.[23] One would anticipate that this fall in consumption would cause a rise in business inventories and lead to a reduction in industrial production. A fall in production of basic industrial products, which began in April 1925, seems to confirm this suggestion, as does the decline in the index of industrial consumption of electricity.[24] These indicators demonstrate that in early 1925, governments' deflationary policies had already combined with declines in domestic consumption and investment to trigger a contraction in the German economy even though unemployment had not yet begun to get worse. The causes of the severe slump the next winter are not entirely clear. The Reichsbank suffered a loss of reserves briefly in the summer of 1925 when the inflow of foreign loans was temporarily halted. This led it to pursue an even more contractionary policy than was its usual wont. Monetary contraction probably made the recession more severe, but the penchant of the Reichsbank for radically altering its reserve holdings and accumulating excess reserves makes any deterministic assumptions about the effects of foreign loan flows suspect.[25] In this particular case, rising interest rates beginning in April 1925 and continuing over the summer, even as the economy slowed down, indicate that monetary factors played an important part in increasing the severity of the recession. Yet perhaps the most important causal factor making the recession so serious is the intangible "rationalization" of production as the economy continued to rid itself of industries which grew up during the inflation, but which could not make a profit after stabilization.

As Germany fell into a sharp recession in the autumn of 1925, German income declined and its balance of trade dramatically improved. Figure 2 plots the trade balance and level of unemployment 1925–27. Although the close relationship between rising unemployment and an improving balance of trade is striking, several other factors which might have contributed to Germany's export surplus need to be mentioned. Prices of essential imports began a decline in late 1925 while export prices held steady. Especially after the turn of the year, this reduced the total value of German imports. Cotton prices fell 15 percent from April 1925 to April 1926, while wool fell 30 percent. The *Reichskreditgesellschaft* credited these declining costs and a reduction in the total quantity of imports for the great improvement in Germany's trade balance.[26] This movement undoubtedly improved German terms of trade and helped the trade balance in the long run. However, it probably contributed relatively little to the export surplus achieved in the first half of 1926, since the terms of trade continued to improve through November 1926, even after the German export surplus disappeared, and Germany had resumed its normal deficit.[27]

Another element that we might have expected to help Germany's trade balance was the increased coal exports made

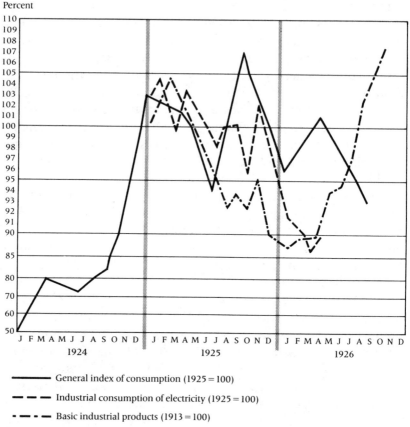

Percent

Figure 3. German Economic Trends, 1924–1926

——— General index of consumption (1925 = 100)

— — — Industrial consumption of electricity (1925 = 100)

— · — · Basic industrial products (1913 = 100)

possible by the British coal strike which began in May 1926. Although the strike stimulated the depressed German coal industry, it failed to produce any decisive improvement in the trade balance. Germany was able to capitalize on British problems by nearly doubling coal exports within three months.[28] Instead of improving, however, Germany's trade balance deteriorated as imports rose even faster to meet the rise in domestic demand as the economy recovered. The British coal strike may have helped the German economy in the spring of 1926, but it was in no way responsible for the trade surplus which in fact began to disappear just as German coal exports rose.

The depression of 1925–26 demonstrates that Germany's trade balance was closely tied to national income, and confirms the argument that adjustments in German income could produce the trade surplus needed to transfer reparations. In the face of falling import costs and artificial stimulation of a major export industry permitted by the British coal strike, Germany's rising national income in the second half of 1926 led the way to a growing trade deficit. Conversely, it is clear that Germany could indeed achieve the export surplus required to pay reparations by reducing national income and the German standard of living. By reducing imports instead of increasing exports, it could even achieve a trade surplus without flooding foreign markets with German goods. But the cost was obviously immense. Falling national income manifested itself by an intolerable rise in unemployment. As figure 2 reveals, only with unemployment well above 10 percent, could Germany balance its trade. To develop any significant export surplus, unemployment in the range of 15 percent to 20 percent was required. It hardly seems unreasonable that leaders of the weak Weimar coalitions would find it impossible to pay this high a price.

The lessons of 1926 were not lost on the officials in the German Economics Ministry responsible for formulating a national economic policy. Although historians have tended to emphasize the views of those Germans who believed that an economic crisis could be used to end reparations, many German leaders understood that it was precisely a crisis that would make Germany capable of paying reparations. In January of 1928, when Reichsbank president Hjalmar Schacht urged an end to foreign loans in order to determine just how much Germany could really pay, he met firm opposition from Economics Minister Dr. Julius Curtius. Curtius warned that an end to the loans would cause an economic crisis, which is perhaps exactly what Schacht hoped. But Curtius did not stop there. He followed the consequences through by drawing on the experience of 1926. He argued that another depression in Germany would lead to an export surplus just as it had in 1926. The result, instead of proving that Germany could not pay, would prove exactly the opposite, and demonstrate that Germany could pay.[29]

As Germany began negotiating for a new reparations settlement (eventually to culminate in the Young Plan), the same considerations arose. Whereas before 1926 Germany had tended to stress that it needed to be protected from a transfer crisis, it now emphasized that, although the economy might be in ruins, transfers could still be made. In January 1929, Stresemann wrote German embassies abroad outlining Germany's negotiating stance. He took pains to explain that an export surplus such as had developed in 1926 was a mark of a cyclical downturn and in no way a fair indication of Germany's capacity to raise the payments by high domestic taxation.[30] In the Economics Ministry, Ministerial Director Hans Schäffer had, by this time, fully accepted the argument that raising the reparations through high taxes would lead more or less automatically to their transfer abroad. Thus, he speculated that Germany had little to gain from the Dawes Plan formula, which separated transfers from the process of raising the payments domestically. Instead, he argued that Germany should press for an index that would allow it to stop collecting reparations-related taxes if the economy fell into a recession or depression.[31]

When reparations negotiations nearly collapsed in the spring of 1929, at least one of Germany's negotiators proposed letting the negotiations fail even if it led to a crisis in the German economy. Heavy industrialist Albert Vögler argued that a crisis would end transfers, and the money which continued to be collected but not transferred could be reinvested in Germany.[32] Wilhelm Lautenbach, of the Economics Ministry, warned that such a policy would lead to disaster. Not only would the German economy suffer, but the very process of suffering would enable the reparations to be transferred. Whether or not all German policymakers were convinced by this argument cannot be known. But Schäffer discussed the problem with everyone in the Economics Ministry, and even his greatest critics could find no way out of the German dilemma.[33]

If Germany enjoyed strong economic growth with full employment, the Allies would insist that it could pay reparations. Conversely, in the event of a severe recession or depression, it would be pointless for Germany to plead inability to pay, since reparations could in fact be transferred. As German national income fell, purchases of foreign goods would fall, and Germany's trade balance would become positive. It now seems likely that during the worst of the Great Depression, the Brüning government recognized this dilemma and chose a deflationary policy to demonstrate to the Allies that the social costs of German compliance with the Young Plan were intolerable.[34] The disastrous outcome of this policy is now obvious. Not so obvious, however, are the alternatives available to German policymakers.

Under these conditions, formulation of an economic policy that could transfer reparations and at the same time solve Germany's perpetual unemployment problem was impossible. Germany's obligations under the Dawes Plan required a balanced budget and a deflationary fiscal policy. Opposite and, as it turned out, stronger pressures within Germany demanded government support in overcoming the ravages of an economy out of control. Put simply, a real fulfillment policy required acceptance of deflation, depression, and unemployment. The domestic political costs of such a policy were virtually intolerable for Germany in the mid-1920s. Someone would have to bear the burden of a depression, and, at least for a time, no social group was powerful enough to force that burden onto any other group. The domestic realities of the German social and political stalemate dictated that the German government attempt to ameliorate the impact of the depression. Not foreign policy ambitions but domestic political and economic weakness determined German reparations policy from 1925 to 1929.

The depression of 1925–26 proved to astute German leaders that Germany could pay and transfer reparations, but that the price of the necessary deflationary policies would be an economic and social crisis. Unable to argue convincingly that Germany could not pay, and unable domestically to put into place the high taxes and budget cuts that would make payment possible, Germany could formulate neither a coherent reparations policy, nor a stable fiscal policy. Under these circumstances, reparations proved to be a constant poison in the Weimar body politic.

German Fiscal Policy
and the Depression of 1925–26

In ending the hyper-inflation in the autumn of 1923, the German government drastically slashed its spending and imposed heavy taxes on the German public for the first time in years. These new fiscal policies were so extreme and so effective that the Reich soon not only ended the deficits of the inflation period, but began running large-scale budget surpluses. As the surpluses mounted, industry began to complain that taxes had been raised excessively and had to be cut.[35] In late 1923 and early 1924, the government's orthodox fiscal policy was countered by a brief period of monetary expansion by the Reichsbank. To everyone's surprise, the economic contraction that had accompanied the stabilization policies in the fall of 1923 gave way to a remarkably strong recovery in early 1924. This recovery was in large part financed by a rapid expansion of Reichsbank credit. While private interest rates ran from 45 percent to 87 percent per year, the Reichsbank maintained a discount rate of 10 percent—a policy not unlike that which it had followed during the inflation and one that obviously helped those large banks and businesses with access to Reichsbank credit.[36] As the money supply expanded and a new inflation threatened, the bank began raising its discount rate. When this failed to halt the rising prices, the bank declared a "credit stop" and simply refused to make any further loans to the German economy.[37]

During the summer and fall of 1924, the "credit stop" effectively ended the last threat of inflation, but also threw the German economy into a sharp recession. Business bankruptcies went from 123 in the first quarter of 1924 to 2,870 in the third quarter. In spite of bitter protests over his credit policies, Reichsbank President Hjalmar Schacht insisted that the Reichsbank would continue to base its policy on the currency position of the bank and not on business conditions.[38]

With the "credit stop," Schacht took the decisive step toward establishing the Reichsbank as a fully independent economic power within German society. With close ties to the pillars of monetary orthodoxy in English and American banking circles, Schacht was able to resist business and government pressure to expand the money supply and reduce interest rates in Germany.[39] Basing his policies occasionally on his intensely nationalistic political beliefs, occasionally on orthodox economic values, and always on personal ambition, Schacht created a power so great that the Reichsbank has been legitimately referred to as a "collateral government."[40]

Although Schacht announced in September 1924 that in the future the bank would try to meet the needs of the economy as much as possible, the tight credit conditions continued until the Dawes loan and private loans improved the reserve holdings of the bank in early 1925. As confidence in the stability of the mark and the German economy rose, the "risk" premium on loans fell and private interest rates declined. By February 1925, market interest rates were lower than the Reichsbank's 10 percent discount rate, so that firms that had borrowed from the Reichsbank earlier began repaying their loans, and the volume of Reichsbank discounts declined. Given these conditions, the Reichsbank slowly moved away from credit rationing and toward a policy of once again using the discount rate to regulate the money supply. In February, it lowered the discount rate to 9 percent.[41] In spite of this reduction, the bank was only following the market interest rate and adamantly refused to help the economy by pursuing a monetary expansion. Rather than trying positively to influence the market interest rate, it continued to follow the market and concentrated on keeping its total volume of discounts fairly constant.[42]

The refusal of the Reichsbank, even after the Dawes Plan was promulgated, to expand the money supply or take the lead in reducing interest rates led to bitter protests from industry, which insisted that it was being starved for both investment and liquid capital. Responding to the political power of business leaders and to the generally threatening economic situation, the German government vigorously took up the issue and pressed the bank to pursue a more liberal policy. When the Reichsbank defended its high discount rate policy by pointing to the potential danger of a rapid withdrawal of short-term foreign loans, Reich Chancellor Luther protested that Germany had to end the "controlled economy" in financial matters immediately, and work to reduce interest rates. If, at some future date, a threat to the Reichsbank's reserve position developed, he insisted that it could then raise the discount rate.[43] The bank leadership refused to be swayed.

Through the last half of 1924 and early 1925, the Reich government tried, rather half-heartedly, to deal with the economic dislocation created by the end of the inflation and the tight credit policies of the Reichsbank. The Labor Ministry especially attempted to increase unemployment pay, with some limited success by January 1925. But the resistance of the Reich Finance Ministry to increasing the costs of government and an economic recovery in the spring of 1925 limited the government's role in the economy.[44] Indeed, the Finance Ministry was correctly charged with being "too fiscal" during 1924 and early 1925. With budget surpluses running at 100–150 million RM per month, by March 1925 the Reich had accumulated surplus funds of a billion RM.[45] This conservative fiscal policy was a major contributor to Germany's economic contraction in 1924–25. But it also provided a cushion which would allow the government to cover fiscal deficits which slowly began to emerge with tax cuts passed in late 1924 and early 1925.[46]

Although these early fiscal deficits were very small and easily covered by the accumulated surplus of the past year, the Reich Finance Ministry was determined once again to impose a balanced budget. As a Finance Ministry official warned the Cabinet, "The surpluses of 1924 have led to a kind of spending hypnosis *(Ausgabenhypnose)* in the Reichstag which has thrown the fiscal estimates overboard."[47] As the economy appeared to recover in the summer of 1925, other Cabinet ministers joined the Finance Minister in opposing any fiscal deficits. The greatest concern was with the problems a deficit would create for German foreign policy. If the Reichstag increased spending, it would cast doubts on Germany's will to balance its budget. This could lead to problems with the Reparations Agent and ruin Germany's attempt to secure American loans. Reich Chancellor Luther shared this opinion and told the Cabinet that "in terms of foreign policy, it is undoubtedly impossible to present an unbalanced budget."[48] With unemployment falling, these foreign policy concerns won the day, and Reich spending was closely restrained.

Although unemployment remained at moderate levels through the summer of 1925, business and industry were not doing well. Government officials blamed high interest rates for the problem and pressed the Reichsbank to reduce its discount rate and make more money available to the economy. But the bank refused to be swayed. Reichsbank President Schacht insisted that any monetary expansion would threaten the stability of the mark, and he would protect the value of the currency even if it created a more severe recession.[49] Schacht's determination to protect his self-proclaimed reputation as the "wizard" who had stabilized the mark took precedence over all other considerations.

By late summer of 1925, German industry was slipping into a severe depression which was not yet fully reflected in unemployment statistics.[50] In response to industrial pleas for help, the government formulated a "price reducing" policy aimed at cutting business costs to make German industry more competitive on the world market.[51] One part of this policy consisted of a further reduction in taxes, while a second and more important effort aimed at reducing German interest rates. When the Reichsbank refused to expand its credit to the economy, the government resolved to use its own resources to circumvent the bank's deflationary policy. The surpluses accumulated by the Reich as well as other branches of the government and public banks would be used to make capital available to industry at reduced interest rates.[52] The Reich also pressed city governments to make funds held by the municipally owned savings and loan banks available to the economy at reduced interest rates. In at least one case, Gustav Böss, mayor of Berlin, attempted to parley his support for the price-reducing policy into a guarantee of Reich support for a Berlin foreign loan. Although he failed to get an open promise of support, Böss did support the government policy, and Berlin did get its loan. Under pressure, the savings banks agreed to cooperate in spite of their "considerable doubts." They felt that efforts to reduce interest rates artificially would fail because private banks would maintain a high markup on funds given to them and would not pass the savings along to investors.[53]

As the "price-reducing" policy developed, it ran into criticism from radically different quarters. The left press refused to acknowledge that there really was any serious economic problem and charged that the entire scheme was merely an attempt to help industry at the expense of the working class. To counter these assertions, the government asked the highly respected moderate economist Moritz Bonn to write an article explaining and supporting government policy. Bonn responded with a scathing letter denouncing Reich economic policy. He attacked the new tariff policies which raised prices on consumer goods and protected industry. He also attacked the government's tax policies and confessed that, although it was hard to know who would really have to carry the burden of high taxes, it appeared that the Finance Ministry had no idea that this even presented a problem. "To me," he wrote, "our entire economic policy seems to be bureaucratic dilettantism responding to the pressures of powerful special interest groups."[54] Needless to say, he did not publish anything supporting government policy.

From another side, the Reichsbank correctly regarded the efforts of the government to force a reduction in interest rates as an attack on its control of the money supply and fought the policy with all the resources at its command. The Reparations Agent also opposed any efforts to reduce taxes and lower interest rates, since both would make Germany less capable of paying reparations. He argued that lowering taxes would reduce the budget surplus required to pay reparations, and lowering interest rates would discourage the inflow of foreign loans which provided the foreign currency required to make reparation transfers. As he wrote to Bank of England Governor Montagu Norman, "In letter and in spirit the policy the German Government is following, violates, it seems to me, the provisions of the Plan, and it comes dangerously near to amounting to a 'financial manoeuver' [to disrupt the Dawes Plan] within the terms of the Plan and the London Agreement." In collaboration with Benjamin Strong, Governor of the Federal Reserve Bank of New York, he encouraged Schacht to fight this attack on Reichsbank sovereignty.[55]

Increasingly, conflicts with German domestic origins were becoming tied up in international power politics. The conflict over financial control of the German economy between the Reichsbank and the Reich government was largely based on differing perceptions of the needs of the domestic economy. To be sure, it involved a crude power struggle between different branches of government, but both sides had good arguments for defending their policies. Although Gilbert found the "price-reducing" plan an affront to the Dawes Plan, there is no evidence that the government intended it as a demonstration of German inability to pay reparations. In fact, there is considerable evidence that if the government had any master plan on reparations revision, it involved waiting a number of years before attempting any such demonstration. Furthermore, the government's efforts to reduce German prices was very much in keeping with classic gold standard remedies for countering a trade deficit. Had the government been successful in reducing German prices and business costs, it would have made Germany more competitive on the international market and would have improved its balance of trade and thus its ability to pay reparations. But the basic driving force behind the government's policy was almost certainly its political need to meet the demands of an economy in crisis.

The Reichsbank, rather like the Bank of England (but unlike the Federal Reserve Bank) saw its primary responsibility as the preservation of monetary stability. Under Schacht's leadership, it fought jealously to protect its absolute monetary sovereignty. The Reichsbank position was greatly strengthened by the power exercised by all central bankers in the 1920s. With the world's economy (and especially European economies) badly out of balance, the central bankers led those who cried that a return to the gold standard would bring back the prosperity of the prewar years. In providing a panacea to the world's economic troubles, the bankers demanded less government spending and stable monetary systems under their own control.

In Germany the domestic conflict between the Reichsbank and the government boiled over into the international arena because of the reparations payments imposed upon Germany. The Reparations Agent believed that the government's policy threatened to wreck the Dawes Plan and he, like many other international bankers, believed that Schacht was the only responsible German official defending a policy of fulfillment. This, as time would prove, was a dangerous illusion. Schacht defended the stability of the mark because it increased his own authority. That this coincided with a policy of fulfillment was purely accidental. When Schacht became convinced that the mark could not be held stable under a fulfillment policy, he would become the leading German spokesman calling for an end to reparations.

In spite of his sympathy for Schacht's position, Gilbert was learning that the Reichsbank president's perception of events was not always reliable. In a letter to Gates McGarrah, explaining the conflict between the Reichsbank and the government, Gilbert tells us a great deal about Schacht. He wrote:

It is natural enough that Schacht should be embarrassed in relation to the Government, for it is his own Government which is doing its best to circumvent the Reichsbank's credit policy by carrying on an independent credit policy of its own. Schacht might be expected to fight this policy of the Government's fairly and squarely, whether there were a reparations problem or not. It would seem to be necessary in his own interest as a central banker.

But, Schacht, caught by his own vanity, which demanded that he act as if he were always in the center of decision making, tried "riding both horses," Gilbert wrote, "and he sometimes gets mixed up in the stories he tells to different people, and even to the same person on different dates." Gilbert provided an example of what he meant. When Schacht first learned about the government's decision to reduce interest rates by lending out government funds, "he was thoroughly disturbed by the statement, and everything he said and did for a few days indicated clearly to those around him . . . that he was perfectly furious that the Finance Minister should have issued such a statement." But two weeks later "he spent half an hour telling me that he had seen the Finance Minister's statement before it was issued and had approved it." According to Schacht's new account it would force the government to make its funds available to the Reichsbank at the same low rate (7.5–8 percent) it was offering to the public. While willing to concede a certain truth to this argument, Gilbert declared that "I cannot believe that Schacht's analysis of it from this point of view is anything more than an afterthought."[56] The story reveals Schacht as a man always ready to defend his interest but quick to change his story in order to save face. With little innate sense of honesty, he probably often failed to understand that the stories he told different people conflicted with each other. He seemed to believe that each statement was true at the time of the telling.

By late 1925, the deepening depression and Schacht's steadfast refusal to provide any relief through an easy money policy led agrarian and industrial leaders to launch a public attack on Schacht's credit policies.[57] This was an attack that hurt, since if Schacht wanted to reduce the money going to cities, he certainly did not want to harm agriculture and industry. He defended Reichsbank policy by pointing out that nearly half of all the loans made by the Reichsbank and the Rentenbank had gone to agriculture, and he insisted that the Reichsbank had encouraged savings banks and insurance companies to make agricultural loans.[58] One of the tragedies of the Weimar economy was that Schacht was correct in saying that agriculture received a massive dose of credit during these years. Almost every traditional economist supported these loans which were supposed to be used by a "productive" sector of the economy and help improve the German balance of trade by reducing imports of food. Unfortunately, ineffective use of this credit by large landowners and falling world agricultural prices which hurt all farmers meant that almost all this money was lost. A vast majority of the agricultural loans had become pratically worthless even before the world depression began in 1929.

In response to the industrial and agricultural criticisms of his policies, Schacht chose a tack similar to that taken earlier by his banking associates. In 1924, when private industry had blamed private bankers for high interest rates and lack of credit, the bankers had countered by charging that the real source of the problem was German city governments which were absorbing all available investment funds. Similarly, Schacht charged that it was not the Reichsbank's credit policies that were harming private industry, but rather the excessive borrowing and spending of the cities. He followed this accusation with a demand that the Advisory Board for Foreign Credits be strengthened and that public borrowing abroad be closely limited by a fixed annual quota. He suggested that 100–150 million Reichsmarks per quarter be the maximum sum that all cities and states could borrow.[59]

Opposition to Schacht's proposal came from two areas and for two very different reasons. Carl Severing, Prussia's Social Democratic Minister of Interior, argued that the Advisory Board as already constituted was functioning very well. He also pointed out that Prussia had initiated municipal loan regulation, had carefully screened municipal requests for foreign loans, and had been very supportive of policies reducing public borrowing. In spite of the fact that over half the population of Germany lived in Prussia, Prussian cities had borrowed only 180 million RM of a total municipal borrowing for all German cities of 550 million RM.[60] Presumably because Prussia was so large and because in Berlin its leaders were in constant contact with the problems of Germany's international position, it worked hard to cooperate with federal policies even though often not socially sympathetic with those policies. Prussian city loans were carefully screened, and in almost every case greatly reduced before being presented to the Advisory Board. The smaller states, even though often more conservative than Prussia, had no incentive to reduce the borrowing of their larger cities, and in fact often encouraged it. They also did nothing to screen out productive from unproductive loans.[61] Despite this, Severing argued with some justice that the Advisory Board had been successful in reducing municipal borrowing and in directing foreign capital into private industry.[62]

Much more aggressive than the criticism from the left was the attack on the Reichsbank from the right. Although industrialists had persistently demanded that municipal borrowing be reduced, they were unwilling to blame the cities for all of Germany's problems. Furthermore, they were affronted by the Reichsbank's desire to expand what they perceived to be an already excessive and rigid system of governmental regulation. Instead, they insisted that the best way to reduce the inflow of foreign capital was to reduce German interest rates, and they demanded that the Reichsbank facilitate this policy by making more credit available.[63] The Reich government fully concurred with the industrialists' analysis since it conformed to the government's continuing conflict with Schacht over control of the monetary resources of the country.[64]

To counter Schacht's unrestrained independence, the government considered legal reforms that would give it a formal role in monetary regulation.[65] But it soon became apparent that a fight with the Reichsbank could not be contained within the domestic arena. Parker Gilbert had already made it clear that he supported a firm Reichsbank control of German monetary policy. If an open fight developed with the Reichsbank, Schacht might call in not only Gilbert, but other foreigners as well to shore up his position. The inflow of foreign loans might be threatened and the Allies might even renew the reparations conflict if the issue became too violent.[66]

The bizarre dependence of the government on Schacht's goodwill is revealed in a report by the German ambassador to the United States, Ago von Maltzan, who had met little but frustration in trying to penetrate the fog around official American foreign policy. He reported that since American officials refused to discuss their policy goals publicly, or with him and his confidants, "it is not easy to establish a clear picture of the real plans of these leading men." But he hoped that his own failure would not cripple the Foreign Office's understanding of American policy since "I assume that the Foreign Office is well informed primarily through Reichsbank President Schacht."[67] Schacht's connections with foreign bankers, most notably his personal friendship with the powerful Bank of England Governor Montagu Norman, and his image as the man who stabilized the mark, gave him vast leverage to resist government pressures. The fact that the Reparations Agent and American bankers believed that his policies were essential to preserve German credit could only strengthen his position. Fearing that an attack on the Reichsbank's monetary authority could have unpredictable and devastating international repercussions, the German government had to give up its plans to use a cheap credit policy to stimulate the economy.[68]

Responding to the business cycle but not to government pressure, the Reichsbank slowly lowered its discount rate during the spring of 1926. The severe depression of 1925–26 reduced demands for money so that, in early January 1926, the bank could end its credit rationing policy and begin a step-by-step reduction in the discount rate from 9 percent in January to 6 percent by July. The bank cautiously followed the market, lowering its discount rate only when the market rate fell and always being careful never to allow its total volume of notes to increase. To the government's constant complaint that the bank's policy was always too little, too late, the bank continued to insist that the downward trend would soon be reversed, and the bank would have to raise its rates.[69] Frustrated in its bid to aid the economy through monetary expansion, the Reich government turned to more unorthodox means to stimulate the economy as recession gave way to depression by December 1925.

When German industry had begun complaining about its economic difficulties in the summer of 1925, labor organizations had insisted that there were no serious problems. The tune changed quickly that autumn as unemployment started its steep climb and the economy sank into full depression. In early December, labor leaders warned the government that "the economic situation in the Rhineland-Westphalia industrial region has worsened to the point that an economic catastrophe with all its dreadful consequences is imminent."[70]

On December 14, 1925, Prussia's Minister President, the Social Democrat Otto Braun, urged Federal authorities to meet with him to discuss ways to speed emergency relief to the Rhineland where the work situation was, he reported, "becoming threatening."[71] Chancellor Hans Luther was inclined to reject Braun's call for expanded productive unemployment projects. As Luther put it, he was convinced that "a sham appearance of economic prosperity created by productive unemployment spending is wrong and economically speaking, simple unemployment pay was the only correct approach." Despite his orthodox economic views, Luther realized that more than just economics was at stake here. As he rather cryptically put it, the "issues concern the masses and could reach political boundaries which would make the fundamental position only conditionally correct." In other words, with the economy in a genuine crisis, one might have to abandon orthodox economic policy in response to growing political pressures for economic relief. Thus, while disapproving of Prussia's demand for greater Reich spending, Luther was afraid to oppose the plan "since that could be a false step politically and lead to uncomfortable consequences." Bowing to political necessity while still determined to uphold fiscal orthodoxy, Luther agreed to the meeting but instructed the Finance Ministry to resist all spending proposals by placing "cold emphasis on the financial considerations."[72]

Despite Chancellor Luther's reservations, the economic crisis was quickly forcing the government to expand its economic relief programs. At a conference held on December 12, 1925, government officials could still insist that caution should guide any future policy. Both Prussian and Reich representatives agreed that Germany could not expand its welfare programs since even richer nations had not been able to afford extensive unemployment support. A week later as the full impact of the crisis began to be felt, Prussian and Reich officials reversed this consensus and agreed that emergency measures had to be put into effect immediately.[73]

As the economic disaster unfolded, Reich and Prussian officials agreed that only the city governments had projects in progress that could be expanded rapidly enough to do any good. As the Prussian Minister of Welfare succinctly put it, the conference held on the twenty-first "was intended to clarify the question of how the municipal governments can be stimulated to undertake more emergency work than previously." As an inducement to the cities to increase their public works spending, the Reich and Prussian governments agreed to use their financial reserves to make loans to cities at 4–5 percent. Although the Reich government encouraged cities to undertake only "productive" projects, it nonetheless pressed the state governments to "remove the obstacles" to increased municipal spending.[74]

By early 1926, Reich authorities were reluctantly coming to agree with Bavaria's Social Minister when he advised the Landtag that "it must be the task of state and municipal governments to do everything to create work and lighten the burden of the unemployed." No clear economic theory lay behind this gradual acceptance of an expanded public role in the economy. Rather, a more negative fear led to the determination that the unemployed could not simply be left to fend for themselves. As Prussia's Minister of Welfare put it, "In the interest of preserving peace and order, finding work for the greatest number of unemployed should not be underestimated."[75]

In the face of these mounting economic and social difficulties and the growing pressures for government aid to the economy, Hans Luther worked to form a new government. On January 20, 1926, he presented his new minority Cabinet, which survived with the passive tolerance of the two largest parties in the Reichstag, the German National Peoples Party and the Social Democratic Party. For the vital position of Finance Minister, which Luther himself had held for the past three months, Luther chose the former Finance Minister of Saxony, Peter Reinhold, who was known to be especially sympathetic to medium-sized industry. In his maiden speech to the Reichstag, Reinhold declared that "it is my conviction that at the present time it is the most important and pressing task of every German to cooperate in overcoming the economic crisis." Luther himself had already taken the position that overcoming the current economic crisis "is the most pressing task of the present time" and promised that the Reich would do everything in its power to "strengthen the productive sections of industry and to alleviate the suffering of the populace."[76] With these announcements, concludes historian Fritz Blaich, "the Reich Cabinet consummated the transition to an active counter-cyclical economic policy."[77]

Despite Luther's and Reinhold's determination to help the economy, their plans in February 1926 remained wed to a very conservative perspective. When Luther promised to help the economy, he made it clear to the Reichstag that he meant that government spending had to be kept to a minimum and taxes which hurt business had to be cut. Reinhold made the point even more bluntly. He declared that the root of the current crisis was the severe capital shortage, and excessive public spending had "not insignificantly contributed to the capital crisis." Repeatedly, he made it clear that his goal was to reduce the costs of production for industry through tax reductions. That this might lead to deficits for the Reich was an embarrassment that Reinhold did his best to minimize by promising to match his tax cuts with reductions in government spending—especially spending by city governments.[78]

In January and February 1926, Reinhold put together his new tax package which he presented to the Cabinet on February 9. The core of his reforms consisted of a 40 percent cut in the turnover tax (what is now called the value added tax); a 50 percent reduction in the tax on business mergers and other reductions of taxes on property, luxury goods, and the stock market.[79] Clearly the primary purpose of the new tax policy was to help industry by cutting costs.[80]

Reinhold estimated that his tax cuts would cost the government half a billion marks. He admitted that he was willing to skate "close to the edge of a fiscal deficit," but he insisted that the Reichstag had to cut spending to match the tax cuts.[81] By cutting both taxes and spending, Reinhold argued that the budget would remain in balance. It is a testimonial to Reinhold's diplomatic skill that he was able to convince the ever skeptical Reparations Agent to support the new financial program. As long as both government spending and taxes were cut simultaneously, Parker Gilbert's orthodox sensibilities could be appeased, and he had enough faith in Reinhold to believe he could accomplish these twin tasks.[80] Unfortunately, the plan immediately fell into trouble for the eternal reason that it is always easier to cut taxes than to cut spending. The tax cuts actually promulgated in the spring of 1926 were not, in fact, offset by any reduction in spending. The fiscal surplus of 1924 and early 1925 gave way to heavy deficits by the summer of 1926.[83]

As the deficits mounted in 1926 and 1927, they raised new problems for the German government in both foreign and domestic policy. No matter how much Peter Reinhold attempted to cut taxes on business, it could never be enough to satisfy the demands of German industrial leaders.[84] At the same time, municipal governments, labor unions, and the Reich Labor Ministry all insisted that the Federal government had to increase funds for city make-work projects and unemployment support.[85] By May 1926 Reinhold would respond to these growing and contradictory demands by appealing to all Germans to accept the spirit of sacrifice that had allowed Finance Minister Luther to save the currency in 1923–24. "I don't need to explain the fateful consequences that a deficit will have," Reinhold wrote the other Cabinet ministers, "the consequences of a budget out of control are fresh enough. I also do not need to repeat that Germany's economic situation cannot be restored to health without a reduction in public spending."[86]

It was not only the domestic economy that was at issue as deficits began to mount. As Reinhold had suggested when he first proposed his tax cuts in February, the new policy would create debts for the treasury that could not be covered on the domestic market. He argued that the cash reserves of the Reich were still so large that no loans would be needed in 1926. Yet Labor Minister Brauns spoke with greater precognition when he warned the Cabinet that by undermining fiscal reserves, the Reich would not be able to respond effectively to future economic problems and its fiscal deficits could induce a revision of the Dawes Plan over which the Reich would have no control.[87] As government deficits grew, Germany would indeed become ever more dependent on foreign capital and would set in motion a revision of the Dawes Plan led by the Reparations Agent.

By May 1926, Reinhold himself began to lose his early confidence that he was in firm control of the budget. Unemployment pay, a source of constant and bitter controversy, had begun to make heavy demands which he warned the Labor Minister, "over the long run, do not appear to be bearable."[88] At the end of May he wrote all the Cabinet ministers, noting that demands for greater spending and larger tax cuts were combining to create a serious problem for the government. He found the most ominous trend in the growing tendency for municipal and state governments to give loans and subsidies to private industry. Although each grant was defended on the ground that it represented an exceptional case, Reinhold warned,

The more the number of such exceptional cases grows, which I have also supported, the greater the danger that the government . . . will not be able to pull back to its former policy and will fall into a subsidy policy which will have fateful consequences not only for the national economy, but also for Reich finances.

Despite his ideological conservatism, Reinhold had helped advance the march toward the modern state with vast leverage over the national economy. Now he began to fear that mounting demands on the state would push it into bankruptcy. When he considered all the new proposals for greater subsidies, more unemployment pay, and larger pensions, he observed, "all these developments create the impression that in parliamentary circles, people do not understand the real situation of Reich finances." The real situation, he now admitted to the other Cabinet ministers, was that the Reich would need 600 million RM in loans to cover its new expenditures, and he had no idea where this money could be found.[89]

Even as Finance Minister Reinhold tried to dam the flood of deficits that he had helped unleash, a new and even more fateful program was being developed in the Labor Ministry. Under broad political pressure, the Reichstag in March had extended unemployment pay from twenty-six weeks to one year. But as Labor Minister Brauns now understood, if the depression continued, an army of unemployed workers would soon lose all support. "We are," Brauns informed the Cabinet, "in an extraordinary state of emergency." Under current procedures, public assistance could help individual unemployed workers, but it was never intended to cover and could not cover the mass unemployment now facing Germany. Until the summer of 1926, the Federal government had been pushing city governments to bear the burden of relief for unemployed workers. But now Brauns argued, the burden had to be spread to "the broader shoulders" of the Federal and state governments.[90] Yet even the states, as Bavaria argued, could not do much more. Until October 1925, Bavaria had covered almost all its unemployment payments by contributions from industry and workers. But this had all ended with the depression of late 1925. By May 1926, it was paying 2 million RM per month but had allocated only half that sum and feared it could not find the money to cover the rest.[91]

On June 28, 1926, Brauns told the Cabinet that "the situation on the labor market is so extraordinarily bad, and one can expect such further unfavorable developments that extraordinary measures are necessary." Moved by the dangers of the situation, the Cabinet, including the Finance Ministry, agreed unanimously to support whatever program Brauns proposed.[92]

After three days of hard bargaining, a massive "work creating" plan was put together. The housing market would be stimulated by 330 million RM in funds made available by Prussia and the Reich. Railroads would spend 100 million RM to rebuild old tracks and provide stimulation for the depressed steel industry. The post office would spend 300 million RM on new facilities and a huge new expansion of German waterways would be set in motion. Municipal governments would be further encouraged to expand their make-work programs, and the Federal government would provide help for them in securing foreign loans if needed to finance the projects.[93] And finally, to oversee the program, the Cabinet created a Ministerial Commission for Work Creation, chaired by Dr. Weigert of the Labor Ministry.

When the spending for the new projects was added to earlier deficits, the Federal government found itself facing a deficit just for 1926 of 1,370 million RM. By the time that state and municipal debts were added to this, it was clear that Germany finally and massively had moved toward a fiscal stimulation of the economy.[94] Finance Minister Reinhold, who in May had been arguing so firmly against further spending, fell into step with the program and even declared that although funds allotted for productive unemployment were already fully committed, he had the authority to overdraw the account and would do so to make money available for the Labor Ministry's program.[95]

There are two tragic aspects of the Reich's move toward heavy deficit spending in the summer of 1926. First, the projects could not be financed within Germany and by forcing the government to borrow the money abroad, Germany became even more dependent on the unstable world money market of the 1920s. Second, and perhaps even more disturbing, the deficits would only begin to have a decisive effect on the economy after the depression had reached its trough and recovery had begun. Thus the benefits were very limited while the dangers were very great.

As initially conceived, the Reich Finance Ministry anticipated that the "work-creating" projects would require about 400 million RM in loans which could, the ministry hoped, largely be financed on the German market.[96] The depression had indeed allowed interest rates to fall and made more money available within Germany than had been the case for years. But Hans Schäffer, Ministerial Director in the Economics Ministry, warned the planners that heavy borrowing would choke off the supply of funds available to industry as the economy began to recover. Government deficits might provide the necessary stimulus to help the economy now, but he worried that heavy domestic borrowing would drive interest rates up and create a new credit crisis as the economy began to recover.[97]

The enormous size of the Reich deficits soon forced the government to consider securing a loan on the foreign market, and this meant scrutiny of the loan by the Advisory Board for Foreign Credit. Even though the Advisory Board should have been dominated by the Reich ministries represented on it, no one was sure whether it would approve a loan for housing projects. In all previous cases, spending for housing had been considered "unproductive" and loans for housing had invariably been denied. If the Cabinet decreed that the decision of the Work Creating Commission could override the Advisory Board's supervision of loans, it was feared that the board would lose its international prestige which gave foreigners confidence in the security of German loans. Furthermore, if the Reich itself decided it could take a loan for housing by justifying it as "productive unemployment compensation," what would prevent every city from doing exactly the same thing? In spite of the Cabinet's decision that the Advisory Board could not refuse a loan which was deemed essential by the Work Creating

Commission and the willingness of the Advisory Board itself to cooperate, no one was really willing to risk reawakening the reparations issue or disturbing the international loan market by pushing too hard. These dangers forced the Finance Minister to declare that the domestic capital market could absorb the Reich loans and "circumstances permitting," also provide capital to private industry.[98]

Even though the Federal government would not look to the foreign bond market, it agreed to support city borrowing abroad. The fears of the Finance Ministry that Germany could not afford the new spending were dismissed by the other branches of the administration. As the Chairman of the Work Creating Commission put it, "The government has already determined that the work creating program will be carried out; thus this question is no longer open to debate. A way to finance it must now be found. If need be, other means than foreign loans must be considered."[99] Yet the foreign market offered the only real hope of long-term credit and, in the end, Finance Minister Reinhold announced that "he was operating on the premise that for both the Economics and Labor Ministries, the advantages of the work creating program outweighed any consideration of financial problems." To overcome the financial problems, he would speak with Schacht and the Advisory Board for Foreign Credit to arrange a program of domestic and/or foreign borrowing to cover the financial needs of the entire program.[100] By the end of August, city and state governments were informed that the Advisory Board would indeed cooperate in securing foreign loans. The local governments were advised to inform the board if new spending projects were designed to relieve heavy pockets of unemployment. In cases where this was true, the board would look more favorably upon a proposed loan even if it was not "productive" in the sense that it improved Germany's balance of payments, which had been the old criteria for securing a foreign loan.[101]

In the fall of 1926, unemployment did begin a significant decline in Germany, and in government circles the work creating program was given some credit for the improvement.[102] Yet, even the Labor Ministry had nagging suspicions that the deficits had really not helped very much. The "natural" recovery of the economy itself, perhaps aided by government policy, had been the decisive factor in promoting growth. In fact, even though Brauns would continue to promote more government aid for the unemployed, the work-creating program and the policies of 1926 seem to have soured somewhat by the end of the year. He summarized the lessons of the experience with this solemn conclusion:

It must be repeatedly stressed with all possible emphasis that it exceeds the power of the State to entirely overcome or even make a major contribution to overcoming this kind of extensive unemployment which is primarily the product of the disorder and upheaval of world economic relations and the national economy . . . Government actions can only partially remove and soften such unemployment. Instead, the fundamental healing must come from within the economy itself . . .[103]

In modern terms, the Labor Minister and the Reich government were still far from a Keynesian perspective. The initial attempts of 1926 to expand unemployment relief had indeed led to a stimulation of the economy, but Brauns was no doubt correct in seeing that the fundamental force affecting the economy was the free market. Over the next three years, the Reich, states and cities would continue to increase the size of their fiscal deficits, but they would never again do so with such far-reaching ambitions as they had in 1926.

In responding to the crisis of 1925–26, the German government was forced to attempt an impossible balancing act which reveals all the tensions inherent in the Weimar Republic. As Finance Minister, Peter Reinhold wanted to cut taxes on industry, thus reducing industrial costs, increasing business profits, and stimulting the economy. He planned to match these tax cuts with reductions in government spending, thus preserving a nearly balanced budget. But this policy in favor of business was matched by the Labor Ministry and union demands that unemployed workers needed immediate relief, not the "trickle down" help that Reinhold's policy promised. In 1926 special interest groups on both the left and the right had enough cohesion and political power to gain government help. To secure social peace, not only did the Reich undertake its belated work creating program, but it also encouraged city governments to expand their spending and helped clear the way for the cities to secure foreign capital to finance their projects.

With Reich finances able to draw on the surpluses of 1924–25, and foreign lenders ready to loan to German cities, the early deficits were easily financed. But as will be seen, a badly undersubscribed Reich loan in February 1927 would demonstrate that German capital available for long-term borrowing was very thin indeed.[104] Thus, the possible benefits of the government deficits were quickly offset by the fact that heavy government borrowing began to absorb the limited capital available to the German economy.

As serious as the economic complications of the deficit spending policy inaugurated in 1926 were, perhaps even more fundamentally, they would point to the political liabilities of the Weimar Republic. The very size of the government as a share of gross national product severely strained the as yet "immature" taxing abilities of the German state. In the years after the Second World War, tax rates much heavier than those of 1924–29 would be easily borne by the economies of Western Europe. But in the Weimar period, when every tax seemed to be a political assault on private industry, the working classes, or other momentarily less powerful groups, relatively modest taxes seemed an unbearable burden. The ability of the state to tax and borrow was limited not only by the capital market and the economy, but, perhaps even more decisively, by the political weakness of the Weimar state and system. The state had neither the crude power to compel private banks or the Reichsbank to extend it credit nor the political credibility to convince investors that it could raise taxes to cover its long-term financial obligations.

Finally, the deficit spending begun in 1926 would be played out in the international political arena as Germany's obligations to pay reparations came into conflict with its domestic fiscal policies. It was in direct response to the continuing and uncontrolled federal, state, and local deficits that the Reparations Agent, S. Parker Gilbert, would reopen the reparations issue and attempt, through the Young Plan, to force Germany to bring its governmental budgets into balance (see chapters 7 and 8 below). It was in response to these deficits begun in 1926 and the demonstration that by 1929–30 they had put the government under the control of the Reichsbank and the international bankers that not Heinrich Brüning but the Social Democratic government of Herman Müller would initiate the deflationary policies that proved so disastrous in the Great Depression.

Chapter 5

Living Without Loans, Spring 1927

In the summer of 1924, Germany's capital weakness had been instrumental in inducing the German government to accept the Dawes Plan. The emergence of government fiscal deficits in the spring and summer of 1926 renewed this dependence on imported capital, since Germany's own financial resources could not cover the public debts. As German fiscal and monetary policy became entangled in the foreign capital market, the reparations issue reemerged, and the agreements reached in 1924 were cast into doubt. Throughout 1927, the Reich government struggled to reestablish its authority over German reparations and fiscal policy but found itself in mounting conflicts with the Reichsbank president and the Reparations Agent. The control and regulation of Germany's foreign borrowing, which had been entrusted to the Advisory Board for Foreign Credit, became the issue that brought this multi-sided conflict into sharp focus. In 1927, all the ramifications of Germany's dependence on foreign capital began to come together. Monetary and fiscal policy, party and interest group politics, foreign and domestic goals all became so bound together that decisions in any one field created unforeseen difficulties in other areas of policymaking.

In the second half of 1926, the German economy finally began the economic recovery that would mark the "golden years" of the Weimar Republic. After ten years of inflation and two years of erratic growth and depression, Germany would briefly enjoy stable growth without inflation. Stimulated by rationalization of industry and large-scale government deficits, unemployment among industrial workers fell from 17 percent in the summer of 1926 to 12 percent in March 1927 and to 5 percent by the summer of 1927 (see chapter 4 above). Real prosperity with growth in production, consumption, and employment seemed finally at hand.[1]

The most remarkable aspect of this economic recovery was that it was largely financed with German money. As late as June of 1926, the German market had been unable to provide any significant investment funds, but due to the depression, there was little demand for capital at that time. In August and September, as the level of economic activity began to pick up, German funds covered most of the new investment.[2] By the end of the year, domestically financed loans had jumped from only 75 million RM in 1925 to 1,485 million RM in 1926.[3]

By the autumn of 1926, the Reichsbank was making loans at 6 percent, and private banks were charging only 1–2 percent above that. In this balmy atmosphere, Ludwig Kastl, business leader of the Reich Association of Industry, announced that "we have strongly approached the relationship of 1913 . . . and . . . are now in the position to place stocks and bonds to a considerable extent on the German market." In October, economist Gustav Stolper commented in *Der Deutsche Volkswirt* on the "surprisingly" rapid increase in domestic capital capabilities, and Parker Gilbert was convinced that the domestic market was once again capable of supplying most long-term German capital needs.[4] By November German banks were offering better terms than American banks, and it was widely believed that Germans were sending their savings abroad to buy German bonds on the American market in order to avoid paying German income taxes.[5]

This improvement on the German capital market coincided with the appearance, for a brief period, of worldwide monetary stability.[6] International interest rates fell, and Germany benefited from these favorable developments. German borrowers who two years earlier had been paying over 10 percent for American loans now found their bonds selling above par when offered at interest rates as low as 6.75 percent.[7] German bonds carrying stock purchase options commanded a premium on the New York market as Americans rushed to take part in the Berlin stock exchange boom which began in the summer of 1926.[8] The recovering German capital market combined with the new American loans to expand the German money supply. In response, the Reichsbank leadership became increasingly agitated at the prospect of losing control over the German money market.

As the foreign capital was converted into marks at the Reichsbank, the bank note circulation expanded. To counteract the inflationary threat of this expansion, the Reichsbank attempted to reduce the money supply by restricting the credit it made available to the economy. This policy soon proved ineffective, since the recovering domestic capital market and continued foreign borrowing supplied the funds that the Reichsbank refused to grant. By holding its discount rate high above the market rate, the Reichsbank simply lost influence over the market. Borrowers repaid their expensive central bank loans and replaced them with loans from the open market. Writing in November 1926, Parker Gilbert took the Reichsbank's side in warning that the growth in foreign borrowing threatened to destroy its control over the money supply. By late 1926, Gilbert would later write, the Reichsbank's efforts to counteract the foreign capital inflow had reduced its holdings of domestic bills to such a low level that the bank's discount rate "was almost without effect upon the German money market."[9]

Testifying before a Parliamentary investigative committee on October 21, 1926, Reichsbank President Schacht charged that the foreign loans had not only destroyed the bank's control over the money supply, but they also created the illusion that Germany could pay reparations. The foreign currency coming into Germany as loans was the same money that flowed out again as reparations. Germany's bank reserves were hostage to the mounting foreign debt, said Schacht, and he warned the

Reichstag that a conflict would soon emerge between loan repayment and reparation transfers.[10] As for expecting help from the United States, Schacht was right when he suggested that the fate of the foreign loans was "apparently 'left in the lap of the gods' by the authorities of the credit giving country [USA].'"[11]

Schacht's anxiety about the foreign loans and belief that Germany could do without them was shared by economists with far more moderate political views. Gustav Stolper warned that in view of the dangers created by the ever-increasing inflow of foreign capital, "it is time for the Reichsbank to give a warning" against further borrowing. Moral suasion, he wrote, had not worked, as "it remains doubtful that the thoroughly correct judgment of the Reichsbank will be able to influence the credit plans of the states, municipalities, and above all, private industry." Stolper suggested that the Reichsbank reduce its discount rate and increase the money supply in Germany. This would help the domestic capital market and reduce the inflow of foreign loans.[12]

A second means of reducing the attractiveness of foreign capital involved suspension of tax advantages given foreign purchasers of German bonds. In August 1925, when the Reich government promulgated Germany's new, post-inflation income tax, the law freed bonds sold abroad from a 10 percent income tax and a 2 percent sales tax paid by domestic bond holders. Drawing on the example of American state bonds, German economists saw that if bonds were made tax free, they could be sold at a lower interest rate and help make cheaper credit available to Germany.[13] Under an agreement worked out with Hjalmar Schacht (whose power here, as so often, extended well beyond his formal mandate), all foreign loans approved by the Advisory Board for Foreign Credit would be freed from the German taxes. Private loans could also be granted the tax concession when their interest rates and use were "productive when viewed in terms of the whole economy."[14] Since Americans were unwilling to pay tax on the interest earned from German bonds, this tax concession was vital to Germany's ability to borrow in New York.

As early as the spring of 1926, falling interest rates within Germany led the *Frankfurter Zeitung* to call for a reduction in German taxes to the same level paid by foreigners since it made no sense to maintain "a capital import premium."[15] After considering the tax issue in a series of conferences, the government decided in May 1926 to support the Reichsbank's position that the time was not yet ripe for a change and that the loan inflow needed to be encouraged by the tax favors.[16]

What the Finance Minister did not add was that any reduction in the tax on capital investments would have to be met by reductions on the taxes paid by wage earners. As Economics Minister Julius Curtius wrote, even though the capital tax raised only 1 percent of total tax revenues, "I do not fail to understand that the abolition of the capital earnings tax would call forth general political objections in view of the equivalent tax on wages." State Secretary Popitz of the Finance Ministry gave the Cabinet a similar warning by reminding it that any effort to repeal the tax on capital would lead to a demand to repeal the income tax on wages.[17] In the fragile balance of Weimar society, even administrations oriented toward private business often hesitated to pursue policies that openly favored business. Subsidies, grants, and tax advantages, while common, were usually given secretly or softened within the context of broad reforms. In this case, even though it was almost universally agreed that Germany needed to encourage capital investment, tax reforms to promote that policy were rejected because the government was unwilling to match it with a reduction of the income tax.

By late 1926, the steady improvement in Germany's capital market had created a consensus among policymakers that Germany could and should reduce its inflow of foreign capital. The Reichsbank initiated a campaign to end the tax advantage given foreign bond holders. Bank director Knaack told a conference called to consider the issue that the bank had reluctantly supported foreign borrowing in the past because of Germany's desperate capital shortage.[18] Now, Knaack argued, the loan's excessive and dangerous growth made a policy reversal essential. He called upon the Finance Minister to end all tax advantages that had been granted foreign loans, and he went so far as to insist that all foreign loans were dangerous and had to be stopped.

The bank's arguments were countered by Reichart of the Economics Ministry. He refused to believe that the situation was as dangerous as the bank asserted. He warned that forcing foreigners to pay income tax on their German bonds would, in practice, mean closing the foreign market entirely. To be sure, he agreed that the rate of inflow must be slowed and urged a more rigorous scrutiny of loan requests to reduce the volume. As he put it, "A brake must be applied; but the brake must not be pulled so tight that the wheel no longer turns." This moderate position that loans should be slowed but not stopped won the support of the Finance Ministry and even the Reichsbank had to accept it as the wisest course.

Drawing on support for this more moderate position, the Reichsbank formally asked the Finance Minister to end the tax benefits granted bonds sold abroad. Ignoring its earlier assertion that all loans had to end, the bank based its demand on the argument that the recovering domestic capital market made it unnecessary and undesirable artificially to stimulate foreign borrowing. It was careful not to imply that Germany could do entirely without imported capital. Their goal, the bank directors wrote, was simply to equalize the real interest rates paid at home and abroad so that Germany could take full advantage of its remarkable recovery.[19] In this the Reichsbank was supported by German private bankers who believed that only the foreign tax advantages prevented them from meeting the needs of the bond market.[20]

On December 4, 1926, the Reich Finance Minister publicly announced that he was no longer able to recommend tax benefits for foreign loans. The policy change was justified by reference to the improvements apparent on the domestic capital market and a desire to reduce the total volume of foreign loans.[21] A week later, a Reichstag committee approved the policy change, and it became official.[22] Representatives of both Prussia and Bavaria declared their support for the new policy. Geheimrat Norden, chairman of the Advisory Board for Foreign Credit, stated that the new policy was not intended to exclude all foreign loans. The goal, he said, was to slow the rate of capital imports by making the borrower carry the tax burden now shouldered by the nation as a whole.[23] In the past, some German borrowers who had been unable to secure tax advantages for their foreign loans had agreed to pay the taxes which were supposed to be carried by the lender.[24] Norden expected that using this formula some loans would continue to be made, but that the total volume would be much less than under the old rules.

A month later, on January 11, 1927, the Reichsbank lowered its discount rate to 5 percent, declaring that this would reduce short-term capital inflows and was a demonstration that Germany had finally reached a point that could be considered normal for the prewar period. Reichsbank president Schacht added that only time would tell if this rate could be maintained, but at least for now Germany would be more dependent on home savings. Whether fully intended or not, the effect of the new policy was, in the words of the Enquête-Ausschuss, to "almost completely cut off the stream of foreign loans."[25] For the next six months, Germany lived without its life-giving foreign loans. Why had it set out on this policy and what were the results?

In his monumental study of German-American relations in the 1920s, Werner Link has asserted that the policies initiated in December 1926 were chosen to demonstrate that Germany could not pay reparations. Ending the foreign loans would deprive Germany of the foreign currency required to pay reparations and prove that German transfer capacity was only an illusion created by the artificial capital imports. He finds support for this conclusion in a statement by Reichstag representative Dr. Hoff, a member of the People's Party and leader in German industrial circles. Hoff, as quoted by Link, asserted that ending the tax-free status for foreign loans was intended "to bring about a certain clarification of the transfer problem."[26] While this is certainly a fair portrayal of part of Hoff's statement, his complete explanation of the new policy was a little more complex and demonstrates that fears about over-indebtedness of the German economy were also important in the discussion. Explaining the origins of the tax policy to the Reichstag Committee on Taxes, Hoff reported, "One wanted to hold back the influx of foreign capital since the impression existed that the domestic capital market could become dominated by foreign capital, and the German economy could become too heavily indebted to foreigners. Moreover, through the embargo, a certain clarification of the transfer problem would be brought about. For when foreign exchange in large quantities flowed into the Reichsbank—as happened in 1926—transferring reparations from these funds was made easier."[27]

The Reichsbank intended to reduce the inflow of foreign loans,[28] and Schacht's aggressive attack on all loans in November 1926 may have been strongly motivated by an attempt to prove that Germany could not pay reparations. Later, in the spring of 1927, the Agent General for Reparations accused Schacht of pursuing policies intended to prevent Germany from paying reparations. However, this accusation centered on policies adopted in May of 1927, not the decisions to tax foreign loans and to lower the discount rate, which were supported by political leaders who were not sympathetic to Schacht's often arbitrary and outrageous behavior.[29] The dominant factor dictating the policy changes in December and January was the changing situation on the money market. Schacht was quite right when he wrote Montagu Norman, "I lost totally control of the market, as our portfolio went down to almost nothing. We therefore were compelled to reduce the rate which I tried to postpone as long as possible as I knew that by such a reduction some wrong impression might be created on our market as to the general interest level for investments. In the first half of January, however, I could not help going to 5 percent."[30] Without any enthusiasm, Schacht was forced by falling interest rates to lower the Reischbank's discount rate in January 1927.

Changes in the international and domestic capital market determined that in the first half of 1927, Germany would find out just how dependent it was on imported capital. As the money market dictated that the capital inflow stop, the Reichsbank and Reich government acceded to that reality. It does not require sinister motives or a determination to overthrow the Dawes Plan to explain German policy in December and

January 1926–27. Yet, the complex interaction between "legitimate" policies intended to promote economic growth and "crisis" policies designed to end reparations would clearly emerge as a consequence of ending the foreign loans. American Undersecretary of the Treasury Ogden Mills was quite right when he observed that "the policy pursued by Dr. Schacht can be explained without any reference whatsoever to the reparations question."[31] Yet it is also true that every action that affected Germany's balance of payments position or the Reichsbank's reserves of foreign currency would also automatically raise the reparations issue. For Hjalmar Schacht, ending the loans served the twin purposes of restoring his control over the money market and testing Germany's ability to transfer reparations without the foreign loans.[32]

In the first half of 1927, the German economy came into full bloom. Production reached "new high levels,"[33] and the crippling unemployment finally seemed to be beaten. During January and February, the domestic capital market remained active and liquid. Large numbers of bonds were floated and foreign capital was not missed. The new monetary policy seemed to be extraordinarily successful. Then, at the end of January the Reich government suddenly announced that it would float the first large-scale loan it had taken since stabilization. Three hundred million RM was to be underwritten by a consortium of eighty banks led by the Reichsbank, while another 200 million RM was to be taken by official agencies, such as the Reich railroad and post office. This huge loan proved far too large for the German money market to absorb, and almost instantly the rosy picture of German financial independence collapsed.[34] The loan was roundly condemned by Parker Gilbert, who felt that until its issue, the domestic market had been strong and growing, but that the Reich loan "marked the turning point," and severely retarded German capital growth. By March, Germany's capital reserves were clearly failing as loan issues fell off dramatically nearly to cease by May. Accompanying this, interest rates turned sharply upward.[35]

The decision to take this Reich loan, with all its unfortunate consequences, must be traced back to the determination to pursue a deficit fiscal policy made in the spring and summer of 1926. By that autumn, it was widely understood that the Reich was interested in securing a loan and would like to place part of it abroad, but in Reichsmarks.[36] In November, Finance Minister Reinhold discussed the possibility of a loan with Parker Gilbert, who was "very reserved" toward Reinhold's suggestion of possible foreign participation in a Reich loan.[37] The *Frankfurter Zeitung* reported that the government was contemplating issuing treasury notes to cover short-term spending, and this is the course that Parker Gilbert would later say should have been followed. Treasury notes would absorb the excess money apparent in the short-term market (funds which were often being used to speculate in the stock market) while leaving the long-term market alone.[38]

In spite of the fact that the Reich government had developed a deficit of 966 million RM by December 1926, Reinhold was still insisting that treasury notes could cover the debt. However, when the Reichsbank discount rate fell to 5 percent in January, and this low rate was matched on the bond market, the prospect of such cheap money was too good to pass up and Reinhold decided to float a long-term bond issue instead.[39] This conclusion is confirmed by a German Foreign Ministry telegram to the Washington embassy. The ministry reported that the proceeds of the government's loan would be used to cover future needs created by the expanded unemployment compensation and "make-work" programs as well as the May 1927 reparations payments. Although there was no pressing need for the funds, the government was anxious to secure a loan at 5 percent. "This," asserted the Foreign Office, "would be a great success for the Reich and its financial prestige. It will mark the capstone in the rebuilding of Reich finances and credit and beyond this will have a favorable impact on general German credit terms abroad."[40]

The decision to take the Reich loan was made by Finance Minister Reinhold acting on his own,[41] and was not seriously discussed in the Cabinet until January 22. When he belatedly announced his intention to seek a loan, Reinhold urged quick action before the money market lost liquidity and prevented such a large issue. Curtius, as Economics Minister, supported his plea, since he agreed the market could change at any time.

The only objection to the loan was a concern that the government might find itself with too much cash. Reinhold quite rightly assured the cabinet that he was not concerned about that eventuality.[42]

Parker Gilbert was unable to understand why such a large loan had been taken "except perhaps Dr. Reinhold wanted to create a sensation before he left the Reich Treasury."[43] Although the Reichsbank took part in the loan and did not publicly oppose it, Schacht told Gilbert that he was "dead against" it, but that the loan had been arranged while he was out of town. Gilbert found it a bit hard to believe that Schacht might really have been so out of touch,[44] but Schacht's repeated and uncontradicted assertions of his surprise indicate that Finance Minister Reinhold "forgot" to tell the Reichsbank that it would be participating in a new Reich loan.[45] In March, Schacht informed the Cabinet ministers that he had been totally surprised by the loan: "I would never have traveled abroad, as I had done on a short vacation, had I known that the Reich loan was coming. I was in Florence when I was surprised to receive an express letter from the Vice-president [of the Reichsbank]. I had no indication that the Reich loan was impending."[46]

Given the government's growing deficit, some form of long-term financing would eventually have to have been arranged.[47] But Reinhold took the loan which broke the German capital market to prove that the German government could get credit at 5 percent and was, therefore, a sound financial risk. To maintain this fiction, the government spent 70 million RM over the next eight months to support the price of the bonds artificially.[48] When the bond price began to fall as German interest rates rose in the summer of 1927, the government went so far as to raise the interest rate on the face of the bonds in order to keep the price at an artificially high level and preserve the image of government creditability. Parker Gilbert complained that "a case such as this was unknown to him in the financial history of any country." When he took the issue up with German officials, "he was told that only two similar cases in the financial history of the world were known. One occurred in Germany in 1918 shortly before the collapse, the other in Guatemala. With some justification, Gilbert declared that these two precedents could not be taken as very encouraging."[49] Eager to prove German fiscal and monetary strength, the Reich instead provided an ominous portent of just how weak both really were.

Monetary Policy and Reparations

Just as Germany set out to test its new economic strength in early 1927, tension over reparations payments began to intrude more vigorously than ever into policy discussions. The issue was intimately entwined with the decision to reduce capital imports and was raised publicly by the new Finance Minister, Heinrich Köhler, in his budget speech to the Reichstag on February 19. From the inception of the Dawes Plan, German economists and officials had anticipated with dread the rising schedule of payments outlined by the plan. Assuming that the German economy would gradually become stronger, the plan set out a progressive schedule marked by a large jump to the normal yearly payment of 2.5 billion RM beginning in September 1928. Convinced that the Reich budget could not endure the strain of this burden, and that transferring the payments to the Allies would be impossible even if it could be raised internally, Germans were pushed to frantic speculation on a way to avoid the impending crisis.[50]

Köhler brought these concerns into the open by telling the Reichstag, "At the present time, in spite of all good will, I see no possible way for us to raise this amount." His pronouncement raised a storm of protest in the foreign press, which saw it as the inauguration of a German effort to revise the Dawes schedule of payments.[51] The German government was quick to deny that it intended any change in its fulfillment policy and pointed out that Köhler's remark had carefully referred to current potential difficulties and emphasized that Germany would do everything in its power to meet its obligations. It defended its concern by pointing to Germany's continued unemployment of 1.8 million, its weak export position, and the fact that a great deal of its industrial capacity remained unused.[52] Von Schubert, State Secretary in the Foreign Office, justified the speech to Parker Gilbert on the grounds that there were wide circles in Germany that were convinced that Germany would never be able to meet the 1928–29 Dawes Plan payment, and one must pay some attention to these groups. Schubert reported that "Herr Gilbert seemed to see this," but Gilbert warned that any discussion of revision had to wait until after the 1928 American elections.[53]

Although in public the government stood united in downplaying Köhler's remarks, in the privacy of government councils, a bitter controversy ensued. Köhler claimed that his statement had been approved by a Cabinet meeting on February 15, which Foreign Minister Gustav Stresemann chose not to attend in spite of being advised that Köhler intended to warn against overestimating the economy's ability to fulfill its Dawes obligations.[54] The Foreign Ministry regarded Köhler's speech as crude and inopportune and said that Stresemann had not attended the Cabinet meeting because a Finance Ministry official had told the Foreign Ministry that Köhler would not raise the reparations issue in his speech. The misunderstanding occurred because Köhler drafted the speech without consulting the reparations division of the Finance Ministry. The Foreign Ministry insisted that since the reparations issue was the central concern of German foreign policy, Köhler should make no further statements on the topic without first consulting the Foreign Ministry. Köhler's disgust with Stresemann's criticism is reflected in his demand a few months later that he be consulted on foreign policy issues concerning reparations since he was the "responsible" minister.[55] Far from pursuing any systematic revisionist policy, the Reich ministers, while agreeing on the long-run goal of ending reparations, were bitterly divided over how to achieve this objective.

As the government contemplated its future reparations course, the German money market took another ominous turn. Volatile, short-term capital, which had been halted by the reduced discount and interest rates early in 1927, began flowing into Germany in unprecedented volumes in March and April. In two and a half months, foreigners sent nearly 800 million

RM in short-term funds into Germany.[56] Stock market prices, which had been rising slowly since mid-1926, began a sharp and accelerating climb in April 1927.[57] German bankers drew heavily on their credit lines from American banks and relent the money at much higher rates to German stock market speculators.[58] This, combined with direct foreign participation in the stock market boom, accounted for most of the short-term capital inflow.

Even as Germany was being swamped with this new capital, interest rates began to rise. Central bankers in the United States, Britain, and Germany believed that the stock market was absorbing funds which should have been invested in industry. Thus, they believed that stock market speculation reduced capital available for legitimate business and artificially raised interest rates. To prevent this from happening, they tried to restrict credit going into the stock market while trying to ensure that credit to other activities remained open. Unfortunately, this policy was based on a misunderstanding of the relationship between capital investment and stock prices. Economists now would argue that buying stocks cannot really absorb any capital, since for each buyer who gives up his funds to purchase a share, there is a seller who receives the money and can, in turn, almost instantly invest the money somewhere else.[59]

In Germany, as in the United States, the stock market boom was closely linked to a movement by industry to free itself from dependence on bank loans and secure investment funds by selling new stock issues. As one observer noted in December 1926, "Although German industry at first preferred to obtain the funds it required by issuing bonds, it has more recently had recourse to issues of new shares on a considerable scale." Shipping companies, banks, iron works, and chemical firms were issuing large volumes of new stocks to finance capital investments.[60] From 1907 to 1914, an average of 600–740 million RM per year in new stocks had been issued. This sum was matched in 1925 and climbed to 1,288 million RM in 1926. From January to April 1927, 460 million RM more stocks were issued for an annual average of 1,400 million RM.[61] While an excessive rise in stock prices might be undesirable, it is evident that a great deal of the money funneled into stock purchases was being passed on into the economy as real capital investment. Furthermore, as the economy grew, demand for capital increased, and rising interest rates were one reflection of this boom.[62] This movement was made more severe by a decline in the German savings rate after January 1927, which reduced capital available for investment, and an inclination of German banks to take advantage of the high liquidity in January–March to make huge new loans which left them overextended and forced a retrenchment later in the year.[63]

As market interest rates rose, demand for Reichsbank discounts still being offered at 5 percent also increased, and the bank soon found its rate the lowest in Germany. Its difficulties were compounded by a rapid loss of gold and cash reserves. Schacht argued that this was, at least in part, due to a repatriation of stock market profits by foreigners. Other experts pointed out that the large passive trade balance of the first half of 1927 had to be paid for with gold and foreign exchange from the Reichsbank. Initially, Schacht remained unconcerned about the loss of reserves since he felt the bank had excess reserves of at least 1 billion RM, which he was happy to see reduced. Only as the outflow continued into April and May did he begin to worry about the Reichsbank's reserve holdings.[64] His determination to stop further short-term borrowing by German banks was solidified when he discovered that Oscar Wassermann at the Deutsche Bank had already permitted the bank to borrow 200 million RM in short-term loans. Schacht declared that if Wassermann had borrowed so heavily, he was frightened to think what others must have done.[65]

Gustav Stolper insisted that the problem could be solved only by an increase in the discount rate and a renewed inflow of long-term foreign capital.[66] Schacht disagreed, believing that not more capital but a better distribution of existing capital was the best solution. If he raised the discount rate, Reichsbank reserves would be protected, but even more foreign short-term capital would be drawn into the German market. In his opinion, the best alternative was a return to direct and specific controls in order to end the excessive stock speculation and free existing funds for productive use.[67] The Reich government also pressed for a low discount rate as a way to provide cheap loans to industry. This would reduce German production costs and make German goods more competitive on world markets.[68]

Responding to these complex pressures, on May 11 Schacht took the unprecedented step of informing the major German banks that henceforth the Reichsbank would not tolerate further speculation on the stock market. Banks which were lending too heavily to stock market speculators would be denied discounting privileges at the Reichsbank. If loans to "legitimate business" continued to be restricted by the private bankers, the Reichsbank would end all discounts to the banks. By this time, the Reichsbank's low discount rate had led the private banks to borrow so heavily at the Reichsbank that they were entirely at Schacht's mercy. They had little choice but to give in to his pressure and the next day, in a joint announcement, Germany's private bankers declared that in June stock market credit would be reduced by 25 percent. Even greater reductions were promised for the future. The immediate result was a near collapse in the stock market, a rapid withdrawal of foreign funds, and a new loss of 110 million RM in Reichsbank reserves.[69]

"Black Friday," as the German stock market crash is known, all but marked the end of the experiment in loan-free living. On June 3 the Finance Minister announced that he was once again compelled to grant tax benefits to foreign lenders in order to encourage the inflow of new long-term loans. On June 10 an increase in the discount rate to 6 percent "had become necessary," Schacht told the Enquête-Ausschuss, "since the exchange reserves of the Reichsbank had fallen to a minimum."

The events of the first half of 1927 provided a blunt demonstration that Germany remained dependent on foreign capital. Schacht's maneuvers in April and May to avoid raising the Reichsbank's discount rate created an international controversy and forced a formal reconsideration within the German government of Germany's future policy toward its reparations obligations. Schacht's determination to end stock market speculation as a means of making more capital available to industry (erroneous though it may have been) found broad support within German economic circles. Georg Bernhard, on the Reichstag's investigative committee, the Enquête-Ausschuss, stood nearly alone in believing that stock market speculation presented no threat to the economy.[70] Within the Cabinet, Schacht was supported by Economics Minister Julius Curtius, who wrote, "Essentially, I was in agreement with the Reichsbank president as he tried to end this drive [to stock speculation]. Whether he chose the right method to use, I leave undecided."[71] The great Social Democratic economist Rudolf Hilferding told the Reichstag that everyone agreed with Schacht that the stock market speculation had to be restrained, but Schacht had chosen a dangerous way to achieve this end. "The goal was right, the methods were wrong," said Hilferding, and as a result investors were reluctant to leave their capital in Germany.[72]

Although his determination to end stock speculation was generally supported, Schacht's refusal to raise the discount rate was attacked by foreign economic experts as well as by liberal economists within Germany. The British embassy felt that Schacht was inconsistant in explaining his policies and reported that his grounds "are frankly not always well founded."[73] The Reparations Agent was even more pointed in his criticisms of Schacht's discount policy. On May 29, Gilbert wrote Montagu Norman,

I am entirely out of sympathy with the Reichsbank. I have said so to Schacht on every possible occasion during the past few weeks, and I think it becomes clearer and clearer every day that the Reichsbank cannot possibly defend its 5 per cent rate under present conditions. . . . I think he does not make sense when he talks of using "direct action" in circumstances like these, and I am personally satisfied that he would have raised his rate at least six weeks ago in accordance with ordinary central banking principles, if it had not been for the question of reparation transfers.[74]

Gilbert's colleague in the Transfer Committee, Pierre Jay, agreed with Gilbert's evaluation. He wrote to Benjamin Strong:

There is no doubt that the loss [of Reichsbank reserves] gave [Schacht] satisfaction from the point of view that it reduced the facility of making transfers. I can't help feeling that he may be a bit imbued with the attitude . . . [of those] . . . who do not wish to have things seem too good in Germany for fear it will help the execution of the Plan. . . . I cannot escape the conviction that any attempt on the part of the German Government or the Reichsbank to lead, as it were, a double life by failing to do what is the best thing for Germany for fear that it may in some way help the carrying out of the Dawes Plan will in the end prove disadvantageous to Germany.[75]

Both internationally and domestically, it was clear that the reparations issue played an important role in the policies of 1927. Yet it would be a mistake to think that reparations alone were involved. First, it should be remembered that there were good economic reasons for ending the tax subsidy granted foreign loans in December 1926. It seemed that Germany was in a position to be less dependent on foreign capital, so there was little reason to continue a policy which was stimulating Germans to send their money abroad. Furthermore, it was not obvious that ending the tax benefits would bring all international borrowing to a halt. As Robert Kuczynski has pointed out, from 1924 to 1926 only 54 of the 69 loans placed in the United States were tax free. On the other 15 loans, the German borrower usually paid the tax.[76]

The failure of the United States to extend long-term loans to Germany in the spring of 1927 was caused not only by developments in Germany, but by changes in the American market as well. As already noted, American interest in German issues had largely fallen off even before the tax benefits were removed. In the first half of 1927, the American market remained uninterested not only in German loans but in other issues as well. Benjamin Strong wrote Norman in March 1927, "Nothing whatever is being done here to stop or impede the issue of Foreign loans . . . I do not know why more Foreign loans have not been issued during the last month or two, a fact which I regret. I believe the main reason to be that the class of loan which has been sought is not up to the banker's standard in one way or another."[77] The assumption that the German policy changes in December and January alone were responsible for the total end of the loans, and that the loans were stopped in order to prove that Germany could not pay reparations cannot be supported.

The real charge that Germany was engaged in a dangerous reparations game was not directed toward the policies that ended the loan inflow in December and January. Rather, what exercised Parker Gilbert and Pierre Jay was Hjalmar Schacht's refusal to raise the discount rate in April and May of 1927. In trying to unravel Schacht's intentions one must always tread very carefully. Schacht was never reluctant to express his doubts about Germany's ability to transfer reparations. He even occasionally advocated a crisis policy to demonstrate that Germany's apparent prosperity was an illusion fostered by excessive foreign borrowing.[78] But the charge that in the spring of 1927 he was principally motivated by a desire to end transfers of reparations fails to take into account the degree to which his policies coincided with policies advocated by other central bankers. Montagu Norman, for example, was apparently quite sympathetic to Schacht's policies in trying to curb stock market speculation without raising the discount rate. He informed Strong that "Schacht has been having his own troubles in Berlin, but for the moment is winning. There is, of course, much controversy about his methods, perhaps due to Dawes and reparations on one side and Central Banking on the other."[79] As Norman himself knew so well, conflicting economic and political needs often made any policy, in part at least, a bad policy. Benjamin Strong, too, was more sympathetic to Schacht than Gilbert was. While agreeing that Schacht "was too slow" in raising the discount rate, Strong noted in a letter to Pierre Jay, "I rather disagree with the argument in Gilbert's letter of May 29 to Governor Norman, and when I finish reading the papers which accompanied his letter, I am going to write him a bit about the bank rate problem as we see it here." And Ogden Mills, as has already been noted, believed that Schacht's policies could be explained without reference to his reparations goals.[80]

Furthermore, in a modern analysis, economist Jörgen Pedersen has argued that raising the discount rate as proposed by Gustav Stolper and Parker Gilbert might have been even worse for the economy than Schacht's "direct action." Pederson argues that the efforts of the United States Federal Reserve Board to use a tight money policy to curb speculation on the

New York stock exchange during the boom of 1928–29 courted economic disaster. Investment funds disappeared as interest rates rose and money continued to go into stocks. The tight money policy made it difficult for industry to secure investment capital but was not effective in halting stock market speculation. Although Pedersen, along with most modern economists, now believes it is incorrect, he recognizes that in the 1920s it was commonly believed that stock market speculation was bad and had to be combated. He wrote that the policy decisions of the Federal Reserve Board (and, one could add, of the Reichsbank) were based on "a deeply seated popular misunderstanding of the functioning of a market economy, especially its financial aspects." Although Schacht initially favored "direct action" to curb speculation while the Americans preferred a tight money policy, their broad policies were surprisingly similar. In a statement which might have been drafted by the Reichsbank, the Federal Reserve Board informed Reserve Banks in February 1929 that "a member [private commercial bank] is not within its reasonable claims for rediscount facilities at its reserve bank when it borrows either for the purpose of making speculative loans or for the purpose of maintaining speculative loans."[81] This announcement expresses almost exactly the Reichsbank's attitude when it tried to force German banks to give up their stock market loans in May 1927. In Germany, the Reichsbank's policy led immediately to a stock market crash, whereas in the United States the Federal Reserve Board reversed its policy and the crash came only months after the attempt to end speculation. It is interesting to note that while the New York Stock Market crash is commonly regarded as an important cause of the Great Depression, the crash of the Berlin market in May 1927 may have unleashed political repercussions but made almost no immediate impact on the German economy.

The Lessons of 1927
and German Reparations Policy

In February 1927, commenting on the public discussion of German reparations capacity, Hjalmar Schacht insisted, "we should not yet even speak of such things."[82] A month later, the growing monetary crisis led him to urge the government to take up the issue of reparations revision with Parker Gilbert, who was, according to Schacht, "inwardly absolutely convinced that we must arrive at a revision of the Dawes Plan." Chancellor Marx agreed with him that Germany could not fulfill its Dawes obligations, but cautioned him that government officials must not say this in public.[83] After the stock market crash in May, Schacht could no longer be restrained by his more moderate colleagues. In public and in private he insisted that Germany needed to formulate a new reparations policy. He lectured the Cabinet on the dangers of foreign loans, arguing that the highly volatile flow of foreign money promoted stock market speculation, overstimulated the economy, and would lead to a crisis if it were suddenly withdrawn. Even worse, during the economic flush created by the loans, foreign governments would think that Germany was enjoying an unprecedented prosperity and "the entire mood in regard to a revision of the Dawes Plan would evaporate because of the phantom [of prosperity] which Germany has created." He insisted that it was wrong to drop hints "here and there" about reparations revision. Instead, the government must formulate an absolutely united policy and then set out to convince others, especially Parker Gilbert, that revision was essential. Until that time, Schacht insisted he would have to maintain a high discount policy in order to defend his reserve position. "This," he declared, "was a completely impossible position."[84]

To the meeting of the Central Committee of the Reichsbank on the day it announced the increased discount rate, Schacht asserted that events since May 12 demonstrated that the foreign capital had completely frustrated Reichsbank discount policy.[85] Prior to May 1927 Schacht had been willing to moderate his more aggressive ideas on reparations and tolerate the fulfillment policy of the government. But the challenge to his authority over the money supply which had been brewing for the past year and reached a peak in the spring of 1927 seemed to unhinge him. He cried that he had "totally lost control of the market" and in a bitter and whining letter to Montagu Norman, Schacht pleaded, "I would like you to tell me how I can manage the currency and how I can control the market if hundreds and hundreds of millions [in] public money is left outside of the control."[86] Although he had persistently criticized government spending and foreign borrowing earlier, Schacht's activities took on new tones of violence after the May crisis. He focused on government spending as the primary source of his frustration and failure. He demanded that the federal government put an end to the "false" credit taking policies of municipal and state governments and insisted that this could be done only if the Advisory Board for Foreign Credit, which he said always opposed him, was reformed.[87]

In the course of the summer, Schacht let anyone who would listen know that changes had to be made. He talked to Parker Gilbert, Benjamin Strong, Emile Moreau (Governor of the Bank of France), Montagu Norman, and Owen Young, and all agreed that Germany had to receive foreign loans to pay for reparations and agreed that close cooperation was necessary to avoid any new crisis. They also agreed that the reparations issue must be kept quiet until after the November 1928 American presidential election.[88] As von Schubert reported, "Schacht explained that these conversations were very important because through them, not only Parker Gilbert, but the other competent Americans and Englishmen shared co-responsibility for the outcome of the next 18 months." After three years of relative peace, the reparations problem once more was becoming a major international issue, and Schacht was in the vanguard bringing it to public attention. While this was clearly a product of the experience of the spring of 1927, it is not so clear that this crisis was created intentionally.

Parker Gilbert remained convinced that in March, April, and May of 1927, when Schacht refused to raise the Reichsbank's discount rate, he "was openly and actively working for a breakdown of reparations transfers."[89] Economics Minister Curtius echoed this charge in November 1927 when he told the other ministers that "the Reichsbank President wanted to carry on Reparations policy independently by creating a preventative crisis to bring about transfer difficulties. But, when the transfer agent withdrew 107 million RM in foreign currency from the German market, he had to give this policy up."[90]

Curtius' assertion might not be entirely reliable, since by November 1927 he and Schacht were in an open feud about Reich economic policies. Further, Gilbert reported that paying the reparations sum in the spring of 1927 caused little trouble, since he had accumulated most of the foreign currency required before there were large withdrawals from the Reischbank reserves.[91] Thus the evidence on whether Schacht did or did not seek a "preventative crisis" in April and May of 1927 is mixed. However, he undoubtedly did believe that in pursuing the policies which he thought were best, the difficulties in transferring reparations would become self-evident. He was willing to face the issue immediately and pursue his chosen policies until the monetary problems which made this impossible were clear for all to see. In this determination to allow an immediate crisis, Schacht ran into solid opposition from the Reich government.

Government reparations policy, while based on the premise that payments would eventually have to be reduced, absolutely rejected any German attempt to induce this revision, at least in the foreseeable future. In terms of a long-run strategy, German reparations goals were outlined most systematically by Hans Simon, from the Foreign Ministry's Reparations Section. First in October 1924 and then again in January 1927, Simon discussed the close connection between foreign loans and reparations. Germany, he wrote, desperately needed foreign capital to rebuild its economy. But the foreign money would also provide the gold required to pay reparations. As long as Germany needed the capital, it would have to ensure that the reparations issue remained quiet. Only after it stopped importing capital could Germany allow its inability to pay to become an issue. At this point, with large volumes of foreign currency required to repay loans, Germany would have little cash left over to make reparations transfers. In October 1924, Simon estimated this change in policy would come in two to three years.[92] By 1927, he suggested that a change in policy was still one or two years away but bluntly wrote, "The greater our private debt, the smaller our reparations burden."[93] He estimated that in two years the cost of servicing Germany's private debt, now 300 million RM/year, would rise to 500 million RM, a sum which he felt was near Germany's maximum reparations capacity. If, by the beginning of the 1928 reparations year (September 1928) foreign loans had not yet declined, the government should consider taking action to reduce the loans, to create a "clear picture" of Germany's transfer capacity. For the present period (1927 to late 1928) Simon wrote that Germany could not argue that it couldn't pay reparations because the loans obviously made transfers possible. Instead, he recommended that emphasis be placed on Germany's low wages and income to argue that Germany could not raise enough taxes at home to pay reparations even in marks. Interestingly, he did not recommend trying to stop the inflow of loans in the first half of 1927, but on the contrary argued that Germany must accept the situation for now and focus on internal problems.[94]

If the long-range plans outlined by Simon were widely accepted in the German government, there was an equal consensus in 1927 that Germany must now do everything possible to avoid any new crisis. In the Foreign Ministry, telegrams from both sides of the Atlantic made it clear that Germany was not seeking any revision. Berlin wired the Washington embassy that in spite of growing "nervousness" in Germany,

At the present time, neither from a consideration of internally raising the reparations, nor from transferring them, can a demand for revision of the Dawes Plan be cogently made. Furthermore, revision of the Dawes Plan is inseparably tied to the interallied debt problem. But this problem cannot be broached with any hope of success until after the American Presidential and Congressional elections. For these reasons any demand now for revision of the Dawes Plan would fail. Therefore, further patience must be shown and the right time awaited.[95]

Maltzan in Washington was in absolute agreement. "It must be clearly established," he wrote, "that the time has not yet come for a revision of the Dawes Plan. For Germany to propagandize for it would be playing with fire."[96]

Perhaps most disturbing to German officials was a document prepared in mid April 1927 by Karl Ritter, the Foreign Ministry's leading expert on reparations.[97] Although one could well doubt whether Germany would be able to pay the normal year's reparations sum of 2.5 billion RM, he argued that "the first two and a half reparations years have shown that the Dawes Plan did not overestimate Germany's capacity to pay, but underestimated it." Furthermore, it would be hard to prove that German taxes were any higher than in the United States and England, and the federal government's reparations payment was little more than one-twelfth of the total budget. Today, he went on, "we can at most say: we don't want to raise the 2.5 billion RM; but we can not say: we can't raise it." Even the transfer problem was currently no problem at all, because of the foreign loans. As in every other official opinion, he argued that the reparations issue simply must not be raised until after the American election. He did, however, urge that private persons such as Warburg and Schacht as well as the International Chamber of Commerce work to show how reparations hurt Germany.

The Finance Ministry was in full agreement with the reservations and cautions expressed by the Foreign Ministry. In a long report on the reparations issue which was circulated widely in government circles, Köhler noted that the fiscal policies of the federal government were a central problem. He wrote, "A balanced budget is a basic foundation of the Dawes Plan. Its maintenance is a crucial duty of the German government. . . . It must be assured that budgetary developments do not force premature negotiations. . . . A fiscal deficit is to be avoided." He warned that if Germany were to assert that its inability to balance the budget made it impossible to pay reparations, "it could result in the opposite side's demanding continued intervention in internal German affairs."[98]

To all Germans, revision of the Dawes Plan had to include not only a reduced annual payment, but perhaps even more crucially, an end to the humiliating supervision foreigners exercised over German internal affairs. Supervisory agents in the Reichsbank, the railroads, and most galling of all the Reparations Agent himself, who could meddle in almost all German affairs, were an open wound reminding Germans of their postwar humiliation and their status as a second-rank power. Germany's dependence on foreign capital and Gilbert's growing influence in the United States gave him real power in German affairs. Ending these controls was a key element of any successful revisionist policy. And, as Köhler so bluntly put it, German governments at every level had to prove their good intentions by balancing their budgets before the controls would be eliminated.[99] The domestic political weakness of the federal government which prevented it from successfully enforcing this balanced budget policy led to its bitterest conflicts with Schacht and Parker Gilbert and inaugurated the tortured process which culminated in negotiation of the Young Plan.

As understood throughout the German government, successful revision of the Dawes Plan depended on a carefully constructed chain of circumstances. First, and above all else, Germany had to convince the world that it was trying its best to fulfill its obligations. The critical element in this endeavor was establishment of a balanced budget.[100] Next, after proving its good will, when at some future date the foreign loans stopped flowing in, Germany would be able to say—See, we've done our best, but we still can't transfer the gold. When the world finally saw and understood this reality, reparations would be scaled down to a realistic and very low level. To almost everyone, actual conscious policy to create this transfer crisis was absolutely unnecessary since all were of the opinion that events themselves, without any deliberate policy, would lead to an eventual transfer crisis.[101] Finally, this entire revision process would have to wait until after the American elections.[102]

Germans were convinced that Americans fully realized that in the long run Germany could not fulfill its reparations debt, and that the Allies could not pay their war debts. But the Republican administration could not undertake revision until after the elections of 1928. The Republicans had failed to achieve their promised armaments reduction and thus were unable to lower taxes as had been hoped. To admit that the Allies could not pay their war debts or Germany its reparations debt would force the administration to tax American voters to make up the deficit. The possibility of a tax increase a year prior to an election was not to be considered. As German ambassador Ago von Maltzan put it, "the contemporary American is against nothing so acutely as an injury to his 'prosperity' and the current administration watches over nothing so jealously, since the maintenance of that prosperity is the only success to which it can point in the next election." Until the elections were over, Germany could do nothing better than to do nothing, and leave any initiative up to Parker Gilbert, who would let the world know when the United States was ready for revision.[103] That Gilbert really shared Germany's views seemed to have been confirmed in March 1927, when he told Reich Chancellor Marx and Schacht in reference to Köhler's assertion that Germany could not pay reparations, "it is not as if one could dispute that this assertion corresponds to the truth. The entire world and especially the experts are convinced of the impossibility of fulfillment."[104]

By June 1927 German dependence on American capital seemed to be an inevitable fact of life. Efforts over the previous six months to reduce the inflow of foreign loans and allow the German capital market to meet domestic needs had been nearly disastrous. Without the steady transfusion of foreign money, investment capital had quickly disappeared, and Germany's hard-won economic prosperity seemed to be threatened. In order to draw foreign capital back into the country, the Reichsbank raised its discount rate and the government once again made foreign bonds tax free. These policies worked precisely as planned, and large volumes of German bonds were soon being sold in New York and other foreign markets. The success on the foreign market was not, unfortunately, matched by a recovery in Germany's domestic capital market, which had been so badly shaken during the spring. While in the previous year, economic prosperity had been accompanied by increased domestic capital supplies, in the second half of 1927 the continued prosperity was constantly threatened by the virtual nonexistence of domestic investment funds.[105] American credits, while more readily available due to a slight recession and falling interest rates in the United States, seemed unable to take up the slack left by the weak German market.[106]

After the failure of the Reich loan of February 1927 and the collapse of the German domestic bond market, the German government would find it impossible to fund its mounting deficits with long-term loans. Instead, it was forced to take short-term loans which had to be constantly renewed. As this debt grew, the Reich would find itself increasingly vulnerable to financial and political pressure and would face mounting problems from a position of desperate financial weakness.[107]

Chapter 6

Domestic Policy and Foreign Constraints, Autumn 1927

The spring of 1927 brought financial troubles not only to Germany, but to Britain as well. In the year since it had returned to the gold standard, Britain had faced a constant struggle to preserve the pound's value against the dollar. The over-valued pound could be supported only by drawing foreign investment funds into London. The Bank of England had accomplished this by holding interest rates above the New York level, but in late 1926 and early 1927 both France and Germany began drawing large volumes of gold out of London, which threatened the pound's stability.

Early in July 1927, the central bankers from Britain, France, Germany, and the United States arranged to meet in an attempt to find a satisfactory way for Europe to draw on America's vast capital reserves to stabilize the international capital markets. The meeting, held at Undersecretary of the Treasury Ogden Mills' home on Long Island, was unique in bringing together Schacht, Norman, Strong, and Charles Rist (assistant to Bank of France Governor Emile Moreau) to discuss the world's financial problems. The meetings were intended to be wide ranging and open, so no records or minutes were kept, and historians can piece together only a fragmentary picture of what went on.[1]

The principal concern of the Long Island meetings was to find a way to buttress sterling's weak position. Although no long-term plans were made, Strong was able to take advantage of an American recession to help his colleagues in Europe. By purchasing $391 million in government securities and lowering the discount rate from 4 percent to 3.5 percent, Strong made more money available to the American economy and took pressure off London and Berlin to raise their interest rates. The policy was in keeping with Strong's long-standing attempts to keep American interest rates low and provide cheap credit for European reconstruction. As he wrote in 1928, "our policy of the last four years has been effective in accomplishing the purpose for which it was designed. It has enabled monetary reorganization to be completed in Europe, which otherwise would have been impossible."[2]

This rather minor attempt at central bank cooperation indicated that when national and international needs conformed, bankers were able to cooperate with each other. But, as Strong would confess, this easy money policy "was undertaken with the well recognized hazard that we were liable to encounter a big speculation,"[3] and in mid-1928 the Federal Reserve moved to reduce speculation on the New York stock market by driving American interest rates upward. Even as Montagu Norman left the Long Island conference, he understood that the agreements reached were only tentative. As he observed in his brief post-conference notes, until war debts and reparation payments were satisfactorily settled, central bank cooperation would remain "rather a pretence! than a deep reality."[4] In the last years of the 1920s, as foreign and domestic interests came into conflict, central bank cooperation deteriorated, and the Federal Reserve proved unwilling to sacrifice American interests for European needs.

When Hjalmar Schacht arrived on Long Island, he was still agitated over his springtime economic and political fights with the German government. He was convinced that government deficits financed by foreign borrowing were creating an artificial and unstable mirage of prosperity in Germany.[5] He was also determined to reduce German borrowing in the United States which, he argued, simply provided the funds that made payment of reparations possible. Schacht did not hide his belief that Germany's foreign loans were being used to pay reparations. He proposed that future loans be "specially earmarked" and made unavailable for transfer abroad by the Reparations Agent.[6]

Soothed by Norman and to a lesser degree by Strong, Schacht had agreed by the end of the Long Island meetings not to raise the loan issue until after the British, French, and American elections which were pending for 1928.[7] But Germany's borrowing would become part of a new international confrontation only months after Schacht had agreed to put it on ice. The moving force behind this new attempt to induce closer control over German borrowing would be S. Parker Gilbert, Agent General for Reparations.

Seymour Parker Gilbert

Until the summer of 1927, German authorities had paid only scant attention to Parker Gilbert. The State Secretary in the Foreign Ministry met with him for the first time in early 1926 after Gilbert had been on the job over a year, and talked with him only once again late in the year. Government files indicate that there was little interest in his views at that time. By mid 1927, this was no longer true and the files began to fairly bulge as Gilbert came to symbolize the twin constraints on German policy imposed by American capital and the reparation debts.[8] As Gilbert established his credentials and reputation as arbiter of the Dawes Plan, his influence increased. Already in February 1927, Ambassador von Maltzan reported from Washington that on American policy toward reparations, Gilbert's influence was "decisive."[9] Later in the year, the German embassy in Washington amplified this impression. It reported that in spite of ready admission from most Americans that at some future date reparations and loan repayments would clash, "at the present time neither those involved in German business, nor public opinion are racking their brain *(zerbricht den Kopf)*. They soothe themselves [in the knowledge] that a confidant of the administration and big finance keeps guard in Berlin as Agent General."[10]

If the Germans respected Gilbert because of his influence on American policy, French observers admired him for broader reasons. Bank of France Governor Emile Moreau wrote in his diary that "M. Gilbert is always very conscientious and very firm in regard to the Germans. In him, we have not only a friend but even more, an excellent agent general of reparations."[11] Gilbert became so friendly with French Premier Raymond Poincaré that Germans regarded them as collaborators, and French Foreign Ministry reparations expert Jacques Seydoux told Germany's ambassador to France that "he held Parker Gilbert in extraordinarily high esteem and could call him his friend."[12]

As Gilbert's ties to French policymakers grew, his relations with British officials, particularly in the Treasury, deteriorated. Gilbert's determination to make the Dawes Plan work was viewed by the Treasury as an impossible task. When he insisted, as he always did, on proceeding about his business without consulting the Reparations Commission, the British resented the very independence that the French applauded.[13] The British expected that the Dawes Plan would fail and that until then the Transfer Committee and Parker Gilbert should keep the issue quiet. Otto Niemeyer observed that "the Transfer Committee is a useful bogey so long as the bogey is kept in a background of helpful obscurity: but if it faces midday sun everyone will see that it is only a turnip draped in a sheet."[14] The American turnip refused to accept the passive role assigned him by the British Treasury and the British were forced to grant him their grudging respect.[15]

In the autumn of 1927, Gilbert's determination to make the Dawes Plan work led him into an open and public conflict with the German Finance Ministry. His relationship with finance bureaucrats deteriorated to the point where Gilbert refused even to speak with some of them.[16] Gustav Stresemann and Erich Koch-Weser believed that part of the reason for the conflict with the Finance Ministry was Gilbert's inability to penetrate Germany's bureaucratic rigidity. As Koch-Weser recorded, "I believe infinitely much is spoiled by treating Gilbert not as a friend but as an adversary, just as the bureaucracy treats anyone who mixes in their affairs."[17] While bureaucratic rigidity was part of the problem, the real issue between Gilbert and the Germans hinged on Gilbert's belief that German deficit spending was violating the rules of the Dawes Plan.

Gilbert's irritation with German fiscal policy became so strong that he openly expressed his regret that the Reparations Agent had not been given the power to control German spending. His only tool was the threat that he would allow all reparation transfers to continue regardless of the consequences. Gilbert anticipated that this threat "would be sufficient to bring them to their senses."[18]

Gilbert's ties to American financial leaders and his influence as Reparations Agent make him arguably the most powerful individual in international financial affairs in the last third of the 1920s. Yet this power was exercised in near total isolation from other policymakers and the public. Rarely has a man had so much authority about whom so little is known. British Ambassador to Germany, Sir Ronald Lindsay, captures the uncertainty that surrounded Gilbert's personality and goals. "As for Gilbert," he wrote:

I am on good terms with him, but God forbid that I should pretend to be able to influence him. I never knew a man who could take his resolutions in such solitude. He is surrounded at his office with Commissioners, but not one of them ever knows what he is planning or thinking. I believe he sinks his character of American—and I say this though I know he is in close touch with Mellon, Ben Strong, and other great ones in New York. He regards himself, I believe, as an international person, charged with the duty of administering THE PLAN, and honestly determined to give it a fair chance.[19]

An American, to be sure, and indeed an American who hoped to become a partner in J. P. Morgan, Gilbert was convinced nevertheless that his duty as Reparations Agent would not be compromised by his upbringing or his aspirations. As Lindsay noted, Gilbert tried to submerge his American character and deal with reparations as a protector of international stability.

German officials assumed that Gilbert's ties to New York financial circles meant that he would protect American investments in Germany. They misunderstood the situation on two scores. First, Gilbert was the innovator in reparations policy and pulled the Americans along behind him. Second, Gilbert's ties in New York were to J. P. Morgan and partners, and these men had, like Gilbert, no sympathy for the "second-rank" banks that were selling German loans. The reality was that American capitalists did not have any agreed-upon policy or interest. Gilbert, like the Morgan partners, was a firm believer in conservative, orthodox fiscal policies and was unsympathetic to governments that tried to finance uncontrolled deficit spending through uncontrolled international borrowing. It was this issue that would thrust Gilbert into the limelight in 1927.

By mid-1927, Gilbert had gone far toward establishing himself as an independent, highly critical observer of German financial policy. Whereas he had been fairly passive during the discussion of railroad bond commercialization in the autumn of 1926, his semiannual reparations reports in November 1926 and June 1927 demonstrated his increasingly active intervention in German affairs. His interest and concern focused on two closely related areas. First and always foremost, Gilbert held the firm conviction expressed by the Dawes Plan itself, that unless the German budget remained balanced, inflation and inability to pay reparations would be the inevitable outcome. The increasing debt of the Reich and its manipulations to hide this debt by expanding the capital budget while leaving the operating budget in balance caused him particular distress. As he wrote in June 1927, "the problem of checking the rising tide of government expenditures has, in fact, become acute."[20]

The Reich's inability to reach a satisfactory financial arrangement with the states and cities was Gilbert's second major concern. The local governments were not providing the detailed budgets needed to reach a final settlement of the tax allocations. Instead, the Reich accepted a temporary settlement and agreed to increase the payments going to the cities and states.[21] Gilbert believed that the new agreement would lead the Reich into serious trouble should its revenues fall during a recession.[22] He complained that, "the whole matter seems to have been allowed to drift . . . and the whole field of public finances of the states and communes remains as obscure as ever." Rejecting a trend which has become standard in almost all modern states, Gilbert argued that "it is, on the whole, a sound principle of taxation that taxes should be levied by the same Governmental authority that makes the expenditures." Since the Reich collected taxes and the local governments spent them, the German system "tends to relieve the states and communes from the pressure for economy in expenditure that would certainly exist if theirs was the responsibility to levy taxes necessary to meet their own expenditures."[23]

By the fall of 1927, the continued and mounting spending by German governments, at the federal, state, and municipal levels, led to an open break with the Reparations Agent, and ultimately to revision of the Dawes Plan. The Reich's decision to increase pay for government employees brought the issue to a head. In spite of Germany's economic recovery, the real salaries of German government employees remained 25 percent lower than before the war.[24] Although their plight was widely recognized, when Finance Minister Köhler proposed a 25 percent pay increase to bring salaries up to former levels, it was obvious that the increase would put a heavy strain on the government's budget. Even more serious, since most state and city wages were pegged to federal wage levels, an increase in federal employee wages would have to be matched by increased pay for local officials and by increased war pensions and family allowances. Since states and cities employed six times more workers than the Reich, Köhler's proposal promised not only to disrupt Reich finances but municipal and state finances as well.[25]

The proposed civil service pay increase generated conflicts within the ruling coalition that nearly tore the government apart. With nearly one third of the deputies to the Reichstag being government employees (156 out of 493), the plan found strong support in the German Nationalist Party, the Peoples Party, and Köhler's own Center Party.[26] Yet the greatest opposition to the plan also came out of the Center Party with its uniquely diverse constituency. The Christian trade unions regarded the pay increase as so excessive that it threatened to raise the national cost of living and thus hurt worker interests. Their opposition was supported by the Bavarian People's Party and many of the state governments, which feared that the increased burden on state budgets would be intolerable.[27] In the following months, the Center Party was convulsed as labor representatives denounced the party's support for the bureaucrats while it failed to support worker interests.[28]

Even some members of the People's Party and the Nationalist Party recognized that the pay raises could topple all the governments over the edge of bankruptcy, but they were unable to slow or reduce the raise for fear of disastrous losses in the upcoming election.[29] Pushed into passing the raise by the hard facts of domestic political life, the Reich government now had to face the fact that its increased spending destroyed the credibility of its fulfillment policy on reparations. Parker Gilbert, as one might well expect, found the huge increase in government spending totally unacceptable. Already concerned about excessive municipal spending, he regarded the civil service pay raise as irresponsible and virtually an attack on the Dawes Plan.[30]

In this case, as with the tax cuts of 1926, increased burdens on government budgets were created by projects supported by the most conservative political groups in Germany. While on the one hand conservatives attacked all government spending, on the other hand they repeatedly demanded increased support for their own pet projects. Their absolute determination to subordinate national policies to their own interests was a major factor in making a comprehensive national policy impossible.

Within the government only Hjalmar Schacht held to his conviction that all government spending had to be reduced. His support of Gilbert's criticisms put him in direct opposition to his nominal conservative allies and demonstrates that, at least in his own way, he was consistent in his criticism of government spending. Finance Minister Köhler's response to Gilbert's criticisms confirms the impression that he was at best fuzzy-headed and at worst incompetent. In his memoirs, he records that he hoped to pay for the increased spending by reducing social welfare and other government payments, and by an unexplained increase in government income. The Dawes Plan, he wrote, "would not be endangered, at the most the supernumerary payments; and perhaps the transfer. But for the latter, the Finance Minister would not be responsible."[31] Surely, in light of his earlier pleas to reduce spending, Köhler understood the implications of a fiscal deficit. Had he argued that he had to grant the raise to meet the demands of his political supporters, his position would have made at least a minimum of sense.

In the late summer and early autumn of 1927, Parker Gilbert and Hjalmar Schacht formed an alliance to pressure the German government to reduce Germany's foreign borrowing and the size of government deficits. In London, both the Foreign Office and Treasury paid close attention to Germany's financial problems and Gilbert's policies. The British had been most favorably impressed by Gilbert's criticisms in his June 1927 report. The Foreign Office, in attempting to understand why the German government seemed incapable of balancing its budget, offered three alternative explanations. "It is not possible," one Foreign Office official wrote,

from the information at present at the disposal of the Foreign Office to suggest with any certainty whether the present budgetary extravagance of the Reich is due merely to mismanagement and lack of foresight or whether this extravagance should not rather be attributed to political and constitutional factors which are beyond the control of the German government, or again, be ascribed to the intentional pursuit of a policy calculated to bring about the breakdown of the Dawes scheme even at the risk of a further internal financial catastrophe.[32]

As the Foreign Office debated German intentions, the Treasury, led by Frederick Leith-Ross, had already made up its mind. While sympathetic to Gilbert's view that German finances were a mess, Leith-Ross saw "no reason to ascribe these tendencies to the international pursuit of a policy calculated to bring about the breakdown of the Dawes scheme." The German government's increasing spending "and the tendency to treat as capital and non-recurrent expenditure, services which ought to be covered by current receipts or entirely abandoned, represent problems with which every European Government has been faced since the war."[33] While Leith-Ross later proved to be perhaps too sympathetic to Germany and too convinced that reparations and war debts had to be cancelled, it is still true that the British Treasury was in an especially good position to understand the German plight, precisely because it faced the same problems.

Discussions within the various branches of the German government offer little evidence that a "crisis" policy was being pursued. In fact, Reich Economics Minister Curtius made the argument that an economic crisis had to be avoided by permitting the loans to continue. He "voiced strong objections against the proposed restrictions on foreign loans, since this would lead to a serious reverse in the business cycle."[34] Germany was more dependent than ever on foreign capital since the domestic market's collapse in the spring. Only 3 million RM in bonds were sold domestically from June to August 1927, whereas in the first four months of 1927 bonds worth 955 million RM had been floated in Germany. As one Foreign Office official observed, the domestic market was "as good as completely closed."[35] State Secretary Trendelenburg and Ministerial Director Schäffer of the Economics Ministry concluded that "insofar as the necessary capital can not be created domestically, foreign capital is essential." Furthermore, they were not convinced that the loans represented any long-run danger to Germany's currency. Vallette in the Foreign Ministry summed up the consensus in government circles when he wrote that "it is entirely erroneous to derive from the fact that the German economy once again finds itself forced to meet its monetary needs primarily from foreign loans, the accusation that Germany is trying to frustrate the implementation of the Experts' Plan."[36]

The German government wanted to ensure the continued inflow of foreign loans out of fear that an end to them would produce an economic recession. But Schacht's determination to impose Reichsbank control over all German funds soon led to a showdown. On September 21, Schacht withdrew his representative from the Advisory Board for Foreign Credit and insisted that the board be given the authority to stop the inflow of foreign capital. He declared that the board as now constituted was unable to protect the currency, the economy, or Germany's political stability. He demanded virtual veto power for the Reichsbank, tighter general loan control, and control over short-term loans. Leaders in the state and city governments joined the Reich Economics Ministry and the Reich Chancellory bureaucrats in rejecting this bid for dictatorial power by the Reichsbank.[37] The mayors of Germany's largest cities countered Schacht with a call for an end to all Advisory Board control over municipal loans, and they insisted that the cities were capable of conducting their finances without the Reichsbank's supervision.[38] The Economics Ministry found Schacht's power grab equally insufferable and pointed out that his attack on long-term loans contradicted his assertion that short-term loans were the real danger to the currency.[39] As Reichardt of the Economics Ministry told the Advisory Board, "When one views the short-term debt as the greater evil, it does not appear right to rigorously dam up long-term borrowing." Reichardt urged the board to reject any policy that would bring a total stop to new borrowing. The board, being more cautious than the Economics Ministry, decided to approve only one further loan— a request from Prussia already under consideration—and then wait for the Cabinet to make a final policy decision.[40]

Schacht's increasingly agitated efforts to stop the loans led the British Foreign Office to further consideration of his motives. One official wrote, "I cannot avoid the impression that Dr. Schacht is up to something. Both he and the Agent-General object publicly to the further extension of Germany's foreign indebtedness, but for different reasons. Gilbert is concerned about priority of reparations and fear of depression." Schacht, while also concerned about a possible depression, was moved "even more" by "consideration that the raising of such foreign loans assist enormously to get the annuity safely across the exchange into allied pockets."[41] Another British official concurred in this evaluation of Schacht's intentions and added, "Up to the present, the Treasury has been inclined to scoff at our fears with regard to the German policy on reparations . . . but the impression left after reading this dispatch is that Dr.

Schacht is up to something, and I agree that we ought to try to get a further pronouncement out of the Treasury."[42]

In a penetrating analysis, Gilbert himself offered some insight into the personality of his apparent ally. He wrote Benjamin Strong, "you may not give sufficient weight to the fact that Schacht is as changeable and moody as can be. He is one thing today and another tomorrow . . . he is temperamental and even mercurial." In order to understand Schacht, Gilbert wrote, "one needs to see him in action day after day for months at a time . . . when Schacht is in New York with you and Norman and the rest he is on his very best behavior." "In Berlin," he went on,

it is quite a different story. He moves up and down in very short cycles, and frequently it is impossible to keep up with him from one day to another. He has gone through particularly violent changes during the past six or eight months, and for a good part of the time I think he followed a perfectly indefensible central banking policy. This was certainly true in March, April and May, and at the very same time he was openly and actively working for a breakdown of reparation transfers. He had a change of heart in June. . . . His trip to America and his talks with you helped very much to confirm his change of heart, and I think that ever since he has been following a more far-sighted policy.[43]

Gilbert meant that Schacht was now maintaining a higher, market-oriented discount rate and agreed with Gilbert that German foreign borrowing had to be reduced. One should keep in mind, however, that Schacht had repeatedly declared that he opposed the loans because he believed that they gave a "false picture" of German ability to pay reparations. He never made a secret of his expectation that if he could reduce the loans, Germany would be unable to pay large-scale reparations. While in a way Schacht was an ally of Gilbert's, we have to look at Gilbert's intentions in order to understand why this was such an uneasy alliance.

While probably correct in believing that Schacht's motives were suspect, the British had not fully understood Gilbert's policies. Gilbert was determined to force the German federal government and the state and local governments to reduce their spending. After a conversation with Gilbert, a German Finance Ministry official understood that he was trying to prevent further foreign borrowing "to force in this indirect way, a reduction in our entire budget and financial behavior."[44] Gilbert explained to Benjamin Strong that "the very great over-expansion of German Government spending is tending to restrict the possibilities of transfer, by over-stimulating internal consumption and encouraging increased imports of commodities for purposes of internal consumption."[45]

Gilbert correctly understood that government deficits were stimulating the economy and inducing greater German imports of foreign goods. He was right in arguing that less spending would automatically improve the balance of payments. In the finest tradition of economists of the day, he ignored the reverse side of this coin which was all too apparent to German politicians. If the government cut spending and increased taxes, it would create greater unemployment and risk the economic crisis that Economics Minister Curtius so greatly feared.

Gilbert was not convinced that the foreign loans helped Germany transfer reparation payments. He explained to Strong, "the advantages of foreign loans from the point of view of transfer are also greatly exaggerated. It is true that the loans do provide foreign exchange in the first instance, but . . . for the most part, the proceeds of foreign loans to Germany go to finance German imports." The problem, from his point of view, was that the foreign loans counteracted the conservative fiscal policies which would allow Germany to pay reparations. The foreign loans, instead of allowing Germany to pay reparations, as Schacht and others, including Benjamin Strong, believed, had the effect, in Gilbert's more theoretical view, of undermining the policies that would allow Germany to pay.[46]

Gilbert was convinced that if he could stop German governments from borrowing on the American market, they would be forced to balance their budgets. By raising taxes and cutting spending, German income would be reduced and this in turn would lead to a drop in imports and an improvement in Germany's balance of trade. Thus, while Schacht wanted to stop loans in order to prove that Germany could not pay reparations, Gilbert believed that by stopping the loans, German income and imports would fall, and Germany would be able to pay. The two men were allied in pursuing the same policy with the ironic difference that they expected precisely opposite results.

Gilbert's determination to reduce American loans to Germany indicates that if he was a tool of American finance capitalists, he was a very odd tool indeed. In this same letter to Strong he pointedly set out the principles which guided his behavior, and one of his firmest demands was that Americans make fewer loans to Germany. One reason for this was a desire to avoid losing American money, but of even more importance was Gilbert's determination to see the Dawes Plan work.[47] Gilbert let his antagonism toward American bankers show when he told Britain's ambassador to Berlin, Sir Ronald Lindsay, that he was using the reparations issue as a way to reduce American loans to Germany "because if he did not, he would 'merely' be clearing the decks for those issuing houses in America" that had to be restrained.[48] In order to make the Dawes Plan work, Gilbert was now prepared to use every means at his disposal to slow or even stop the flow of American money to Germany.

America Stops the Loans

In late September 1927 the New York financial district was stunned by the announcement that the State Department had forbidden Harris Forbes to float a loan for the state of Prussia, with the implication that a ban on all German financing had been intended. The State Department's precipitous action, apparently taken without consultation with the Commerce Department and while Secretary of State Kellogg was out of town, seemed to bode a new determination to implement the controls over American lending which had been ineffectual for so long. As Werner Link has written, "Never before had the State Department intervened so directly."[49]

Although the State Department had repeatedly warned American bankers that it did not like their extensive German loans, it had also continued to state that it had "no objection" to them. In the first half of 1927, the State Department had even been moving toward a termination of the nominal review process that had existed since 1922.[50] The dramatic reversal of this drift and the determination to block the Prussian loan came about not because of changes within the United States but as a result of Parker Gilbert's growing feud with the German government over its financial policies.[51]

As Gilbert's irritation grew, the Advisory Board for Foreign Credit was preparing to approve Prussia's loan as its last act before the German Cabinet took up Schacht's demand for a more restrictive policy. But the Prussian loan more than any other offended Gilbert because the request for $30 million to cover the state's deficits came just as he was pressing to reduce government spending. Gilbert wrote the Finance Minister protesting the Prussian loan, and the next day the Reichsbank withdrew from the Advisory Board and demanded that the board be vastly strengthened. In a rage, Gilbert also wired the Federal Reserve Bank in New York and urged the Americans to help force financial discipline on Germany. He wanted the American administration to threaten to close New York to future German loans. Failing this, he sarcastically added, "even if the Department of State interposes no objections to the present Prussian loan, I should think that it might at least make this an occasion for the strongest possible representations to the German Government as to the necessity of effective control of these issues at their source in Germany." Benjamin Strong telephoned William Castle at the State Department (Kellogg being out of town) but was informed that State had already told Harris Forbes that the loan was unobjectionable.[52]

Continued pressure from Gilbert, who was supported by Strong, forced the State Department to reverse its position and inform Harris Forbes that the Prussian loan was not acceptable. Yet even in this apparently decisive action, the State Department quickly tried to soften its decision and, following Gilbert's advice, push Germany to exercise its own control. Castle told the German consul in Washington that he had the impression that the Advisory Board which had formerly been so reliable had become too soft in approving public loans. "The American administration," Castle said, "would of course prefer it if the initiative to solve the current situation came from the German Government," and he asked Kiep to relay this opinion to his government. To reporters asking for a clarification of its policy, the department said it had not altered its policy, but did disapprove of certain types of loans such as that to Prussia.[53] Having created a minor crisis, the State Department almost immediately began to back away from the firm position it had apparently assumed.

American bankers, according to Benjamin Strong, were now pressing for some solid clarification of government policy. Whereas "in the early days they resented the intervention of the Department of State and claimed to be willing and able to exercise their own judgement as to the propriety and goodness of loans to German borrowers, this incident has now rather led them to desire more specific and definite direction from the Department as a guide to their policy." As for the possibility of getting this firm policy statement, Strong was doubtful. "I feel equally certain that it is unlikely that our Department of State, after the conversations which have already occurred, will take a definite and affirmative position with the bankers." Furthermore, since some of the bankers were willing to ignore the government's disapproval, "unless the position of the State Department is much more definite than has yet seemed to be possible . . . we must . . . conclude that if a suitable control is to be exercised it must be brought about in Germany."[54]

Strong warned Gilbert that "on the whole, I cannot but regard the present situation as extremely unsatisfactory." He feared that if the impression grew that Gilbert, Strong, and the American government opposed German public loans, the whole market could be upset. This, in turn, could make it impossible to transfer German reparation payments and "precipitate the test of the Dawes Plan at least a year earlier than seems to be desirable and possibly necessary."[55] Having supported Gilbert's attack on the Prussian loan, Strong now sought a retreat to his earlier position that the loans were necessary, that the government must not get too involved, and that, in any event, real control had to come from Germany.

Perhaps overly optimistic, but basically correct, German consul Otto Kiep decided a month later that the United States was not going to institute any new and rigid regulation of foreign loans. Reviewing the differences between the Commerce Department, which wanted a ban on "unproductive" loans, and Kellogg's conviction that in practice the State Department could not regulate the loan market, he found no reason to anticipate a new American policy. The firm opposition of men like Senator Carter Glass to any commitment by the government to accept responsibility for ensuring the security of the loans made an active policy even more improbable. The controversy surrounding the loans led Kiep to conclude:

This discussion and the subsequent press reports have, however, as I positively believe to be true, neither in the Cabinet nor in the responsible departments (State Department, Treasury, Department of Commerce) led to an authoritative clarification and determination of the fundamentals of loan policy. Rather, for the future it has been left with the previous general formulation. And it would appear that for the future, no serious dissension [with this policy] is growing notwithstanding the general uncertainty in regulating past foreign loans.[56]

As an after effect of the State Department's opposition to the Prussian loan, general criticism of the department's interference in the private economy grew, and there was some discussion of relaxing even the weak controls now existing. Benjamin Strong, however, agreed with Kiep that little change either in the form of stronger or weaker regulation was likely. He repeated his oft-expressed view to Lindsay of the British Foreign Office that "if dollar loans to Germany were to be stopped or checked it was only in Berlin, and it was not in America that useful action could be taken." Lindsay, while sympathetic to Gilbert's demand for greater fiscal restraint on the part of the German government, was not at all convinced that Strong was right in expecting some positive action from Berlin. Such determination was unlikely since, as he wrote, "the German Government is weak . . . [and] anxious to get popularity in the country and willing to pay for it."[57]

Reform in the Advisory Board for Foreign Credit

Under pressure from the Reichsbank and the United States, the German government began an intensive reconsideration of its loan policy in October 1927. Schacht, by this time, seemed to have moved into complete agreement with Gilbert and was following Gilbert's prescription of "correct" central bank policy. With market interest rates rising and Reichsbank loans increasing, Schacht raised the discount rate from 6 percent to 7 percent on October 4.[58] He also urged Strong to raise the Federal Reserve's discount rate as this would discourage German short-term borrowing in New York. He added that if "a raise in your rate would lead to a withdrawal of American funds from our market, I would be rather satisfied and I think that the [reparation] payments then to be made can easily be met out of the new long-term foreign loans which have been contracted these last weeks." Schacht now convinced Pierre Jay that he was acting in full support of the Dawes Plan. Jay wrote Strong that Schacht's

attitude with regard to transfers . . . seems to have changed quite recently, that the one thing Germany mustn't do is to let transfers break down. This agrees entirely with the views expressed . . . in . . . your letter of July 21 and it seems to me an entirely sound view, although only if carried into effect in a reasonable way.[59]

Jay revealed his limited confidence in Schacht in his phrasing that "quite recently" Schacht had been reasonable and the worry that even a sound policy might be harmful if not carried out in a "reasonable way"—obviously a reference to Schacht's tendency to extreme and erratic behavior.

Within Germany there was less enthusiasm for the "new" Schacht. A memorandum in the Foreign Ministry noted in reference to the October 4 discount rate increase, "voices are not lacking which impute to the Reichsbank president the intention of suppressing the economic upswing which he regards as unnatural."[60] Finance Minister Köhler told the Reich ministers that Schacht was consciously trying to exploit his connection with Parker Gilbert to embarrass the Reich government, and that the two men were "to a remarkable degree in accord" in their demands for less public spending, less public borrowing, and a unified administration of public funds under the Reichsbank's control.[61]

Dr. Curtius had mixed feelings about Schacht's intention. While still believing that in the spring Schacht's action had been motivated by a desire to prove that Germany could not pay reparations, and hinting at the possibility that this remained behind Schacht's current policy, he agreed with Pierre Jay's estimate that Schacht had probably changed his mind. Today, he said, Schacht seemed to believe that "a revision of the Dawes Plan and a transfer crisis can come into question only after the 1928 elections in the United States, France, and Germany."[62]

Schacht himself, in arguing with leaders of the Association of German Cities, tried to sway them with an appeal to the tactics of revisionism. He warned them that "in future negotiations on the Dawes Plan, Germany will be reproached for the excessive foreign indebtedness of the public corporations. The Allies and associated powers, especially France, could successfully place Germany in the moral wrong" if these loans were not controlled. Schacht also warned the cities against borrowing short term in order to finance long-term projects, and he ended with the threat that if the cities didn't follow his advice, "then the Reparations Agent and Poincaré would give them the necessary lesson."[63]

Despite the widespread opposition to Schacht's demand that the Advisory Board be reformed, there was also some considerable agreement that a compromise had to be worked out.[64] On October 7, the Cabinet and Schacht met and agreed that Germany, including the cities, was not yet over-indebted, and that it still needed some long-term foreign capital. As prearranged by the leading permanent bureaucrat in the Reich Chancellery, State Secretary Herman Pünder, everyone also agreed that the Advisory Board would have to be reformed in order to reduce the volume of loans. Pünder advised municipal leader Konrad Adenauer not to worry about the reforms though, since "I do not believe it will involve incisive changes."[65]

Schacht, Curtius, and Köhler worked to reform the Advisory Board regulations so that it had to take into account the entire economic situation before approving a loan request.[66] Schacht intended this to mean that if too many loans were coming into Germany, even productive loans would be forbidden. But the Economics and Labor Ministries insisted that consideration also be given to developments in the labor market. City leaders added their voices to the demand that more loans be allowed them.[67] The SPD especially demanded more foreign loans to stimulate the economy and asked if it wasn't time to permit loans to build better housing in Germany. Even the Reich Association of Industrialists found it hard to understand Schacht's position, and business leader Dr. Jacob Herle asked Paul Silverberg if it wasn't possible that Schacht was being pushed by his need to work with the Agent General.[68]

Finance Minister Heinrich Köhler engineered the promised changes in the Advisory Board by warning the states on the one hand that they must agree to some reforms or risk losing all future credit, and on the other suggesting that massive public opposition to the Reichsbank made other minor concessions to Schacht bearable without loss of face.[69] Under the old rules, the board judged a loan strictly on its own merits. If the loan was offered at an acceptable rate of interest and was to be used for a "productive" purpose, the board had little choice but to approve it. Under the new guidelines, the board could refuse even a sound, productive loan if further borrowing threatened the economy or the stability of the currency. For the first time, the Advisory Board was really given authority to take into account the broader impact of capital imports on the whole economy. The voting rules were also changed to give the appearance of greater control over the states. But, as Board Chairman Arthur Norden observed, "the intention was to sharpen the guidelines . . . [but] . . . certain promises were made to the States that in consolidating short-term debts, accommodations would be made."[70] Schacht understood that the practical result of the new regulations was a defeat for his efforts to increase control. He vented his spleen by taking his stand to the public via speeches and newspaper articles which were unexcelled in their violence.

The Reparations Agent's Memorandum

On October 20, 1927, Parker Gilbert delivered a memorandum on German financial policy to Reich Finance Minister Heinrich Köhler. Although he intended it to remain secret, a *New York Times* reporter found out that a memorandum had been sent and guessed that it was highly critical of the Finance Minister's policies. Köhler attempted to prevent publication of the memorandum by telling his fellow Cabinet ministers that Gilbert opposed its publication and that releasing it to the press would violate his confidence. This assertion appears to have been a total fabrication on Köhler's part, since two days later Gilbert wrote him a letter with a copy going to the Reich Chancellor stating that "I have no objection to the publication of the full text of the Memorandum," and adding that he had already verbally informed Köhler of this. Several days later the full text of the memorandum was published, revealing that its criticisms of Reich policy were even sharper than press reports had guessed.[71]

Gilbert charged the German government with "developing and executing constantly enlarging programs of expenditure and of borrowing, with but little regard to the financial consequences of their actions." As he had in the past, Gilbert warned that "if present tendencies are allowed to continue unchecked, the consequence is almost certain to be serious economic reaction and depression." His principle concern was with growing Reich deficits and the Reich's agreement to increase state revenues without reaching a financial settlement. In spite of higher payments to the cities and states, and in spite of the Reich's assumption of more unemployment relief, the cities and states were borrowing more than ever. "The question underlying state and communal borrowing," he wrote, "is not whether individual loans should be placed in the domestic market or in the foreign market, or at short or long term, but whether they should be placed at all."

He then went on to criticize the civil service pay raise which had initially been proposed as a reasonable 10 percent in July and then had suddenly become the dangerously expensive 18–25 percent increase which was finally passed. This, plus plans to compensate owners of private property damaged during the war and plans for school reforms could lead Germany into a fiscal catastrophe. Gilbert warned that "the Reich, by failing to exercise proper restraint in its expenditures, is endangering the stability of its budget, the establishment and maintenance of which is the cornerstone of the expert's plan." Gilbert, like most conservative, orthodox economists, was further concerned that this growing public outlay deprived agriculture and industry of the investment capital essential for a healthy economy. Finally, he mentioned the failure of the Reichsbank to control all public funds, which made an effective credit policy impossible. Summing up his impressions, Gilbert wrote, "These tendencies, if allowed to continue unchecked, are almost certain, on the one hand, to lead to severe economic reaction and depression, and are likely, on the other, to encourage the impression that Germany is not acting with due regard to her reparations obligations."

As might well be expected, publication of this critique had widespread repercussions. American investors became even more nervous about German bonds when this report came so close on the heels of the Prussian loan incident. Prices for many German bonds fell several points in the next weeks and issue of new bonds was ended.[72] The memorandum created new divisions within the German government and generated a great deal of bitterness toward Köhler. The Foreign Ministry particularly found Köhler's handling of Gilbert embarrassing. In early October, Stresemann had approached Gilbert to try to patch up relations and get a feel for what he was really after.[73] Gilbert complained that he didn't understand Köhler and Köhler didn't understand him. He agreed with Stresemann's suggestion that things had been much better when Peter Reinhold had been Finance Minister. Gilbert suggested that what was really needed was a State Secretary in the Finance Ministry to handle reparations problems and give the ministry some sense of direction. Closer and more open communications between Gilbert and the German government were also essential. Stresemann did not fail to quote Gilbert, who added that "it would be extraordinarily pleasing to me, if I had the opportunity to speak with you more often about these things," and concluded that if Stresemann were Finance Minister they could no doubt soon reach an understanding.

When it became apparent that Gilbert had written the memorandum because Köhler had ignored verbal warnings, irritation with Köhler was increased. Gilbert told State Secretary von Schubert that he had had many conversations with Köhler, "perhaps too many," and had suggested that the differences might be clarified if he presented his views in writing—to which Köhler had agreed. Karl Ritter, head of the German Foreign Ministry's reparations division, told British consul Finlayson that things had been going smoothly until that "old muddle-headed fool" Köhler asked for Gilbert's complaints in writing.[74] He added that "even cumulative stupidity could be productive of real good. The 'Dummheit' of Dr. Köhler had produced the Gilbert memorandum, for which Ritter was truly thankful, since some objective outside judgement was necessary to bring the Reich Finance Ministry to a proper sense of its duties." Lindsay, too, found Köhler hard to understand. He wrote, "I have much sympathy with [Gilbert's] difficulties. Before Dr. Köhler's unfailing aimiability [sic], his ceaseless volubility, and his complete disregard of all suggestion, combined with the utter disorganization of the Ministry, Mr. Gilbert has been absolutely baffled." He added as a final coup, "Dr. Köhler's personality and incompetence is [sic] an important and unpleasant feature of the situation." Pierre Jay wrote Benjamin Strong that "one of the jokes going around German banking circles is that it would be a good thing for Germany if Gilbert were Finance Minister and Köhler were Agent General."[75]

German industrialists, in July 1927, found Gilbert's interference in German domestic affairs and insistance that Germany could pay reparations so offensive to German national pride that they joined together to create an "anti-reparations agent," who would mount a propaganda campaign to isolate Gilbert. Now in November, they fell all over themselves supporting his attack on public spending. Gilbert reported that shortly after he presented his memorandum, he had been visited [by a] very important German industrialist, a man of almost violent Nationalistic policies, whom he had never made the acquaintance of. This gentleman had called uninvited to say that it was high time the German Government was called to order in Finance, and to express the hope that his, Mr. Gilbert's, memorandum was couched in the strongest possible language, as nothing else could have any effect.

Gilbert added that eight or ten of the most powerful industrialists in Germany had hired Hans Luther to head a private lobby to force a reduction in government spending.[76]

The leadership of the Reich Association of Industrialists (RDI) concluded that "the discussion and conclusion of the Reparations Agent coincide with the fruitless demands made not only by industry but by all circles of the economy for the past two years." And they speculated that unless government spending was brought to heel, foreign faith in German credit could be entirely destroyed. The industrialists even went so far as to accept the fulfillment policy toward reparations that had come to dominate government thinking. They agreed that Gilbert's accusation that Germany was not practicing fiscal responsibility, "must, unfortunately, be seen as a sign that all future prospects for a revision of the Dawes Plan, at least insofar as raising the funds internally is concerned, has been very seriously endangered if not completely ruined." Government spending had to be cut as only this would "let foreigners and especially the creditor states see that we are serious about our obligations and that we will strive to fulfill them."[77] Germans, of course, expected that even their good faith effort at fulfillment would lead to failure, but German industry was willing to throw its support behind Gilbert in order to further its attack on government spending. Gilbert indeed was delighted by his new support and felt confident in reporting that he was "sure that the Germans didn't mind his 'kicking them in the pants pretty hard and strong'; indeed, they appeared to like it."[78]

If it was a sorry spectacle to see German conservatives supporting the Reparations Agent while attacking their own "bourgeois" government and spending policies which often were designed specifically to aid those who were now so critical of the administration, it was equally ironic to find Liberals and Socialists lining up in defense of that administration. Georg Bernhard, a leading democratic publicist, charged that Gilbert's note had actually been inspired by Köhler and Schacht, who presumably intended to use it to force a reduction in the government's budget. *Vorwärts,* the SPD mouthpiece, usually so conciliatory, supported a sharp rejection of Gilbert's right to interfere in the economy. The Center Party's newspaper, *Germania,* wrote that the most objectionable part of the warning was its attack on pending legislation, namely, the school reform which the Center Party was so actively pushing.[79]

Not only did Gilbert's memorandum expose German political divisions but it also revealed the complex financial arrangements which had developed by the mid-1920s. As Rudolf Hilferding told the Reichstag, probably 80 percent of municipal loans had been employed in ways to help industry. Creation of electric works, better transportation, and similar projects were largely undertaken in order to encourage industry. Prior to the war, he pointed out, it was very common for large industries such as AEG or Siemens to take out loans to finance municipal construction of worthwhile projects. Now, the general financial weakness made this impossible and forced cities to assume the burden directly. Hilferding might have added that even in the twenties, many of the municipal loans for electrification were taken with guarantees from AEG and Siemens, and tied to private industry's participation in the projects.[80] Even some industrial circles openly supported municipal spending. The Association of Sachsen Industrialists in Dresden urged the RDI to explain to Gilbert that the problems created by the war, the Treaty of Versailles, and the postwar economy were the causes of German borrowing and spending policies. He must be made to understand, they wrote, that "the spending of the states and municipalities is to a considerable extent to be seen as a product of the last war."[81] This attitude on the part of Saxon industrialists was undoubtedly influenced by Saxony's leadership in using state loans to provide credit to private industry. Paul Silverberg also urged the RDI to pursue a moderate course with the assurance that, as everyone knew, no one was more firmly opposed to excessive governmental intervention in the economy than he. "But," he insisted, "these conditions cannot be changed over night." He pointed out that in keeping with German tradition, cities would always have a role in capital investment, but a limited one.[82] These industrial voices of moderation were, however, in the small minority.

Gilbert's note divided Germans along ideological lines, while the practical thrust of the government's real activities was largely ignored. Social Democrats and German municipal leaders supported greater governmental responsibility, and thus ended up defending Köhler, even though a large share of the Reich's deficit was created by projects designed to help conservatives. The 1926 tax cuts, agricultural loans, and the civil service pay raise were projects directed toward helping industry and conservative political groups. Conservatives, in spite of the practical effects of government policies, opposed its expansion in principle—being careful, of course, to single out for support projects that helped them personally. While clearly beneficiaries of the government deficits, they demanded a balanced budget and supported Gilbert's criticisms, even if with some embarrassment. Most conservatives also opposed making reparation payments. But the balanced budget they demanded was the basic step needed to ensure that Germany could pay.

As a result of the furor created by Gilbert's memorandum, Stresemann began to sit in on meetings between Gilbert and the Finance Minister. This seemed particularly necessary, since Gilbert told a number of people that he could no longer talk to the representatives of the Finance Ministry, and he especially did not want to see Geheimrat Karlowa again. The government took Gilbert's complaint to heart and within months Karlowa either quit or was removed from his post as one of the Finance Ministry's most powerful bureaucrats, transferred to the Foreign Service, and sent to Mombassa, East Africa, as Consul.[83] Stresemann also asked to have a Foreign Ministry representative placed on the Advisory Board for Foreign Credit, since "as a result of the well-known events of the past weeks, these foreign loans have become a critical aspect of foreign policy." Both the Economics and Finance Ministers argued that the state governments would never allow another Reich representative on the Board.[84] The Economics Ministry, while sympathetic to

Stresemann's arguments, feared any confrontation with the states. Furthermore, it was felt that if any new representative were to be added to the board, it should be from the Labor Ministry because of the critical impact loan regulation had on the labor market. Stresemann had to settle for a non-voting seat on the board.[85]

Finance Minister Köhler, obviously stung by the ferocity of the attacks on his personality and policies, circulated a letter to the other Reich ministers tracing the origins of the current financial problems and, for the first time, revealing their real severity. The deficit spending, he reported, had begun with the tax cuts promulgated in the spring of 1926 and the decision made then to cover spending in the capital budget by loans instead of by surpluses from the operating budget. He felt this had been a perfectly legitimate decision, since the investments covered under the extraordinary budget were for housing, industrial development, and other projects which would have long-range benefits. Since future generations would be helped by these investments, it was only fair that they should help pay for them as the long-term loans were repaid. But the unemployment of 1926 had been so severe that the Reich budget had been strained to the point where it now had an uncovered debt of over 900 million RM, of which half had already been spent. Its problems were compounded by the necessity to spend large sums to support the Reich's loan of February 1927.[86]

The current inability to float a long-term loan, and the rapid exhaustion of support from treasury note issues, meant that coverage of the deficit might soon become impossible. As Köhler wrote, "In this event, the Reich Government would find itself in an extraordinarily difficult situation." The only relief possible would be a radical cut in spending à la 1923, to balance the budget. He therefore asked that the government agree to reduce spending, especially grants made to the Labor and Transportation Ministries for the 1926 work creating program. "For reparations policy reasons," he concluded, the government must avoid taking any further loans in 1928. As for the security of existing loans, Köhler argued with real accuracy that the largest and most dangerous volume of short-term loans was not held by cities, but by German agriculture. A debt already reaching 4.2 billion RM had to be consolidated into long-term loans or risk disaster.[87] Unfortunately even long-term loans could not make German agriculture profitable.

The German government's determination to adopt Gilbert's fiscal policies and balance its budget was confirmed in a telegram that Ritter sent to the major embassies abroad. He noted that although most other European nations maintained a capital budget covered by borrowing, Germany's weak financial market made this impossible. Allocations not already spent would have to be cut or postponed. "The capital budget," he promised, "will be radically cut back . . . and . . . we have absolutely ensured that the ordinary budget will be held in balance under all circumstances." He reported that the budget already had been cut 300 million RM while tax receipts would be 200 million RM greater than expected. Ritter's approach to fiscal policy was conveyed in remarks he made to Finlayson a few days later. Ritter explained that he had opposed the government's decision to repay part of the debts wiped out during the inflation. "One had to let the past be done," he said; "if people died of hunger, it was a thousand pities, but the state could not help them."[88] Like Parker Gilbert, Ritter, as an "apolitical" bureaucrat, had little but disdain for the weakness of politicians who gave in to voter pressure and refused to follow "correct" economic policies.

Although German officials were determined to cooperate with Gilbert, they were not unhappy to learn that the British Treasury was very critical of him. By late 1927, Gilbert and Frederick Leith-Ross were verging on an open feud. Leith-Ross resented Gilbert's autonomy and was convinced that both reparations and war debts had to be cancelled before international monetary stability could be restored. He, along with German officials, also believed that domestic economic needs might well differ from the policies that Gilbert demanded to make the Dawes Plan work. As one German official wrote, "It is not always the case that a sound financial and economic policy from our point of view is identical with one which makes transfers easier."[89]

The crisis induced by Gilbert's memorandum forced Germans to think about the ties between their own national goals and the American loans. Some officials clung to the belief that American bankers would protect their loans by forcing a lower reparations settlement. Hans Luther, past Chancellor, future Reichsbank president, and in 1927 employed as a propagandist for German industry, shared this opinion. But far more perceptive (although perhaps less well understood) was a counter view which circulated in industrial circles. The United States had loaned to many nations, with Germany taking about one quarter of America's foreign loans, so the Americans had interests in many markets, and J. P. Morgan had no interest in protecting Germany. Thus, as one observer put it, Luther's faith in American help was more an "illusion" than a reality.[90]

How successful were Gilbert's pressures in forcing the German government to balance its budget? Despite the apparent desire of most German officials to meet his demands, it was not to be. Referring to Gilbert's June 1928 report, which contained no further criticism of municipal borrowing in spite of its continued volume, Ritter commented, "this sympathetic attitude deserves special interest when we realize that . . . when one critically considers the results, the actual development of the issues raised in the memorandum and the last report have not been entirely in line with the wishes expressed in the memorandum." Especially noteworthy was the fact that public loans had become even a greater share of total borrowing than they had been before the memorandum. Ritter summed up Gilbert's dilemma with the observation, "Just as in the conversations on Reich finances, the Agent General had to bow to the force of reality . . . the law of supply and demand has once again soon prevailed."[91]

Parker Gilbert and the Birth of the Young Plan

After the long and bitter exchanges between the Reparations Agent and the German government, German officials were surprised by the moderate tone adopted in the Agent General's report of December 1927. Even more surprising were Gilbert's suggestions that the time for consideration of a final reparations settlement had come and his emphasis that in this settlement the transfer protection given to Germany under the Dawes Plan must be ended.[92] In a memorandum presented to the Reparation Commission, Gilbert spelled out clearly and precisely why he was now convinced that revision was necessary.[93] He wrote that one of the foundations of the Dawes Plan was the concept "that Germany herself should exercise prudence in the management of her affairs and not dissipate her resources and her credit through overspending and over-borrowing by the public authorities." In his memorandum to the Finance Minister in October and in his December report, he had "made it clear that the transfer protection which is given to Germany by the Plan involves reciprocal obligations on the part of the German Government, and . . . presupposes that Germany on her part will do everything within her power to facilitate transfers on reparation account." Gilbert argued that the Dawes Plan itself was partially responsible for the problems he was now having with the German government. "The very existence of transfer protection, for example, tends to save the German public authorities from some of the consequences of their own actions." He all but charged that the growing Reich budget was permitted because German officials hoped that when a transfer crisis came, the transfer clause would be used to end reparations payments.

Somewhat more sympathetically, Gilbert noted that uncertainty over the final reparations debt made it difficult to carry through such essential reforms as the final financial settlement with the states and cities. Until the Reich knew what its reparations debt would be, it could not agree to fixed payments to the local governments. Summing up his concern, Gilbert wrote, "In other words, there will surely come a time, and in the not too distant future, when the system of protection established by the Plan will be less productive of reparations for the creditor Powers themselves than a system which gives Germany a definite task to perform on her own responsibility, without foreign supervision and without transfer protection."

The last point was so important that Gilbert said it twice. The entire thrust of his argument was that transfer protection had to be ended and this would force Germany to accept the "responsible" policy which he so unsuccessfully had been promoting during the past year.

The motive force, then, behind Gilbert's call for a new reparations settlement came from his experience with German finance and his inability to induce a more conservative policy. In the summer and autumn of 1927, as a transfer crisis seemed to be brewing, Benjamin Strong urged him to seize the initiative in heading off a crisis. Less hopeful than Gilbert that Germany could pay large reparations, Strong did concede Gilbert's point that conservative fiscal policies could greatly strengthen German transfer capacity.[94] While hoping that Gilbert's quick action might prevent a transfer crisis, Strong was not sanguine about the possibility. "I am not," he wrote Pierre Jay, "looking forward with any comfort or satisfaction to the possibilities of any sort of crisis, but this transfer problem is of a sort which usually cannot be solved without the influence or impact of some sort of a crisis . . . I see no possibility of anticipatory action," he went on, "except through the intervention of Gilbert."[95]

While in the United States in December and January, Gilbert talked with a number of American officials. A consensus emerged that some sort of settlement was desirable, and that the American capital market was now strong enough to absorb the bonds which would be a crucial part of any settlement.[96] Gilbert had consistently believed that, in revising the Dawes Plan, "the fundamental thing from every standpoint is that there should be a final settlement." Germany, he insisted, had the most to gain by this final settlement because it would remove the uncertainties plaguing Reich financial policy. But, he warned, "Germany must be prepared to pay, and to pay high, for the sake of getting a settlement." He added, "I think it is clear also that in order to get a settlement, Germany must depend largely on the use of her credit. It is vitally important, therefore, to keep Germany's credit at the highest possible level and to deal with the whole situation while her credit is unimpaired."[97] Gilbert used this promise of large volumes of negotiable German bonds to win French support for a Dawes Plan revision. The security and immediate availability of the funds made the option very attractive to French officials who, as always, found themselves in financial trouble in late 1927.[98]

Germans who hoped that Germany had indebted itself so heavily to the United States that Americans would demand a lower reparations settlement to protect their private loans soon saw their dreams begin to sour. Secretary of the Treasury Andrew Mellon publicly and firmly refused to consider any connection between reparations and allied debts.[99] Only if the Americans reduced their demands on the Allies could Germany realistically hope that reparations would be reduced. In a public letter to Dr. John Grier Hibbon, president of Princeton University, Mellon already had argued that American demands on the Allies were modest and legitimate. And he pointed out that only by increased taxes on Americans could the Allied debt be reduced. Mellon added that when the House of Representatives approved the French debt settlement, the debate "indicated that an overwhelming majority . . . were opposed to more lenient terms." In rejecting any further reduction in the Allied debt, Mellon concluded, "It must also be obvious that if the amounts paid by all our debtors are to be reduced and a corresponding reduction is to be made in the amount of reparations to be paid by Germany, the net effect of this change will be to transfer the burden of reparation payments from the shoulders of the German tax payer to those of the American tax payer."[100]

Germans found it nearly impossible to believe that the American government would continue to insist that there was no direct link between reparations and war debts, but Mellon's position remained firm. His view, like Gilbert's, was based on the belief that, given the correct fiscal and monetary policies, Germany could raise and transfer very large sums. In Gilbert's view, the British "had always underestimated German capacity to pay." And in the final settlement which he had in mind, Germany's obligations would be nearly equivalent to those under the Dawes Plan.[101] The next year demonstrated that Gilbert and the American government would hold to their long-standing reparation and war debt policy, and that Germany's hope that the large volume of American loans would win American support for a vastly reduced reparations settlement was badly misplaced.

Chapter 7
Twilight of the "Golden Years," 1928–1929

In late 1926 and 1927 Germany's fragile economic recovery allowed a brief period of political tranquility. But real social cooperation was far from established and beneath the surface calm, bitter struggles were developing. For a time, fiscal deficits made possible by the inflow of American capital allowed Germany to invest and consume well beyond its own internal capacity. But, by late 1927, industrialists were concluding that even with the Nationalist party in the ruling coalition, they would not be able to win the total control of the state that they sought.[1] As conservatives mounted a campaign against the entire democratic structure of the Weimar Republic, the political peace began to break down. When Schacht and Gilbert successfully stopped the inflow of foreign loans, they brought the simmering conflict to a boil. The key years, 1928 and 1929 linked the recovery and "tranquility" of 1926 and 1927 to the open social warfare of the depression years of the nineteen thirties.

Developments after Gilbert's Memorandum

In the aftermath of the Reparation Agent's memorandum condemning German borrowing and fiscal policies, the American market refused further loans to Germany. During the entire month of November 1927, only a single loan was successfully floated. As a Foreign Ministry memo declared, "The foreign market has been almost completely closed to German loan requirements." The weak demand for German bonds was demonstrated when the price of Prussian bonds fell three points as soon as the bank syndicate which had sold the bonds and had artificially supported the price was terminated.[2] With this example as a warning, no further effort was made through the turn of the year to determine just how badly the autumn controversies had damaged the market.

After over two months of drought, Harris, Forbes decided in January 1928 that the time for a new German loan had come and launched an aggressive campaign to sell bonds for the Westphalian United Electric Power Company. In developing a large-scale public promotion campaign, Harris, Forbes drafted a series of fliers to convince its salesmen that German bonds were a sound investment for Americans. Their publicity line focused on the profits and growth of the German firm while downplaying the high interest rates earned on German loans. Vigorously pushed by Harris, Forbes, the bonds were successfully sold in short order. The firm then reminded its employees that "the quick sale of any issue is always a highly desirable thing, but in this case, the bonds being the first German offering since the reaction last fall, the quick sale is of especial importance and should remove any doubt as to the reception American investors are ready to give sound German securities."[3]

Harris, Forbes was quite right in asserting that German bonds could still be sold in the United States. During the first quarter of 1928, over 374 million RM in bonds were sold—a rate much above the lean first quarter of 1927 and even better than the more "normal" years of 1925 and 1926. These loans were not, however, the same type that had been common earlier. Many of the bonds, including the Westphalian electric loan, were for public utilities, while only one city was able to secure a foreign loan. German banks also took a larger share of new loans than ever before and used these funds to provide building mortgages and agricultural loans.[4]

During the first half of 1928, while foreign markets were reopened to private and utility loans, selective restraint by the German government for the first time effectively prevented long-term municipal borrowing. The indebtedness of German banks to foreign lenders, already an important phenomenon, became all the greater as they began to act as intermediaries for city and private borrowers. Not only did this increase German bankers' dependence on foreign capital, but the fact that many of these loans were short-term meant that this dependence carried greater danger with it. Undoubtedly, for a handsome profit, German bankers were assuming the risk for cities and other borrowers by taking short-term American loans and relending them in Germany for long-term projects.[5]

The American government remained concerned about the German public loans. In early January the State Department inquired how Germany proposed to handle two loans then pending. The loans in question were from "semi-public" corporations which were officially private, but in reality controlled by German cities. Specifically, the Americans wanted to know if the loans would be reviewed by the Advisory Board for Foreign Credit. As Poole of the American Embassy tactfully put it, the State Department "intended to make its own decision more or less dependent on the position taken by the *Beratungsstelle* [the Advisory Board]." Aware that the board probably did not have control over legally private industries, Poole added that "if the *Beratungsstelle* lacks authority, he would appreciate a statement from the government itself." He made it quite clear that what the Americans were after was a firm statement on how far the reforms of the Advisory Board would go and on Germany's future loan plans.[6]

German officials may have been unaware that the Americans were suffering their own internal inability to formulate a policy, but they were correct in looking upon the State Department's request as a product of Gilbert's effort to clarify the reparations issue and force Germany to conform to his ideas of an honest fulfillment policy. "Through this apparently harmless question," reparations expert Ritter noted, "we are presented with two problems; a domestic political question whose implications are probably unknown to the State Department, and a question of reparations policy which the State Department probably knows about after Gilbert's presence [in the United States]." The domestic problem of how to deal with semi-private industries was still to be worked out, but the reparations problem had now begun to haunt Ritter and other German policymakers. They suspected that Gilbert had put the State Department up to asking the question so that "when the [German] government approves these two loans . . . and a large number of similar loans in the future, the reproach could later be made against us: 'You were asked by the State Department in every individual case, and you should not have approved them had you not been certain that service on these loans could be transferred along with reparation payments.' "[7]

For Germany, the loans were becoming a real threat with no easy solution. They gave Germany a false image of being able to transfer reparations easily and thus undermined German claims that transfers were impossible. Schacht had constantly harped on this theme, while the government had tried to make the best of the situation by arguing that the debts would tie the United States to a low reparation settlement. But now Ritter began to see that Germany was in a worse trap than the Americans. If Germany owed too much, when the time to renegotiate came, the demands of loan repayment would be so great that very little would be left over for reparations. Although this might appear to be good, Ritter warned that "the danger exists that so little transfer capacity will be left over for the final settlement . . . that a final settlement would no longer seem attractive enough to the other side." In this eventuality, the issue might simply be left to drag on and on with its continuing destructive impact on German policy and society unrestrained.[8]

Forced to recognize that domestic financial policies entailed dangerous and unpredictable risks in foreign policy, the German government moved, for the first time, to stop foreign loans to German cities and other fully public agencies. This would at least remove some of the power from foreign criticisms since sharp attacks had consistently focused on the public debt. But, as Ritter had pointed out, even the private loans carried dangers if they became so large that German transfer capacity was seriously threatened.

With most loans practically halted since Gilbert's memorandum, pressure within Germany to allow a renewed inflow of capital was strong. The Labor Ministry, which had won a seat on the Advisory Board in late 1927, attacked the board's inclination to wait for guidelines from Gilbert and the Reichsbank. Labor's representative exhorted board members to remember that "the Advisory Board must also take into account domestic policy considerations. It is a fact to take into consideration that the labor market has very considerably worsened." Cities were delaying projects that could help the employment situation because they could not find adequate financing. He urged the board at least to begin hearings on new loans. These concerns of the Labor Ministry were shared in the Economics Ministry, which also attacked the government's weak inclination to wait for Parker Gilbert to make a decision for it.[9]

The mounting pressures within the ruling coalition were a clear reflection of the broad demands within Germany calling for expanded social and spending policies. Although the government found it impossible to ignore these pressures and the demands of agriculture and industry for further financial aid, it became increasingly difficult to find acceptable compromises. Particularly on the international front, the situation had by this time become so serious that the domestic arguments for further public spending were losing influence.

Assuming his oft-taken role as Gilbert's confidant, Schacht, in mid January, asked for a meeting with the Cabinet to discuss instituting controls on so-called "mixed" loans—those of public utilities, transportation companies, and industrial corporations which were largely publicly owned but legally private.[10] Schacht said that he agreed with Gilbert's desire to slowly reduce German borrowing in order to clarify Germany's transfer capacity. If Germany would regulate its own borrowing, Schacht suggested, it would free itself from foreign controls and still be able to meet its reasonable needs for foreign loans.[11]

Economics Minister Curtius rejected Schacht's proposal with the argument that a reduction in loans would cause an economic crisis in Germany. This would not only force consideration of a new reparation settlement prior to the 1928 elections in France, Germany, and the United States, but even worse, an economic crisis would cause Germany to develop a huge export surplus. Drawing on the lessons of 1926, Curtius argued that an economic crisis would enable Germany easily to transfer reparation payments.[12] This brilliant insight was ignored by Schacht as he explained that both he and Gilbert were primarily concerned that Germany avoid any transfer problem since this in itself could create a crisis in the German economy. Gilbert's hope, said Schacht, was to induce the Allies to discuss a new reparations settlement before transfers could be endangered. Schacht added, "I only believe that this conviction of Gilbert's, that a break in transfer would have devastating effects for Germany, is correct."

In addressing another of Schacht's suggestions, that the tax on capital be ended to induce more domestic saving, Finance Minister Köhler rightly noted that the problems were as much political as economic. To be sure, he admitted, Germany needed both to save and invest more, but the capital tax was a part of the political compromise which kept the Weimar government afloat. Any effort to end the capital tax would have to be matched by elimination of the income tax.[13]

Unable to formulate a policy that could meet both the political realities and the economic necessities, the Cabinet once again chose the option of inaction. By both political inclination and economic orientation, this conservative government believed that it was important to reduce foreign borrowing and increase domestic savings, but Germany's political fragmentation prevented any forthright stand on the issues.

During the next months, as the government tried to decide on a new policy, public loans were effectively barred by Advisory Board delays. After almost two months of hesitation, a climactic meeting of the government's Committee on Reparations broke the deadlock by setting a firm policy of institutionalizing the indecision.[14] After a discussion with Gilbert, Finance Minister Köhler came away convinced that Germany now had a chance for a favorable revision of the Dawes Plan. But, he said, "this must be accomplished by a reduction in spending and restraint in loan policies." Even as the Finance

Minister urged restraint, his State Secretary, Johannes Popitz, warned the other bureaucrats and cabinet officials that although Gilbert was pressing for less municipal borrowing, any attempt to exert real control which might end in a failure "could be a serious setback in the [upcoming] electoral campaign." The government would be accused of having campaigned on the promise of promoting local self-government and having betrayed that promise by preventing municipal borrowing. Furthermore, even if the control were to be effective, Popitz warned that the cities would compensate for their loss of long-term loans by taking even more dangerous short-term loans. Economics Minister Curtius affirmed Popitz' political prognosis and again urged some sort of moderate policy with the plea that "in all events we must avoid falling into a crisis." To this, the vice-president of the Reichsbank reassured Curtius that "the Reichsbank is also opposed to inducing a transfer crisis wantonly." The government thus found itself trapped by foreign policy considerations which dictated that no loans be permitted, while domestic politics demanded that cities be allowed to borrow abroad.

The solution to this dilemma quite obviously was to create a great show of activity, while assuring that nothing really happened. As Popitz suggested, by careful scrutiny of each of the 235 pending municipal loan requests, one could make a show of determining the entire amount of money being requested while also delaying any effective decision. As the board renewed its deliberations, municipal officials would be reassured that some loans would be permitted and they would be more willing to reach a compromise with the Reich to hold down the total demand.[15]

As for the "semi-public" utility loans, the government, in spite of all the foreign pressures, would not budge. To regulate them would create another constitutional crisis, since critics would charge that the government was trying to expand its control over private loans.[16] In this case, domestic considerations won out, since it was simply too dangerous to expand the loan control to cover semi-public firms. By this decision, the government gave in to conservative, industrial power by shying away from control of private loans. But it also made a concession to municipal governments which were increasingly using semi-public corporations to take foreign loans.

Domestic considerations were not alone in determining this Reich policy. The exceedingly complex nature of German reparation policy is revealed by the way in which it, too, played an important role. The Foreign Ministry advised its Washington embassy that if Gilbert succeeded in forcing the German government to commit itself to approving all loans, "the reproach could be made, that . . . we had assumed the responsibility that repayment of the loans would not endanger reparation transfers."[17] On the one hand, Germany had to be careful not to borrow too much, but on the other, it wanted to permit some loans (both to help the economy and for reparations purposes) while being sure that the government was not held responsible for those loans. The dangerous game Germany had hoped to play was becoming ever more complex. The risks were becoming increasingly clear as critics within the German bureaucracy pointed out that if Germany could not pay enough, the allies would not accept a final settlement, and Parker Gilbert strove to force the German government to accept full responsibility for ensuring that transfers could be successfully completed. Convinced that both a moderate volume of loans and reparations could be paid by Germany, Gilbert's problem now was to force the German government to adopt a "responsible" (read deflationary) policy.

Municipal Debt

In the early weeks of 1928, the Advisory Board for Foreign Credit, while not discussing or approving individual loans, was not totally inactive either. It undertook a survey of municipal loan requests and needs, which produced some interesting results. First, cities had already requested 1.5 billion RM in new loans, a sum considerably larger than they could hope to receive. The short-term municipal debts, while large, were not dangerously so, and surprisingly, most of them were domestic. The lion's share of the municipal short-term debt had been issued by larger cities with populations over 80,000. Of a total floating debt of 700 million RM, these large cities held 503 million RM. Again, of the 700 million total debt, 624 million RM was held domestically—with German public and private banks nearly splitting the share of short-term advances. The board concluded that if cities were granted a total of 600 million RM in new foreign loans, their short-term debt could be consolidated while the Reichsbank's concerns about excessive borrowing could be mollified. It was hoped that careful state scrutiny of loan requests, especially by the responsible Prussian administration, might further reduce this sum.[18] Through March and April, the board's continued investigation into general municipal credit needs was used to justify its inaction in the case of individual loan requests.[19]

In early May the Cabinet decided that it had to permit some city loans in order to defuse a potentially dangerous election issue.[20] It agreed that for the coming year, the cities could sell a maximum of 350 million RM in foreign bonds. This fixed sum was set with the open understanding that it conformed to Parker Gilbert's desires. Schacht told the Cabinet that "we must be in agreement with Gilbert," and the Cabinet itself concluded that it "must not make any difficulties with the Reparations Agent."[21] That Gilbert had actually helped set the precise terms of this quota seems doubtful since he repeatedly protested that he would not talk specifics with anyone. But at some point, his agreement with the quota was given or implied since, over a year later, the Finance Ministry continued to feel itself bound not to exceed the 350 million RM in loans which had been "agreed to with the Reparations Agent."[22]

Americans were aware that it was Gilbert's pressure which had succeeded in forcing this new loan policy. Pierre Jay, who worked in Gilbert's office, boasted to Benjamin Strong that "the German Government has taken a firm stand for the control of foreign borrowing. By dint of much conversation Gilbert has gotten them to recognize their responsibility in this matter, and they are going at it full tilt." Jay was optimistic that this new policy would be successful and declared, "I think they will stick to it."[23] When the influential liberal economist

Robert Kuczynski attacked the Advisory Board's restriction of municipal loans as a concession to the demands of German private industry, one official in the Foreign Office observed, "this is a logical result of the fact that he does not perceive the important reparations policy connections or the range of the pressure from abroad."[24]

For the first time, international relations really had played a more important role in policy decisions than domestic affairs. Despite the increasingly shrill demands by private industry that public spending and borrowing be reduced, it was the foreign pressure which provided the final incentive to action. Fear that Gilbert might be able to close the foreign market if some moderate policy changes were not adopted and the dawning realization that the foreign loans carried dangers as well as benefits combined to produce the reforms. But there was one final consideration that led the Reich Cabinet to approve a reform that once again admitted a moderate inflow of foreign capital to city treasuries. Since the Dawes Plan expressly committed the Reich and states to paying reparations before all other debts, publication of Gilbert's memorandum in the fall of 1927 had effectively closed the foreign market to them. When, during the spring, the Advisory Board had also forced cities off the international market, their additional demands on the domestic market threatened to deprive the Reich and states of this last remaining source of capital.[25] For the sake of Reich finances, the cities had to be allowed back on the international market.

Hjalmar Schacht took advantage of the halt in long-term municipal borrowing from December 1927 to May 1928 to reject the charges of his detractors who said that he wanted to stop the loans in order to create an economic crisis. He mocked *Vorwärts* and other leftist newspapers which had predicted that an end to the loans would create an economic disaster, but now had to admit that the economy was doing very well without the foreign capital.[26] Schacht asserted that recent growth proved once and for all that the economy was resting on a sound foundation independent of the artificial stimulation of foreign loans. Now going through a phase of utmost reasonableness, Schacht assured the Cabinet that both he and Gilbert were trying to prevent a collapse of German finance and economic disaster.[27]

All of Schacht's earlier pronouncements indicate that he had expected economic and reparations problems if the loans were ended, but he was now willing to take the credit for policies that did not seem so disastrous. He told Rowe-Dutton in late March that he was now "completely satisfied" with the Advisory Board and as a result, it was possible to "relax pressure a little" to permit a "certain amount of foreign borrowing, [since] the public authorities had learnt their lessons." Rowe-Dutton, often concerned that Schacht might do anything to end reparations, found him very reasonable on this occasion. "The whole conversation," he reported, "gave me the impression that Dr. Schacht is convinced that the measures which Germany must take in her own interests are exactly those measures which are in the interest of the allies. . . . I should say he would be willing that the allies should benefit on condition that Germany benefits more."[28] The new regulations imposed by the quota system satisfied both Schacht and Gilbert and permitted an important step to be taken toward a Dawes Plan revision.

Although the restraint on municipal spending and borrowing created by the new regulations was largely dictated by foreign policy considerations, it quite naturally had support from within Germany as well. The big Berlin banks, represented in the *Seehandlung*, had suggested as early as January 1928 that the best way to permit some loans, but not too many, was to allow the Reichsbank to set a quota for each year.[29] More conservative elements, however, were not yet satisfied. The *Deutsche Tageszeitung*, a newspaper representing agrarian, especially large landholders' interests, commended the Reichsbank's long-standing policy of trying to reduce public spending and taxes, but found the new municipal loan policy far too generous. Schacht, the article asserted, had made an unwise compromise in permitting this additional public debt of 350 million RM.[30] The new policies, while no doubt conservative, were far from representing the more reactionary desires of some German groups.

Increasing Sophistication
in Capital Movements

The new municipal loan policy, for all that it was politically motivated and in good part forced upon the German government by Gilbert, was the culmination of three years of learning which had produced a highly sophisticated procedure for channeling international funds into the German economy. With total public borrowing set by a fixed allocation, the sum was carefully divided among various groups of borrowers. The very largest cities—Berlin, Cologne, Frankfurt a.M., and Munich—were allowed to negotiate their own loans using their already well-established connections. Another 135 cities participated in a unified loan under the umbrella of the German Savings Bank and Clearing Association—the national organization representing German municipal banks. All these loans were to be taken in two parts, the first half in the summer of 1928, with a second loan being issued in the fall.[31]

This consolidated loan for the smaller German cities demonstrated the remarkable evolution in loan negotiations since 1924. Earlier efforts at this type of loan had foundered on the reluctance of American buyers to purchase bonds that were not guaranteed by one identifiable authority. With the Savings Bank Association acting as loan agent, the smaller cities were able to play in the foreign loan game and secure an attractive price for their bonds. The key to making it work was the willingness of the Reich government to accept an active part in coordinating the loan requests.

Unfortunately, the new system of loan regulation instituted in May 1928 suffered from the same major weakness as the old haphazard system. When the capital market itself dictated that capital should move from Americans who were eager to lend, to Germans, who were ready to borrow, governments were hard pressed to halt the flow. When cities were prevented from issuing long-term bonds, they managed to take short-term loans, often through German banks. As the German government tried to crack down in 1928, these evasions became greater and more ingenious. As one promoter wrote Cologne's mayor Konrad Adenauer, "it is more or less an unspoken secret that these difficulties can be gotten around and indeed have already been gotten around repeatedly."[32]

The most common form of evasion involved a complicated process whereby German banks acted as intermediaries between German cities and foreign lenders. In the typical case, a city would take a loan from a German bank in exchange for promissory notes in Reichsmarks. The bank would then sell the Reichsmark notes to foreign investors, usually in Holland. The city was able, in this way, to insist that it had only borrowed domestically and therefore did not require Advisory Board approval. The cities, when caught, denied any devious intent and, at least in one case, the city of Münster convinced the Prussian Interior Ministry that it had been unaware that the bonds were being sold abroad.[33]

An example of the extremes cities might go to in order to secure foreign credit is revealed by the case of the city of Lüneburg. A former great trading city in the Hanseatic League, Lüneburg lies about forty miles south of Hamburg. As in many other cases, Lüneburg's effort to circumvent Advisory Board control was reported by the Reichsbank, which acted as a watch dog over municipal irregularities. According to the Reichsbank's report, the Lüneburg affair began when a firm called the Lüneburg Salt and Chemical Company took a 6 million RM foreign loan. Passed off as a private firm, the city in reality owned 50 percent of the Salt and Chemical Company. As the Reichsbank understood the plan, the Salt and Chemical Company was to keep only 1.5 million RM while passing the remaining 4.5 million on to another firm called the "Lüneburg Power, Light, and Waterworks Corporation." This second dummy corporation had been created the previous October and was supposed to pass 3.9 million RM of the loan directly on to the city administration, which would use over half the proceeds to pay off short-term loans taken from the municipal savings bank and already spent on water and electric works.[34] This fabulously complicated scheme would provide laundered funds directly to the city while avoiding any public scrutiny of the loan.

When called upon by the Advisory Board to investigate the Lüneburg plot, the Prussian government took months to unravel the threads. The city magistrates denied that they would receive any of the proceeds from the reported loan, but finally revealed that the plan was even more complicated than the Reichsbank had suspected. An umbrella company by the name of *Gemeinwirtschaftliche Interessengemeinschaft Lüneburg* was to be the initial borrower, and it, in turn, was to pass on the proceeds of the loan to the two firms named in the Reichsbank report. Furthermore, the loan was to be taken through a Berlin bank, but in reality would come from an American bank. Even though the entire project was obviously controlled by the city government, it could not be stopped since the city had effectively isolated itself from the legal borrower.[35] Even more amazing, four months later the Lüneburg Power, Light and Waterworks Corporation was able to float a long-term bond issue in the United States for over a million dollars.[36]

The Lüneburg loan was not an isolated incident. The city of Düsseldorf also received funds when the "private" *Rheinischer Bahngesellschaft* took a $4 million, one-year loan in the United States and then reloaned the entire sum to the city. In this case, the railroad corporation was even supposed to secure a long-term loan to pay off this short-term debt. When it was unable to do so, Düsseldorf was forced to reveal the scheme and seek a public loan to cover its debt.[37]

Given the financial strains on most city governments, and the reports of massive hidden loans, the cases in which cities were caught remained surprisingly low.[38] It is even possible that like the rumors of huge loans in early 1925, there was a great deal more smoke than fire in all of this. Two things, however, were clear. First, German cities and banks were increasingly turning to short-term loans when they could not secure long-term bonds. And second, those cities that were caught, managed in most cases to keep their ill-gotten funds. The most extensive violations of Advisory Board control came, according to the Reichsbank, only after the depression was well under way in late 1931, as the "standstill" agreements were being negotiated.[39] In spite of ever tougher controls, the Reichsbank's vice-president was probably right in complaining that the Board would never be able to stop municipal borrowing, "because the cities have again and again circumvented the governing regulations and contrived ways to get around any bothersome control."[40]

Industrial and Agricultural Loans

The process which had culminated in unified municipal loans, thereby making funds available to small cities on good terms, was repeated in agriculture and industry. In early 1925, as German industry looked to the American market, only the very largest firms had any chance of securing an American loan. A special commissioner sent to New York by the German government wrote the Finance Ministry in January 1926 that there were only ten to twenty German firms large enough to take loans of $5 million or more, which could interest the American market.[41] Even banks which hoped to secure foreign credits to reloan to smaller industries were unsuccessful. One banker spent three months in New York and gave up when he became convinced that only a state or city guarantee could provide the security demanded by American investors. Although they were anxious to help smaller German firms, the Americans were not willing to do so without securing solid mortgage guarantees.[42]

These kinds of pressures induced the Economics Ministry to concoct a scheme to create an investment company which would channel foreign funds to smaller industries. In 1925, heavy industry in alliance with the Reichsbank managed to stop the plan and prevent governments from getting involved in the finances of private industry.[43] By mid-1926, the Reich Association of Industry reversed its position and began to ask the government to help small business secure foreign loans.

Although the association was closely tied to large-scale industry, it needed to retain the support of smaller firms which provided its mass base. The increasing demands and frustrations of small firms led the association's business manager Ludwig Kastl to advise the association that "on the basis of previous negotiations, it must be accepted that the credit needs of small industry can only be satisfied by founding state credit institutions."[44] Government officials who had faced the sharp and aggressive opposition of the Reich association in the past met its new call for government help with open bitterness. Director Ritscher declared "that it surprised him to hear this suggestion from precisely the source which had previously protested so sharply against every economic activity of the state. . . . It is remarkable," he went on, "that the same circles which are perpetually opposed to the state mixing in the private economy, in this case, to be sure only as a last resort, call for state help."[45]

In every discussion of state help for private investors, proponents of the plan referred to the one positive model that demonstrated how the scheme could work.[46] The Saxon Mortgage Institution, initially founded in June 1925 to supply credit to Saxony's farmers, soon began making industrial loans as well. It drew its credit from the sale of mortgage bonds secured by the combined value of all the farms receiving credit. Under this scheme, each farmer was essentially liable for the entire debt of all participating borrowers. In November 1925, the bank requested permission to float a $10 million bond in the United States, specifically to help industry and trade in Saxony. Although the Advisory Board was not willing to establish a precedent allowing other states to follow this course, it decided that Saxony was suffering such a severe credit crisis that it would have to approve a $5 million loan.[47]

The Reich Association of Industry refused, at first, to believe that the Saxon model could provide the key to helping small industry. But the demands of small industry and the quick success of the Saxon bank in securing its American loan soon turned this criticism into praise. Other states followed Saxony's example and the industrialists took over the plan and tried to present it as their own.[48]

Within a year, Bavaria sought and secured a loan for 20 million RM to give to small industry, and obtained an equal sum through the Bavaria Mortgage and Exchange Bank.[49] A total of twelve other state banks received shares of a $10 million loan taken from Lee, Higginson in October 1927. As with the Saxon loan, these funds were meant to be used by "small and middle-sized" firms, and a maximum of 500,000

RM was set on loans to any one company. By mid-1927 the Reich Association of Industrialists, while not always assuming credit for making these loans available, was at least actively supporting them and announced hopes of creating upwards of 200 million RM in credit by 1928.[50]

By the end of 1927, perhaps as much of $84 million had been borrowed by German banks with the expressed intention of relending the proceeds to small and middle-sized industry.[51] This not inconsiderable sum is an important share of the total borrowing of private industry, which reached about $147 million in 1926–27.[52] Thus, somewhat surprisingly, German foreign credit was distributed over a fairly large group of borrowers and through these loans smaller industries were able to find cheaper capital than was available in Germany. The fact remains, however, that the lion's share of American credit went only to the very largest firms and no doubt strengthened them relative to their smaller competitors. Even within the sums taken for "small and middle-sized" industry, it is probably safe to assume that large "second-rank" industry was able to secure more than businesses which could fairly be termed "small industry." Moreover, this $84 million was spread among many more firms than the $63 million taken by big industry.

This trend toward greater government aid to industry continued through early 1928, but the increasing difficulty of obtaining loans in the United States brought the projects effectively to a halt by the end of the year. Yet, it was notable that German private industry had gone far toward accepting large-scale government support in coordinating foreign borrowing. State banks and municipal savings and loan banks were the primary agents raising and distributing foreign capital to middle- and small-sized German industry. This activity was condoned and encouraged by the Reich government and even the Reichsbank, acting through the Advisory Board for Foreign Credit. Much as the Reich Association of Industry may have been unhappy about this expansion of "cold socialization," it accepted the help and tried to make the most of it.[53]

While the Reich government worked to reduce municipal loans and only hesitantly and indirectly promoted industrial loans, from the very beginning it took a far more active role in helping German agriculture. Not only Germans, but foreign financiers as well, regarded agricultural investments as sound and highly desirable. It was commonly believed that making German agriculture more productive would not only stimulate the German economy, but also improve Germany's balance of trade and make loan repayment easier. With this broad support, the Rentenbank became a conduit to funnel 131 million dollars in foreign money into German agriculture between 1925 and 1928. On top of this, state and municipal banks borrowed another 66 million dollars directly for agricultural improvement.[54]

In spite of this massive state aid, German agriculture failed to prosper. Indeed, by 1927–28, German farmers were in a severe crisis, a fact that was to have tremendous impact on Weimar society as agrarians turned to the Reich government for relief.[55] The greatest problems emerged on the largest estates. While small farms of under fifty hectares (about 125 acres) made a profit in 1928–30 of about 82 marks per hectare, large estates were losing vast sums.[56]

When the German National Peoples Party joined the Reich Cabinet in January 1927, and Martin Schiele took the post of Minister of Agriculture, the Reich government began to develop a vast array of programs to help agrarians. Schiele wanted to stabilize prices, regulate production, and raise tariffs. But the core of his plan was creation of a 200 million RM fund to convert short-term agrarian loans into long-term loans. In 1928 alone, the Reich appropriated 465 million RM to aid German farmers. These huge sums not only increased the burden on government budgets and absorbed scarce investment credit, they also entirely failed to satisfy or effectively help German farmers.[57]

By the spring of 1928, this new spending by the Reich led to another altercation with Parker Gilbert. The Reparations Agent objected to the fact that a "settlement loan"—intended to finance the moving of farmers into under-populated areas of East Prussia—had been guaranteed first by a mortgage on the settlers, then by the Rentenbank, and finally by the Reich itself. Gilbert was informed that only the Reich guarantee made selling the bonds possible, but he insisted that if the Reich was going to reduce spending as recently promised by the Finance Minister, such guarantees could not be given.[58] With all its other difficulties, the Cabinet refused to get into a fight with Gilbert over the settlement loans and decided that if his approval could not be won, negotiations "must immediately be broken off, since all difficulties with the Reparations Agent on account of the settlement loans are to be avoided."[59]

By this time, Gilbert's power over the foreign capital market was so great that German officials were afraid to resist his demands. When Finance Minister Köhler promised to reduce spending and borrowing in a speech which was not widely reported, Gilbert forced him to repeat the announcement and ensure that it was given appropriate publicity. A series of meetings with Gilbert led Köhler to warn his colleagues that they must use the greatest care in dealing with the Reparations Agent, "because the smallest error could induce Gilbert to some sort of act which could endanger this loan and, moreover, endanger the entire further loan policy."[60]

Despite these precautions, the government's commitment to agricultural resettlement was so strong that it resolved to seek funds domestically if the foreign market proved unavailable.[61] When the domestic market proved too weak to supply the required funds, the government turned to a bizarre scheme to come up with the cash. Suggested and developed by the Labor Ministry, the Cabinet hoped to exploit the Rentenbank's well-established foreign connections to secure money which the Reich government itself could not provide. The first step of the plan called for the Rentenbank to take a 35 million RM foreign loan which it would immediately reloan to the government. Since this sum alone would not be adequate, further steps called for the Rentenbank to accept 25 million RM in municipal obligations in return for more cash. The great majority of the debt (20 million RM) was currently held by the Reich so the real recipient would be the Federal government. As to the actual value of the municipal bonds, even the Labor Minister had to confess that they were of only nominal market value. As he wrote the State Secretary in the Reich Chancellery, "Even though the communal obligations presently have no real possibility of realization, in the course of time it may be possible to dispose of them [sie abzustossen]."[62]

Unable to raise even 20 million RM by itself for a project deemed absolutely essential, the Labor Ministry proposed that the Reich induce the Rentenbank to advance it the funds using nearly worthless municipal bills as collateral. If even contemplating the scheme seems unbelievable, even more unbelievable is the fact that the Cabinet and eventually even the Finance Ministry agreed to the plan. The outline of the plan, at least in some vague way, may even have been discussed with Gilbert,[63] but this was most likely limited to his understanding that the Rentenbank and not the Reich would seek a foreign loan for agricultural resettlement. The entire episode reveals not only how dependent Germany was on Parker Gilbert's approval, but also the extraordinary financial weakness of the Reich government even in the midst of economic prosperity. Notwithstanding these problems, the Reich remained absolutely committed to pouring more and more money into agriculture.

As Robert Kuczynski noted, while Gilbert and Schacht shouted about the dangers of public loans, they never mentioned the much more insecure agricultural loans.[64] By the end of 1928, German agriculture had borrowed 7.5 billion RM, of which only 1.5 billion had actually been productively invested. The vast majority of the funds, over 6 billion RM, had simply been lost.[65] In January 1928, the Minister of Agriculture admitted that three fourths of the amount borrowed for agriculture had "disappeared never to be seen again, lost through bad crops, large and unfavorable investments, and the excessive interest charges."[66] Despite the mounting defaults, agrarians continued to find banks and governments willing to extend them credit. By late 1930, they had short-term debts of 4.2 billion RM, a sum which exceeded the debts of German cities and the Reich, and was both more insecure and more pressing.[67]

The End of American Loans

In mid-1928, as Germany struggled to use foreign capital more effectively and make it available to smaller borrowers on better terms, the American market began to tighten. In the spring, American interest rates slowly edged upward, although money remained widely available. By the end of the summer, it was becoming clear that Germany and other foreign borrowers were in trouble if they had to meet their capital needs on the American market.

Continued slow bond sales, in spite of falling prices and rising interest rates, led an American investment firm, Lawrence Stern and Company, to conduct a survey of American bankers to find an explanation for the poor performance.[68] Of 650 banks responding to the questionnaire, a majority believed that bond prices would remain depressed and not recover their former high levels. The bankers blamed the bond companies themselves for much of the problem. They believed that excessively sharp competition had led dealers to accept more overpriced bonds than they could sell. Further, they felt that bond syndicates had not provided prolonged market support after the bonds had been sold. Investor confidence was shaken when prices often fell soon after the bonds were issued. But, for all these faults, the bankers placed the burden of blame on high American interest rates and the shifting of more and more capital into the stock market.

As had happened in Germany in 1927, foreign and domestic funds were flowing into the stock market, and as the central bank attempted to restrain stock speculation, interest rates were pushed upward with the discount rate in the United States hitting 5 percent by July 1928.[69] Leading American economists like Benjamin Anderson and Professor O. M. W. Sprague were convinced that the speculative market was inducing stock brokers to borrow far more than they safely should and was pulling funds away from more honest investments.[70] As Lester Chandler has noted, the pull of the stock market had a devastating effect on Federal Reserve Bank credit policy. Benjamin Strong had wanted to keep interest rates low to stimulate the American economy and allow Europeans to borrow cheaply on the American market. But, as Chandler writes, "in the end it was primarily stock speculation that led the Federal Reserve to restrict credit so much as to jeopardize its other objectives, both domestic and international."[71]

The tightening American capital market soon began to make its pressure felt in Germany. Whereas in June 1928, Germany was able to borrow 249 million RM in the United States, in July this figure fell off to only 6 million RM.[72] During the first six months of the year, twenty-nine long-term loans were taken in the United States, but in the second half of the year, only six loans were floated.[73] German willingness to pay high interest rates briefly opened up some secondary markets in Britain, France, Holland, and Switzerland, but these centers were unable to take America's place.[74] Some of the German bonds sold in London were actually coming from New York where falling bond prices made them attractive to British investors, and the Dutch market was actually a channel for short-term American funds.[75] By early 1928, world interest rates began to rise as gold flowed into the United States and central bankers were forced to raise their discount rates.[76] Domestically, Germany found little relief as only 28 million RM in bonds were sold in Germany from July to September 1928.[77]

By autumn 1928 the American bond market was effectively closed to German borrowers. Even the highly regarded second tranche of the consolidated municipal loan had to be cancelled for lack of American buyers. Cities which had counted on this money now found themselves in a desperate financial situation. The Association of German Cities urgently requested permission for the cities to take short-term loans until the bond market improved.[78]

The mayor of Mainz explained how his city fell into trouble. His story illustrates how the impact of the tight capital market made itself felt only after a long delay. Mainz had been granted 5 million RM in the consolidated loan and had received 2 million of that in the first tranche. Since it had expected to receive another 3 million in the autumn, the city borrowed that money ahead of time as expensive, short-term obligations. By December 1929, when the second tranche still had not been sold, the short-term debts were coming due, the banks might not refinance them, and they were too expensive anyway. To bail itself out, the city requested permission to take a loan in Holland bearing a real interest rate of 8 percent. The Advisory Board refused to grant permission to take the loan, even though some members were sympathetic. The problem with permitting Mainz to take an unacceptably expensive loan, one member observed, was that there was nothing unusual about Mainz's situation since most cities had exactly the same problems.[79]

For a brief period in late 1928 and early 1929, the domestic German capital market showed signs of a small recovery.[80] But this liquidity could not be interpreted as a unilaterally favorable development. As the directors of the Rhenish State Bank explained, their increased liquidity was a product of both good and bad developments. To the good, a large harvest had allowed agriculture more money than was common, while the Reichsbank currently was holding large reserves which permitted it a liberal discount policy. Unfortunately, the main reason for the increased liquidity was that the economy had already begun to go into a recession. This, plus the labor conflict and lockout in the Ruhr coal and steel areas, meant that demand in the German economy was falling, and consequently credit pressures were reduced. In the bank's view, the relatively good credit situation would be threatened only if city governments were to turn to the domestic market with excessive demands.[81]

Germany's weak capital market led to the almost universal expectation that the end of the American loans would cause a disastrous rise in German interest rates. This did not happen. Instead, continued short-term borrowing delayed the moment of crisis for over a year. But even more important, the German economy was already going into a recession, so that reduced demand for investments more than compensated for the reduction in capital imports.[82] Germany was momentarily saved from a capital crisis by the expedient of taking dangerous short-term loans and by the onset of the great depression.

Reparations Revision: The Young Plan

As German leaders struggled to deal with the faltering economy and complex capital problems, they entered into negotiations for a new reparations settlement. German plans for reparations revision, so carefully outlined in June of 1927, had, by the end of the year, already begun to unravel (see chapter 5 above). The basic prerequisite of a balanced budget had foundered on the shoals of special interest group pressures, continued economic difficulties, and the basic political weakness of the Reich Government. The second essential condition, that renegotiation be put off until after the American elections, had also failed, since Parker Gilbert, disgusted by German financial policies, began to prepare for a new and final plan at least a year earlier than expected.

The only trump card left in the German hand was the hope of exploiting the American private investment in Germany to win support for reduced reparations. Since this was Germany's last remaining hope, German officials planned to play it to the maximum. The hope was based, however, on three serious misconceptions about American policy. The first was the notion that American private bankers could dictate American reparations policy. Perhaps deceived by the bankers' apparent success in preventing either the State or Commerce Departments from instituting any effective regulation over foreign loans, German planners hoped the bankers would now be able to protect their loans by forcing lower reparations. As we have seen, the inability to formulate a positive policy of loan regulation was based on far more than banker opposition. Further, it is much easier for a "negative" lobby to prevent a government from instituting new policies or regulations than it is for an "affirmative" lobby to force a new policy.

Germany's second misconception was the expectation that American bankers were united enough effectively to exert what influence they theoretically might have. New York investment bankers were largely isolated from and even antagonistic toward inland bankers. Furthermore, the most influential banking house of them all was not sympathetic to the other New York bankers. For years, partners in J. P. Morgan had, both publicly and privately, warned against excessive loans to Germany. The firm had only limited interest in the German loans and, while probably not willing to pursue any policies directly inimical to the loans, was also unlikely to base its policies on their preservation (see chapter 3 above).[83]

Finally, American policymakers were far more concerned about domestic tax cuts, which might have to be abandoned if Allied debts were reduced, than they were about protecting private loans made to Germany. As Gilbert bluntly told British Ambassador Sir Ronald Lindsay, "The mere existence of [American] investments in Europe would not suffice to keep alive any beneficent interest in European affairs. Their loss would affect a couple of hundred thousand bondholders only and would cause a great outcry; but what would continue to interest the broad mass of American opinion would be the regular collection of the debts from the European Governments, which would affect the millions of taxpayers."[84] With Herbert Hoover likely to become President, it was even less likely that the United States would reduce its war debt demands.

As an American, Gilbert undoubtedly wanted to prevent wholesale defaults on American loans. But his broader concern was a determination to preserve world-wide financial stability which he believed was threatened by irresponsible German fiscal policy and irresponsible American loan policy. In view of these cross currents of pressures and interests, German plans to exploit the American loans were, at best, a gamble. Against these low odds, Germans entered into reparations revision with surprisingly high hopes.

Parker Gilbert, at first gently but eventually with great vigor, seized and held the initiative in the reparations negotiations. German officials, reading his annual report of December 1927, which first called for consideration of a new plan, were confused. State Secretary Schubert hoped to find enlightenment from American Ambassador Schurman. He confessed to Schurman that "what Herr Gilbert said in the last chapter of his report is clear to me, but what is less clear to me, is *why* he said it." Schurman was unable to offer any clarification. Falling back on traditional American insistence that the Allied debt and reparations were two separate and distinct problems, Schurman seemed to know nothing about Gilbert's move, and wanted to know nothing.[85]

Schurman's uncertainty was well justified, since it is still not clear how Gilbert planned to solve the perplexing problems surrounding the Allied debts, reparations, and loans. In conversations with Mellon, Strong, Young, and others, Gilbert and the American leaders agreed that the time for revision had arrived. Whether Gilbert was instrumental in pushing the plan or whether all had come to the same conclusion individually is not clear. But a conjuncture of several factors made the moment auspicious. Beyond Gilbert's growing concern about German finance—a concern shared by many others[86]—conditions in the United States contributed to the decision to tackle the problems at that time. American bankers, with a temporary, as it proved, excess of capital ready to invest, were urging Washington to pursue political settlements that would reduce international instability and expand foreign investment opportunities.[87] This pressure was primarily directed toward normalization of relations with France and to a lesser degree toward final settlement of German reparation obligations.[88]

In order to finally eliminate the politically and economically destabilizing influence of reparations and war debts, the Americans discussed and may have tried to formulate a comprehensive and final settlement. As generally interpreted, this plan called for a revision of the Dawes Plan to reduce reparations and end foreign intervention in German affairs. Yet, the American, or "Gilbert," plan was never fully spelled out, and if indeed there was such a thing, it soon was superseded by events. The one thing Gilbert made clear was that he primarily wanted to force Germany to balance its budget and help transfer reparations. But far wider schemes may also have been involved. Gilbert had long insisted that Germany must save its railway and industrial bonds created by the Dawes Plan to be used in the "final" settlement. Now Germany might sell these bonds—worth nearly 16 billion RM—on the American market and turn the proceeds over to the Allies as reparations. The Allies, in turn, could approach the American Treasury with cash in hand and offer to repay their war debts early in return for a "substantial discount."[89]

British officials were quite rightly very skeptical of the whole scheme. Treasury officials argued that "the marketing of German bonds is a delusion which, since 1920, has repeatedly excited the appetites of French Governments, and there is little more prospect of their expectations being realized today than on previous occasions." Gilbert proposed the deal, according to the Treasury's interpretation, because it was the only way to get around American insistence that the Allies pay for sixty-two years. If this were true, the scheme in effect may have been intended as a way to permit the United States to agree to a substantial reduction in Allied war debts by allowing a heavy discount in return for a large cash payment. In any event, the British were convinced that the huge sums involved could never be sold, and any attempt to do so would create a "world shortage of credit."[90] When Gilbert insisted that the Allies should first reduce reparations and then see if the United States wouldn't reduce war debts, the British responded that they would never allow the United States to say to them, "open your mouth and shut your eyes and see what I will give to you."[91]

Gilbert flatly denied that there was any "Gilbert Plan" for revision and quite obviously was not wedded to this scheme. By mid-1928, hopes of selling any large volumes of foreign bonds on the American market began to fade.[92] Growing stock market speculation in the United States led the Federal Reserve to raise interest rates in the full knowledge that this might strain European resources. As Strong made abundantly clear, he wanted to help Europe but could not permit foreign considerations to dictate bank policy.[93] The changing conditions of the American capital market ended any hope, however unrealistic, of massive bond sales, and by the end of the year the entire plan simply faded from view.[94]

Amid rumors, plans, changes, and revisions, German officials desperately tried to pin Gilbert down to determine exactly what he and the Americans wanted. At one point, Schubert, Hilferding, and Schacht, driven to desperation by their inability to understand Gilbert, hatched a plan whereby the three would interrogate Gilbert individually and then compare notes to see if they could patch together a coherent analysis.[95] While the outcome of Schacht's and Hilferding's efforts are lost (one suspects they may never have talked to

Gilbert), Schubert's conversation reveals frustration, misunderstanding, and confusion on all sides. Schubert pressed Gilbert to clarify why, after repeatedly warning Germans that revision must wait until after the American elections, he now was calling for negotiations to begin prior to the elections and was even encouraging Germany to take the lead in settling the issue. Gilbert responded with the observation that elections in Germany and France were now over so negotiations could proceed—as if he had never intended to wait for American elections! The only thing Gilbert did make clear is that he believed Schacht was still arguing that Germany could not pay, and Gilbert felt this kind of attitude could only hurt German interests. He even, "very confidentially," expressed objections to Schacht having any important role in revision discussions because Schacht was "extraordinarily jealous of Herr Stresemann and . . . Schacht worked much too much with numbers and digits *(Zahlen und Ziffern)."* Schubert's response to this conversation and other talks with Gilbert, and his inability to draw any conclusions about Gilbert's goals, were summarized in a preface he gave to a later discussion with Gilbert. "I give the content of this discussion," he wrote, "which, as usual, was in part, quite *(recht)* complicated."[96]

German leaders need not have been so uncertain of Gilbert's intentions had they thought about the analysis of their own experts, but they would also have been less hopeful about the ultimate outcome of the new negotiations. As Foreign Ministry reparations expert Karl Ritter so rightly pointed out, German officials themselves were largely responsible for Gilbert's determination to seek a new reparations agreement. Ritter argued that Gilbert meant what he said when he insisted that the central goal of revision must be to give Germany itself full and sole responsibility for collecting and transferring reparations.[97] In order to get the United States and the Allies to accept this modification, Gilbert began to play down his conflict with the Germans over financial policies. His report of December 1927 was much milder than his highly critical October memorandum. In his report of June 1928, he barely acknowledged the existence of any conflict, even though neither municipal nor Reich finances had been significantly reformed.

In preparing for a final reparations settlement, German officials may have been confused about Gilbert's goals, but they were relatively certain of their own. Although different officials may have emphasized different goals, all agreed on three principle aims. Probably most important for Gustav Stresemann was a determination to eliminate the office of Agent General. Gilbert and his staff were seen as agents of Allied economic espionage. But far more critically, their existence represented, as one official would later write, Germany's "disgraceful financial dependence on a representative of the victorious powers . . . whose entrenchment in the long run would have destroyed Germany's character as a sovereign state."[98] To free Germany from its subservience to foreign capital and from Gilbert's influence, Germany had to accept revision of the Dawes Plan. Beyond this, Germans were anxious to end Allied occupation of the Rhineland as quickly as possible. Finally, Germans, of course, also hoped to reduce the amount they had to pay in reparations. This took on special emphasis in 1928–29, since it was feared that once Germany had actually made its full payment under the Dawes Plan, it would become more difficult to claim that it could not pay that sum.

With assurance from Hjalmar Schacht that he would be able to win a massive reduction in reparation payments and the fear that if they rejected Gilbert's offer, they might never have another chance at revision, the Germans plunged into the swirling political currents.[99] Schacht hoped to pay as little as 700 million RM a year, a sum considered even by most other Germans to be unrealistically low.[100] In order to win a reduction in reparations, Germans still hoped to exploit the influence of American bankers to their advantage. This took two forms. First, the bankers' plans to make more German loans in the future meant, as Hans Schäffer confided to his diary, that "one must use the greed of the bankers. Without agreement of the Germans to dispense with transfer protection, no loans. Without a reduction in the annual payment, no agreement to dispense with the transfer protection."[101] Thus, the desire of American bankers to make new loans might be exploited to reduce payments, and the transfer clause could be used as a powerful bargaining chip. Schacht, in typical fashion, informed British Treasury official Ernest Rowe-Dutton that Germany was willing to give up transfer protection, "but," Schacht said, "the Allies must realize that Germany would ask *very many things* in return." Rowe-Dutton refused to take this statement at face value and observed, "Such was the force with which he uttered those words that I was led to form the personal opinion . . . that Germany is in fact anxious to abandon transfer protection, in order to regain her complete independence. If she appears to cling desperately to protection, it will be in order to exert maximum compensation for what is, in effect, the only apparent concession she has to make."[102]

While the desire to link future loans to a favorable settlement was not often so explicitly stated, German hopes that existing American loans could be favorably exploited was much more common. Stresemann, in a more subtle way than Schacht could ever manage, explained exactly how Germans saw the role of the United States in the new reparations plan. In a statement to the press on 14 November 1928, Stresemann said,

As regards the capacity of Germany to pay, it is the American and not the German view of this point that will carry weight. This will be the main business of the American observer, as is explained by the large investments of American money in Germany. On this matter there have been some very interesting utterances from America, from which it would appear that the American observer has been instructed to point out that America is concerned to see that no obligations are imposed on Germany beyond her capacity to pay, otherwise, the American loans would depreciate.[103]

German hopes that bank pressure would serve German interests no doubt led them to overestimate the power of American bankers. German policymakers conveniently forgot that a low settlement would have to be based on a reduction in Allied war debts, which the United States was not ready to accept.

Even within German councils, cooler heads saw that Germany's foreign debts were not going to be that easily exploited. In the Reparations Policy Committee, the twin dangers of the foreign loans were becoming clearly understood. In the early years, as the loans came into Germany, they had provided the foreign capital needed to transfer reparations and thus made transfers appear easy. But now, as the loans had to be repaid, they drained German foreign currency so that very little would be left over to pay reparations. While on first thought this might appear to be good, since it would permit Germany to argue that it could not pay very much, on second thought, it could be very dangerous. As Ritter warned, "The danger exists, that so little transfer capacity will be left over for the final settlement, that a final agreement will not be attractive enough to the other side."[104] Later, as negotiations got underway, Curtius came to a similar realization. He told the Cabinet, "One of the strongest trumps for our experts in Paris will undoubtedly be this prior burden on the German economy of interest charges" from the foreign loans. But what would happen, he asked, "if one of the members of the reparations conference were to say: the Germans are themselves responsible for that, since they perpetually drove the interest level to artificial heights. . . . Then", Curtius exclaimed, "with one blow this argument will be thrust aside," and the conference will say that Parker Gilbert was right in asserting that Germany's excessive borrowing had undermined its economy. For Curtius, this threat to Germany's reparation plans and the fear that mounting interest payments would overburden the German economy, forced him to conclude that Germany had to curb its foreign borrowing.[105]

Schacht, if no one else, considered the possibility of inducing or at least permitting an economic crisis as a means of proving that Germany could not pay any significant level of reparations.[106] In typical fashion, he vacillated between calling for a crisis policy and claiming that his only goal was to avoid any crisis. To a British official, he "voiced his readiness, even his anxiety to revise and even to smash the Dawes Plan at the first opportune time."[107] But later, announcing his agreement with Gilbert, he told the Cabinet that his only goal was to avoid any crisis. Any appeal that a crisis policy might hold was undercut by the probability that the Allies would never agree to a small settlement. As one Foreign Office official put it, "the danger is much greater that the doctors will refuse to perform the operation on the sick body and will again accept a provisional solution and postpone a final settlement for years."[108]

Parker Gilbert persistently warned German officials that if they waited for an economic crisis, they would only find more trouble. In 1928–29, many American and British officials believed that the world economy and especially the German economy, was headed for a crash. The difference between Americans like Gilbert and Benjamin Strong, and British leaders, most notably Frederick Leith-Ross, the Treasury's leading reparations expert, was that the Americans desperately hoped to avoid the crisis by arranging a reasonable reparations settlement, while the British tended to feel that only a crisis could end all the international debts, and thus clear the air for sane policies.[109] As it became apparent that Gilbert would be successful in inducing a new conference, Leith-Ross grudgingly agreed to cooperate if it would postpone a crisis for three to four years. But, he observed, "our main interest is to see that we are not committed too deeply either to sanctions in the event of a German default or to lending to a Germany burdened with such a debt. Let the Yanks and the French lend her the money necessary to keep her on her legs." Then he added the coup de grace: "The French have always had a sure instinct for investing in bankrupt countries and their recent transfer of funds to Germany may be an instance of the operation of this instinct."[110]

Gilbert repeatedly urged the Germans to work for a final settlement before events made it impossible. On occasion, he left this as a vague threat for German officials to ponder in perplexity, while at other times he spelled out his fears. He assured von Schubert "that even an expensive arrangement would be cheaper than not coming to a settlement in the near future. . . . In particular," he warned him, "it must be avoided that an arrangement be put off until such a time as the German economy declines, that would be the most dangerous for Germany."[111] He urged Stresemann to ignore the theory of the British Treasury (Leith-Ross) that if Germany would wait four or five years, it would suffer an economic crisis and then receive a more generous settlement. Such a hope was "entirely wrong" and would cost Germany all the economic progress it had made in the past four years. He added that France would never make a settlement in the face of a German collapse.

Stresemann refused to accept Gilbert's alternatives and observed that based on Allied needs and demands, "a final total may be expected of between 2.1 and 2.2 milliards," and he added, "I am staggered by the suggestion that a burden of more than two milliards yearly should be laid on Germany's shoulders." Gilbert admitted that the settlement would be expensive but said that, "Germany has the choice between a costly settlement and a settlement at a time of crisis." To this implication that Germany was economically stable, Stresemann could only protest that the German economic recovery was an illusion and, he declared, in reality, "Germany is dancing on a volcano."[112] Stresemann spoke far more accurately than even he might have guessed.

Germans, having continuously complained that they wanted a new reparations settlement, were now swept along by forces out of their control and unsympathetic to their position. Gilbert's chief and, indeed, only support, came from French President Raymond Poincaré. In turn, Gilbert's praise for Poincaré as the only man who could solve the reparations dilemma became so profuse that von Schubert commented that he had "hardly ever seen a man so wrapped up by Herr Poincaré as Parker Gilbert was," and Stresemann charged that Gilbert had lost his earlier objectivity and had become simply the "pace-maker" for French objectives.[113] By late 1928, Gilbert was indeed totally committed to reparation revision even when agreement seemed impossible. His desperate effort to avoid what he feared could become a world-wide financial crisis was perhaps supplemented by his desire to protect his personal prestige and ambitions as he struggled to bring the negotiations to a successful conclusion.[114]

To protect themselves from this seemingly uncontrolled rush, German officials tried tactfully to warn Gilbert that they would cooperate in a new settlement only if it was clearly to their own advantage.[115] Gilbert's efforts to convince the Germans that even an expensive settlement was better than waiting for a crisis, and the Germans' efforts to impress upon the American that only a cheap settlement was acceptable, flew past each other with scarcely any impression until April 1929, when the issue brought Young Plan negotiations to an abrupt deadlock.

To clear the way for a new conference, Gilbert met with Winston Churchill (Britain's Chancellor of the Exchequer) and Poincaré to find an agreement on what the Allies would expect from Germany. Gilbert then informed German Foreign Minister Stresemann, Finance Minister Hilferding, and Chancellor Herman Müller that Britain and France expected Germany to cover all Allied war debt payments to the United States plus something beyond this to cover French reconstruction costs.[116] The Germans knew from other sources as well that the settlement would have to be around two billion marks per year to be acceptable to the Allies.[117] Within the German Foreign Ministry, officials were able to estimate with astonishing accuracy the schedule most likely facing Germany. Based on Allied debts to the United States, they saw that payments would have to begin at 1.67 billion RM in 1929, climb to 2 billion RM by 1935, and hit a peak of 2.2–2.3 billion in 1970–75.[118] That these figures so nearly match the Young Plan schedule ultimately agreed upon is no accident and is a testimony to the ability of German specialists to analyze the situation accurately.

Yet the fact remains that the Germans refused to recognize this reality. This was in good part a product of their own blindness, but also a result of the way Gilbert had gone about setting up the negotiations. Although the Germans were informed that the British and French had certain expectations, they persisted in the illusion that an impartial committee of experts would reduce reparations to a modest sum. As one Finance Ministry official would write in the midst of the economic crisis of 1931, if all the experts had had the courage and impartiality of Britain's Sir Josiah Stamp, Germany's economic problems would have forced the world to see that it could not pay as much as the French and Gilbert expected.[119] The ability of both sides to ignore the implications of the other side's remarks allowed the misunderstanding to go on until the entire negotiations nearly collapsed. It permitted Gilbert to conclude that the Germans knew the final cost would be around 2 billion RM annually, while Stresemann and other Germans felt that no specific sums had been agreed upon and believed that their reservations had been recorded.

Germany's choice of negotiators made compromise even more difficult than it need have been. With Hjalmar Schacht, we are already familiar. In constant conflict with the Reich government, Schacht was undoubtedly selected to represent Germany because of his enormous stature in foreign circles, and his confidence that he could win a drastic reduction in the reparation payments. Germany's second negotiator had no such credentials. Albert Vögler had little experience in international negotiations, and his chief claim to fame was as a hard-nosed representative of Germany's coal and steel industry. A British consul in Berlin reported Vögler's appointment with ominous warnings. Vögler, he wrote, "knows nothing except the coal industry and brutality." Vögler and all German heavy industrialists, he continued, "are the most unsuitable people for international negotiations, because they cannot get away from the idea that they are presiding at a meeting of shareholders who are present solely for the purpose of being browbeaten." As for why a Social Democratic government would appoint men like Schacht and Vögler to represent it in international negotiations, he explained that "the socialists, as so often in the past, have shirked the responsibility of being associated with a difficult task which may turn out badly."[120] This attack on socialist timidity may be well-founded, but it was only part of the explanation. Long-standing distrust of international bankers led Germans to seek experts who were not tied to high finance and who could defend the German economy. As one writer in the German Foreign Ministry expressed it, only someone with a real feeling for the needs of the economy could successfully represent Germany; "someone who determines German economic development . . . namely someone from industry."[121] Also, after the difficulties in securing approval for the Dawes Plan, German moderates undoubtedly hoped that participation of industrialists in the negotiations would force German industry to accept any agreement reached. The expectation was certainly reasonable; the reality was much different.

As negotiations for the Young Plan got underway in Paris in February 1929, Germany soon played the one card it held and on which such high hopes had been placed. Schacht informed the allies that Germany had to pay one billion marks a year to service its 13 billion mark foreign debt. Based on his assumption that Germany had a total transfer capacity of two billion marks, Germany could pay only one billion marks a year in reparations.[122] While American experts worried about Schacht's economic argument, the Europeans simply ignored it. They made it clear that political considerations and Allied debts to the United States would set the rate of German payments. With hardly a second thought, German hopes to exploit the loans to reduce reparations were dashed.[123]

When it became clear that the Allies would not even consider the low offers being made by the Germans and, indeed, were upping the ante, Schacht nearly ended the conference. On April 17, 1929, he offered to pay 1.65 billion RM but added the crucial reservation that Germany could pay this much only if the Polish corridor was returned and Germany was granted new overseas colonies.[124] The public expression of these demands came as a shock both to the Allies and to most members of the German government. That Schacht privately believed these to be critical issues was well enough known, since he had expressed his opinions earlier to a dismayed J. P. Morgan, Owen Young, and Thomas Lamont.[125] Some members of the German Cabinet knew that political demands would be included in Schacht's proposal, but the full content evidently was not known. When it became clear that the political demands would destroy the negotiations, the Cabinet refused to support Schacht's position and was desperately worried that collapse of the negotiations would lead to a financial crisis within Germany.[126]

After having pushed with almost frantic haste to get the negotiations underway, Gilbert saw all his plans begin to fall apart.[127] He charged German officials with bad faith and rightly insisted that Müller, Schacht, and Hilferding all had been informed of what they could reasonably expect to pay.[128] Schacht, in typical fashion, denied having any knowledge about any prior agreement and implied that the Cabinet had perhaps made a deal behind his back. Both Müller and Hilferding also denied any such agreement and maintained that no German would ever have agreed to such high payments.[129]

Having already counted on reduced reparations to save the tottering federal budget, the Reich Cabinet was forced to accept a compromise proposed by Owen Young. Schacht in turn agreed to sign the plan if, and only if, the Cabinet accepted full responsibility.[130] Under the new agreement, annual payments started at 1.7 billion RM, rose to 2.43 billion and then fell slowly until all reparations were to be paid off at the end of fifty-nine years. Payments averaged 2.05 billion RM.[131] Vögler was at first willing to accept the plan but succumbed to the pressures of his industrial and conservative allies and resigned rather than sign the agreement.[132] This was only a hint of the violent attacks on the Young Plan and the democratic government being prepared by the political right.[133]

Modern historians have been inclined to point out the many benefits Germany gained from the Young Plan.[134] The advantages were indeed substantial. Payments were reduced from the Dawes schedule and Germany was not required to give up transfer protection on the entire sum. One third of each annuity was to be paid under all circumstances; two thirds had a modified transfer protection in case Germany was unable to raise the foreign currency required to pay. More immediately, Germany was saved from a potential financial crisis, since a limited volume of foreign lending was once again begun. And perhaps most important, Allied interference in German affairs through the Reparations Agent and other agencies finally was terminated. Yet, the fact remains that from the very beginning the issues were as much political as economic. And politically, Germany, and especially the democratic government, lost heavily. At their most optimistic, German officials argued that the Young Plan represented an improvement for the first ten years and after that new negotiations might rectify the excessive payments.[135]

The Cabinet found itself in deep embarrassment as it prepared for the Parliamentary debates over the plan. Julius Curtius, as one of the representatives of the German Peoples Party, agreed to speak for the plan but emphasized that he could give it only a mild recommendation and at that he would only say it was an improvement over the Dawes Plan. Even Chancellor Müller suggested that "we have no interest in a prolonged debate," which could only call attention to the plan's failings.[136] Most Germans would have agreed with Schacht that it was "absolutely impossible" for Germany to pay the Young Plan sums. Schacht admitted, however, that failure to sign could force foreign capital out of Germany and wreck the German economy. "The result," he concluded, "would be privation, economic and social shocks—a crisis in the real sense of the word."[137] Far from a success, the Young Plan represented a necessity for which all officials tried to avoid responsibility.[138] Maneuvered into negotiations by Gilbert, Germany was forced to accept the plan or face unknown disasters.

　　German hopes to exploit the American loans to reduce reparations had failed. While the Young Plan payments were lower than those under the Dawes Plan, they were well above what Germans thought they could afford and had hoped to pay. Reparations remained fixed by Allied war debts, and the Americans refused to even consider any adjustment in that field. As Schacht so accurately observed, the Allies had entered negotiations with a fixed idea of how much they would accept, and they would not accept less.[139] German faith that the end sum would be set by American policy was not entirely wrong. Their error came in believing it would be set on the basis of American desire to protect the German loans. Instead, the war debts remained the key consideration, and the German gamble on the loans was lost. The interests of the American government came ahead of the interests of American bankers.

　　For Germany, the Young Plan culminated a series of misjudgments and misfortunes in both economic and political fields. As Jon Jacobson has argued, the political antagonism which became so apparent during the Young Plan negotiations effectively signalled the end of the period of international understanding begun with the Dawes Plan and the Locarno Agreement.[140] Parker Gilbert's determination to force the German government to accept responsibility for its fiscal policies and foreign loans had finally been successful. But right-wing attacks on the Young Plan would bring industrialists and agrarians to the final break with the Weimar system and begin the process that would lead the Nazi party into alliance with more traditional rightists. The political price paid for the Young Plan would symbolize the conjuncture of Germany's failed attempts to stabilize its internal social system through deficit spending, and its foreign position through a policy of fulfillment. The two policies were inherently contradictory, and failure to come to terms with this reality led to defeat both at home and abroad.

Chapter 8

The Loans, the State, and the Depression

During the winter of 1928–29, the German economy first began to show clear signs of the decline that would ultimately lead to the Great Depression. With some economic indicators already turning downward in 1927 and others not declining until the summer of 1929, it is impossible to pinpoint the moment at which the depression "began" in Germany. But, when unemployment reached 3 million over that winter of 1928–29, it was clear that the economy was in trouble.[1]

The recession began as a normal cyclical inventory recession in industry. But government policy and Germany's monetary weakness combined to deliver the fatal hammer blows that made this depression worse than any previous capitalist experience.

Theodore Balderston has recently demonstrated that a drastic investment collapse in German railroad construction, public utilities, house building, and government spending was critical in setting Germany off as the nation that, along with the United States, would suffer the most severe effects of the Great Depression.[2] What is remarkable about all four of these areas is not only that high interest rates would cause a decline in spending, but also that all four areas of investment were heavily determined by government policy.

In 1929, all the economic and political liabilities which had grown up since the stabilization came due, and the Weimar Republic proved incapable of covering its debts. The mounting public deficits which had been political necessities earlier and which had been so helpful to the economy in 1926 and 1927 had now become dangerous political and economic burdens. The political right reasserted its demands that the state remove itself from the economy, and even political moderates had to admit that the deficits were out of control and were becoming international political liabilities.

As short-term borrowing took the place of the no longer available long-term bond issues, the debts became ever more unstable. By late 1929, the government found that its only possible response to the growing depression was a vigorous deflationary policy in a desperate attempt to regain fiscal control. Political weakness combined with the capital stringency to produce a policy of despair and disaster.

Foreign Loans and the Onset of the Depression

The breakdown of the international financial system in the early 1930s made a major contribution in turning local depressions into a prolonged world-wide depression, and the end of American long-term lending in late 1928 was instrumental in setting up that financial crisis.[3] Yet it is less clear how Germany's failure to secure long-term loans after mid-1928 contributed to its economic difficulties. Despite the virtual cessation of long-term capital imports, German interest rates did not climb in 1928 and, indeed, even fell slightly in early 1929. However, this was not due to the recovery of Germany's own capital market but to the fact that the German economy was already sliding into the depression so fast that the demand for money was falling. Only with the near breakdown of the Young Plan negotiations in April and May 1929 did German interest rates show a marked rise—hitting 9.38 percent for day-to-day funds but then declining to around 8 percent throughout the rest of the year.[4] With the turn of the new year, 1930, German interest rates began to show the full impact of the spreading depression as demand fell and interest rates declined to 4 percent.[5] This trend strongly indicates that because Germany was already moving into a depression, the termination of capital imports did not directly induce a rise in German interest rates. Instead, the major upward pressure on German rates was political and not economic. The near breakdown of reparations negotiations in the spring of 1929, and the Nazi electoral victories in September 1930 immediately caused large capital outflows and higher interest rates.[6] As we shall see, this does not mean that capital was readily available in Germany in 1929. Many complaints of capital shortage were voiced, and many borrowers found themselves unable to fulfill their commitments. In all of this, however, politics played as important a role as capital supplies.

The fact that generally declining interest rates did not induce economic recovery in 1929–30 may in large part be explained by problems concentrated in agricultural and governmental sectors of the economy. In both agriculture and government finance, long-term problems came to a head in 1929 and produced powerful downward pressures throughout the economy. In both agriculture and government, German domestic policies were closely tied to the international capital market. In the case of fiscal policy, as we have already seen, decision making was further complicated by Germany's reparations obligations. While fiscal excesses and irresponsibilities abounded, it was not just "unwise" spending that created these problems. Public finances carried political implications which made them the center of a heated debate.

At every level of German government, finances were in better order than those of German agriculture. In fact, unlike agricultural bonds, which were going bad already in 1929, almost all public bonds continued to be serviced in marks and were often sound investments for Germans throughout the years of depression. This disclaimer notwithstanding, public finances were often weak enough to threaten default, and they lent themselves to political pressures which became apparent with the termination of American lending.

State and municipal governments found themselves in dangerous financial positions by 1928–29. The state governments complained that they had never received the taxes they required to meet even their most basic demands.[7] But the cities found themselves in even more desperate straits. The cities' largest and most responsible national organization, the Deutsche Städtetag, found itself in a difficult situation as it tried to defend municipal finances. On the one hand, the Städtetag lobbied the Reich to provide greater funds for the cities and to reconsider the entire municipal-Reich financial relationship in order to stabilize city budgets. On the other hand, it urged municipal leaders to cut spending, to rationalize budgets, and, in general, to practice the greatest possible frugality.[8] Municipal governments responded to these pressures with the claim that they could not ignore demands for improvements in streets, transportation, public utilities, housing, and expanded resettlement—all of which created expenses that could not be met out of current taxes.

But by 1928 the dominant expense faced by city governments was the mounting cost of unemployment compensation and welfare.[9] Cologne, for example, spent only 21 percent of its tax revenues on welfare in 1913. Under the Weimar system, this outlay climbed to 57 percent in 1928. As the depression began to force even greater welfare spending, it climbed to 65 percent of Cologne's tax revenue in 1929, to 69 percent in 1931, and finally, at the depths of depression in 1932, Cologne was spending 90 percent of its tax income on welfare.[10] Led by the rising costs of unemployment support, German welfare spending more than doubled between 1925 and 1930.[11] Obviously, this burden would strain even a well-run finance system. In the case of Cologne and many other public bodies, this initial strength was not present.

The actual size of municipal debt was not so large that it should have presented any untoward dangers. Compared to prewar levels, it was even very modest, since earlier debts had been wiped out by the inflation. Prior to 1913, municipal debt totalled 10.5 billion RM and was growing at the rate of 500–850 million RM per year. In 1929, the total municipal debt was a much smaller 6.5 billion RM, but this had been accumulated in the brief span of five years, and the debt was increasing by 1.5 billion RM per year.[12] The crux of the problem, therefore, did not lie in any excessively large accumulated debt, since cities had less debt in 1929 than they had had prior to the war. Rather, the problem centered on the rapid increase in municipal debt, the increasingly short-term nature of the debt, and, more critically, the financial and capital weakness which underlay this increase.

Parker Gilbert and other critics of municipal spending were partially correct when they asserted that cities were happy to increase their spending rapidly since they did not have to collect the taxes to pay for that spending. Instead, cities turned to the federal government and demanded an ever larger share of federal tax receipts.[13] Probably much more important, however, was the fundamentally changing role of governments which had been given a huge push by the World War and which was in the process of making itself felt in all industrial societies. In Germany, prior to the war, governments spent about 17 percent of the Net National Product. During the inflation period 1919–1923, government spending on goods and transfer payments accounted for 38 percent of NNP. This declined to 30 percent in the later twenties but still represented nearly a doubling of government's share of the prewar economy.[14]

This growth in government spending and income redistribution obviously gave the government a central role in the national economy. And the city governments made up the most active element in this public spending. Government investment was larger than industrial investment throughout the second half of the twenties, and the cities accounted for 70 percent of all government investment.[15] Similar trends were taking place in other industrial countries. In England, for example, national and local governments spent between 30 and 35 percent of national income during the interwar years.[16] For German governments, this apparently irreversible and irresistible growth in government came at a time when political and financial weakness made paying for it nearly impossible. The chances of avoiding a crisis under the best of circumstances were low, and Germany hardly faced the best of circumstances. The ultimate weakness of municipal finance in the later Weimar years centered on Germany's impoverished money market and the cities' growing dependence on short-term loans. Although it is difficult to estimate exactly how large or how dangerous the short-term loans were, available information yields some strong suggestions. Studies in early 1928 reported a surprisingly small volume of municipal floating debt. The Advisory Board for Foreign Credit was informed that all cities with populations over 25,000 had a combined short-term debt of only 700 million RM. The great bulk of this debt was held by large cities with a population over 80,000 (530 million RM). Of the total debt, 525 million RM was owed to German banks (about half to public banks and half to private banks) while only a very modest 175 million RM was owed short-term to foreign lenders. Other estimates at the same time placed the municipal short-term debt even lower.[17]

Dow Jones and Company published a list of German city and state foreign loans due for repayment in 1928 and reported a total of only $29,906,500, or about 120 million RM.[18] Evidently, all the loans listed with the exception of two by the city of Leipzig had been submitted to the Advisory Board for approval and were perfectly legal. The board did write Saxony requesting that it investigate the Leipzig loans, and asked the state government to ensure that no further foreign loans were taken without first getting board approval.[19]

Until 1928, then, the total volume of municipal short-term debt as exposed by various investigations appeared remarkably small. Speaking in late 1931, Reich Chancellor Brüning asserted that up to 1928, it had been common practice for cities to begin projects with short-term financing and then convert the debt into long-term loans. In 1928, he said, hopes that a renegotiated reparations settlement would reduce international interest rates led cities to delay converting their short loans in the expectation of better terms after the reparations settlement. But, Brüning concluded, "when the Young Plan was signed, the international capital market had suffered to such an extent from depression that conversion was impossible.''[20]

Brüning may have been right in his portrayal of earlier policies, but his explanation of the increasing short-term debt is not entirely convincing. As already noted, by the summer of 1928 it was difficult to place German bonds on the American market, and many cities, locked into expensive projects, were forced to expand their short-term borrowing. As early as the spring of 1928, Cologne City Treasurer Wilhelm Suth was warning his mayor, Konrad Adenauer, that "the outlook for a foreign loan this year is thoroughly unfavorable. We will thus have to make do with further short-term credits for all the fixed expenditures. But, you can see where that could lead by looking at the example of Düsseldorf which has placed itself under the quasi-legal control of the bankers."[21] Thus Cologne, whose finances will be discussed more fully in a moment, was, already in the spring of 1928, moving toward expanded short-term borrowing, and Düsseldorf was already so heavily indebted that German bankers were supervising its finances.

Other bits of information indicate that the short-term debts of German cities were more serious than the official surveys revealed. When the Reich Finance Ministry proposed a large long-term loan to consolidate only the debts of cities with populations over 80,000 (the cities assumed to have the great bulk of the short-term debts), a number of letters were sent to the National Association of German Cities protesting the exclusion of smaller cities from the project. One letter, insisting that smaller cities also needed help, revealed that "the three mid-sized cities in Oldenburg alone have a short-term debt of 10 million RM and they need a consolidation of this debt just as much as the cities with 80,000 and more inhabitants."[22] The cities' association, like other agencies, had assumed that smaller cities owed much more modest debts, and the surprise registered by this 10 millin RM debt of three small cities was indicated by three exclamation marks in two different colors beside the passage.

Obviously, short-term debts were much larger than cities had openly admitted. This was in good part a result of the effort of the Advisory Board to reduce foreign borrowing. Again and again, the board recognized the need for city projects, approved them in principle, and then reduced the size of the acceptable loan to about half the sum requested.[23] This policy permitted cities to undertake projects but denied them the means to finance their work safely. In spite of inadequate long-term support, cities tended to proceed with their plans and hope they could somehow secure the residual. Most often, this involved an increase in their short-term debt. This policy of approving inadequate loans for many projects may have helped keep the foreign market open to large numbers of German borrowers, but it also greatly weakened the financial position of most city governments. Their short-term debts, which were more expensive and less secure than bond issues, were thus increased by the Advisory Board's policy. In this case, the control of foreign loans had contributed to greater economic instability within the German economy.[24]

Given these problems, it is hardly surprising that when the depression began to reduce municipal incomes and increase welfare payments, city governments found themselves in financial difficulties. For some cities, the depression was not even required before they faced default. In December 1927, Chemnitz and Hannover announced to the Advisory Board that they were unable to cover short-term notes which were coming due immediately. Since their problem remained isolated, some relief could be provided. The central organization of German public banks arranged a loan for one of the cities and even managed to secure board approval for the transaction. The Advisory Board's main concern was that the bailout operation neither be made public nor be too vigorously hidden. As the board expressed itself, "the affair, even if it is not permitted to become publicly known, should not be surrounded by a veil of secrecy which could awaken the suspicion of American bankers that the Advisory Board is doing something improper."[25]

If municipal short-term debts in 1928 were larger and more dangerous than Germans were willing to admit, they were still relatively modest when compared to those about to develop. We have already seen the impact on Mainz's finances when the American loan market was closed to German bonds.

But the forces that dominated fiscal and financial policies in the coming year ran much deeper than just the international loan market, and the impact of policy decisions extended throughout the entire economy. By examining first the financial position of the city of Cologne as an example of municipal developments, and then turning to how German cities united in response to their problems, a better picture of municipal finance can be presented. This in turn sets the stage for a discussion of state and Reich fiscal policies, which were often similar to city policies, but, while perhaps of less economic importance, were even more destabilizing politically.

Cologne

As early as the spring of 1928, Cologne had already begun to find it difficult not only to balance its budget, but to find financing for its deficits. By September, when it was becoming clear that Cologne would not be able to cover its floating debt with a long-term foreign loan, the city fathers had already approved uncovered deficits of $46 million and had spent $27 million of that sum. The years 1927 and 1928 alone had seen the creation of half of this debt, while half had been carried over from earlier years. The largest share of spending had gone into street cars, road construction, land purchases, housing, and canals—all projects the Advisory Board would have found to be "unproductive."[26] Although city leaders were becoming concerned about this continuing debt, it was not until late 1929 that Cologne really got into trouble. At that time, a 38 million RM ($9 million) short-term loan taken from German banks in 1926 fell due, and the city was unable to either pay off the debt or refinance it. According to city officials, the original loan had been made necessary when the Advisory Board refused to approve a large enough external loan in 1926. They also claimed that Reich leaders had approved the expedient of seeking a domestic short-term loan to supplement the 40 million RM foreign loan approved by the board. The city justified its position with the assertion that "every responsible authority gave his agreement that the debt would soon be covered by a long term loan, without one voicing even the slightest objection."[27] Yet the debt coming due was far greater than just the 38 million RM the city was willing to defend. To consolidate its floating debt, the city asked for a long-term foreign loan of 75–80 million RM, to be taken "if and when market conditions would permit it and subject to the approval of the Advisory Board."[28]

By late October 1929, with few foreign loans being made, Cologne began to really feel the pinch.[29] The American banking house of Lee, Higginson wanted to float the Cologne loan, now raised to 100 million RM, but stipulated that it would only do so if this loan consolidated Cologne's entire floating debt and, if in the future, the city would "abstain from borrowing and proceed with a balanced budget."[30] This determination by American bankers to use their financial power to force a reduction in German government spending echoed Parker Gilbert's demands on the Reich in late 1927.

Bankers Trust, which soon became interested in Cologne's affairs, made even more far-reaching demands. No longer willing to make loans merely on the basis of the city's "good credit," Bankers Trust demanded that the city pledge its public utilities to support any future loan. Stating that "Cologne's finances have been handled almost as badly as Berlin['s]," Bankers Trust's Berlin representative Parker McComas urged his firm to move very cautiously. With grim clarity, McComas also revealed that Bankers Trust had more than financial interests in mind when offering to deal with Cologne. He wired the firm's home office that the "chief idea [of] our stepping in was to get [a] hold on Utilities." McComas was willing to work with Lee, Higginson only if the banks and the city could agree on a loan secured by a claim on the public utilities.[31]

McComas was constructing his plans in a back door alliance with two of Germany's most powerful private businessmen. He believed that Werner Kehl, a director of the Deutsche Bank, and industrialist Paul Silverberg would use their influence with Reichsbank president Schacht to kill any loan unless Cologne gave up its utilities. He concluded that, "association [with Lee, Higginson] without getting hold on utilities [is] directly counter [to the] interests [of] Kehl, Silverberg, [and] ourselves." He spelled out Bankers Trust demands directly by informing Cologne that the bank wanted options on "all electrical as well as straight city business." And he let the city leaders know that "[we] would not do such credit under any circumstances without full knowledge and consent [of] Schacht and Silverberg."[32]

Convinced that the Advisory Board would not approve a long-term loan under any circumstances, Cologne was saved from this blackmail when Lee, Higginson decided to extend credits worth 41 million RM for nine months.[33] The attempt by Bankers Trust to force Cologne to give up city ownership of its public utilities is one of the few cases where American bankers directly interfered in German social policies. It came at a time when the city found itself in desperate financial straits and was, presumably, open to blackmail. The circumstances are similar to the Thyssen loan of early 1925, when a desperate German borrower faced the threat of no loan unless it altered its basic political orientation. As with the Thyssen loan, this threat also collapsed when other American lenders proved willing to extend credits without the strings. In the Cologne case, though, Lee, Higginson had made one demand that the city was forced to accept—that the city take measures to balance its budget. This, as it turned out, was probably a more important demand than that made by Bankers Trust, but the city's determination to meet this condition had less to do with the Americans' insistence than with Cologne's own situation.

In February 1930, Cologne's finance committee was informed that the city would have to make major changes in its budget and taxes. Burgermeister Konrad Adenauer stated that just to meet the city's most pressing needs, it would have to collect 22.5 million RM more in taxes in the coming year than it had in the past. He gave three reasons for this change—presumably in descending order of importance. First: the deficits of past years had now caught up with the city, and it had to begin to repay old loans. Second: since the city would no longer be able to take new loans, it had to increase taxes not only enough to meet payments on its old loans but it now had to raise taxes in order to meet the expenses that had driven it to borrow in years past. He declared, "We must break with the previous system and we must meet expenses out of current income." Thus, past spending and the ending of the loans placed the greatest burden on the city's budget, but, to this Adenauer added a final factor: the effects of the depression had already vastly increased the cost of unemployment compensation, and to cover these costs, the city had to increase its tax receipts.[34]

Over the next year, Cologne did try to increase its tax income. It raised city property taxes 10 percent *(Realsteuer)* in the hopes of gaining 6.4 million RM. It also doubled its beer tax. On top of this, the city appealed to Prussia for an extra 2.8 million RM. Since even these measures would not be enough to balance its budget, the city also tried to cut spending by 10 million RM. Adenauer appealed to Chancellor Brüning for support for the tax increases as the only way to save the city from financial disaster.[35] Despite these efforts at financial retrenchment, time was running out. In January 1931, only six months prior to the currency crisis that virtually destroyed the German financial system, Cologne carried an ever growing short-term debt—by now up to 155 million RM.[36] And the city's debt continued to mount as it ran a deficit of 33 million RM in 1931 and 24.7 million RM in 1932. In spite of its efforts to cut spending and raise taxes, the pressures of depression made budget balancing almost impossible despite the most strenuous efforts. By late 1931, the city was on the verge of default, as it was unable to repay a large short-term loan and was forced to ask for an extension.[37]

City Finances and the Construction Industry

In looking at Cologne, we see for the first time a pattern that will repeat itself with depressing regularity. Government deficit spending from 1926 to 1928 stimulated the German economy and helped promote recovery from the depression of 1925–26. However, continued and even mounting deficits after the economy had moved close to full employment created financial problems when the depression of 1929 began to make itself felt. Although most of these deficits were financed within Germany (by 1931, all of Cologne's short-term loans were made by German banks),[38] the availability of American capital had played a critical role in permitting this debt accumulation. By late 1929, the thrust of government policy was radically altered by increasingly burdensome public debts, the incipient depression, which eroded the tax base and increased unemployment expenses, and, finally, the end of the American loans. Over the coming years, just as the depression reached its worst, cities, states, and the Federal government all found themselves forced to begin financial retrenchment to avoid bankruptcy— not always with success. Thus, just as governments had stimulated the economy from 1926–28, they acted to depress it in the following years. Following a textbook case of what not to do, governments bowed to the force of circumstance, and systematically exaggerated the impact of the already unstable German business cycle.

Just as Cologne had slowly found itself forced to make unpleasant policy choices, so too were most other German cities forced to rationalize their finances. In the summer of 1929, pressure to reduce unstable and expensive short-term debts forced Frankfurt am Main to cancel all new construction projects even though city officials were well aware that the action would increase unemployment in the city.[39] By late that year, with a total long- and short-term debt of over a billion RM, Berlin and its city-owned businesses were simply unable to meet their bills.[40]

To deal with the mounting crisis, the municipal governments turned to the one source of credit they themselves could control. With foreign capital markets all but closed, and the domestic market too weak to offer any relief, the cities decided to tap the funds held by the municipally owned savings and loan banks. A plan was suggested by Oskar Wassermann of the Deutsche Bank, and presented to the powerful National Association of Municipal Governments by Konrad Adenauer. The directors of the association suggested that cities employ 50 percent of the new deposits placed in their savings and loan banks to consolidate their short-term debts.[41] The president of the association, Oskar Mülert, wrote city mayors not only urging that they employ savings and loan funds to consolidate their short-term debts, but also calling on them to reduce their total spending. Warning that the very existence of municipal self-government was at stake, he exhorted them to take the necessary actions to solve their financial problems themselves before higher authorities stepped in.[42] Recognition that city budgets were overstrained prompted widespread support for the association's plan, and cities with populations over 50,000 agreed without exception to reduce their spending.

As had been true in Frankfurt, the initial impact of the new austerity programs centered on the construction industry.[43] But the impact on construction did not stop with the reduction in municipal construction projects. The employment of savings and loan funds to purchase city bonds had an even more serious impact. Since the savings and loans had been the primary source of home construction loans, the absorption of those funds created a second and decisive pressure on the construction industry. By March 1930, the construction industry had fallen into such a severe crisis that the Reich Labor Minister felt compelled to urge a modification in municipal financial policies.[44]

In view of the general trend of the German economy in 1929–30, it would be unfair to blame municipal policies for the entire depression in the German construction industry. Yet the recent emphasis on the importance of the collapse in construction and government's role in creating it indicates how important the interaction between politics and economics was in making the German depression more severe.[45] With the cities planning to take 500 million RM out of the savings and loans in 1930 and eventually cover most of their 1.8 billion RM floating debt in this way, the home building industry faced a massive squeeze.[46] The end of the cities' own building and their absorption of savings and loan funds combined to produce a compounded downward pressure on the German economy. The deficits of 1926–28 were now forcing city governments into policies that would make the depression worse, and the city governments were not the only branch of government pursuing retrenchment policies.

Bavaria

While German city governments worked their way into the depression, some of the state governments followed policies that made the most precarious city budgets appear sound. Perhaps the most extraordinary example of the budgetary problems faced by German governments, and the elaborate measures taken to relieve them is provided by the state of Bavaria. The second largest of German states, and certainly, after Prussia, the most powerful, Bavaria emerged in 1924 from the inflation and stabilization in remarkably weak financial condition.

To cover what it claimed were expenses incurred in promoting industrial expansion, Bavaria negotiated a large American loan in the summer of 1925. While admitting that it already had uncovered short-term debts of 23.5 million RM, the Bavarians convinced the Advisory Board that promoting state-owned hydroelectric projects was essential for the coal starved Bavarian economy. Further, the board professed to believe that by reducing German coal consumption and improving the water transportation system, the hydroelectric projects could help strengthen Germany's balance of payments. In an argument that promoted a more active role of the state in the economy, board chairman Norden even stated that private construction projects were best undertaken by loans through the state, since it would allow the state greater supervisory rights and reduce overall costs.[47]

The loan which Bavaria secured with these arguments was, in fact, neither so rational nor so constructive as the Advisory Board professed to believe. Admitting that Bavaria intended to use the funds to cover already incurred short-term debts, the board wanted to believe that the funds really would be productively employed. The truth was far different. "The question of how the loan will be employed," wrote one expert, "can most simply be answered by saying that the Bavarian state just needs money for the most varied purposes; above all to get rid of its pressing short-term obligations." To be sure, he said, the hydroelectric projects would also benefit, but they were being pushed into the foreground "since people did not want to emphasize the poor public financial situation, and it makes a better impression if it can be demonstrated that the loan will be used for productive purposes."[48]

Having secured this first loan by pleading that it was needed to pay for big and essential public projects, Bavaria returned the next summer to inform the Advisory Board that it now needed another $10 million to complete these projects. More than this, the Bavarians argued that in undertaking these projects, Bavaria was doing the Reich a big favor. Pointing to the Reich's new deficit spending policies inaugurated in mid-1926, the Bavarian Finance Ministry argued that Bavaria's spending would pay for some of the projects the federal government was planning and would also help stimulate the economy. The Bavarians called attention to rumors that the Reich hoped to take a huge foreign loan to pay for its proposed projects and observed, "We are thus assuming, if I may say so, a part of the Reich's responsibility and are working with the same financial strength, toward the same goal as the Reich."[49] This observation is interesting not only because it demonstrates how the Bavarians sought to turn the Reich's problems to their own advantage, but even more because it indicates a widespread understanding that deficit spending by German governmental agencies was a legitimate and acceptable means of stimulating the economy and relieving problems created by the depression.[50]

As will quickly become apparent, Bavaria's loans continued to be used for far more than financing the much-discussed water projects and were in fact employed to cover a chronic and growing fiscal deficit. In any event, this second loan, like that a year earlier, was approved and sold on the American market with great success. The Bavarian press was full of praise for this demonstration of financial acumen on the part of the state's Finance Minister Krausneck. Particularly appealing was the condition that during the first four years of the loan, Bavaria had to pay only interest charges. Only in

1930 would the payment rate go up as repayment on the bonds really began.[51] It is, perhaps, unnecessary to suggest that by 1930 Bavaria was far less able to afford a higher payment schedule than it was in 1926.

Even this loan of July 1926 could not bail Bavaria out of its deficit woes, and in December 1926 it informed the Reich that it was taking another $10 million loan, this time from the Dresdner Bank. Bavaria insisted that technically it did not require Advisory Board approval since it was a domestic loan. But even the Bavarians had to admit that the bank had every intention of selling the treasury bills it received as collateral in America. When Bavaria's state bank president and Advisory Board representative insisted that the loan could and would be easily repaid, the board felt compelled to accept the argument and let the issue drop. Almost immediately thereafter Bavaria took a 75 million RM internal loan which, once again, was a huge "success." This time, first amortization payments would come in 1932.[52]

By the summer of 1927, Bavaria was living precariously by converting one short-term loan into another. To repay its $10 million loan from the Dresdner Bank, in June it took another $20 million loan from the American firms Equitable Trust and Harris, Forbes. This time the Reich Finance Ministry found Bavaria out of line and insisted that the loan should have been approved by the Advisory Board. Convinced that short-term loans of Bavaria, Saxony, and Prussia had saturated the foreign market, the Reich Finance Minister called for an end to such dangerous, unregulated short-term borrowing.[53]

Unable to balance its budget or cover its deficits domestically, Bavaria refused to accept this appeal. Its operating budget for both 1927 and 1928 showed large-scale deficits, while its capital budget for the two years increased the debt by another 116 million RM.[54] In early 1928, with its $20 million American loan falling due in June 1928, the Bavarian Finance Ministry informed the Reich that "Bavaria is not in a position" to repay the loan. Its increasing debts made it impossible "either completely or in part" to cover the debt.[55] Arguing that a new loan it was negotiating was not a new debt but merely the extension of an existing loan and that taking a long-term loan would help defend the stability of the mark, Bavaria pleaded for an exemption from existing rules. Citing the Americans' willingness to cover the old debt with a new three-year loan and their desire to make all arrangements several weeks before the old debt was due in order to hide the connection between the two loans, Bavaria called for quick Advisory Board approval of its request.

When the board decided to permit Bavaria to issue only one-year treasury notes instead of the three-year loan requested by the state, Bavaria reacted in panic. A one-year renewal, it warned, would solve nothing since other notes were falling due all the time. Much more ominously, Bavaria all but threatened to go bankrupt if its loan was not approved. State bank president Wolf, representing Bavaria, wrote the board that "if the states are not permitted to take any more foreign loans . . . the states would have no further interest in maintaining their good credit standing abroad. Such a mentality would not only make things difficult for state governments which are being pressed for the greatest possible savings, but could also prejudice the credit of the Reich." Under this threat, the board agreed the next day to allow Bavaria to take either a one-year loan of $20 million, or a three-year loan of $15 million.[56]

With the certain knowledge that it had won, Bavaria proceeded to take what it wanted. It made arrangements with Bankers Trust Company for the Bavarian State Bank to take $20 million for six months with guaranteed renewals for two years. So Bavaria got its $20 million and got it for more than a year. The Advisory Board approved the loan, said Norden, "because as a purely bank credit—the Bavarian State Bank will be the borrower—it will not come into public view."[57] To hide Bavaria's virtual default, the Reich government, at the very height of the greatest economic boom of the 1920s, was forced to condone this subterfuge. As economic conditions deteriorated, state incomes fell, and when Bavaria's deferred loan repayments fell due after 1930, there could be very little doubt but that worse troubles lay ahead.

At the depth of the depression, in late 1931, Bavaria did in fact refuse to repay the short-term loans it had taken in 1928. The Bavarian State Bank claimed that the funds fell under the so-called "Standstill Agreements" which stopped short-term loan repayments after the German banking crash of June 1931. The American bankers felt the loans were not covered and should be repaid. It soon became apparent, however, that while the Bavarians sought legal grounds for not paying, the real problem was that they could not pay.[58] Indeed, by January 1932, the Bavarian State Bank, as the agent for the state of Bavaria, was one of only three German borrowers unable to meet its foreign debt obligations.[59] Bankers Trust representative John Stahl was being neither facetious nor inaccurate when he concluded a report to his colleagues in New York, "In closing, all I can say is that the mad Ludwig of Bavaria had nothing on the fellows who are running Bavarian affairs today."[60]

Reich Finances, 1929

Just as municipal finances reached a turning point in late 1929, so too did Reich finances begin to break apart. The decisions in 1926 and 1927 to ease the impact of the "stabilization crisis" by reducing business taxes and implementing large-scale "make work" projects inaugurated government deficits which became increasingly onerous. Hidden from view by inclusion in the "extraordinary" budget, Germany continued to insist that its operating (and public) budget was in balance. In 1927 alone, the extraordinary budget carried a deficit of 1.5 billion Reichsmarks. While a third of this was covered by the Reich loan of February 1927, two thirds were completely uncovered.[61]

Despite Finance Minister Köhler's repeated assurances that he would balance the budget and his demands that the government support him in this policy, the deficits mounted. By the spring of 1928, Democratic Party leader Erich Koch-Weser found the dangers of the continued deficits so great that he seemed to hope that the Reparations Agent would interfere again to force greater moderation. The explanation for the continuing deficits, he felt, lay in the basic weakness of the German political parties and in Köhler's personality. He wrote,

"Recently, there has developed a downright race between the various parliamentary factions to make themselves popular by distributing money. Finance Minister Köhler says to everyone 'yes and amen' and finances are being untenably disordered."[62]

But the problems with Reich finances lay deeper than Köhler's personal weakness and the floundering party system. When the Social Democratic coalition government came to power in the spring of 1928, the new Finance Minister, Rudolf Hilferding, found himself fighting a losing battle to restrain Reich spending. He charged that the government bureaucracy itself was partially responsible for the problem since every branch of the government tried to increase its own budget and pay.[63] Hilferding pressed the Cabinet to control spending and went so far as to announce in January 1929 that the Reich budget for 1929 really would be balanced. He offered a tough sounding formula to prove it. He told the press that the federal budget would be aided by 500 million RM in new taxes and a reduction in transfers to the state governments of 120 million RM. He said that the new taxes were made necessary by the high reparations payments which demanded "sacrifices from the economy which were so heavy that he doubted that they could long be borne." The taxes were now so high that he worried that the economy could not bear them for more than one year without a crisis.[64]

Whether one believes that the government's tax policy really threatened to destroy the economy or not, it is indisputable that the tax income was not great enough to cover the state's outlays. In fact, it was precisely at this time that the government finally began to realize just how serious its financial problems were.

By April 1929 it was becoming apparent that Hilferding had failed in his reform attempts, and a brief report on his inability to secure a loan to cover the Reich's immediate cash needs set in motion an intensive investigation of the situation. Fearing that the Cabinet and Reichstag were not being fully informed about the seriousness of the Reich's financial position, Chancellor Müller asked for a complete analysis.[65] Responding to Müller's request, State Secretary Herman Pünder reported that rising unemployment, falling taxes, and excessively generous government budgets were creating problems that reached well beyond the short-term cash needs and had to be solved by fundamental long-term changes. He wrote, "it is my firm conviction that in reality, the problems are more serious now than anything endured in the past ten years, including the difficult period of the inflation and going over to the new currency."[66]

The mounting deficits and the government's inability to finance them with safe long-term bonds were combining to create a fiscal crisis of the German state.[67] This basic weakness was compounded by the weak political position of the Cabinet. When the Young Plan negotiations deadlocked in the spring of 1929, the rush to withdraw money from Germany further undermined German monetary reserves and added a political dimension to the basic capital shortage. This political element became even more direct when German bankers and industrialists refused to cooperate in helping the government unless its generous social policies were reversed.[68]

Within a week of Müller's request for information, the Finance Ministry provided confirmation of his worst fears. State Secretary Popitz informed the Cabinet that it could anticipate a Reich deficit for the coming year of nearly a billion RM.[69] In fact, even this horrifying sum turned out to be too optimistic. In the fiscal year running from April 1929 to April 1930, the Reich ran a deficit of over 1.6 billion RM. When this was added to the deficits of German city and state governments, the total public debt stood at just over 3.1 billion RM.[70] This represented over 3 percent of German Net National Product. The importance of these deficits becomes clearer when we consider that the much discussed $200 billion deficit of the United States government in 1984 represented about 5.7 percent of GNP but was offset by a $50 billion surplus by state and local governments. Thus in 1984 the United States ran combined deficits of about 4 percent of GNP.

To cover the Reich debt, the Finance Ministry proposed a combination of tax reforms and treasury note issues. But Pünder found the Finance Ministry's proposals wholly unrealistic. He informed the Chancellor that "the entire extremely pessimistic exposition is based on the completely uncertain and optimistic assumption that prior to the summer recess, the Reichstag will pass a reform law on unemployment insurance and that tax receipts will not fall below the estimates which are well known to be very high." He added that Popitz had independently concluded that the entire budget problem could not be resolved through normal parliamentary legislation, but, like the stabilization laws of 1923, could only be solved through an enabling act which allowed the government to rule by decree. Pünder not only agreed that an emergency law was necessary, he was afraid that the "flight into real values" which would accompany a new inflation had already begun.[71] The idea that Germany was teetering on the edge of a new hyperinflation was a gross misunderstanding of the situation but was based on the perception that state deficits were rapidly getting out of control and that it was this same development that had led to the monetary collapse of the early 1920s.

As the Finance Ministry struggled to meet its daily operating expenses, it found that it could no longer borrow on the domestic capital market. Hilferding advised the Cabinet that the big private banks were unwilling to extend any more short-term credit to the government because they were concerned about their own liquidity and the danger of monetary instability which might arise if the reparations negotiations collapsed. But another "unofficial" source of their reserve was their sympathy with the demand of private industry that the Reich end the capital profits tax, eliminate the *Reichskreditgesellschaft* (a major source of government loans) and reduce state ownership of industries.[72] Although the social demands set the framework for private bank reservations about further governmental loans, it is likely that their lack of liquidity was the real determining factor. This supposition is supported by the fact that the Association of Publicly Owned Credit Institutions was even more active in discouraging further government borrowing than the private bankers. The public association wrote Hilferding that any further state loans would ruin the market for mortgage loans. "We remember in this regard," they wrote, "that the capital market collapse in 1927 was similarly introduced by the issuing of a 500 million RM loan of the Reich. The situation today is only different in that the money situation is incomparably worse, the mortgage debentures in circulation a great deal larger and the ability of the banks to absorb short-term securities a great deal smaller."[73]

Hilferding worked to secure a domestic loan in the face of mounting Reichsbank opposition and uncertainty over Germany's ability to absorb a loan.[74] When this effort failed, he turned to the international market. But here, too, sailing was far from smooth. Reparations uncertainties and the American stock market boom combined to retard interest in German loans. Beyond that, Reichsbank president Schacht began once again to attack Reich borrowing. After a conversation with Parker Gilbert, he let it be known that he (and presumably Gilbert as well) was convinced that German interest rates were high only because of the monetary demands of the Reich. He added that "he had to ask himself the very serious question, if the Reichsbank could continue to cooperate" in meeting the financial needs of the Reich.[75] With far more subtlety than he normally exhibited, Schacht maneuvered to fulfill his threats. Over the summer, rumors began to circulate that Americans would not consider floating a new reparations loan until Reich finances were reformed. Furthermore, Americans reportedly believed that the essential reforms would never be introduced under a Social Democratic government and especially not as long as Hilferding served as Finance Minister. From a number of sources, Social Democratic Reichstag deputy Rudolf Breitscheid concluded that Schacht had initiated these ideas. Breitscheid assured Reich Chancellor Müller that he had effectively countered this latest effort by Schacht to use international pressures to force changes in German domestic policies.[76]

Despite Schacht's efforts and the general inclination of Americans not to lend more to Germany at that time, in June 1929, Hilferding was able to secure a one-year $50 million loan from Dillon Read.[77] The loan was arranged without Schacht's knowledge. While unhappy about the loan because, he said, "he held Dillon Read to be a second-class firm," Schacht did not take a public stand against the loan.[78] It is also interesting that, while German bankers had demanded extensive changes in Reich policy before they would lend their own money, both Mendelssohn and the Deutsche Bank acted as intermediaries for the Dillon Read loan.[79] For a commission, it would appear that the German banks were willing to put other people's money where they would not put their own.

The loan from Dillon Read, while providing a brief respite, was far from solving the Reich's financial problems. With income falling as the depression reduced business activity, the Reich was pinched by the costs of rising unemployment payments and the need to begin paying back loans taken over the previous four years.[80] By August 1929, Finance Minister Hilferding felt compelled to inform the Chancellery that Germany had to accept the Young Plan regardless of legitimate reservations, or "incisive measures on both the income and expenditure side will become necessary if suspension of payments which the Reich is legally obligated to make is to be avoided."[81] But Hilferding's own Social Democratic Party could not tolerate any reduction in unemployment support which was becoming the critical issue in the budget. Labor Minister Rudolf Wissell threatened to resign and bring down the government if workers were not given better support.[82]

The regime survived only because a Cabinet crisis would have destroyed the final Young Plan negotiations taking place in The Hague, and Germany would lose the reduction in reparations which was now absolutely vital to its budget. In mid-August, Wissell and Interior Minister Carl Severing traveled to The Hague to hammer out a compromise with the other Cabinet leaders who were in the midst of negotiations with the Allies. A shaky agreement, unsatisfactory to all parties, was finally accepted which raised employer contributions to the unemployment insurance fund and extended the waiting period before workers would receive aid. The deal was accepted because, as one minister put it, "the problem of reform of the unemployment insurance is certainly of great importance. But a success at The Hague conference is even more important. Therefore whatever else happens a Cabinet crisis at the present time must be avoided."[83] Through the fall and winter, the unemployment issue festered as Finance Minister Hilferding, perhaps under the influence of his State Secretary, Johannes Popitz, struggled to keep the government afloat financially and the Labor Ministry fought to help the mounting millions of employees thrown out of work by the depression.[84]

Hilferding found himself under particular pressure from Parker Gilbert to keep German finances under tight control. Should foreign lenders become convinced that the German government's finances were not sound, they would refuse to purchase the Young Plan bonds and the entire reparations reform would collapse. Specifically, Gilbert insisted that Germany not seek any foreign loan until after the Young Plan bonds had been sold.[85]

Despite Hilferding's assurances that he was not in the market for a foreign loan, Gilbert continued to worry that he might consummate a loan through the Swedish match king and financial manipulator, Ivar Kreuger.[86] Germans continued to look for some ulterior motive behind Gilbert's concerns. They recognized that he was determined to see the Young Plan successfully sold but thought that he might also want to prevent a Reich loan from competing with a French loan being floated in the United States by J. P. Morgan. Von Schubert at the Foreign Office judged that a Reich loan "would be seen [by Gilbert] as a disagreeable competitor for the project of the House of Morgan, to which he is known to be close."[87] However much Gilbert may have actually wanted to support Morgan, it hardly seems possible that German leaders could ignore the fact that Gilbert had consistently tried to reduce Reich spending as a way to ensure reparations transfers. This was surely still his central concern.

Gilbert was not the only one worried about Reich attempts to seek a foreign loan. The French Cabinet was determined to accept the Young Plan and evacuate the Rhineland only if the Young bonds could be sold.[89] In response to these concerns, the German Cabinet instructed its ambassador in Paris, Leopold von Hoesch, to assure the French that only the Kreuger loan was being considered, and it would not affect the American market. He was authorized to state that reports that Hilferding was considering another loan from Dillon Read or any other American bank "can be characterized as absolutely untrue." Hilferding also told von Schubert that Gilbert "knows that the offer from Dillon Read will not be accepted." Von

Schubert himself not only reassured Gilbert that the Reich was not interested in further foreign borrowing, but also informed him that the disagreements between Schacht and Hilferding over short-term borrowing of the Reich had been resolved. On November 21, Hoesch reported back to Berlin that he had carried out his instructions and had informed the French that Germany was entirely sympathetic to French fears about ensuring successful sales of the Young loan and would not be borrowing on foreign markets.[89] The issue seemed closed and groundless fears laid to rest.

If this had been the end of the story, it would hardly be worth the telling, but of course nothing effective had been done to reorganize Reich finances, which remained in a condition that prompted Sir Horace Rumbold, British Ambassador to Germany, to observe that "one is reminded of a similar state of affairs in pre-war Turkey."[90] Nor had relations between Schacht and Hilferding reached quite the high level of amicability suggested by von Schubert. Indeed, Rudolf Hilferding and Hjalmar Schacht seemed made to fight. As the most brilliant economic theorist of Social Democratic ideals, Hilferding represented everything that Schacht hated. On top of this ideological antagonism, Hilferding, as heir to the Finance Ministry's old deficit policies, moved into a slot which by its very nature promised conflict with the orthodox demands of the Reichsbank president. When Hilferding continued and even expanded the fiscal deficits, Schacht in turn expanded his assaults on Reich policies.[91]

Hilferding became the lightning rod that attracted Schacht's rage for affronts that went far beyond Hilferding's personality or personal policies. Schacht, as chief German negotiator for the Young Plan, had been unable to force the allies to make the concessions he had sworn to win. In order to save face and produce an acceptable compromise, a number of important issues were left unresolved pending further negotiations. After Schacht stepped down as Germany's representative, he began to demand that Germany win all the issues he had been forced to leave unresolved or betray the victory which he claimed to have won in the earlier negotiations. This antagonistic stance, produced by Schacht's determination not to accept responsibility for a treaty, which was already under vicious conservative attack, led to Schacht's exclusion from information on the course of further negotiations. Schacht responded to this in typical fashion by bitter complaints about his abused status. When the new Economics Minister, Paul Moldenauer, took the occasion of a dinner party encounter with Schacht to ask for his views, Schacht "told me bitterly that I was the first Minister in many months that had actually asked his advice."[92] Schacht's rage was so great that at another evening get-together with a number of politicians and bankers, he put on an "absolutely unbalanced performance." Complaining that the government completely ignored him, he proclaimed that a new inflation was directly ahead, spoke of raising the discount rate in spite of the faltering economy and "carried on like a Wilhelmian decadent [Epigon]." The bankers viewing this performance were "absolutely shocked," partially by the pessimism of Schacht's pronouncements, and partially by his crazy behavior, behavior which one of the observers could only account for by believing that Schacht had been drunk.[93]

Schacht's attacks on Reich authority not only led him into conflict with Hilferding, but with high officials of the Reich permanent bureaucracy as well. Hermann Pünder felt compelled on at least one occasion to rebuke Schacht for his interference in govenmental affairs and took steps to make it clear to Schacht that he was not invited to be a regular participant in Cabinet meetings.[94] But Schacht came into most direct conflict with Johannes Popitz, the leading bureaucrat in the Reich Finance Ministry. Moldenhauer even believed that Hilferding had been led into the fight with Schacht by Popitz, and found Popitz to be the dominant force behind the Reich's conflict with Schacht. In Moldenhauer's judgment, "Popitz saw in Schacht the man who injured the state's authority. To him, the Reichsbank was a subordinate agency which did not have the right to criticize the government, but rather, had the obligation to fulfill the orders of the government."[95] This growing conflict based on ideological, political, and personal disagreements culminated in a dramatic showdown between the Reich Finance Ministry and the Reichsbank in December 1929.

Having assured all interested parties in mid-November, 1929, that the Reich would seek no further foreign credits, Hilferding was forced in less than a month to renege on his promise. He once again went after the long pending loan from Dillon Read which he had so recently assured Gilbert was a dead issue. Hilferding blandly informed the Cabinet that "I am not worried about difficulties from the Reparations Agent especially because his legal position over short-term loans is not very strong. But beyond that he wants to avoid a collapse of Reich finances." Once the loan was in hand, Hilferding was confident that the Reich would be able to cover its future payments. Chancellor Müller was closer to the truth when he objected that "I don't think it is so certain that we can borrow the 1250 million [RM]."[96]

Opposition to the Dillon Read loan from Reichsbank president Schacht created more problems for Hilferding. Schacht insisted that a half billion RM sinking fund be created to start paying off old debts before he would tolerate a new loan. The government felt it could not possibly give in to this demand since the ruling coalition would collapse and the entire German state might be paralyzed if any changes were introduced to the tenuous tax compromises already reached.[97] Under pressure from bankers Paul Warburg and Oskar Wassermann, Schacht tentatively agreed to keep quiet about the Dillon Read loan.[98]

Early on the morning of 16 December 1929 Reich Chancellor Hermann Müller went to Reich President Hindenburg and informed him that in the coming weeks the Reich would be unable to meet its cash requirements. The Reichsbank's uncooperative position on the Dillon Read loan threatened to push the Reich into default. Hindenburg offered to talk to Schacht, but despite his repeated appeals that a failure to secure a Reich loan "would result in a financial crisis with incalculable consequences," Schacht remained unmoved.[99] His only concession was a promise that as long as no one asked him about the loan, he would not oppose it. But if asked about it, Schacht warned he would have to say that until the Reich balanced its budget and created a special fund out of tax surpluses to consolidate its debts, the Reich was a poor credit risk.

During the course of the day, Schacht repeated his stand, first to Müller, then to the Cabinet, and, finally, at 8:00 that evening to an assembly of the party leaders of the ruling coalition. At each conference Schacht stated that the Reichstag had to accept its responsibility and move to balance the budget. And at each meeting Schacht was informed that it had been nearly impossible to reach the compromises which allowed any financial policy at all, and it would be impossible to formulate any drastic new policy.[100]

Schacht's attacks on government policies were most firmly rejected by the most conservative elements of the coalition. Heinrich Brüning of the Center Party condemned Schacht's demands while People's Party spokesman Curt Hoff clearly explained why businessmen were sympathetic to Hilferding's policies (if not to Hilferding personally). Hoff stated that the business interests "lived from the hope" of a tax cut and any delay in granting the tax cut would produce the "most severe suffering." "If this hope [of a tax cut] were to disappear," he said, "it would be all over for capital liquidity and business."[101] Schacht rejected this argument, too, with his traditional stand that it was the huge government floating debt that drove up interest rates and was the source of business suffering.

Surprisingly, Schacht found more sympathy from Social Democrat Carl Severing. For years as Prussian Minister of Interior, Severing had tried to reduce municipal spending. Now, as Reich Interior Minister, Severing was sympathetic to Schacht's insistence that Reich finances be put in order. He could not, however, agree with Schacht's demands for instant action since it would destroy the ruling coalition, cause a breakdown in the Young Plan negotiations, stimulate political activities of both right and left radicals, and perhaps lead to civil war. Instead, Severing said, Schacht had to help the Reich solve its current problems.[102]

Severing, like Hilferding, had learned from hard experience that unstable government deficits were dangerous. The deficits did not seem to help the economy, they weakened the government's political power both at home and abroad, and they had not solved the social and economic problems that had produced the initial deficits. Just as Germany was falling into the depression, Severing so poignantly noted, everyone had learned that the Reich had to balance its budget. This meant that taxes must be raised and spending cut—actions which in the face of spreading depression could only add to the national misery. With disastrous accuracy, he observed, "From the present situation, all concerned parties have learned so much that earnest measures to rationalize conditions will be taken."[103]

After Schacht left the evening conference, Chancellor Müller informed the Cabinet that it had to go ahead and try for the Dillon Read loan. Hilferding supported the move with the assurance that Dillon Read had agreed to make the loan even if Schacht opposed it.[104] Early the next morning, December 17, Hilferding sent a secret telegram to Germany's ambassador in the United States, Friedrich Wilhelm von Prittwitz, asking him personally to call on Clarence Dillon, head of Dillon Read. He was to inform Dillon that "all constitutional factors" had been cleared to legalize a short-term loan of $75 million from Dillon Read to the Reich. Von Prittwitz was to include in his remarks the observation that Dillon "did not need to doubt, that this introductory agreement between his house and the Reich would continue and expand into other credit arrangements." Finally, von Prittwitz was reminded that "the greatest speed in discussions is urgently requested."[105]

Within six hours of the time that Hilferding sent this secret telegram, French authorities were fully informed of the situation. The French had already warned Germany's Ambassador von Hoesch that American bankers would never float the Young loan if Germany now took another foreign loan, and von Hoesch had reassured them that nothing involving the American market was in prospect. Now von Hoesch was summoned to meet with the top French leadership, Foreign Minister Briand, Minister President Tardieu, and Finance Minister Chéron, to explain what Germany meant by the wire to Dillon Read. Before the uninformed Hoesch could get instructions from home, the French leaders bluntly informed him that even a short-term loan would "severely harm French interest in the Young Plan," would ruin German credit, and would make it impossible to sell the Young Plan bonds. Believing that the loan contract already lay before Clarence Dillon, the French insisted that decisions had to be made within hours and had little use for von Hoesch's weak explanation that, "it is well known that the cash situation of the Reich is, at the moment, catastrophic."[106]

So poorly had the German government prepared for its desperate financial gamble that it was only the next day that Berlin finally provided von Hoesch with the official explanation of Reich policy. The cash situation had reached a point, he was instructed to tell Briand, that a total collapse of the treasury was threatening and a "State crisis" would soon follow a treasury collapse.[107]

The next day, at a meeting with Hilferding, Popitz, and Moldenauer, Schacht insisted that the Reich's credit was now ruined and demanded that it create a special fund of 500 million RM to begin servicing its floating debt. This would not only involve giving up Moldenauer's pet project of a tax reduction for industry, but might even force the Reich to increase taxes. Moldenauer, like others in the Cabinet, had not fully appreciated how serious the Reich financial situation was until he found out that Popitz had been working until 6 P.M. the previous evening to "hunt up" 9 million RM due the next morning. In spite of the dawning realization that Schacht was not making up the crisis, the Cabinet successfully prevailed upon him to give his word that he would not attack the loan as long as no one asked him about it. Schacht's word was good for as long as it took him to reach the nearest newspaper office. At 11:30 that night, Moldenauer was awakened by Hans Schäffer, who informed him that, immediately upon leaving the meeting, Schacht had given the press a long, typed memorandum attacking the Reich government's "pump economy."[108]

Schacht had widespread support in demanding that the Reich balance its budget. Pierpont Morgan sent Schacht a telegram supporting his stand, while the positions of Gilbert and the French government provided strong moral support for his resistance to Reich policies.[109] On the same evening (December 18) that Schacht was preparing his assault on the Reich government, Parker Gilbert was also making the rounds trying to make sense of German policies. In meetings with Müller and Hilferding, and later with the State Secretary in the Foreign Ministry, von Schubert, Gilbert both opposed the Dillon Read loan and insisted that the Reich could and, indeed must, find the cash within Germany to meet its obligations. Von Schubert found the entire situation especially frustrating because he had long believed that cooperation with Gilbert could have been easily arranged if only the Germans would work at it a bit. In late November, when Gilbert had all but forbidden an earlier Dillon Read loan, von Schubert had appealed to Hilferding to talk to Gilbert. But, after two weeks of inaction, Hilferding blandly told him that he had not seen Gilbert, but there was no longer any problem with the Reich being able to meet its payments, and Hilferding "believed full well, that in the mean-time, Gilbert had satisfied himself on this score." That was December 5; now two weeks later, Gilbert found himself forced to tell von Schubert once again that the Reich must not seek a foreign loan.[110]

At the same time, Gilbert's complex cooperation with Schacht was falling apart. Gilbert told von Schubert that he had not spoken to Schacht in a long time. Furthermore, the Reich must not back down to Schacht and, instead, must formulate its plans and make him agree to cooperate. "One must not let Schacht dictate terms as had been done in the past" he told von Schubert.[111] As Gilbert became increasingly convinced that Schacht was attempting to sabotage the Young Plan, he supported the policies Schacht wanted, but insisted that the German government formulate those policies itself. His comments to von Schubert were intended to reduce Schacht's power while supporting his policies. In the short run, Gilbert only strengthened Schacht's position; in the long run, he helped remove Schacht as Reichsbank president.

On the morning of 19 December 1929, the German government was brought to its knees. When Ambassador Pritt-witz took Hilferding's loan request to Clarence Dillon, the American backed out of his commitment. He justified his refusal to grant the Reich a loan by pointing out that the German banks which were going to handle the funds on the German side had been forced to withdraw under pressure from Schacht.

Dillon said he had been willing to grant the loan if Schacht remained neutral, but he had not expected Schacht's vigorous opposition.[112] With the Finance Minister already telling German local governments that they would receive only half the funds due them from the Reich, the Cabinet had to come up with money immediately.[113] Frantic negotiations over the course of the day led to the agreement that although in normal times the Cabinet ought to resign, in view of the present crisis, it must first raise enough money to avoid default. The only way to do this was to reach an agreement with Schacht.[114]

When Chancellor Müller, hat in hand, asked Schacht for his terms, Schacht insisted that before the Reichsbank would make any credit available, the government would have to establish by law a 450 million RM sinking fund to pay off its debts. After the Cabinet agreed to this demand, Müller had to try to convince the coalition parties to go along.[115] Here, he ran into trouble. Led by representatives of the Center Party and German People's Party, the party leaders refused to trust Schacht's commitment that if the Reichstag first passed the new tax laws and ended its efforts to pass a tax reduction, he would grant the Reich the required credits. Without hearing him personally commit himself, the politicians were not prepared to trust Schacht. To satisfy their demands, the meeting was adjourned for two hours while Schacht was found and brought forth to assure them that he would make no further demands. With this assurance, the party leaders either pledged their party's support or went off to try to convince their waiting delegations to swallow the bitter pill.[116]

Two days after Hilferding's rush to secure the Dillon Read loan, von Schubert in the Foreign Ministry could declare, "The Dillon Read loan is as good as dead. A direct demand on the foreign market by the Reich government for either long- or short-term funds is no longer a possibility." The implications for government policy were much broader than that. As Foreign Minister Julius Curtius advised his ambassador in Paris, "With this action, we have taken a decisive step toward further rationalization of the Reich finances. But, creation of the debt repayment fund means that the program of a tax reduction and reduced burden on industry will probably have to be delayed for months."[117] Schacht's action clearly hurt the interests of German industry and was the last blow that finally forced the Reich to retreat from its long-standing deficit fiscal policies. The deliberate policies, which had stimulated economic growth for the past four years, but which had caused increasing concern in responsible leaders of every political persuasion, had now come to an end.

On December 20, Rudolf Hilferding offered his resignation as Reich Finance Minister. In his brief letter, Hilferding wrote:

The policies I have followed had the following goals: The progressive consolidation of the floating debts—a policy which had already been introduced by securing the Kreuger loan: Employment of the savings from the Young Plan to repay the budget deficits of 1928 and 1929 as well as to reduce the burden on industry through a tax reduction of effective dimensions at an early time.

This policy has been destroyed by outside intervention and therefore can no longer be carried on by me.[118]

Initially, few politicans had seemed inclined to demand Hilferding's resignation. Instead, blame for the disastrous fiscal policies was placed on his State Secretary Johannes Popitz. Popitz long before had alienated leaders of state governments by his efforts to force the states to yield to Reich financial control. Acting through the Reichsrat, the crisis in Reich finances now gave the states a lever to demand his resignation. Social Democratic Labor Minister Rudolf Wissell also denounced both Hilferding and Popitz for following policies that could only appeal to the conservative German People's Party. Although Social Democrats in general continued to support Hilferding, Wissell found no opposition when he declared that Popitz had to go.[119] When the two People's Party Ministers, Moldenauer and Curtius, threatened to resign if Hilferding didn't accompany Popitz, Hilferding's fate was also sealed. His resignation was accepted and his term as Finance Minister came to an end.[120]

Aftermath

The distress suffered by the German government in December 1929 heralded the Weimar Republic's final economic crisis. As the Reich, the state, and the city governments began vigorous fiscal retrenchment, and the rest of the world began its slide into depression, the German economy all but collapsed. Perhaps the most immediate product of the Reich's fiscal crisis was the determination by federal leaders to rid themselves of Hjalmar Schacht and a Reichsbank that seemed set on humiliating the government.

Meeting in early January 1930, leaders of the Social Democratic Party resolved to use their position in the Cabinet to attack Schacht and reestablish the government's authority over fiscal policies. They further insisted that the Cabinet force the Finance Ministry's representative in the Advisory Board for Foreign Credit to support renewed municipal foreign borrowing and help circumvent the Reichsbank's incessant veto there. But, in this effort to strengthen municipal finance, the cities themselves presented as great an obstacle as the Reichsbank president's temper, since, as Chancellor Müller himself was forced to confess, "at the present time the finances of most cities are so unfavorable that these cities will not be able to secure foreign loans. When the cities can hardly pay their employees and when hospital wings must be closed because there is no money, where will one be able to find a guarantee on the interest" of a foreign loan?[121]

It was this financial weakness of the cities and the Reich which gave Schacht the power over German finance so abhorred by the Socialists and other political leaders.[122] As Müller noted, "the struggle of the government against Schacht will first be accompanied by success when Reich finances are reformed." Only when the government did not need to seek any help in covering its expenses could it overthrow Schacht's financial dictatorship. To accomplish this, new taxes would have to be passed and rigorously collected. Until finances were reformed, the Reich would remain hostage to Schacht's demands.[123] The conviction that government deficits had to be ended was not held by the Socialists alone. Leaders of the other parties in the coalition government raised the same issues and said, too, that before Schacht could be confronted, the Reich would have to put its own financial house in order.[124]

The winter's crisis had not only demonstrated the inability of the deficit policies to provide long-term support for the economy, it had also revealed the terrible political weakness that undermined Germany's foreign and domestic policies. German leaders were compelled to believe that only by reestablishing a balanced budget could Germany repair the economic damage done over the past years. Of perhaps even more importance, a balanced budget was the first crucial step toward German independence from the bonds of foreign and domestic bankers.

In the winter of 1929–30, as German politicians resolved to rid themselves of the Reichsbank's oppression, it became clear that German industrial and banking leaders were no longer enamored of Hjalmar Schacht. His demands for high taxes, his lofty independence, and his limitless ambition left him isolated now even among the circles that formerly had seen themselves as his close allies.[125]

Schacht's support from foreign banking circles also collapsed in the aftermath of the December crisis. Schacht had long been able to call upon the forces of foreign fiscal orthodoxy for support in his internal German feuds. Now those foreign supporters began to suspect him of heresy. Since the spring of 1927, Parker Gilbert had worried that Schacht was intent on creating an economic crisis in order to demonstrate that Germany's reparations burden was intolerable. For a time, the united efforts of Schacht and Gilbert to force Reich authorities to balance their budget overshadowed this underlying disagreement and allowed Gilbert to ignore his fears. But Schacht's position during the Young Plan negotiations ended this cooperation. Gilbert now saw that Schacht was determined above all else to end reparations—a stand which not only threatened to undermine Gilbert's support of the French government and Raymond Poincaré, but also threatened to destroy Gilbert's hope of ending his mission with a ringing success.[126]

By the end of January 1930, Social Democratic Reichstag leader Rudolph Breitscheid was pleased to observe that Schacht was losing his influence abroad and had to be fired. Schacht, he proclaimed, "has become an economic and financial burden to Germany since foreigners have doubts that Schacht really will carry out the new plan with good will."[127] Breitscheid was absolutely correct in perceiving that Schacht had lost his former American allies. Support that Schacht had received from J. P. Morgan in his confrontation with the Cabinet in December 1929 was downplayed and all but denied by Morgan two months later.[128] Morgan's retreat was almost certainly a product of Parker Gilbert's increasingly blunt criticism of Schacht and Schacht's reparation policies. By February 1930, State Secretary von Schubert reported that Gilbert told him, "Schacht continues to claim that he has support from the Americans. He [Gilbert] could assure me that this claim of Schacht's was entirely false."[129] Shortly thereafter, Gilbert flatly accused Schacht of being a chronic liar who could never be believed. Gilbert's change of heart had been solidified when Schacht tried to sabotage the Young Plan loan by informing American negotiators that he personally would not give a penny for German government bonds because the government was no longer credit worthy.[130]

　　With the inauguration of the Young Plan, Parker Gilbert had won most of what he had sought. Reparations had been reduced, but Germany was still required to more than cover the Allied war debts to the United States. More importantly, the Reich government was now legally required to supervise its own finances and could be held solely accountable if its budget deficits created international complications. This victory had been threatened by Schacht, who had agreed with Gilbert that budgets had to be balanced but refused to agree that Germany could then pay reparations and refused to accept responsibility for a settlement that was under increasing conservative attack within Germany.[131]

　　In a telegram to Owen Young, at the end of February 1930, Schacht claimed that concessions forced on Germany during the final round of negotiations for the Young Plan had so mutilated the original agreement that he would "decline any responsibility whatsoever" for the final pact.[132] As Schacht moved toward resignation rather than accept the new plan, the Reich worked to soften the impact of his resignation. In spite of his loss of influence with Gilbert and Morgan, Schacht retained high standing with the banking world, and the government had been warned that his resignation would lead to a panic and endanger the mark's stability. To counter this danger, the Reich searched for a successor to Schacht with a strong enough personality that any notion of a collapse could be immediately dismissed. It found its man in former Finance Minister and Chancellor Hans Luther, who had a well-deserved reputation for fiscal and financial orthodoxy and hard headedness.[133] When Schacht finally did sign the Young Plan agreement and then offer his resignation on March 7, the Cabinet quickly accepted it and just as quickly put Luther in his place. Despite all fears, Schacht's resignation had almost no impact on the money market or the mark's value.

In March 1930, the crumbling Weimar coalition collapsed, and the last parliamentary Cabinet in Germany was terminated. The final issue destroying the coalition was produced when Social Democrats refused to permit unemployment benefits to be cut as the principal means of reducing expenses.[134] In spite of this last effort to defend their own interest group, the Social Democratic leaders largely followed the new Chancellor, Heinrich Brüning, as he imposed an increasingly deflationary fiscal policy on the federal budget.[135] With Brüning's rise to power, the Reich took the final step away from the policies pursued over the past five years and entered a new era of nearly unrelenting deflation.[136]

Conclusion

Germany accepted the Dawes Plan and the obligation to pay reparations in 1924 because German leaders knew that only by ending the economic struggle with France was there any hope of rebuilding the German economy or stabilizing German society. Domestic needs dictated a major concession in foreign policy. But in accepting the Dawes Plan, Germany also accepted the obligation to pursue a fulfillment policy with severe deflationary implications. By 1925–26, German officials realized that fulfillment would force Germany to endure high unemployment and renewed domestic conflict. The dilemma facing German policymakers by 1928 had come down to this: to solve domestic problems they had pursued international policies that briefly reduced domestic conflict, but soon began to create even more severe social and economic problems. By accepting large volumes of American loans, Germany could temporarily get around its dilemma and both pay reparations and finance large-scale government deficits. But this alternative, too, proved more dangerous than helpful, since even before Americans stopped making loans, the loans themselves had become the center of social conflicts within Germany and of foreign policy conflict with the Reparations Agent.

To some extent Germany's problems from 1924–29 were unique products of Germany's internal social-financial weakness and its international obligations in the aftermath of the Dawes Plan. But, on a more fundamental level, Germany's dilemma illustrates the reality faced by policymakers who must pursue domestic and foreign policy objectives that are inconsistent with each other. Historians are inclined to talk as if either foreign policy or domestic politics hold a primary place in shaping national goals. In Germany in the Weimar period, it is the interplay and conflict between domestic and foreign policy that is most important.

Within Germany, attempts to regulate the capital imports from 1924–29 illuminated two central and related themes: the growing social conflict and the reemergence of a government active in influencing the national economy. The depression of 1925–26 led to a reversal of the contraction in government spending that had been a key victory for conservatives during the stabilization crisis. As government spending grew in the late twenties, conservative disenchantment with the Weimar Republic focused on restricting the state's influence in the economy. Despite the fact that government provided extensive aid to industry and agriculture, leaders in these powerful sectors issued increasingly shrill denunciations of the state. Growing government spending and deficits from 1927–29 not only undermined Germany's foreign policy, they also became the focus of the social conflicts within Germany that would destroy the Weimar Republic.

But the growth of the German government was far from a unique phenomena. All across Europe and in the United States, attempts were underway to redefine the role of the state in a modern economy. The Weimar Republic led the way toward the creation of modern welfare capitalism backed by a powerful and interventionist government. Yet even as Weimar pushed into the forefront of state economic activity, the Weimar state was the most unstable of the West European governments. In part it was this very weakness that led the German government to offer subsidies and support to a broad range of special interest groups. Weakness, not strength, led to the expansion of the state in the mid nineteen twenties, and growing resentments against this expansion led to the final assault on the Weimar system when the depression discredited the state in the early thirties.

The nineteen twenties were a period of transition in modern capitalism from the relatively open market liberalism of the nineteenth century to the welfare statism of the post-World War Two era. Neither the political left nor the political right was prepared to accept this new role of the state. The right continued to contain a strong faction that believed that the reforms of the revolutionary period could be repealed and workers could be returned to their absolute dependence on the factory owner. The left, even in the SPD, continued to talk as if they still believed in revolution long after the party had in reality given up its revolutionary ambitions. Both the left and the right viewed Weimar politics as a zero sum game where every benefit for one side was a loss for the other. Without real support from either side, Weimar's emergent welfare state tottered along for several years, but was finally and fatally undermined by the inability to reconcile the extremes or to establish the solid tax base needed to finance the new state activities safely.[1]

In a society where powerful interest groups view every tax on themselves as a mortal blow to their existence and view every subsidy or benefit to other groups as imposing an intolerable burden upon themselves, the chances of political stability are obviously slim.[2] In this environment, it was easier to increase unemployment pay, government salaries, or subsidies to industry and agriculture than it was to increase the taxes needed to pay for these grants. It takes time and a willingness to make political compromises to stabilize the expanded state and neither was available to the Weimar Republic.

Indeed, political moderates joined reactionaries in regarding the new and larger state as a major contributor to the final economic crisis to beset the Weimar Republic. With the onset of the Great Depression in 1929, conservatives seemed to have history on their side when they surveyed the faltering German economy and declared that the uncontrolled government deficits had created this economic disaster.[3] Socialists as well accepted this lesson of history and agreed that only balanced budgets could serve Germany's vital international and domestic interests. Thus, in the face of the mounting depression, efforts to reduce government spending and increase taxes were doubled and redoubled. The deficits of 1926–30, built up during a period of relative prosperity, had never been adequately financed, justified by economic theory, or politically accepted. They had become an immense liability that Germany was forced to confront at its economic and political nadir.

By 1928–29, Germany's financial weakness had become a major independent constraint on government attempts to stabilize Weimar's social system. The state's inability to finance its deficits gave growing power to the Reichsbank, the Reparations Agent, and foreign bankers. This financial and international dependence undermined any last hope of holding the Weimar Republic together.

The inability of industrialists and agrarians to preserve their control over the Weimar state and the inability of the left to consolidate their gains led to a political stalemate by 1929. In this stalemated system, the greatest weakness was not that any one group exercised dominant power, but that a number of interests were engaged in a life-and-death struggle over the body of the German state.[4] Realizing this, it becomes more understandable why, after years of irresolvable conflict and frustration, Germany could turn to the Nazi solution. Offering at least verbal concessions to almost everyone, Hitler promised a social peace which had eluded Germany for fifteen years. The realization both that the Nazi state was dedicated above all else to its own form of anarchic political power and that it would nearly cost Germany its very existence as a sovereign state led post-World War II leaders to seek the very settlements and compromises which had not emerged in the 1920s. The social conflicts of the twenties and the terrible cost of not finding compromise solutions are the direct antecedents of the cooperation which produced the stability of post-World War II West Germany.

Against the background of domestic pressures shaping German economic policy, it is not surprising that the United States, despite its enormous financial power, found it difficult to alter German policies along lines desired by Americans. But the nature of American policymaking also made a major contribution to reducing American ability to use its power to gain its ends. The Republican administration was reluctant to use government to make decisions that could be made by the free market. The leading, and indeed sole, advocate of an active government policy was Herbert Hoover. Hoover had no sympathy for the big New York banks and feared that their excessive foreign lending would lead to loans with little chance of future repayment. He was anxious to reduce the flow of American capital abroad and to use the government in an advisory role to see that only sound loans were made. But Hoover was also concerned that government not dominate the economy or accept responsibility for guaranteeing the security of any foreign loans. Too active a policy might lead to an obligation on the part of the government to act as international collection agent for the New York banks in the event of future defaults. With Benjamin Strong at the Federal Reserve Bank opposed to any government regulation of the banks while the Treasury and State Departments were worried about loan security but reluctant to fight against Strong, Hoover's ambiguous feelings produced a policy of allowing the banks and the market to regulate American capital flows.

For the most part, private American banks were left alone to undertake the task of international financial stabilization in the second half of the nineteen twenties. But the bankers were interested in making money, not policy. In several isolated cases, New York bankers tried to impose political conditions on German borrowers before making a loan. But American attempts to force German heavy industry to accept a commercialization of the Dawes Plan or to force city governments to give up their control of public utilities failed when competing American banks offered to make the loans without the political strings. Competition and division among the bankers left Germans free to use the loans as they saw fit.

This pattern of American unwillingness to impose restraints or regulations on Germany was reversed when the Reparations Agent, Parker Gilbert, became concerned about German municipal borrowing. By later 1927, Gilbert, acting as a technical expert most concerned with reparation payments, had assumed a dominant role in American policy formation despite the fact that he held no official position in the United States government. In the absence of anyone else willing to make hard political decisions, Gilbert used his ties to Secretary of Treasury Andrew Mellon, the Governor of the Federal Reserve Bank of New York, and the senior partners in J. P. Morgan, as well as his "moral" authority as enforcer of the Dawes Plan to pressure Germany to change its policies. Gilbert's conviction that excessive public borrowing was undermining German fiscal stability and thwarting the payment of reparations led him to risk an international crisis in order to reverse German spending habits.

Gilbert viewed his job in much the same way that the Dawes Committee had viewed theirs. As financial experts uninterested in politics, these orthodox bankers hoped to cut the gordian knot that had bound international relations since 1919. Like the Dawes Plan experts, Gilbert assumed that there was some real, absolute amount that Germany could afford to pay in reparations and that this issue was one that had to be solved by economic experts without regard to political considerations.

In his devotion to this task, Gilbert was willing to push harder than any other American to counter what he regarded as German irresponsibility. In effect, Gilbert took the position assumed by the International Monetary Fund in the 1980s. As a proponent of fiscal responsibility, Gilbert, like the IMF, represented the school of international bankers who viewed respect for the sanctity of contracts as the primary responsibility of all governments. The complex and deadly links between international finance and domestic politics were not the concern of these monetary authorities.

Appendix

1. German National Product and Government Spending
   (1913 prices, billions of RM)

	1925	1926	1927	1928	1929	1930	1931	1932
Net Social product	45.5	43.7	51.8	53	53.6	50.3	45.2	41
Government spending	11.8	14.4	15.2	16.2	16.5	16.8	15.8	14.6
Government income	11	13.1	14.1	14.6	15.1	15.8	15.5	13.7
Fiscal deficit	.85	1.26	1.16	1.67	1.41	.97	.32	.94
Deficit as % of NSP	1.9 %	2.8 %	2.2 %	3.1 %	2.6 %	1.9 %	.7 %	2.2 %

SOURCE: Peter-Christian Witt, "Finanzpolitik als Verfassungs- und Gesellschaftspolitik," tables 2 and 5. Figures have been rounded.
NOTE: Fiscal year 1925 ends April 31, 1926

2. German Long-Term Bond Issues by Borrower (millions of RM)

	1925		1926		1927		1928
	Issued in Germany	Abroad	Issued in Germany	Abroad	Issued in Germany	Abroad	Issued in Germany
Reich, cities and states	75	654	1,485	788	1,063	331	1,176
Private (excluding mortgages)	79	491	322	659	194	550	285

SOURCE: Enquête-Ausschuss, *Die Reichsbank,* p. 98.

Notes

Abbreviations Used in the Notes

AA: Politisches Archiv des Auswärtigen Amtes-Bonn
BA: Bundesarchiv Koblenz
BHsa: Bayerisches Hauptstaatsarchiv—Munich
DBFP: Documents on British Foreign Policy
FRBNY: Federal Reserve Bank New York
FRUS: Foreign Relations of the United States
HA GHH: Historisches Archiv der Gutehoffnungs hütte
HHPL: Herbert Hoover Presidential Library, West Branch, Iowa

Idw Köln: Institut der Deutschen Wirtschaft Cologne
LA Berlin: Landesarchiv Berlin
NA: National Archives, Washington, D.C.
PRO: Public Records Office, London
RAM: Reich Labor Ministry
RDI: Reichsverband der deutschen Industrie
RFM: Reich Finance Ministry
RK: Reich Chancellory
RWM: Reich Economics Ministry
SAA: Siemens Archiv Akten
SS: State Secretary

Introduction

1. AA WR 14D, vol. 1, telegram Dufour (London) to Berlin, no. 658, 18 October 1924, and in the same file, Ludwig Bendix report no. 73, 20 October 1924.

2. Knut Borchardt, "Real Kredite- und Pfandbriefmarkt im Wandel von 100 Jahren," in Rudolf Haas, Ernst Knacke, and Knut Borchardt, eds., *100 Jahre Rheinische Hypothekenbank.*

3. William Appleman Williams, *The Roots of the Modern American Empire,* and *The Tragedy of American Diplomacy,* esp. ch. 4, "The Legend of Isolationism." Studies supporting and expanding on Williams' general thesis include Carl Parrini, *Heir to Empire: United States Economic Diplomacy 1916–1923,* and Robert Freeman Smith, *The United States and Revolutionary Nationalism in Mexico, 1916–1932.* By far the most complete study in this genre dealing with German-United States relations is by the German historian Werner Link, *Die amerikanische Stabilisierungspolitik in Deutschland 1921–32.*

4. Stephen Schuker, *The End of French Predominance in Europe: The Financial Crisis of 1924 and the Adoption of the Dawes Plan;* Melvyn Leffler, *The Elusive Quest: America's Pursuit of European Stability and French Security, 1919–1933;* Michael Hogan, *Informal Entente: The Private Structure of Cooperation in Anglo-American Economic Diplomacy, 1918–1928,* and Frank Costigliola, "The United States and the Reconstruction of Germany in the 1920's."

1. Power and Politics in the Weimar Republic

1. Charles Maier, *Recasting Bourgeois Europe: Stabilization in France, Germany, and Italy in the Decade after World War I;* Claus-Dieter Krohn, *Stabilisierung und ökonomische Interessen: Die Finanzpolitik des deutschen Reiches 1923–1927;* Gerald Feldman, *Iron and Steel in the German Inflation 1916–1923;* and Gerald Feldman, "The Social and Economic Policies of German Big Business, 1918–29."

2. On the Städtetag, see Otto Ziebill, *Geschichte des deutschen Städtetages;* on Böss, see Christian Engeli, *Gustav Böss Oberbürgermeister von Berlin 1921 bis 1930;* on Landmann see Dieter Rebentisch, *Ludwig Landmann: Frankfurter Oberbürgermeister der Weimarer Republik;* on the broad political alliance in Hamburg, see Ursula Büttner, *Hamburg in der Staats- und Wirtschaftskrise 1928–1931;* on municipal policy in general see the articles in Karl-Heinrich Hansmeyer, ed., *Kommunale Finanzpolitik in der Weimarer Republik,* and Wolfgang Hofmann, *Zwischen Rathaus und Reichskanzlei.*

3. Engeli, p. 167.

4. *Ibid.,* p. 134 and pp. 139–140. Engeli notes that already in 1918 Berlin was in a catastrophic financial position. See also *Denkschrift über das Arbeitsgebiet und die Tätigkeit der Beratungsstelle für Auslandskredite vom 1. Jan. 1925 bis zum 30. September 1926,* in *Verhandlungen des Reichstags,* Anlagen zu den Stenographischen Berichten, III Wahlperiode 1924/27, Band 413, Drucksache no. 2897, p. 3.

5. BA R431/2324, Geschäftsbericht des Preussischen Städtetages 1 April 1922–1 April 1925.

6. Engeli, p. 168.

7. Krohn, pp. 64 and 146, Peter-Christian Witt, "Reichsfinanzminister und Reichsfinanzverwaltung 1918–1924," pp. 19–22, 60–61.

8. Bernd Weisbrod, *Schwerindustrie in der Weimarer Republik,* p. 191 note 111 and p. 375. Also Dieter Hertz-Eichenrode, *Wirtschaftskrise und Arbeitsbeschaffung,* p. 89.

9. BA R431/962, letter Reichsbank directors to Reich President, 4 December 1923.

10. AA, RM 45, vol. 1. Telegrams from Sthamer (London) to AA, no. 625, 7 December 1923, and no. 630, 8 December 1923. Also Note by von Maltzen, 14 December 1923.

11. Otto Braun, *Von Weimar zu Hitler,* p. 64.

12. *Akten der Reichskanzlei . . . Die Kabinette Marx I und II*, 1:146, n. 1.

13. BA R431/962, Reichsbank Directors to State Secretary in the Reichskanzlei, 17 December 1923.

14. *Kreuz-Zeitung*, 24 December 1923, clipping in BA R431/962, p. 102.

15. See letter from Reichsbank employee Max Immanuel to Carl Severing, 2 August 1948, in Ebert Stiftung, NL Severing, Mappe 106.

16. BA R431/962, p. 128, Vermerk 6 August 1926. In the most recent study of Schacht, Heinz Pentzlin argues that the charges against Schacht were entirely groundless and based on a personality clash with his superior in Belgium. Unfortunately, Pentzlin uses very little documentation and cites no source for this information. His study is further flawed in being almost entirely an apology for Schacht, who was Pentzlin's superior in the Economics Ministry during the 1930s. Heinz Pentzlin, *Hjalmar Schacht; Leben und Wirken einer umstrittenen Persönlichkeit*, pp. 27–28, 60. For Pentzlin's relationship with Schacht, pp. 7–8.

17. Schacht, *Account Settled*, p. 13.

18. Paul Silverberg, *Reden und Schriften*, p. 49. Speech before the general meeting of the Reichsverbandes der Deutschen Industrie, Dresden, 4 September 1926; and p. 78, speech at the general meeting of der Vereinigung von Banken und Bankiers in Rheinland und Westfalen, Cologne, 1 March 1926.

19. BA, NL Koch-Weser/34, p. 249, Vermerk 12 June 1926.

20. Reichsverband der Deutschen Industrie, Geschäftliche Mitteilungen, 2 October 1928, no. 22, p. 181.

21. Gerd Hardach, "Reichsbankpolitik und Wirtschaftliche Entwicklung 1924–1931."

22. Knut Borchardt, "Real Kredite- und Pfandbriefmarkt im Wandel von 100 Jahren," in Rudolf Haas, Ernst Knacke, and Knut Borchardt, eds., *100 Jahre Reinische Hypothekenbank*, p. 207.

23. Enquête-Ausschuss, *Die Reichsbank*, pp. 61–63.

24. Harold James, "The Causes of the German Banking Crisis of 1931," table 1, p. 76. The American Council of Foreign Bond Holders set America's share of the German loans at $1.25 billion. See the article by Dr. W. Skaupy, a lawyer for the American bondholders, "Der Bereinigung deutscher Dollarbonds in den Vereinigten Staaten," in *Die Betriebs Berater*, Heft 15, 30 May 1954, pp. 458–459. Loan expert Robert Kuczynski's final summation also is very close to this, at $1.29 billion. See Kuczynski, *Bankers' Profits from German Loans*, pp. 4–5. In Department of Commerce notice, "German Borrowing in U.S. Shown in Commerce Department Study," Grosvenor Jones, head of the Finance Division reported that prior to the Young Plan loan, Germany had taken $1.179 billion in the United States. Adding in the Young loan of $85 million, Jones would yield a total of $1.26 billion. A copy of this report is in AA, WR 2A, vol. 4. British and Dutch shares were reported in *The Economist*, 22 August 1931, Annex 6, p. 7.

25. *The Economist*, 22 August 1931, Annex 5, p. 6. Rolf Lüke, p. 216, estimated that Germany's short-term debt to the United States was 1.7 billion RM while Cleona Lewis, *America's Stake in International Investments*, p. 388, estimated a much higher sum of $3 billion or 12.6 billion RM.

26. *Kapitalbildung und Investitionen in Deutschland 1924–1928*. VZKf sonderheft 22, p. 25.

27. These figures are reached using Kuczynski's estimate of German borrowing in the United States from 1925 to 1929 of $1.197 billion, and estimates in the Chase

Economic Bulletin 81 (14 March 1930), 10(1):8, that in the same period foreign securities sold in the United States were worth $5.869 billion.

28. Carl-Ludwig Holtfrerich, *Die deutsche Inflation 1914–1923. Ursachen und Folgen in internationaler Perspektive*, pp. 266 and 273.

29. Untersuchungsausschuss für das Bankwesen 1933, "Wirkungen des Krieges und der Kriegsfolgen auf das deutsche Bankwesen," by Dr. Franz Grüger, p. 12, in BA RD51/8, and Constantino Bresciani-Turroni, *The Economics of Inflation: A Study of Currency Depreciation in Post-War Germany 1914–1923*, pp. 279–280, 352.

30. Grüger, in *Untersuchungsausschuss für das Bankwesen*, p. 13. Hjalmar Schacht also noted the early loss of bank reserves but emphasized the continued losses right up to the stabilization. See his comments in memo by Finlayson of conversation with Schacht, 1 May 1924, in PRO, FO–371/9793.

31. Grüger, in *Untersuchungsausschuss für das Bankwesen*, p. 15.

32. Krohn, *Stabilisierung*, p. 138.

33. Theodore Balderston emphasizes this problem in "The Origins of Economic Instability in Germany 1924–1930. Market Forces versus Economic Policy."

34. See, e.g., Rolf Lüke, *Von der Stabilisierung zur Krise*, pp. 40–44; Carl Schmidt, *German Business Cycles 1924–1933*, pp. 72–73; H. G. Moulton and C. E. McGuire, *Germany's Capacity to Pay*, p. 122; James W. Angell, *The Recovery of Germany*, p. 115; and *Kapitalbildung und Investitionen in Deutschland 1924–1928*, VZKf sonderheft 22, p. 23.

35. Feldman, *Iron and Steel*, and Gerald D. Feldman, "The Large Firm in the German Industrial System: The M.A.N., 1900–1925," pp. 252–253.

36. Harold James has pointed out that in the case of textiles and agriculture, part of the explanation for German bankers being willing to grant large loans was that with the Reichsbank unwilling to act as the lender of last resort after 1924, the banks were forced to loan to firms which could issue bills against real goods and had the political power to force the government to aid them in the event of economic problems. Harold James, "Did the Reichsbank Draw the Right Conclusions from the Great Inflation?" pp. 21–22.

37. Carl-Ludwig Holtfrerich, "Amerikanischer Kapitalexport und Wiederaufbau der deutschen Wirtschaft 1919–1923 im Vergleich zu 1924–29," pp. 499–500.

38. Allied Powers Reparations Commission, Transfer Committee Economic Service notes, note 42, by Constantino Bresciani-Turroni, 12 April 1927.

39. Schmidt, pp. 72–73.

40. Holtfrerich, "Amerikanischer Kapitalexport."

41. German bankers told Stresemann that 6 milliard RM had been sent to Germany by foreigners, and about half of this had been destroyed in the inflation. See comment by Director Mosler in AA NL Stresemann 278 "Visit from Representatives of the Banks" (Mosler, Goldschmidt and Wassermann) 11 Feb. 1925.

42. Holtfrerich, "Amerikanischer Kapitalexport."

43. See also Erich Welter, *Die Ursachen des Kapitalmangels in Deutschland*. Welter argues that on the supply side, the capital shortage in the mid-1920s was largely caused by high taxes which reduced savings, by reparations payments and by high wages which cut the income of the rich who would have saved a large share of their income. On the demand side, he emphasizes lack of investment during the war and its resultant increase after stabilization, and misinvestment in agriculture. He doesn't mention misinvestment in industry or capital flight out of Germany.

44. Schucker, *The End of French Predominance*.

45. Leffler, *The Elusive Quest*, p. 87.

46. J. P. Morgan suggested the actual procedure used, whereby the Reparations Commission appointed representatives to the Dawes Committee and asked the American government to permit American citizens to sit. Germany also asked Washington to permit American participation, so that all interested states joined in the request. PRO, T-160/178/F.6970, 1:24, telegram to Crewe, 3 Dec. 1923, and pp. 50–51, Chilton to London, 11 Dec. 1923.

47. PRO, T-160/178/F.6970, 1:28. Foreign Office minute, 24 Nov. 1923.

48. AA, RM 27, vol. 3, letter Wiedfeldt (Washington) to Maltzen (Berlin), 6 November 1923.

49. Detailed narrative and analytical discussions of the Dawes Plan negotiations are available in a number of recent works: Stephen A. Schuker, *The End of French Predominance in Europe;* Melvyn P. Leffler, *The Elusive Quest;* and Werner Link, *Stabilisierung.*

50. AA, Ritter-Rep, vol. 1, copy of W. Rep. 3811–memo by Hamm to Reich Chancellor, I.G. no. 1619, July 1924.

51. AA, RM 27, vol. 4, telegram Wiedfeldt to Berlin, no. 167, 14 June 1924; Schubert to Washington, no. 140, 19 June 1924; and Schubert to London, no. 308, about 30 June 1924.

52. See the exchange of letters between Norman and J. P. Morgan in mid-June 1924 in Lamont papers, file 176–10.

53. The files in the Lamont papers 176–8 and 176–9 are filled with criticism of the plan, its impracticality and likelihood of failure. See especially memorandum by Leffingwell, "The Dawes Report," 18 April 1924, in 176–8, and Lamont to J. P. Morgan, 21 April 1924, in 176–9.

54. J. P. Morgan to J. S. Morgan Jr., 3 July 1924; Morrow to Grenfell, 8 July 1924, and J. C. Grenfell and Lamont to J. P. Morgan, 8 July 1924, all in Lamont papers 176–11. For a more complete discussion of the problems faced in naming the Agent General, see Schuker, pp. 284–289, and Kenneth Paul Jones, "Discord and Collaboration: Choosing an Agent General for Reparations."

55. Lamont to Morgan, 12 August 1924, in Lamont papers 176–25.

56. AA, RM 27, vol. 4, Maltzan (Berlin) to Botschaft (Paris), no. 672, 22 August 1924.

57. AA, RM 5, vol. 20, Ruppel (Paris) to AA, no. 419, 27 August 1924, and vol. 19, Sthamer to AA, no. 523, 18 August 1924.

58. Leffingwell to Whigham, 13 August 1924, Lamont papers 176–25.

59. Heinrich Köhler, *Lebenserinerungen des Politikers und Staatsmannes 1878-1949,* pp. 241–242.

60. BA R431/2359, Note by Min. Dir. Schäffer of conversation with Marcus Wallenberg, 28 September 1925, and BA R431/275, memo SS in Reichskanzlei to Min. Rat. Dr. Wachmann, 28 October 1925.

61. BA, NL Moldenhauer, 3, p. 28.

62. PRO, T-160/262/F.10457, vol. 3, Lindsay to Leith Ross, 28 December 1927.

63. Schuker, pp. 264–265.

64. Stresemann speech to the Central Committee of the DVP, 6 July 1924. BA R45II/39, pp. 285, 297–299, and 309.

65. Ritter memo "Endsumme," written 26 or 27 August 1927, in AA, RM 5, vol. 20.

66. Stresemann to Central Committee of the DVP, 6 July 1924, BA R45II/39, pp. 285–287.

67. Robert P. Grathwol, *Stresemann and the DNVP*, provides a detailed discussion of the events leading up to the critical vote. pp. 32–52. See also Henry A. Turner, *Stresemann and the Politics of the Weimar Republic*, p. 173.

68. S. V. O. Clarke, *Central Bank Cooperation*, pp. 74–78.

69. Costigliola, "The United States and the Reconstruction of Germany," p. 494.

70. Robert Kuczynski, "Die Reparationsanleihe," in *Finanzpolitische Korrespondenz*, 10 April 1925, AA, WR 140, vol. 1.

71. AA, WR 140, vol. 1, telegram Dufour (London) to Berlin, no. 658, 18 October 1924; and in the same file, Ludwig Bendix report no. 73, 20 October 1924.

72. *Ibid.*, Ludwig Bendix report no. 73, 20 October 1924, and J. P. Morgan and Company to Morgan Harjes and Company, 14 October 1924, in Lamont papers 178–6.

2. The Origins of Loan Control

1. Carl Holtfrerich, "Amerikanischer Kapitalexport und Wiederaufbau der deutschen Wirtschaft 1919–23 im Vergleich zu 1924–29."

2. Link, *Amerikanische Stabilisierungspolitik*, and "Der Amerikanische Einfluss auf die Weimarer Republik in der Dawesplanphase (Elemente eines penetrierten Systems)," in Hans Mommsen et al., eds., *Industrielles System und politische Entwicklung in der Weimarer Republik*, vol. 2, emphasizes the American pressures but ignores Germany's own interests served by loan regulation.

3. A number of works have dealt with Hoover's role in the government and his economic and social visions. See especially Ellis Hawley et al. in J. Joseph Huthmacher and Warren I. Susman, eds., *Herbert Hoover and the Crisis of American Capitalism*; Gary Dean Best, *The Politics of American Individualism: Herbert Hoover in Transition, 1918–1921*; Joseph Brandes, *Herbert Hoover and Economic Diplomacy*; Joan Hoff Wilson, *American Business and Foreign Policy 1920–1933*; Carl Parrini, *Heir to Empire: United States Economic Diplomacy, 1916–1923*; Evan B. Metcalf, "Secretary Hoover and the Emergence of Macroeconomic Management".

4. See especially Hawley and the other articles in Huthmacher and Susman; also Robert Sobel, *Herbert Hoover at the Onset of the Great Depression 1929–1930*.

5. Herbert Hoover, *The Memoirs of Herbert Hoover*, 2:13.

6. FRBNY, Strong Papers 012.5, letter Gilbert to Strong, 21 May 1921.

7. Wilson, p. 106; Parrini, pp. 185–186.

8. Wilson, p. 106.

9. NA RG 59 800.51/503 letter Morgan to Harding, 6 June 1921; copy contained as enclosure in letter Lamont to Kellogg, 6 March 1925.

10. FRBNY, Strong Papers 012.5, Gilbert to Strong, 21 May 1921.

11. *Ibid.*, 28 May 1921.

12. *Ibid.*, Strong to Gilbert, 13 June 1921.

13. See for an example of this view, Strong to Mellon 21 September 1925 in NA RG 39 Box 220, file Strong, Benjamin, correspondence re France—Sept.-Oct. 1925.

14. See banker testimony before the United States Senate Committee on Finance: *Hearings pursuant to Senate Resolution 19 on the Sale of Foreign Bonds and Securities in the United States*, pts. 1–4.

15. Robert Kuczynski documents the profits in *Bankers' Profits from German Loans;* the refusal to accept responsibility is the central theme of Charles Kindleberger's excellent study, *The World in Depression 1929–1939.*

16. Parrini, *Heir to Empire,* pp. 186–187.

17. Herbert Hoover Presidential Library (HHPL), Commerce Papers, OF-State Department, misc., Hughes to Hoover, 7 December 1921.

18. *Ibid.,* Mellon to Hughes, 9 December 1921; Hoover to Hughes, 13 December 1921, and Hoover to Hughes, 31 December 1921. For Hughes' opposition see Hughes to Hoover, 24 December 1921, in the same file and in HHPL Commerce Papers, personal-Hughes, Charles E., letter Hughes to Hoover, 16 December 1921.

19. Hoover, *Memoirs,* 3:85–86.

20. HHPL, Foreign Loans São Paulo, Brazil, memorandum Jones to Hoover, 1 April 1922.

21. *Ibid.,* Jones to Hoover, 5 April 1922.

22. *Ibid.,* Commerce Papers, OF-State Department, misc., letter Hughes to Hoover, 20 April 1922, and the memorandum by Strong in HHPL, Foreign Loans São Paulo, Brazil, as enclosure to Hughes letter of 20 April 1922.

23. FRBNY, Strong Papers 011.1, Strong letter to Hughes, 9 June 1922.

24. HHPL, Commerce Official-foreign loans, São Paulo, Brazil, letter Hoover to Hughes, 29 April 1922; and Hoover telegram to Willis K. Clark, 8 March 1922.

25. *Ibid.,* Hoover letter to Hughes, 29 April 1922.

26. *Ibid.*

27. *Ibid.*

28. See especially Holtfrerich, "Amerikanischer Kapitalexport"; also the older but still outstanding work of Constantino Bresciani-Turroni, *The Economics of Inflation: A Study of Currency Depreciation in Post-War Germany,* pp. 251–252.

29. HHPL, Gen. Acc 300-Fed. Res. Bank of N.Y., Strong-Norman Correspondence, letter Strong to Norman, 9 July 1924.

30. Wilson, *American Business and Foreign Policy,* p. 113.

31. See the memorandum reviewing the loan policy by Grosvenor Jones, 8 February 1929, in NA RG 151, 640-Foreign Loans-Germany.

32. Hoover, *Memoirs,* 2:88.

33. *Deutsche Bergwerks Zeitung,* 31 July 1924.

34. Public Records Office (PRO), FO-371/9793. Memo by Findlayson of conversation with Oberregierungsrat Husslein of the German Treasury, 2 May 1924.

35. AA, SW FW2A, 17 April 1924; 6 May and 4 April 1924.

36. HA (Köln) 902–207-1, p. 173, 15 November 1923.

37. *Deutsche Bergwerks-Zeitung,* 7 July 1924.

38. FRBNY, Strong Papers 1012.5, Strong letter to Gates McGarrah, 24 November 1924.

39. BA-NL Silverberg, vol. 299, "Aufzeichnung über die Sitzung der Finanzierungskommission" (of the RDI), 24 October 1924.

40. HHPL, Commerce Papers, Bureau of Foreign and Domestic Commerce, Dr. Klein, daily report to the Secretary, 13 June 1924.

41. AA, SW FW2A, Foreign Office Circular to RDI, Deutscher Industrie und Handelstag, Deutscher Städtetag und Deutschen Landwirtschaftsrat, 22 July 1924.

42. For Severing's control of the Prussian bureaucracy, see Hagen Schulze, *Otto Braun: oder, Preussens demokratische Sendung,* pp. 302–303, 566–567.

43. Stuttgart, E151dI-54. Württemberg Girozentrale Rundschreiben no. 323, 22 September 1924.

44. Stuttgart, E151dI–54. Letter Prussian Interior and Finance Ministers to the "Ober- und Regierungspräsidenten," 11 October 1924. The order was reported in *Vossische Zeitung*, 14 October 1924.

45. AA, SW FW2A, Prussian Ministry of the Interior Ministerial paper no. 42, 21 October 1924; and Stuttgart, E151dI–54, p. 143.

46. BA R2/2000, "Referentenaufzeichnung über die Frage der Auslandsanleihen der Länder und Kommunalverbände," RFM Abteilung 5, 16 October 1924.

47. See, e.g., Link, *Stabilisierungspolitik*, pp. 399–400, 441–442.

48. Quoted in Hermann Dietrich-Tröltsch, "Kommunalkredit, Reparationen und föderalistisches Prinzip," p. 589.

49. Claus-Dieter Krohn, *Stabilisierung und ökonomische Interessen: Die Finanzpolitik des Deutschen Reiches 1923–1927*, p. 97.

50. BA R2/2000, note dated 22 October 1924 on meeting held 17 October.

51. *Ibid.*, Reichsbank Directors to Reich Finance Minister, 17 October 1924.

52. DZA Preuss. Min. des Innern #227, Bd. 1, Beiheft 11, cited in Dietrich-Tröltsch dissertation, p. 413, n. 1.

53. BA R43 I/640, pp. 342–345. Protokoll über die Sitzung des Zentralausschusses der Reichsbank, 28 October 1924.

54. BA R2/2000, Vermerk, 25 October 1924, summary of conference held 23 October 1924; Reich Finance Minister to state governments, 25 October 1924. Stuttgart, E151dI–54; and Prussian Finance Minister to states, Reichsbank, RFM and RWM, 29 October 1924, AA, SW FW2A.

55. Stuttgart, E130b–1340, Württemberg representative to the Reichsrat, report to the Württemberg Finance Ministry, 31 October 1924.

56. BHsa-MF67540—notes on the meeting in RFM, 31 October 1924.

57. BA R2/2001, Reich Economics Minister, 1 November 1924, "Foreign loans and the danger of inflation."

58. BA R2/2000, Aktenvermerk W. Rep. 5880. (unsigned, undated—about 1 November 1924).

59. BA R2/2000, "Auszug aus dem Protokoll der Sitzung des Reichsministeriums vom 31 Oktober 1924."

60. Stuttgart, E130b–1340, "Sitzung des Staatsministeriums Stuttgart," 6 November 1924.

61. Kabinette Protokolle. From records of the German Foreign Office received by the Department of State, 1756/D762755. See also Heidegret Klöter, "Der Anteil der Länder an der Wirtschaftspolitik der Weimarer Republik 1919–1933," pp. 166–175.

62. NA, RG 151, Box 2965, undated report by Warren D. Robbins. Britain's financial expert in Berlin, H. C. F. Finlayson, was very indignant about the size and unproductive nature of the Anhalt loan and approved the government's taking charge. See report by Finlayson, 1 November 1924, in PRO-T160/216F. 7969, vol. 1.

63. BA R43 I/2236, p. 196. Reich representative in Munich to the Reich Chancellery, 3 November 1924. See also the formal protest of the Bavarian People's Party over the use of Article 48, in BA R2/2000, p. 51.

64. Stuttgart, E130b–1340, Württemberg Gesandtschaft München, 6 November 1924.

65. LA Berlin, DST B3682, letter DST to Deutschen Sparkassen und Giroverband, 22 November 1924.

66. BHsa Ma103859, Krausneck, 10 November 1924.

67. Württemberg did not regard the use of Article 48 as illegal. See Stuttgart, E130b–1340, "Sitzung des Staatsministeriums Stuttgart, 6 November 1924.

68. BA R43 I/2358, letter Luther to State Secretary in the Reich Chancellery, 26 November 1924.

69. BA R2/2000, note by Fischer, 8 November 1924; and German Consulate (New York) telegram to Foreign Office, 5 November 1924.

70. NA RG151, Box 2965, G. Jones to Stokes, 21 November 1924.

71. Letter Hughes to Mellon and Hoover, 15 November 1924, NA RG 59 862.51/ 1839.

72. AA, SW FW2A, Luther telegram to German ambassador to U.S., 14 November 1924.

73. Dietrich-Tröltsch, pp. 589–591.

74. BHsa MF 67540, Wolf to BsMdF, 11 November 1924; BA R2/2000, meeting between the states and RFM, 23 December 1924, and Kabinette Protokolle 1756/ D762779–D762788.

75. *Verhandlungen des Reichstags* (1924), 384:626.

76. See memo in AA, WR 2A, vol. 3, dated 19 May 1928.

77. BA R2/2000, Reich Economics Minister, no. 2070, 15 April 1924, letter to national organizations of industry, trade, and banking warning them to avoid loans that did not generate their own repayment in foreign currency.

78. *Ibid.*, note on the conference to discuss private foreign credits held 12 January 1925; and Aufzeichnung, 14 January 1925.

79. Idw Köln-II, "Geschäftliche Mitteilungen für die Mitgleider des RDI," 14 February 1925, p. 19. See also the circular sent by the Zentralverband des Deutschen Bank -und Bankiergewerbes to member banks, 2 February 1925, copy in BHsa Mwi 453.

80. BA R43 I/633, Reich Finance Minister to State Secretary in the Reich Chancellery, 12 February 1925; and unsigned memo to Reich Chancellor, 12 February 1925.

81. BA R2/2000, Husslein report, 9 March 1925.

82. *Verhandlungen des Reichstags* (1924), 384:626, and Enquête-Ausschuss, *Die Reichsbank*, p. 46.

83. Denkschrift über das Arbeitsgebiet und die Tätigkeit der Beratungsstelle für Auslandskredite vom 1 Januar 1925 bis zum 30 September 1926, in *Verhandlungen des Reichstags*, Anlagen zu den stenographischen Berichten, III Wahlperiode 1924/ 27, Band 413, Drucksache no. 2897, p. 10.

84. *Ibid.*, p. 3, and statement by Norten in Enquête-Ausschuss, *Die Reichsbank*, pp. 96–98.

85. BA R2/2000, "Stellungnahme der Industrie- und Handelskammer zu Altona zu der Verordnung . . . vom 1 November 1924."

86. The social issues of "Kalte Sozializerung" or more colloquially "creeping communism" in American parlance are taken up extensively in the next chapter.

3. Politics and Foreign Loans, 1925

1. LA Berlin, DST-B3682, letter Stadtdirektor Gera to DST, 25 March 1925.

2. *Ibid.*, Adenauer to DST, 23 December 1924; this file contains a number of letters, but see especially Girozentrale Kommunalbank für die Provinz Sachsen, Thüringen und Anhalt, 16 December 1924; and DST to Oberbürgermeister Gera, 29 March 1925.

3. Allied Powers Reparations Commission, Transfer Committee Economic Service, n. 47; besides Cologne, Berlin's loan was also only short term. LA Berlin, DST-B3682, letter Magistrat Berlin to DST, 28 April 1925.

4. Robert Kuczynski, *Deutsche Anleihen im Ausland, 1924–1928*, p. 30. A letter from the Reichsschuldenverwaltung to the Reich Finance Minister, 18 February 1925, reports a loan of the city of Saarbrücken which is not reported elsewhere. BA R2/2001.

5. FRBNY, C261, German government, letter Strong to Stewart, 11 May 1925.

6. Thyssen, A1–846, report on "The Thyssen Concern," 1924.

7. Thyssen, A1–849, letter Thyssen AG to Barth, 8 April 1924.

8. Thyssen, A1–847, memo of conference 18 December 1924 of Deutsch-Lux, Phoenix, Stinnes, and Thyssen.

9. *Ibid.*, letter Rabes (New York) to Thyssen, 22 November 1924.

10. *Ibid.*, letter Fiske (of Dillon Read) to Vögler, 26 November 1924.

11. *Ibid.*, Tagebuch Walter Barth, pp. 4 and 5–6.

12. *Ibid.*, pp. 5–6.

13. SAA 11/Lb 946, vol. 2, letter Köttgen to Siemens, 21 October 1924.

14. Thyssen, A1–847, Tagebuch Barth, entries for 9 and 16 December, and in the same file letter Rabes and Barth to Clarence Dillon, 16 December 1924.

15. Thyssen, A1–848, letter Appleton, Buttler, and Rice to Rabes, 13 January 1925; Thyssen, A1–847, letter August Thyssen Hütte Gewerkschaft to Price Waterhouse and Co., 13 March 1925.

16. Thyssen, A1–847, Tagebuch Barth.

17. Siemens also used other banks to pressure Dillon Read into better terms. See Haller Aktennotiz, 4 December 1925, in SAA 11/Lb 946 vol. 2.

18. See AA, SW FW2, vol. 2, telegram Maltzen to Ritter, no. 147, 11 September 1925; Simon (AA) to Kastl, 14 September 1925; Kastl to Simon, 7 October 1925; RWM letter IB no. 11539 of 9 October 1925, and RFM to AA V.C. 14763, 22 October 1925.

19. Most recently see Frank Costigliola, "The United States and the Reconstruction of Germany in the 1920's," pp. 494–496.

20. HA GHH 4001012000/15 telegram Harrison to Reusch, 11 March 1925; BA R2/2001, Reichsschuldenverwaltung to RFM, 18 February 1925; *Handels-Zeitung des Berliner Tageblatts*, 20 June 1925, article by Dr. Felix Pinner; LA Berlin, DST-B3682, Magistrat Berlin to DST, 28 April 1925; and Gerd Hardach, *Weltmarktorientierung und relative Stagnation*, p. 58.

21. AA Aktengruppe III—Pol. USA Z. D. politik 2, Maltzan to AA, 30 April 1925.

22. BA R43I/634, p. 68. Conference on financial policy, 17 April 1925, and BA R43I/640, p. 369, meeting of the Central Committee of the Reichsbank, 28 July 1925.

23. Carl Böhret, *Aktionen gegen die "Kalte Sozialisierung" 1926–1930; ein Beitrag zum Wirken ökonomischer Einflussverbände in der Weimar Republik*, pp. 24 and 30.

24. Hansmeyer, ed., *Kommunale Finanzpolitik*, p. 174, and Ursula Büttner, *Hamburg in der Staats- und Wirtschaftskrise 1928–31*, pp. 28–35 and 79–82.

25. Otto Ziebill, *Geschichte des deutschen Städtetages*, pp. 233, 240.

26. Hansmeyer, ed., *Kommunale Finanzpolitik*, p. 174.

27. Böhret, *Aktionen gegen die "Kalte Sozialisierung,"* p. 53.

28. Johannes Pfitzner, *Deutschlands Auslandsanleihen*, p. 41.

29. Otto Braun, *Von Weimar zu Hitler*, p. 217.

30. Böhret, *Aktionen gegen die "Kalte Sozialisierung,"* p. 55, and Joseph Schumpeter, *Business Cycles*, 2:760.

31. BA-NL Silverberg 299—RDI Geschäftsführung an die Fachgruppen und Landschaftlichen Verbände des RDI, 28 July 1924.

32. Krohn, p. 138.

33. BA-NL Silverberg 299—"Niederschrift über die Sitzung vom 4 September 1924 des Ausschusses für Bank- und Kreditfragen" of the RDI.

34. BA R11/1423, p. 339. "Zentralverband des deutschen Bank- und Bankier gewerbes an den deutschen Industrie- und Handelstag," 26 November 1925, and BA-NL Silverberg 360, pp. 11–15, letter RDI to members of the executive board etc., 23 June 1926.

35. Böhret, p. 17, and Lüke, p. 227. Both indicate that Schacht probably coined the term and certainly did much to popularize it.

36. See extensive records in BA R11/1423 and BA-NL Silverberg, vol. 360.

37. BA R11/1423, see letters from Handelskammer, Karlsruhe, Nordliche Niederschleisen, etc., and Handelskammer Bremen, 23 April 1926.

38. NA RG151, Box 2966, letter Grosvenor Jones to Hoover, 10 December 1925.

39. BA R11/1423, "Aktennotiz über die Besprechung in Sachen "Kalte Sozialisierung," 16 February 1926; comments by Dr. Sagemeier. The Reich also provided considerable support to industry. By mid 1926, one report listed Reich subsidies and loans to 17 firms or business groups for a total of 171 million RM. See the photocopy entitled "C. Dritte gruppe: Zuwendungen an private Unternehmen" in BA-NL Silverberg 250, pp. 38–40.

40. See Lother Schön, *Studien zur Entwicklung hydroelektrischer Energienutzung: Die Elektrifizierung Irlands* and the comments by C. F. von Siemens to his Aufsichtratssitzung in May 1929, cited in Ernst Waller, *Studien zur Finanzgeschichte des Hauses Siemens*, 5 Tiel, 1918-1945, p. 161.

41. A classic example of this may be found in DVP Party member Heyl's letter to Dingeldy calling for state aid for the Hessian fishing industry. BA NL Dingeldy, 72, p. 202, letter dated 10 July 1926. Leaders of the iron and steel industry were divided on the issue. Peter Klöckner wanted state loans made to Rhine and Ruhr cities for bridge construction as a way to increase demand for steel. Paul Reusch wanted no government interference at all. Weisbrod, *Schwerindustrie*, p. 236.

42. Böhret, *Aktionen gegen die "Kalte Sozialisierung,"* pp. 59, 67, 75, 32, 95.

43. German Consul New York to Foreign Office, 17 October 1924, in AA, SW/FW2A.

44. Wiedfeldt to Foreign Ministry, 15 December 1924, in AA, RM/27, vol. 4. This led Stresemann to attack Wiedfeldt for allowing the statement to go unchallenged. Wiedfeldt, a director of Krupp, and Stresemann hated each other and took nearly any opportunity to blame the other for foreign policy fiascoes with the United States. In this file, see the exchange on the monarchist charge and the uproar when the German embassy in Washington failed to fly its flag at halfmast after Woodrow Wilson's death in 1924.

45. *Journal of Commerce*, 17 October 1924. The announcement was reported to the German Foreign Office the same day by the New York Consulate, in AA, SW FW2A, 17 October 1924.

46. Senate Committee on Finance: Hearings on the Sale of Foreign Bonds, etc. (1932), p. 32.

47. Wiedfeldt believed this meant Morgan was directly taking part in the German loans; see his report to the Foreign Ministry, 15 September 1924, in AA, RM 27, vol. 4.

48. Archdeacon letter to Lippincot and McComas, 19 June 1929, in BA R111/ 218. The records of the Bankers Trust Company's office in Berlin were confiscated during the Second World War and are now available in the Bundesarchiv Koblenz. They provide some interesting details on American financing in Germany, but are particularly strong for the period after 1929.

49. See the "very confidential" memorandum dated 14 February 1931 in BA R431/2392. The close tie between Morgan and Lee, Higginson was personified by George Murnane, who was acting director of Lee, Higginson and one of the directors of Bankers Trust. This did not, however, preclude keen competition between the two firms in seeking to secure German clients.

50. Speech was reported in AA, RM5, vol. 20, Wiedfeldt to AA no. 281, 14 December 1924.

51. Norman H. Davis Papers, Box 27, letter Davis to Cordell Hull, 8 January 1925. Hull made the same accusation in a speech to the House of Representatives, 19 December 1925, *ibid.*

52. AA, Botschaft Washington: Deutsche Anleihen 1, p. 13. Wiedfeldt to AA no. 89, 30 January 1925.

53. Herring's report is in HHPL, Commerce Official, Foreign Loans, Germany, 2 January 1925.

54. Jones to Herring, 20 February 1925, and Herring to Jones, 25 March 1925, NA RG 151, General Records Foreign Loans—Germany—640.

55. NA RG 151, Box 2966, letter G. Jones to Herring, 2 February 1925.

56. NA RG 39, Box 85, *file* G743.2, Hoover to Wadsworth, 4 February 1925.

57. *Ibid.*, note dated 10 February, and Wadsworth letter to Hoover, 14 February 1925. Hoover's hesitation to have the government commit itself too firmly in guaranteeing loans is revealed in a letter from Lewis Einstein, U.S. legation Prague to Kellogg, 16 June 1925, forwarded to Hoover, and Hoover's reply to Kellogg, in HHPL, Commerce Official, Foreign Loans, São Paulo, Brazil.

58. NA, RG 151, Box 2966, letter Grosvenor Jones to Charles E. Herring (Commerce Attaché Berlin), 9 April 1925.

59. Kuczynski, *Deutsche Anleihen im Ausland,* pp. 30–31.

60. NA, RG 151, Box, 2966, memo Herring to Grosvenor Jones, 14 March 1925, and letter Jones to Herring, 24 April 1925.

61. *Ibid.,* Jones letter, and in HHPL, Commerce Official, Foreign Loans, Germany, draft of the letter to U.S. manufacturers, Grosvenor Jones memo "Economic effects of dollar loans to German industry."

62. NA, RG 151, Box 2966, letter Jones to Herring, 9 April 1925, and Jones to Herring, 24 April 1925.

63. *The Chase Economic Bulletin* (8 October 1931); 9(4):7–8.

64. See comments on Herring's report in letter from L. E. Lyon (U.S. Trade Commissioner, London) to Grosvenor Jones, 5 August 1925, NA, RG151, Box 2957.

65. *Papers Relating to the Foreign Relations of the United States* (FRUS), 1925, 2:174–175.

66. *Ibid.,* p. 175.

67. William Castle, head of the West European Section of the State Department, had been worrying about the German loans for months. See his letter to Grew, 4 December 1924, in NA RG 59 862.51. HHPL, Commerce Official, Foreign Loans,

Germany, State Department letter to Hoover, 19 October 1925; FRBNY, Strong Papers 1012.1, letter Strong to Gilbert, 7 November 1925, p. 2, and Arthur Young Papers, Box 3, file "German loans in the U.S. from 1925," report titled "German loans," dated 5 October 1925.

68. NA RG 59 800.51/509½ AN. Young memorandum, "The Department of State and the Flotation of Foreign Loans," 2 April 1925, and RG 59 800.51/507½, letter Assistant Secretary of State to Secretary of State, 10 April 1925.

69. The quote is from Young to Secretary of State, 11 March 1925, in RG 59 800.51/503. Secretary of State Kellogg's acceptance of this view is reflected in his letter to Lewis Einstein of 9 July 1925 in RG 59 800.51/516. Young held to this view through the year, Young to Secretary of State, 7 August and 15 September 1925, NA RG 59 862.51.

70. NA RG 59 800.51/518, Winston to Kellogg, 26 August 1925, and Kellogg to Mellon, 20 October 1925.

71. Arthur Young report, "German loans," 5 October 1925, in Young Papers, Box 3, file "German loans in the U.S. from 1925."

72. HHPL, Commerce Official, Foreign Loans, Germany, letter Kellogg to Speyer and Company, 9 October 1925.

73. A. N. Young Papers, Box 3, file "German loans in the U.S. from 1925," record of conversation among James Speyer, Henry W. Taft, Secretary of State, and Arthur Young, 12 October 1925.

74. *Ibid.*, telephone conversation Young with Speyer, 6 or 16 October 1925.

75. Gilbert to Kellogg, 16 October 1925, NA RG 59 862.51.

76. FRBNY, Strong Papers, 1012.1, letter Gilbert to Winston, 18 October 1925; Gilbert to Winston, 29 October 1925; Gilbert to Strong, 5 November 1925; Gilbert to Strong, 29 October 1925; Winston to Gilbert, 15 October 1925.

77. *Ibid.*, Strong to Gilbert, 7 November 1925. See also file "Germany 1924–28," letter Strong to Winston, 19 November 1925, and Strong Papers, 610.2, letter Strong to Leffingwell, 2 November 1925.

78. BA R431/652, p. 127, letter Schacht to Bayerische Gesandtschaft (copy to Reichskanzlei), 23 September 1925. The problems of monetary policy are discussed in the next chapter.

79. AA, WR 2A, vol. 1, 6 October 1925. In a speech at Karlsruhe, Schacht supported long-term private loans, called for an end to short-term loans, and demanded less public borrowing. Allied Powers Reparations Commission, Transfer Committee notes, n. 17 reported a conference with State Finance Ministers in which Schacht and the RFM called for less public spending. In AA, RM 27, vol. 5, telegram Washington embassy to AA no. 431, 21 October 1925, Schacht reported that he had talked to Charles Mitchell while in Berlin to try to slow municipal borrowing.

80. AA, RM 27, vol. 5, telegram Schacht to AA no. 70, 24 October 1925. Another motive attributed to Schacht was a desire to interest the United States in a revision of the Dawes Plan, for which Schacht was supposed to represent the German government. See AA SS-C, vol. 11, Ruppell (Paris) to AA, 22 Otober 1925, for report of such rumors in *Petit Parisian* and *Le Temps*. The Foreign Office quickly instructed Schacht to deny such reports and issued a denial itself. As Ritter succinctly summed up German policy, "As is well known, it is the Reich government's policy not to take the initiative in altering the Dawes Plan now or later, but rather to leave the initiative up to the other side." AA, Ritter Reparations: 1, Ritter to German Consulate New York (for Schacht), no. 93, 5 November 1925. Whether Schacht had intended to broach the reparations issue or not is uncertain, but he evidently did not, in fact, ever get

a chance to do so. See AA, WR-FVallg 14 Am, vol. 4, Dieckhoff (Washington) to AA no. 897, 24 October 1925.

81. AA, RM 27, vol. 5, telegram Botschaft Washington (Schacht) to AA no. 431, 21 October 1925. Benjamin Strong supported Schacht's proposal but probably did not understand the internal German issues raised by it. See his letter to Parker Gilbert, 7 November 1925, in FRBNY Strong Papers, 1012.1.

82. FRBNY "Germany 1924–28," Strong to Winston, 19 November 1925, and Strong Papers, 1012.1, Strong to Gilbert, 7 November 1925.

83. Letter Mellon to Kellogg and Hoover, 3 November 1925, in NA RG 39, Box 85, file G743.2. For Hoover's concurrence, in the same file, see Hoover to Mellon, 6 November 1925. See also Kellogg to Mellon, 9 November 1925.

84. AA, RM 27, vol. 5, Schacht to AA no. 70, 24 October 1925.

85. AA, SW FW2, vol. 2, telegrams Reichsbank to Schacht, 27 October 1925, and AA to Schacht, no. 339, 27 October 1925. See chapter 2 above for details.

86. AA, SW FW2, vol. 2, telegram AA to Schacht, no. 339, 27 October 1925.

87. Arthur N. Young Papers, Box 3, file "German loans in the U.S. from 1925," Young memo of conversation with Mellon and Gerrard Winston, 20 November 1925.

88. NA RG 39, Box 85, file G743.2, Strong to Winston, 20 January 1926.

89. Hoover wrote Henry M. Robinson, "We have not yet come to any decision with regard to German loans and do not think we are likely to. It seems clearly outside our function." HHPL, Commerce Official, Foreign Loans, Germany, Hoover to Robinson, 23 October 1925. Castle told Bergmann that he would be more comfortable if the U.S. Government was not involved in loan regulation (although the State Department still did not agree). AA, SW FW2A, 30 March 1926. And G. Jones reported that lawyers hired by the bankers had advised them that the State Department letter was not so explicit as to "deter them from offering any German loans which they considered safe." NA RG 151, Box 2965, file 640, Germany, Jones to Herring, 4 December 1925, and Box 2966, file 640, Germany, G. Jones to F. W. Allport, 2 June 1926. Schurman and Parker Gilbert also found that the control within Germany was weak and unlikely to change, FRUS (1926), 2:202–203, and Kellogg agreed, NA RG 39, Box 85, file 743.2, Kellogg to Mellon, 30 March 1926.

90. See, e.g., BA R43I/653, pp. 358–359, letter Norden to State Secretary in Reichskanzlei, 3 December 1925, and Schacht's self-absolution of responsibility for demanding fewer loans in LA Berlin, B8784 II, "Niederschrift über die Besprechung betr. der Aufnahme von kommunalen Auslandsanleihen zwischen den Vertretern des deutschen Städtetages, des Reichsfinanzministers und dem Reichsbankpräsidenten," 28/29 September 1927.

91. *Akten, Kabinette Luther I and II,* 1(1):25; BA R2/2112, "Vermerk über einen Vortrag des Reichsbankpräsidenten in den Reichskanzlei am 5 Dezember 1925," and Stuttgart, E130b-1340, Ministerialabteilung für Bezirks- und Körpershaftsverwaltung an das Ministerium des Innern, 11 Dezember 1925.

92. BA R43I/2359, "Stenographische Niederschrift der Besprechung der Reichsregierung mit den Staats- und Länder," 2 October 1925, and Stuttgart, E130b-1340, letter RFM to state governments, 12 November 1925.

93. Stuttgart, E130b-1340, "Württembergische Bevollmächtigte zum Reichsrat (Schick) an das Württemberg Staatsministerium," 14 November 1925.

94. Denkschrift, in *Verhandlungen des Reichstags,* 1924/27, Band 413, no. 2897, p. 4.

95. Jon Jacobson, *Locarno Diplomacy.*

4. 1926: Depression, Reparations, and Fiscal Policy

1. Walter A. McDougall, *France's Rhineland Diplomacy, 1914–1924: The Last Bid for a Balance of Power in Europe;* Marc Trachtenberg, *Reparation in World Politics: France and European Economic Diplomacy 1916–1923;* Hermann J. Rupieper, *The Cuno Government and Reparations 1922–1923: Politics and Economics;* and Charles S. Maier, "The Truth about the Treaties?" pp. 66–67.

2. This is a central theme of Stephen A. Schuker, *The End of French Predominance in Europe: The Financial Crisis of 1924 and the Adoption of the Dawes Plan,* and a call for more work in this area is made by Peter Krüger, "Das Reparationsproblem der Weimarer Republik in Fragwürdiger Sicht."

3. Sally Marks, "Reparations Reconsidered: A Reminder." Trachtenberg has argued that even this assumption is wrong (p. 385, n. 85).

4. Etienne Mantoux, *The Carthaginian Peace of the Economic Consequences of Mr. Keynes,* pp. 115–117. Mantoux estimates German national income in 1925 at 65 billion RM. The highest possible reparations demanded under the Versailles Treaty would have been 8.6 billion RM annually, or 14.3 percent of German national income. The Dawes Plan payments of 2.5 billion RM were about 4 percent of GNP. He adds that, according to Hitler, Germany spent 15 billion RM / year on rearmaments in the 1930s; funds which, he suggests, could have gone to paying reparations. Gerd Hardach, *Weltmarktorientierung und relative Stagnation: Währungspolitik in Deutschland 1924–1931,* p. 146, estimates the Dawes Plan payments at 1.6–2.9 percent of German GNP and 9.7–14.3 percent of German exports.

5. See the articles by Ohlin, Rueff, and J. M. Keynes in *The Economic Journal,* June and September 1929. Fritz Machlup developed the analysis most completely in "Foreign Debts, Reparations and the Transfer Problem," written in 1928 and available in Machlup's book, *International Payments, Debts and Gold.*

6. Trachtenberg, *Reparation in World Politics,* pp. 337–342, notes that in the context of the 1920s, the income effect might not have worked automatically to transfer reparations. But he finds the main problem in transfer to have been German unwillingness to pay and allied unwillingness to receive reparations.

7. Schuker, *The End of French Predominance,* p. 16.

8. Peter Krüger, *Deutschland und die Reparationen 1918/19.*

9. Carl-Ludwig Holtfrerich, "Internationale Verteilungen der deutschen Inflation 1918–1923," and *Die deutsche Inflation 1919–1923: Ursachen und Folgen in internationaler Perspektive.* Holtfrerich estimates that from 1919 to 1923 between $1.7 and $1.9 billion was invested and lost in Germany—more than the $1.3 billion given to Germany under the Marshall Plan following World War II.

10. See especially Hardach, *Weltmarktorientierung,* pp. 126–127.

11. Charles S. Maier, *Recasting Bourgeois Europe,* p. 252. Maier is aware of the possibility of a "recessionary spiral into unemployment" (p. 253), but concludes that "reparations claims were not really extreme." Charles S. Maier, "The Truth about the Treaties," p. 56.

12. Machlup, *International Payments,* p. 385.

13. Trachtenberg, *Reparation in World Politics,* pp. 158–173.

14. Claussen to Schäffer, 9 March 1929, Schäffer-Claussen Schriftwechsel, in Hans Schäffer Papers, Institut für Zeitgeschichte, Munich. This is only the most emphatic of a whole series of similar reports. Rupieper, *The Cuno Government,* p. 8, finds the same resistance on the part of industry in 1921.

15. Schuker, *The End of French Predominance,* p. 279.

16. This, of course, was especially true of Britain. See D. E. Moggridge, *The Return to Gold, 1925;* Donald Winch, *Economics and Policy;* and Sidney Pollard, ed., *The Gold Standard and Employment Policies between the Wars.* All three authors agree that Britain's return to parity in 1925 overvalued the pound and forced a deflationary policy. Moggridge (p. 18) notes that American prices rose until 1925 and then began a slow fall for the rest of the Weimar period.

17. Monthly data confirming the importance of reductions in imports in determining trade surpluses of 1926 and 1930-31 are contained in *Monatliche Nachweise über den auswärtigen Handel Deutschlands,* reports for 1925-1932.

18. This seems to be the policy suggested by Charles Maier, although he, too, notes the risk of unemployment. *Recasting Bourgeois Europe,* pp. 252-253.

19. Marc Trachtenberg, *Reparation in World Politics,* p. 161, points out that briefly in 1921, Seydoux considered offering subsidies to German industrialists to artificially induce payment in kind. But the project was never developed. It is interesting to note that in 1925 France was reselling some of its coal deliveries from Germany at up to a 30 percent discount from the price Germany was credited with. This may have been one of the reasons that France found deliveries in kind to be unacceptable later. See the letter Strong to Mellon, 21 September 1925, in NA RG 39, Box 220, file Strong, Benjamin, correspondence re France Sept.-Oct. 1925.

20. *Vierteljahrshefte zur Statistik des Deutschen Reichs,* 36 Jahrgang, erstes Heft, p. 185.

21. Reichskreditgesellschaft, *The Economic Development of Germany during the First Six Months of 1926,* p. 12. Using a base of January 1922, average total employment for the second half of 1925 was 105.5. This fell to 83.4 in January and February 1926 and then rose to 98.8 in May 1926.

22. Allied Powers Reparation Commission, Transfer Committee Economic Services, note 18, "Prussian Finances" of January 1926, and note 25, "Declaration of the Finance Minister on the Balancing of the Budget," both written by Gaillet-Billotteau.

23. *Ibid.,* note 27, "Some Data on Consumption in Germany," 25 August 1926, p. 55, by Bresciani-Turroni.

24. Reichskreditgesellschaft, *The Economic Development of Germany during the First Six Months of 1926,* p. 7, reports industrial consumption of electricity, and *Germany's Economic Position at the Turn of the Year 1926/1927,* p. 36, reports the index of production of important industrial basic products.

25. The origin of the recession of 1925-26 and the Great Depression of 1929-33 is the subject of a series of articles by Peter Temin, M. E. Falkus, and T. Balderston in *Economic History Review.* Temin's article, "the Beginning of the Depression in Germany," appears in vol. 24, no. 2 (May 1971); Falkus offers a monetary explanation of the recession and depression in "The German Business Cycle in the 1920's" (August 1975), vol. 27, no. 3. All three offer comments in vol. 30, no. 1 (February 1977).

26. RKG, *The Economic Development of Germany during the First Six Months of 1926,* pp. 49-50.

27. RKG, *Germany's Economic Position at the Turn of the Year 1926/1927,* p. 58.

28. *Ibid.,* p. 5.

29. "Stenographische Niederschrift des Berichts des Herrn Reichsbankpräsident," 20 January 1928. BA R431/635.

30. Stresemann telegram to German embassies in London, Paris, etc., 3 January 1929. AA, RM5, vol. 24.

31. Schäffer to Claussen, 24 February 1929. Schäffer-Claussen Schriftwechsel, vol. 1.

32. *Ibid.*, Schäffer to Claussen, 1 May 1929 (morning).

33. *Ibid.*, Schäffer to Claussen, 1 May 1929 (afternoon).

34. Hardach, *Weltmarktorientierung,* pp. 126–127.

35. BA R43I/876, p. 281, Sitzung des Reichsministers, 31 October 1924; BA R43I/2396, pp. 4–8, Reich Finance Minister to Aussenhandelsverband, 22 November 1924.

36. This point is made by Heinz Habedank, *Die Reichsbank in der Weimarer Republik,* p. 101.

37. Enquête-Ausschuss, *Die Reichsbank,* pp. 61–63.

38. Fritz Seidenzahl, *100 Jahre Deutsche Bank (1870–1970),* pp. 274–275.

39. Habedank's assertion that industry supported the credit stop is entirely without foundation (p. 109). A flood of letters protested the policy. See the collection in BA R43I/1135.

40. Helmut Müller, *Die Zentralbank — eine Nebenregierung; Reichsbankpräsident Hjalmar Schacht als Politiker der Weimarer Republik.*

41. BA R43I/640, pp. 350–351, ''Protokoll über die Sitzung des Zentralausschusses der Reichsbank,'' 26 February 1925, and Enquête-Ausschuss, *Die Reichsbank,* p. 63.

42. Theodore Balderston has brilliantly argued that Reichsbank policy was not responsible for high interest rates on Germany's long-term bond market. The real problem which would force both industry and government onto the foreign bond market was the weakness of Germany's capital resources due to destruction of savings during the inflation and the unwillingness of Germans to buy long-term bonds. T. Balderston, ''The Origins of Economic Instability in Germany 1924–1930. Market Forces versus Economic Policy.''

43. BA R43I/634, ''Stenographische Niederschrift der Besprechung über währungs- und finanzpolitische Angelegenheiten,'' 17 April 1925.

44. BA R43I/2029, p. 112, and *Akten der Reichskanzlei, . . . Luther I and II,* p. 11, see p. 22, for opposition of RFM to further spending.

45. BA R43I/1135, p. 99. Prussia had also accumulated a large surplus. See BA R43I/2030, pp. 165–166.

46. Tax cuts favorable to business were partially offset by tax increases on consumer goods, BA R43I/2396, pp. 4–8 and 267. In mid 1925, the RFM estimated that in the budget year 1925/26 the Reich would have a net deficit of only 10 million RM. BA R43I/877, pp. 21–22.

47. ''Protokoll der Sitzung des Reichsministeriums,'' 22 July 1925, in BA R43I/877, p. 67. Comment by Ministerialdirektor Lotholz.

48. *Ibid.*, p. 72, letter RFM to Reichskanzler, 30 July 1925; p. 68, Sitzung des Reichsministeriums, 22 July 1925.

49. Schacht offered economic justifications for his policy in BA R43I/640, ''Protokoll über die Sitzung des Zentralausschusses der Reichsbank,'' 28 July 1925. But he called forth the threat of inflation when he explained his policy to Benjamin Strong, FRBNY, Strong Papers 1000.6, Strong report of conversation with Schacht, 11 July 1925.

50. By August 1925, production of basic industrial products had fallen over 10 percent from a peak in January 1925. Whereas unemployment, which would reach 22 percent in January 1926, was at a minimal level of only 4 percent in August 1925. For industrial production see Reichskreditgesellschaft, *Germany's Economic*

Position at the Turn of the Year 1926–1927, p. 36. For unemployment among union members see *Vierteljahreshefte zur Statistik des Deutschen Reichs*, 36 Jahrgang erstes Heft, p. 195.

51. The policies of 1925–26 are analyzed in considerable detail by Dieter Hertz-Eichenrode, *Wirtschaftskrise und Arbeitsbeschaffung*.

52. FRBNY, Strong Papers 1012.1, letters Gilbert to Strong, 10 September 1925, 13 September 1925, and 17 September 1925. Gilbert estimated funds available to the government at 2–3.5 billion RM (13 September letter), and Strong to Gilbert, 30 September 1925. Also see *The Economist*, 26 September 1925.

53. BA R43I/653, "Vermerk Min. Rat. Dr. Wachsmann," 5 November 1925; "Sprechzettel: Min. Rat. Dr. Schippel," 30 September 1925.

54. BA R43I/2359, letter Dr. Kempner to Bonn, 1 September 1925; and Bonn to Kempner, 4 September 1925.

55. FRBNY, Strong Papers 1012.1, Gilbert to Norman, 17 September 1925; Strong Papers 1116.5, Strong to Norman, 2 October 1925.

56. FRBNY, Strong Papers 1012.1, Gilbert to McGarrah, 16 October 1925.

57. BA R43I/640, "Protokoll über die Sitzung des Zentralausschusses der Reichsbank," 3 December 1925. BA R13I/100, "Verein Deutscher Eisen- und Stahlindustrieller: Aufzeichnung über die Sitzung des Hauptvorstandes und des Fachgruppenauschusses," 16 December 1925, and Fritz Blaich, *Die Wirtschaftskrise 1925/26 und die Reichsregierung; Von der Erwerbslosenfürsorge zur Konjunkturpolitik*, pp. 59–105.

58. BA R43I/654, letter Schacht to Reich Chancellor, 4 January 1926. Schacht said that total loans made by the Reichsbank and Rentenbank amounted to 2,280 million RM of which 1 billion RM had gone to agriculture.

59. *Akten . . . Kabinette Luther I and II*, letter Reichsbank directors to the Reich Chancellery, 24 January 1926; BA R2/2126, "Niederschrift über die Sitzung der Beratungsstelle," 22 January 1926.

60. BA R2/2001, letter Prussian Minister of Interior (Severing) to Reichsbank directors, 11 February 1926.

61. BA R2/2126, comments by Norden, "Niederschrift über die Sitzung der Beratungsstelle," 23 January 1926.

62. BA R2/2001, letter Severing to Reichsbank directors, 11 February 1926.

63. BA R13I/100, "Verein Deutscher Eisen- und Stahlindustrieller: Aufzeichung über die Sitzung des Hauptvorstandes und des Fachgruppenausschusses," 16 December 1925, and BA R43I/635, "Notiz für den Reichskanzler zur Reichsbankbesprechung," 12 February 1926, quoted by Gerd Hardach, p. 68. Hardach argues that the government's pressure on the Reichsbank to reduce interest rates was primarily intended to reduce the inflow of foreign capital. As has been argued here, it is much more likely that the government's real concern was to stimulate the economy and fight Schacht's power grab.

64. See the unsigned memo from the Reich Chancellery questioning the motives of the high discount policy and arguing that the grounds for such a policy were erroneous, BA R43I/635, memo dated 4 December 1925.

65. BA R43I/655, memo, 15 April 1926.

66. BA R43I/654, memo, 8 April 1926; see Stresemann's comments to the Cabinet, 25 June 1926, BA R43I/1413.

67. AA, WR-FV allg. 14 Am., vol. 6, letter von Maltzan to AA no. 691, 22 June 1926.

68. BA R43I/1413, 25 June 1926.

69. See BA R43I/641, "Protokoll über die Sitzung des Zentralausschusses der Reichsbank," 26 March, 7 June, and 6 July 1926; and memo prepared in the Reich Chancellery, 11 June 1926.

70. BA R43I/2030, pp. 125–130, letter AfA bund to Reich government, 5 December 1925. Similar fears and calls for more government help were made by the Christian labor unions, see memo by SS in RK to Reich Chancellor, 19 September 1925, in BA R43I/1136, and the Reich Labor Ministry, see RAM memo, 4 December 1925, in BA R43I/2030, p. 122.

71. BA R43I/2030, p. 141, letter Prussian Minister President to Reich Chancellor, 14 December 1925.

72. *Ibid.*, p. 147, Vermerk, 18 December 1925.

73. *Ibid.*, pp. 155–157, Aktenvermerk, 17 December 1925, on conference held 12 December; and p. 160, Reich Chancellery memo, 21 December 1925.

74. *Ibid.*, p. 165, Prussian Minister of Peoples' Welfare, Aktenvermerk, 21 December 1925; and pp. 202–203, letter RAM to state governments, December 1925; pp. 256–257, letter RAM to Reichspräsident, 20 January 1926, for proof of Reich pressure on Berlin to speed up its implementation of expanded emergency make-work projects.

75. *Ibid.*, p. 243, Reich Representative to Munich (Haniel) to Reich Chancellor, 13 January 1926; and p. 157, Aktenvermerk, 17 December 1925.

76. *Verhandlungen des Reichstags,* Wahlperiode 1924, 338:5402 and 5146.

77. Blaich, *die Wirtschaftskrise 1925/26,* p. 109.

78. *Verhandlungen des Reichstags* (1925), 338:5147, 5403–5407 and 5476.

79. *Akten . . . Kabinette Luther I und II,* p. 1128.

80. BA R131/68, pp. 153–156, meeting of VDESI and Fachgruppe des Eisenschaffenden Industrie beim RDI, 10 March 1926.

81. Blaich, p. 116.

82. Von Schubert conversation with Gilbert, 22 February 1926, AA, SS-Ggil., vol. 1, and Hertz-Eichenrode, *Wirtschaftskrise,* p. 92.

83. Reich Minister of Finance letter to Reich ministers, I/22003, 1 November 1927, AA, Ritter-R. fin und Rbank, vol. 1. For a general review of the size of government deficits and efforts to hide them, see Rolf Lüke, *Von der Stabilisierung zur Krise,* pp. 87–96, and Carl Böhret, *Aktionen gegen die "Kalte Sozialisierung",* p. 37.

84. For examples of the insistent industrial demands for greater reductions in government spending and arguments that Reich fiscal policy was unresponsive to industrial needs, see: RDI letter to Reich president, 29 December 1925, in BA R43I/1136, pp. 214–224; Wolff's Telegraphisches Büro release, 4 March 1926, "Die Wirtschaft zu den Steuermilderungen," in BA R43I/2397, p. 160; and speech by Kastl to RDI, 3 September 1926, copy in BA NL Silverberg, 235, p. 30.

85. See letter Vorstand Deutscher Städtetag to RAM, 8 March 1926, in BA R43I/2031, pp. 99–100; and note by Stresemann, 24 January 1926, in AA NL Stresemann/279.

86. Letter RFM to Reich ministers, etc., 21 May 1926, in BA R43I/877, pp. 290–291.

87. *Akten . . . Kabinette Luther I und II,* pp. 1105; and 1109, Ministerbesprechung, 9 February 1926. The only occasion which I have found that indicates that the deficits might have foreign policy advantages came in a discussion of the budget on 5 February 1926. When Reinhold suggested that the budget for 1926 would remain balanced despite the tax cuts, but that deficits might emerge by 1927, Foreign Minister Gustav Stresemann observed that if he remembered correctly, "in his reparations

report, Parker Gilbert wrote that the Germans could pay more in reparations than they were now paying and perhaps Germany's capacity to pay had been underestimated. When one thinks about this, one should consider if it would not be opportune to conclude a budget with a deficit" (p. 1086). This observation was not followed up by others at the meeting, remained more hypothetical than concrete, and came only after it was becoming clear that domestic political and economic considerations made a deficit policy necessary.

88. BA R43I/2031, p. 103. RFM to RAM, 14 May 1926.

89. BA R43I/877, pp. 287–289, letter, RFM to Reich ministers etc., 21 May 1926.

90. BA R43I/2031, pp. 122–124, letter RAM to Reich ministers etc., 15 June 1926; and p. 293, Vortrag des Referenten, 11 August 1926.

91. *Ibid.*, pp. 127–131, letter Bayerische Gesandtschaft to Reichskanzler, 14 June 1926.

92. *Ibid.*, pp. 162–163, Ministerbesprechung, 28 June 1926.

93. *Ibid.*, pp. 170–186, Chefbesprechung, 5 July, 6 July, and 7 July 1926. Reported by Wolff's Telegraphisches Büro, 8 July 1926.

94. *Ibid.*, pp. 242–245, Besprechung der Min. Komm. für Arbeitsbeschaffung, 13 July 1926. State borrowing was estimated to be an additional 300 million RM (p. 264), report of conference in RFM, 21 July 1926. I have not seen any estimate of municipal spending emerging specifically from these decisions.

95. *Ibid.*, p. 165, Ministerbesprechung, 28 June 1926.

96. BA R2/2001, RFM memo, 15 July 1926.

97. *Ibid.*, Aktenvermerk, "Besprechung über die Finanzierung der Arbeitsbeschaffung," 21 July 1926, and Reich Minister of Finance letter to Reich ministers, 1 November 1927, in AA Ritter-R. fin und Rbank, vol. 1.

98. BA R2/2001, meeting of the ministerial commission for work creation, 13 July 1926; Reich Finance Minister Vermerk, 15 July 1926; letter from Minister Director von Brandt (RFM) to Reg. Rat. Weigert in the Labor Ministry, 20 July 1926; and note on the discussion on financing the work creation, 21 July 1926, and BA R43I/2031, p. 243, meeting of Ministerial Commission for Work Creation, 13 July 1926.

99. BA R43I/2031, p. 243, meeting of the Ministerial Commission for Work Creation, 13 July 1926.

100. BA R2/2001, note on the discussion on financing the work creation, 21 July 1926, and BA R43I/2031, p. 227, letter RFM to SS in RK, 20 July 1926.

101. BA R43I/2031, p. 21, letter RAM to state governments, 31 August 1926.

102. *Ibid.*, p. 71, Resortsbesprechung, 21 September 1926.

103. *Ibid.*, pp. 257–285, letter RAM, 24 December 1926.

104. Balderston makes this point in "The Origins of Economic Instability."

5. Living Without Loans, Spring 1927

1. Carl Schmidt, *German Business Cycles 1924–1933*, pp. 44–45, 62–63.

2. "Niederschrift über die Sitzung der Beratungsstelle," 18 June 1926, in BA R2/2127; and "Protokoll über die Sitzung des Zentralausschusses der Reichsbank," 28 September 1926, p. 17, in BA R43I/641.

3. Enquête-Ausschuss, *Die Reichsbank*, p. 87.

4. Finanz- und Handelsblatt der Vossischen Zeitung, 4 September 1926, report of Tagung; *Der Deutsche Volkswirt*, 1 October 1926, p. 5; and *Report of the Agent General*, June 1927, p. 64.

5. Transfer Committee Economic Service, "Credit and Financial Summary, November 23, 1926," reported in NA RG39, box 85, file "Credit and Financial Summary June 1926–Nov. 1926"; *Frankfurter Zeitung*, 5 December 1926, p. 4; Chefbesprechung, 16 October 1927, remarks by RFM Köhler, BA R43I/656, p. 294; and letter Shepard Morgan to Kenzel, 11 March 1927, in FRBNY, Germany 1924–28.

6. Stephen V. O. Clarke, *Central Bank Cooperation: 1924–31*, p. 106.

7. Memo, 11 July 1926, in AA, SS-C, vol. 12, and RFM report "Steuerlich begünstigte Auslandsanleihen," 1 February 1929, in BA R2/2136.

8. Report in the *Financial News*, 22 July 1926, copy in BA R2/2001.

9. *Report of the Agent General*, November 1926, p. 60, and June 1927, p. 64.

10. *Ibid.*, and AA, WR-2A, vol. 1, 24 October 1926.

11. Quoted from an article by John Elliott in the *New York Herald Tribune*, 23 February 1927, clipping in AA, WR-FV allg. 14 Am., vol. 10a.

12. *Der Deutsche Volkswirt*, 1 October 1926, p. 5.

13. BA R2/2001, letter Reichsschuldenverwaltung to RFM, 18 February 1925, and BA R2/2005, memorandum 29 May 1925.

14. BA R2/2005, memo dated 14 December 1925, covering a meeting held 11 December 1925 with the Reichsbank president on the tax considerations for foreign loans.

15. *Frankfurter Zeitung*, 8 April 1926, no. 258. Another proposal for tax reduction was made in a letter from the Industrie und Handelskammer of Frankfurt a.M. to the RFM, 7 April 1926, in BA R2/2005.

16. BA R2/2005, Vermerk, RFM VC 11690, 11833, 10 May 1926, report on conference in Abt. V of the Reich Finance Ministry.

17. Letter, Reich Economics Minister to Reich Finance Minister, 20 May 1927, BA R2/2008; Popitz's remarks are in the minutes of the Report of the Reichsbank president, 7 March 1927, BA R43I/635, p. 88.

18. "Niederschrift über die Besprechung mit den Vertretern der Ressorts . . . Betrifft: Steuerliche Begünstigung von Auslandsanleihen," 18 November 1926, BA R2/2006.

19. Stuttgart, E151d I-54, letter Reichsbank Directors to Reich Finance Minister, 23 November 1926.

20. Letter Coffin to Secretary of State, 21 January 1927, in NA RG 59 862.512/304.

21. Memo, Reich Finance Minister to the Reichsrat, 7 March 1927, "Steuerliche Begünstigung von Auslandsanleihen," Stuttgart, E130b–1342.

22. "Aufzeichnungen über: a) eine Sitzung des Reichstags- Unterausschusses, b) des 6 Ausschusses," 14 December 1926, BA R2/2007.

23. Württembergische Gesandtschaft (Berlin) to Württembergische Staatsministerium, no. 5495, "Betreff: Steuerliche Begünstigung von Auslandsanleihen," 10 December 1926, Stuttgart, E151d I-54.

24. Robert Kuczynski, "Norden's Antwort" in *Finanzpolitische Korrespondenz*, 16 May 1928.

25. "Protokoll über die Sitzung des Zentralausschusses der Reichsbank," 11 January 1927, BA R43I/641; Enquête-Ausschuss, *Die Reichsbank*, p. 84.

26. Quoted by Link, *Stabilisierungspolitik*, p. 406.

27. "Aufzeichnung über eine Sitzung des Steuerausschusses des Reichstags," 8 July 1927, BA R2/2008.

28. See Paul Silverberg's speech to RDI, "Die Lage der deutschen Wirtschaft im Urteil des Generalagenten," etc., 21 October 1927, BA, NL Silverberg 10, as well as sources already cited.

29. Gilbert letter to Strong, 8 September 1927, FRBNY, Strong Papers 1012.2.

30. Letter, Schacht to Norman, 21 May 1927, FRBNY Germany 1924–28. Even in late November some German banks agreed that German interest rates were bound to rise as the economy recovered. See article in the *New York Times*, 22 November 1926, "Berlin expects easy money period to end."

31. Mills to Kellogg, 15 July 1927, in NA RG 39, Box 85, file G743.1.

32. "Protokoll über die Sitzung des Zentralausschusses der Reichsbank," 10 June 1927, BA R431/641, p. 46.

33. Reichskreditgesellschaft, *Germany's Economic Development* (1927), pt. 1, p. 2.

34. *Deutsche Volkswirt*, 28 January 1927, p. 528; and *Frankfurter Zeitung*, 3 May 1927, p. 30.

35. *Report of the Agent General*, June 1927, p. 80.

36. AA, WR-2A, vol. 1, September 1926, and report by Kastl to RDI, July 1926, BA NL Silverberg 248, pp. 15–33.

37. Meeting between RFM and Gilbert, 12 November 1926, AA, SS-C, vol. 12.

38. *Frankfurter Zeitung*, 12 January 1927, p. 3, and *Report of the Agent General*, June 1927, pp. 75–76.

39. Memo by Finlayson on German internal loan of January 1927, dated 28 January 1927, PRO, FO-371/12140.

40. Telegram, Ritter to embassy, Washington, no. 41, 23 January 1927. AA, Botschaft Washington Deutsche Anleihen 2, p. 288.

41. This is the assertion of Reinhold's successor Heinrich Köhler in a conversation with Erich Koch-Weser. See Vermerk, 28 April 1927, BA, NL Koch-Weser 36, p. 127. In late October 1926, the Finance Minister assured the Reich Chancellor that no loan would be considered prior to the end of March 1927. Any funds needed would be raised by treasury bills. See the note from Pünder to Marx, 22 October 1926, in BA R431/877, p. 351.

42. Kabinettesprotokolle, from Records of the German Foreign Office received by the Department of State, 1842/D771489.

43. Finlayson report of conversation with Gilbert, 12 February 1927, report dated 18 February 1927, PRO, FO-371/12140.

44. Reichsbank, *Verwaltungsbericht*, 1927, p. 130; Finlayson conversation with Gilbert, 12 February 1927, PRO, FO-371/12140.

45. Lindsay to Chamberlain, 28 October 1927, PRO, T-160/262F.10457, vol. 1.

46. Report of the Reichsbank president 7 March 1927, BA R431/635.

47. Popitz said that by April 1927 the loan was needed to cover deficits, but Schacht countered that since the Reichsbank had taken 300 million RM worth of the loan anyway the government could just as well have borrowed short term from the Reichsbank to meet its needs. *Ibid.*, p. 88.

48. Reich Finance Minister note, 1 November 1927. AA, Ritter-R. fin und Rbank, vol. 1. The difficulties in selling the bond and supporting the price are related in the report of the Bavarian representative to the Reichsrat, 25 March 1927, in BHsa/MF 66833.

49. Memo, Hortsmann conversation with Gilbert, 31 October 1927, AA, SS-C, vol. 13.

50. Ritter to German embassy (Washington), 9 April 1927, AA, RM5, vol. 21.

51. Ritter (Berlin) telegram to German embassies in Paris, Washington, etc., 19 February 1927, AA, RM-5, vol. 5, and Köhler, *Lebenserinnerungen*, p. 233. But it was reported to the State Department without apparent concern by American ambassador Schurman. Schurman to State Dept., 16 February 1927, paraphrase in NA RG 39, Box 85, File G743.1.

52. Ritter to German embassies in Paris, Washington, etc., 19 February 1927, AA, RM-5, vol. 5.

53. Records of the State Secretary for Foreign Affairs, from Records of the German Foreign Office received by the Department of State, 2232/E100844–E100845.

54. Köhler, *Lebenserinnerungen*, p. 233.

55. Vallette Aufzeichnung, W. Rep. 258, 9 February 1927, AA, SS-C, vol. 12. Also see the memo drafted by Ritter and Schubert to be sent to Köhler. Although this copy remained unsent, the issue was obviously raised in some other manner. See Köhler's letter criticizing the Foreign Office's negotiations for a loan to stabilize the Romanian currency without consulting the Finance Ministry, 25 March 1927, AA, Ritter-Rep., vol. 2.

56. Enquête-Ausschuss, *Die Reichsbank*, p. 198.

57. *Frankfurter Zeitung*, 2 May 1927, p. 3.

58. Enquête-Ausschuss, *Die Reichsbank*, p. 199.

59. Fritz Machlup, *The Stock Market, Credit and Capital Formation*, p. 299; also, Carl Iversen, *Aspects of the Theory of International Capital Movements*.

60. Allied Powers Reparations Commission, Transfer Committee Economic Service, Note 34, 20 December 1926, p. 27.

61. Reichskreditgesellschaft, *The Economic Development of Germany During the First Six Months of 1927*, p. 38.

62. See Gerd Hardach, *Weltmarktorientierung*, p. 80, for a good explanation of the process.

63. Reichskreditgesellschaft, *The Economic Development of Germany During the First Six Months of 1927*, p. 37. In 1913 the saving rate was about 84 million RM per month. Through most of 1926 it ran at 130–150 million RM per month, rose to 350 million RM in January 1927, and then declined to 127 million RM in April. See also "Bericht der Generaldirektoren der Landesbank über die Verwaltung der Landesbank der Rheinprovinz—1927," p. 133, in HA Köln, 902–91–3.

64. Enquête-Ausschuss, *Die Reichsbank*, pp. 193–195.

65. Lüke, *Stabilisierungspolitik*, p. 235.

66. *Der Deutsche Volkswirt*, 13 May 1927, p. 1,027.

67. Enquête-Ausschuss, *Die Reichsbank*, p. 67, and *Report of the Agent General*, June 1927, p. 72.

68. See Stresemann's report of the stormy Cabinet meeting of 22 June 1927, in *Gustav Stresemann, His Diaries, Letters, and Papers*, p. 277.

69. Enquête-Ausschuss, *Die Reichsbank*, pp. 67–68.

70. *Ibid.*, p. 201.

71. Julius Curtius, *Sechs Jahre Minister der deutschen Republik*, p. 57.

72. *Ursachen und Folgen. Vom deutschen Zusammenbruch 1918 und 1945 bis zur staatlichen Neuordnung Deutschlands in der Gegenwart*, 6:238.

73. Report, British embassy in Berlin to Principal Secretary of State for Foreign Affairs, 24 June 1927, PRO, FO-371/12140.

74. Letter, Gilbert to Norman, 29 May 1927, FRBNY, Germany 1924–1928.

75. Jay to Strong, 22 June 1927, FRBNY, Strong Papers 1012.3.

76. Kuczynski's article, "Norden's Antwort," *Finanzpolitische Korrespondenz*, 16 May 1928.

77. Strong to Norman, 25 March 1927, FRBNY, Strong Papers 1116.7.

78. Reichsbank Directors to Reich Chancellor, 27 June 1927. Copy in BHsa MW 454.

79. FRBNY, Strong Papers 1116.7, letter Norman to Strong, 22 May 1927.

80. FRBNY, Strong Papers 1012.3, Strong to Jay, 10 November 1927; and Mills to Kellogg, 15 July 1927, in NA RG 39, Box 85, file G743.1.

81. Jørgen Pedersen, "Some Notes on the Economic Policy of the United States during the Period 1919–1932," pp. 473–494, the quote is from p. 483.

82. Records of the State Secretary for Foreign Affairs, 2232/E100840, comment by von Schubert.

83. Report of the Reichsbank president 7 March 1927, in BA R431/635.

84. *Akten zur deutschen auswärtigen Politik 1918–1945, aus dem Archiv des Deutschen Auswärtigen Amts*, series B, 5:391–394.

85. Enquête-Ausschuss, *Die Reichsbank*, p. 68.

86. Letter, Schacht to Norman, 21 May 1927, FRBNY Germany 1924–1928.

87. Schacht conversation with von Schubert, 1 August 1927, AA, SS-Ggil, 1:28.

88. *Ibid.*, pp. 26–28.

89. Letter, Gilbert to Strong, 8 September 1927, FRBNY, Strong Papers 1012.2.

90. BA R431/2360, p. 25, "Aus dem Protokoll der Sitzung des Reichsministeriums," 30 November 1927.

91. See Vallette's memo to Ritter, 4 April 1927. AA, Ritter-Rep., vol. 2. On April 1, Gilbert already had 70 million RM in foreign currency and needed only 30 million more from Reichsbank reserves to make the transfer. On 29 April he made the transfer. AA, Ritter-Rep., vol. 3, Vallette to Min. Dir. and SS, 29 April 1927. Robert Kuczynski, however, stated that this transfer caused a "menacing" rise in the price of the dollar. That this was a decisive factor seems doubtful at a time when the Reichsbank was losing 1 billion RM. Robert Kuczynski, "American Loans to Germany," in *Foreign Investments*, p. 183.

92. Simon memo, 25 October 1924, AA, WR-FV Allg. Geheim, vol. 2, cited by Link, *Stabilisierungspolitik*, pp. 399–400. Link believes that this report and Simon's report of January 1927 reveal Germany's basic reparations policy.

93. Simon's report entitled "Vermerkungen zu dem letzen Jahresbericht des Generalagenten und über die Möglichkeit der Revisionspolitik," 11 January 1927, AA, SS-C, vol. 12.

94. *Ibid.*, Link's emphasis on Simon's long-range policy may be correct, but it seems erroneous to think that this long-range plan had anything to do with the crisis of early 1927.

95. Ritter (AA) to Botschaft Washington, 9 April 1927. Copies in several files including AA, RM-5, vol. 21; AA, SS-C, vol. 12.

96. Maltzan to AA, 18 April 1927, AA, WR-FV Allg. 14 Am., vol. 10.

97. Ritter memo, "Soll die Revision des Dawesplans jetzt beantragt werden," 18 April 1927; the memo was given to the State Secretary, Stresemann, and Vallette. AA, Ritter-Rep., vol. 2.

98. RFM memo, "Überblick über gegenwärtigen Stand und nächste Zukunft der Reparationsfrage," 12 July 1927; copies of this memo are located in BA R431/ 275; AA, RM5, vol. 21, and AA, Ritter-Rep., vol. 3. Köhler made similar although

less forceful arguments in a letter to the other Reich ministers, 14 April 1927, in BA R431/878, p. 99.

99. Wolf to Bavarian Foreign Minister, 21 October 1927, reported comments made by Köhler, BHsa MW 454.

100. In March 1927, the Cabinet discussed the possibility of submitting a deficit budget but decided that it was too soon to admit that the government couldn't balance its budget. See the brief report of the Reich Ministers meeting, 24 March 1927, in BA R431/878, pp. 86–87.

101. On January 26, 1926, the German embassy in Washington sent the Foreign Ministry an article from the *New York American* with this note attached, "The article is noteworthy in that it renders German policy in regard to the Dawes Plan essentially correctly in two sentences: 'The ruling circles in Germany are determined not to permit a break down of the Dawes Plan to be blamed on German sabotage. Behind this determination, however, lies the hope that the plan itself will demonstrate the impossibility of its continued functioning.' " In AA-Botschaft Washington, Reparations, Dawes-Plan, vol. 4.

102. Report Maltzan (Washington) to AA no. 463, 18 April 1927, AA, RM5, vol. 21.

103. *Ibid.*, p. 8. see also Kiep to AA 763, 24 July 1927, which urges Germany to wait on Gilbert's initiative. AA, WR-FV allg. 14 Am., vol. 11.

104. Note signed by Marx of a conversation among Marx, Schacht, and Gilbert, 11 March 1927, in BA R431/275, pp. 270–272.

105. See the letter by Deutschen Städtetag, Landeskreistag, etc., to Deutschen Sparkassen- und Giroverband, 16 July 1927, and the Sparkassen answer, BA R2/2002, p. 71.

106. Clarke, *Central Bank Cooperation*, p. 128.

107. Harold James makes this point in his soon to be published dissertation, "The Reichsbank and Public Finance in Germany, 1924–1933," pp. 103–104.

6. Domestic Policy and Foreign Constraints, Autumn 1927

1. Clarke, *Central Bank Cooperation*, pp. 123–124, Lester V. Chandler, *Benjamin Strong Central Banker*, p. 375, and R. S. Sayers, *The Bank of England*, 1:336–346.

2. Strong to Gilbert, 14 July 1928, FRBNY, Strong Papers 1012.2.

3. *Ibid.*

4. Norman's handwritten notes, written after the conference, are photographically reproduced in R. S. Sayers, *The Bank of England*, vol. 3, appendix 17. These impressionistic notes are the only record of positions taken at the meeting.

5. See the letter from the Reichsbank directors to the Reich Chancellor, 27 June 1927, copy in BHsa MW 454.

6. *New York Journal of Commerce*, 4 October 1927, reported by E. Howard to FO, 17 October 1927, PRO, FO-371/12147.

7. Letter Leffingwell to Lamont, 12 July 1927, in Lamont Papers 103–12, and Norman's notes on the Long Island conference in Sayers, vol. 3, appendix 17.

8. The most important file on Gilbert is AA, SS-Ggil, "die wichtigsten Gespräche mit dem Reparationsagenten Parker Gilbert."

9. Maltzan telegram to AA (Ritter) 155, 21 February 1927, AA, WR-FV Allg. 14 Am., vol. 11. This is confirmed by Norman's comment that Benjamin "Strong

leaves all decisions up to P.G.," in notes on the Long Island conference in Sayers, vol. 3, appendix 17.

10. AA WR-FV Allg. 14 Am., vol. 11, Kiep (Washington) report to AA no. 763, 24 July 1927.

11. Moreau diary, p. 416, quoted in Lüke, *Stabilisierungspolitick*, p. 147.

12. AA-Botschaft Washington, Reparations, Dawes Plan vol. 4, Hoesch to AA, 24 November 1925.

13. PRO, T—160/216 F. 7969, vol. 1, Report of the British delegation to the Reparation Commission, 29 September 1926, and letter Orme Sargent (FO) to Secretary to the Treasury, 12 October 1926.

14. *Ibid.* Niemeyer to Sir John Fischer Williams, 6 October 1926.

15. PRO, FO-371-12141, letter, Warren Fischer, Chancellor of the Exchequer to P.M., 9 November 1927.

16. Memorandum, Ritter to Stresemann, 21 October 1927, AA, RM5, vol. 21.

17. Memorandum, 4 February 1928, p. 63, BA NL Koch-Weser 37.

18. Finlayson report of conversation with Gilbert, 12 February 1927. Report dated 18 February 1927, PRO, FO-371/12140.

19. Sir Robert Lindsay to William Tyrrell, 23 November 1927, PRO, FO-371/ 12142.

20. *Report of the Agent General*, 10 June 1927, p. 47.

21. *Ibid.*, 30 November 1926, p. 35.

22. Privately, Gilbert expressed all his concerns in a letter to the Reich Finance Minister, 17 March 1927, AA, SS-C, vol. 12. Publicly, he repeated them in his report of 10 June 1927, pp. 49–50.

23. *Report of the Agent General*, 10 June 1927, p. 51.

24. Allied Powers Reparations Commission, Transfer Committee, Economic Service, note 46, "Status and Salaries of Officials of the Reich from 1924 to July 1, 1927: A Comparison with 1913" (p. 20). The comparison was based on purchasing power rather than a straight monetary comparison.

25. *Ibid.*, pp. 24–25.

26. Otto Braun, *Von Weimar zu Hitler*, p. 232.

27. Braun, p. 232, and Allied Powers Reparations Commission, Transfer Committee, Economic Service, note 54. In December 1925 the state governments had even successfully prevented a civil service pay raise on the grounds that their budgets could not bear the added costs. See *Akten . . . Luther I und II*, p. 987.

28. For a comprehensive discussion of the internal political crisis that this issue created in the Center Party see Michael Stürmer, *Koalition und Opposition in der Weimarer Republik 1924–1928*, pp. 236–241.

29. Stürmer, p. 237.

30. See correspondence on how to deal with Gilbert's antagonism to municipal spending: Landman to Mulert, 29 July 1927; "Vermerk über eine Besprechung mit Ministerialdirektor Dr. Zarden," 4 August 1927; and Mulert to Landman, 13 August 1927, in LA Berlin, DST-B6131.

31. Köhler, *Lebenserinnerungen*, pp. 251 ff., and 244.

32. Memorandum by E. Howard Smith to Sir Ronald Lindsay and the Treasury, 4 August 1927, in *Documents on British Foreign Policy 1919–1939*, Series I A, 3:503–504. The suspicion that Germany was running large deficits to prove that it could not pay reparations was voiced by the *New York Herald Tribune* and reported in Maltzan to AA 339, 14 June 1927, AA, SS-C vol. 12.

33. Treasury (Leith-Ross) to FO, 16 August 1927, PRO, FO-371/12141.

34. Report to State Secretary and Reich Minister, 29 September 1927, citing Curtius' letter of 18 September 1927, AA, WR-2A, vol. 2. Curtius' letter calling for a ministers' conference to discuss loan reduction and its harmful effects on the economy is in AA, RM-RM16, vol. 3, Curtius to State Secretary in the Reich Chancellery, 18 September 1927.

35. AA, WR-2A, vol. 2, memorandum by Vallette, 22 September 1927.

36. Memorandum given to the Reich Chancellor, 24 September 1927, BA R43I/656, p. 229; memorandum, Vallette, 22 September 1927, AA, WR-2A, vol. 2.

37. Letter Schacht to Reich Finance Minister, 22 September 1927, AA, RM-RM16, vol. 3; Helmut Müller, *Die Zentralbank—eine Nebenregierung*, p. 66; and memorandum, State Secretary in the Reich Chancellery, 29 September 1927, BA-R43I/656, p. 242.

38. Gisela Upmeier, "Schachts Kampf gegen die kommunalen Auslandsanleihen," in Hansmeyer, ed., *Kommunale Finanzpolitik*, p. 165.

39. Memorandum, State Secretary in the Reich Chancellery, 29 September 1927, BA R43I/656.

40. Reichardt (Economics Ministry) comments in "Niederschrift über die Sitzung der Beratungsstelle," 20 September 1927, BA R2/2128. The debate in this meeting led to Schacht's withdrawal from the board when it approved the Prussian loan.

41. Note by J. V. Perowne attached to memorandum by "E. Howard" to FO, 17 October 1927, PRO, FO-371/12147. This is recorded in slightly altered form in DBFP, Series I A, 4:53, and dated 18 October.

42. *Ibid.*

43. Letter, Gilbert to Strong, 8 September 1927, FRBNY, Strong Papers 1012.2.

44. Note by Karlowa "streng vertraulich," 24 August 1927, in AA, Ritter-Rep., vol. 3. The same motive was attributed to Gilbert in a report to the State Secretary and Foreign Minister, 20 September 1927, in AA, WR-2A, vol. 2, and was alluded to by British Ambassador Sir Ronald Lindsay after a conversation with Gilbert, reported in DBFP, Series I A, 4:57.

45. Letter, Gilbert to Strong, 8 September 1927, FRBNY, Strong Papers 1012.2.

46. *Ibid.*, p. 5. "The tendency, in other words, is for the foreign loans to set into motion within Germany forces which run entirely counter to the forces which one would theoretically expect to be set in motion by the internal process of collecting funds for reparations purposes." Gilbert had come to this understanding a year earlier when he explained to Schurman that collecting taxes would reduce German purchasing power and thus help transfer reparations. Schurman to Secretary of State, 31 March 1926, in NA RG 39 box 85, G743.1 (Problems arising under the Dawes Plan—General). For Strong's view, see his letter to Pierre Jay, 21 June 1927, FRBNY, Strong Papers 1012.3.

47. Gilbert to Strong, 8 September 1927, FRBNY, Strong Papers 1012.2.

48. Sir R. Lindsay to Sir A. Chamberlain, 24 October 1927, DBFP, Series I A, 4:57.

49. G. Jones to Hoover, 26 September 1927, HHPL, Commerce Papers, OF Secretary of State Kellogg; letter, Strong to Gilbert, 24 September 1927, FRBNY, Strong Papers 1012.2, pp. 1 and 8; Kiep (Washington, D.C.) to AA, 26 September 1927, AA, WR-2A, vol. 2; memorandum by Castle, 26 September 1927, NA RG 59 862.51; and Link, *Stabilisierungspolitik*, p. 414.

50. See the memorandum by Leland Harrison, 28 January 1927, in NA RG 59 800.51/558, and by A. N. Young, 21 March 1927, in NA RG 59 800.51/560.

51. Strong to Gilbert, 24 September with a postscript dated 29 September 1927, FRBNY, Strong Papers 1012.2, and Ruppel (Paris) to AA, 23 September 1927. Report of conversation with Gilbert, AA, WR-2A, vol. 2.

52. Telegram Gilbert to FRBNY, 24 September 1927, NA RG 39, box 85, file 743.2; Strong letter to Gilbert, 24 September 1927, FRBNY, Strong Papers 1012.2.

53. Kiep (Washington, D.C.) to AA, 26 September 1927, AA, WR-2A, vol. 2; memorandum by Castle, 26 September 1927, NA RG 59 862.51; letter, Strong to Gilbert, 24 September 1927; this section was written 29 September, FRBNY, Strong Papers 1012.2.

54. Letter, Strong to Gilbert, section written 24 September, pp. 6–7, FRBNY, Strong Papers 1012.2.

55. *Ibid.*, p. 7.

56. Kiep to AA, no. 1106, 24 October 1927, AA, WR-2A, vol. 2.

57. Strong to Norman, 18 October 1927, FRBNY, Strong Papers 1116.7; Lindsay to Chamberlain, 24 October 1927, DBFP, Series I A, vol. 4.

58. "Protokoll über die Sitzung des Zentralausschusses der Reichsbank," 4 October 1927, BA R43I/641.

59. Letter, Schacht to Strong, 15 October 1927, FRBNY, Germany 1924–28; Pierre Jay to Strong, 24 October 1927, FRBNY, Strong Papers 1012.3.

60. Note (unsigned), 7 October 1927, AA, WR-2A, vol. 2.

61. Chefbesprechung, 6 October 1927, BA R43I/656, pp. 291–292.

62. *Ibid.*, p. 298.

63. *Ibid.*, Köhler's interpretation of Schacht's remarks and RFM to State Secretary in Reich Chancellery, 4 October 1927.

64. *Ibid.*, Chefbesprechung, 6 October 1927; also Schäffer seems to have agreed that some greater control was needed. See Schäffer diary, 9 October 1927, 3:74.

65. Letter, Pünder to Adenauer, 10 October 1927, in HA Köln, 902-207-2. See also Upmeier, p. 166, in Hansmeyer, ed., *Kommunale Finanzpolitik.*

66. "Niederschrift über die Sitzung der Beratungsstelle." 11 October 1927, BA R2/2128.

67. Letter, Reich Labor Minister to RFM, 12 October 1927, BA R43I/656, p. 318; Upmeier, p. 167, in Hansmeyer, ed., *Kommunale Finanzpolitik.*

68. SPD memo on the Economy, 13 October 1927. *Verhandlungen des Reichstags,* Bd. 418 (Anlagen), no. 3650. Letter, Herle to Silverberg, 15 October 1927, BA, NL Silverberg 10.

69. Württembergische Bevollmachtigte zum Reichsrat to the Württembergisches Staatsministerium, 20 October 1927, report on meeting of the State Representatives with Köhler, Curtius, and Schacht, 19 October, in Stuttgart, E130b–1341; and Chefbesprechung, 6 October 1927, BA R43I/656.

70. "Niederschrift über die Sitzung der Beratungsstelle," 4 November 1927, BA R2/2128.

71. Lindsay to Chamberlain, 31 October 1927, PRO, FO-371/12141; Köhler remarks, "Protokoll der Ministerbesprechung," 24 October 1927; and letter Gilbert to RFM, copy to Reich Chancellor, 26 October 1927, BA R43I/176. The full text of Gilbert's memorandum is published in the *New York Times,* 6 November 1927, pp. 1 and 24.

72. Letter, Harrison to McGarrah, 11 November 1927, FRBNY, C261, German Government.

73. Memorandum by Stresemann of conversation with Gilbert, 6 October 1927, AA, SS-Ggil, 1:30–33.

74. Von Schubert conversation with Gilbert, 14 November 1927, AA, SS-Ggil, 1:34; Lindsay report on the Agent General's memo, 8 November 1927, PRO, FO-371/ 12141, partially reprinted in DBFP, Series I A, 4:82–84. Köhler tried to imply that he had asked for Gilbert's views in writing, but apparently it was Gilbert who took the initiative. See Lindsay to Chamberlain, 27 October 1927, in PRO, T-160/262 F10457, vol. 1.

75. Lindsay report, 8 November 1927, PRO, FO-371/12141; Jay to Strong, 13 November 1927, FRBNY, Strong Papers 1012.3.

76. Lindsay report, 8 November 1927, PRO, FO-371/12141. What Gilbert did not add and may not have known is that Luther had originally been hired to attack the Dawes Plan and act as "anti-reparations agent." See the remarkable collection on the formation and function of "Buro L" and Bundes zur Erneuerung des Reiches in HA GHH 400101293/15.

77. BA NL Silverberg 227, pp. 315–319, RDI aide-memoire, November or December 1927, report of meeting of RDI presidium, 18 November 1927.

78. Lindsay to FO, 11 November 1927, reports comments made by Gilbert to Finlayson, PRO, FO-371/12141. For further evidence of industry's opposition to city spending and support for Gilbert's criticisms, see Ludwig Kastl's address to RDI during conference of 2–3 September 1927 in *Geschäftliche Mitteilungen*, September 1927; and memorandum, unsigned but probably by Ritter, 2 November 1927, in AA, Ritter-Rep., vol. 3.

79. Reported in *New York Times*, 7 November 1927, p. 1.

80. Hilferding to the Reichstag, 3 December 1927, in *Ursachen und Folgen*, 6:239–241; on loan use see the records in BA R2/2128.

81. Letter, Association of Saxon Industrialists to RDI, 7 October 1927, BA, NL Silverberg 10.

82. Silverberg speech to RDI, 21 October 1927, BA, NL Silverberg 10.

83. Memorandum, Ritter to Stresemann, 21 October 1927, AA, RM5, vol. 21. Letter, Jacob Gould Schurman to Kellogg, 18 April 1928, Arthur N. Young Papers, Box 1, file "Reparation Developments, 1924, after the Dawes Plan." Karlowa said he had asked to be transferred to the Foreign Service because he was fed up with Finance Ministry incompetence. See notes by Finlayson, 11 November 1927, in PRO, T-160/ 262F 10457, vol. 2, and 7 December 1927, in vol. 3.

84. Letter, Stresemann to RFM and RWM, 17 November 1927, AA, Ritter-R. fin und Rbank, vol. 1; letter Schäffer (RWM) to AA, 26 November 1927, and Köhler to AA, 30 November 1927.

85. Memorandum, 22 November 1927, and note by Stresemann, 16 December 1927, BA R431/656, p. 401.

86. RFM to Reich Ministers, I22003, 1 November 1927, AA, Ritter-R. fin und Rbank, vol. 1. The support already had cost over 70 million RM.

87. Government's answer to Parker Gilbert, 5 November 1927, BA R2/3139.

88. Telegram AA to Germany embassies, W. Rep. 1714, 8 November 1927, AA, Ritter-Rep., vol. 3 and Lindsay report to FO, 8 November 1927, PRO, FO-371/12141.

89. "Aufzeichnung zu dem Bericht des Generalagenten," December 1927, written in January 1928, AA, WR-2A, vol. 3. See also Tyrrell to Lindsay, 17 November 1928, in DBFP, Series I A, 4:93. The increasingly bitter antagonism between Gilbert and Frederich Leith-Ross of the British Treasury can be followed in PRO, T-188/273.

90. Note by Ministerial Director de Haas, 18 November 1927, AA, SS-C, vol. 13, and the report of Luther's comments to a "small circle" of leading German industrialists in letter Sogemeier to Reusch, 29 October 1927. Sogemeier apparently

approvingly sent criticisms of Luther's view written by professor Schumacher. HA GHH 400101293/15.

91. Memorandum by Ritter, W. Rep. 1840/28, June 1928, AA, Ritter-Rep., vol. 5.

92. *Report of the Agent General,* 10 December 1927. Gilbert explained to Strong that ending transfer protection would be the key to restoring control over the German budget. Gilbert to Strong, 14 November 1927, NA RG 59 862.51.

93. Agent General for Reparations memorandum for the Reparation Commission, 24 February 1928, copy in AA, SS—Ggil, vol. 1.

94. Strong to Jay, 8 July 1927, FRBNY, Strong Papers 1012.3, and Strong to Gilbert, 13 September 1927, FRBNY, Strong Papers 1012.2.

95. Strong to Jay, 10 November 1927, FRBNY, Strong Papers 1012.3.

96. Telegram, Kiep (Washington, D.C.) to AA 24, 17 January 1928, in AA, WR-2A, vol. 3; also Link, *Stabilisierungspolitik,* pp. 411–418. Link argues that Strong was the original proponent of revision in order to protect American ability to continue to lend to Germany and protect past loans. Jon Jacobson, *Locarno Diplomacy,* p. 143, places the responsibility more directly on Gilbert but is not clear on Gilbert's motives. Melvyn Leffler, in *The Elusive Quest,* finds Gilbert the prime actor and the desire to protect American investments only one of several motives—the prime concern being rationalization of German fiscal policies (pp. 182–187).

97. Letter, Gilbert to Strong, 10 July 1928, FRBNY, Strong Papers 1012.2.

98. Harold James, "The Reichsbank and Public Finance," pp. 57–59.

99. Mellon made favorable remarks on Gilbert's December 1927 report but also firmly rejected any connection between reparations and war debts. Since the connection was so obvious to Germans, they were unable to understand what Mellon really wanted. See AA memorandum, 27 December 1928, AA, SS-Ggil, vol. 1.

100. Letter, Mellon to Hibbon, 5 March 1927, copy in AA, Ritter-Rep., vol. 2.

101. DBFP, Series I A, vol. 5. Lindsay conversation with Gilbert, 29 May 1928, pp. 78–82. Gilbert made similar comments to British financial adviser E. Rowe-Dutton, p. 57.

7. Twilight of the "Golden Years" 1928–29

1. This disillusionment with the results of DNVP participation in the government is explicitly expressed in a pamphlet issued by the Arbeitsausschuss Deutschnationaler Industrieller, "Zur Lage (Nr. 7)", December 1927, HA GHH 400101293/8b. See also the complaints filed by iron industry representatives over high wages, social costs, and public spending in a meeting with the Reichspräsident, November 1927, in BA R43I/1137, pp. 206–207. The growing determination of heavy industrialists to attack Weimar's wage and arbitration system is chronicled in Weisbrod, *Schwerindustrie,* pp. 333–363.

2. Note, 2 December 1927, and report, Embassy Washington, D.C., to Berlin, no. 444, 21 November 1927, AA, WR-2A, vol. 2.

3. AA, WR-2A, vol. 3, see the series of fliers by Harris, Forbes for internal information to salesmen about new bonds. The quote is from the flier dated 7 February 1928.

4. *Handelszeitung des Berliner Tageblatts,* 1 April 1928, and comment on this report, W. Rep. 828, 1 April 1928, in AA, WR-2A, vol. 3.

5. Dietrich-Tröltsch, "Kommunalkredit," pp. 1544–1548.

6. Foreign Ministry memo to German Embassy Washington, W. Rep. 412, 22 February 1928. AA, WR-2A, vol. 3, and note by de Haas, 10 January 1928, AA, SS-C, vol. 13.

7. "Aktenvermerk über die Sitzung des R.P.A.," 14 January 1928, by Ritter, in AA, WR-2A, vol. 3.

8. *Ibid.* That others in the German government were equally concerned that approval of all loans could undercut German reparations hopes is confirmed in a Foreign Office telegram to the German Embassy in Washington, W. Rep. 412, 22 February 1928.

9. BA R2/2128, remarks by Stephen of the Labor Ministry, minutes of the meeting of the Advisory Board, 18 January 1928, and meeting of the Advisory Board, 10 February 1928.

10. AA, WR-2A, vol. 3, letter Reichsbank directors I/931, 18 January 1928.

11. BA R431/635, minutes from the report of the Reichsbank president to the Reich government, 20 January 1928.

12. *Ibid.,* p. 210.

13. *Ibid.,* p. 217.

14. AA, SS-Ggil, vol. 1, meeting of Committee on Reparations, 22 February 1928.

15. *Ibid.*

16. AA, WR-2A, vol. 3, telegram AA to German Embassy Washington, D.C., W. Rep. 412, 22 February 1928.

17. *Ibid.*

18. BA R2/2128, minutes of the meeting of the Advisory Board, 18 January 1928, remarks by Norden and report by Prause. Public banks had loaned cities 240 million RM; private banks had loaned 211 million RM and the remaining 74 million was listed as "other."

19. AA, WR-2A, vol. 3, Stresemann remarks in W. Rep. 948, 18 April 1928.

20. Rowe-Dutton wrote Waley of the British Treasury that "the Advisory Board's refusal to grant new loans was causing loud municipal protests, especially as they are . . . being besieged by American bankers offering them favorable terms." Dutton to Waley, 22 March 1928. PRO, FO-371/12876.

21. Report on Cabinet meeting, 3 May 1928, in Hans Schäffer diary.

22. BA R2/2028, unsigned memo read and initialed by many Finance Ministry officials, 29 November 1929.

23. FRBNY, Strong Papers 1012.3, letter Jay to Strong, 20 May 1928.

24. AA, WR-2A, vol. 3, note, W. Rep. 1229, 23 May 1928.

25. *Ibid.,* Reich Finance Ministry memorandum, IC 3803, 16 April 1928.

26. Minutes of the report of the Reichsbank president to the Reich Government, 13 April 1928, 11 A.M. BA R431/635, p. 297. Pierre Jay also found it very encouraging that in spite of reduced municipal spending, unemployment was declining. FRBNY, Strong Papers 1012.3, letter Jay to Strong, 20 May 1928.

27. BA R431/635, p. 303.

28. PRO, FO-371/12876, memo by Rowe-Dutton of conversation with Schacht, 23 March 1928.

29. BA R2/2128, comments by President Schröder of the Seehandlung in minutes of the Advisory Board meeting, 18 January 1928.

30. Article by Freiherr von Richthofen (Md. R.), *Deutsche Tageszeitung,* 6 July 1928.

31. For negotiations on individual loans see BA R2/2128. The agreement on the total sum of the loans was reported in minutes of the Advisory Board, 3 May 1928, BA R2/2128, and in the prospectus of the "$17.5 million German consolidated municipal loan, 1 June 1928," BA R2/2013, p. 285. That a second part would be issued in the fall was confirmed by Reich Finance Ministry memorandum, IC 4651, 12 May 1928. AA, WR-2A, vol. 3.

32. Letter from Heinrich Maus, from the publishing house of the *Kölnische Volkszeitung* and the *Kölner Lokal-Anzeiger* to Adenauer, 25 June 1928. HA Köln, 902-207-2, p. 245.

33. BA R2/2142, letter Prussian Minister of Interior to RFM, 28 November 1927.

34. BA R2/2111, letter Reichsbank directors to the Advisory Board, 20 December 1927.

35. See letter from Norden to Prussian Minister of Interior, 23 December 1927, his reminder that he had still not received an answer on 2 February 1928; and letter Prussian Minister of the Interior to RFM, 22 February 1928, in BA R2/2111.

36. Kuczynski, *Deutsche Anleihen in Ausland*, p. 37.

37. BA R2/2142, memo Höth, 18 November 1928, and letter RFM to Prussian Minister of the Interior, 12 December 1928.

38. Beyond the cases already cited, Bremen, Hamburg, and Karlsruhe were reported, but the first two successfully argued that their loans really were only short-term. See RFM letter to Bremen, 13 August 1928; Bremen telegram to RFM, 2 October 1928, and RFM to Hamburg Senate, 23 October 1928, in BA R2/2142.

39. BA R2/4070. Reichsbank directors to RFM, 15 February 1932.

40. BA R2/4067, p. 38, note by Hülse, "Zur Frage der Aufnahme von Krediten im In- und Auslande durch die öffentliche Hand." Written in January or February 1930.

41. BA R2/1859, letter Krüger to Finance Minister, 15 January 1926.

42. Article by Dr. Görnandt in *Industrie und Handels Zeitung*, 16 June 1926, clipping in AA, WR-2A, vol. 1.

43. BA R43I/654, note by Grävell, "Betriff: Gründung einer Investment Company," 23 January 1926, and note by Pünder, 30 January 1926.

44. BA, NL Silverberg 300, "RDI Committee for Banking and Credit Questions," 3 June 1926.

45. BA R43I/655, "Niederschrift über die Besprechung vom 22 Marz 1926 über Kreditversorgung der Klein- und Mittelindustrie."

46. See, for example, references to the Saxon State Mortgage bank in the article by Dr. Rudolf Görnandt in *Industrie und Handels Zeitung*, 16 June 1926; support and criticism are voiced in the RDI Committee for Banking and Credit Questions, 17 October 1925, in BA, NL Silverberg 300. A more positive stand was taken at the meeting of 29 January 1926. Its success is reported in Krüger letter to RFM, 15 January 1926, in BA R2/1859.

47. BA R2/2005, letter Sächsische Landespfandbriefanstalt to RFM, 7 November 1925; and *Denkschrift*, in *Verhandlungen des Reichstags*, 1924/27, Band 413, no. 2897, p. 10.

48. RDI Committee for Banking and Credit Questions, meetings of 17 October 1925 and 29 January 1926. At least Bavaria and Thuringia hoped to create similar banks. BA, NL Silverberg 300.

49. BA R2/2136, letter Bayerische Vereinbank to RFM, 29 August 1927, and Gutachten der Beratungsstelle, 14 October 1927.

50. See Reichsverband der deutschen Industrie, Die Geschäftsführung an die Fachgruppen und landschaftlichen Verbände, etc., *Tagebuch,* no. 1741 III, 13 October 1927, and no. 1616 III, 14 September 1927, in HA Köln, 902–91:3; Die Geschäftsfuhrung of the RDI an die Fachgruppen, etc., *Tagebuch* no. 231 III, 13 February 1927, in BA NL Silverberg, vol. 301; and finally RDI *Geschäftliche Mitteilungen* no. 22, 2 October 1928.

51. This includes $9 million by the Saxon State Bank, $20 million by Bavaria, $20 million by the Bavarian Mortgage and Exchange Bank, $10 million by the Landesbankzentrale, and a $25 million loan by the Deutsche Bank intended for middle-sized industry. For use of this last loan see BA, NL Silverberg 81, p. 194, report from Deutsche Bank, September 1927.

52. Kuczynski, *American Loans to Germany,* pp. 56–59. There is some overlap as the Deutsche Bank loan is probably included by Kuczunski as part of the $147 million whereas the state bank loans cited above (n. 51) probably were not.

53. BA R2/2121, minutes of the Advisory Board, 4 July 1927; and RDI, *Geschäftliche Mitteilungen,* 7 March 1928, report no. 112, "Vorstandssitzung des Reichsverbandes am 24 Februar 1928," by Kastl.

54. Kuczynski, *Deutsche Anleihen 1924–29,* Rentenbank loans are reported on p. 85. Other loans are numbers 70, 73, 84, 94, and 108 as listed by Kuczynski.

55. Dieter Gessner, *Agrarverbände in der Weimarer Republik,* pp. 152 and 266.

56. F. C. von Zitzewitz-Kottow, "Kapitalbeschaffung, Zinsverbilligung, Entschuldung," in Fritz Beckman et al., eds. *Deutsche Agrarpolitik im Rahmen der innern und äusseren Wirtschaftspolitik,* 1:549. Cited by Robert Gates, "German Socialism and the Crisis of 1929–33."

57. Gessner, *Agrarverbände,* pp. 150–180; and Karl Hochdörffer, "Die staatlichen Subventionen der Nachkriegszeit in Deutschland," pp. 50–58 and 113–114. Hochdörffer estimated that total government help extended to agriculture came to 2 billion RM by 1929.

58. AA, SS-C, vol. 14, Ruppel (Paris) report to AA, 4 April 1928, of conversation with Gilbert.

59. AA, WR-2A, vol. 3, extract from the minutes of the Reich Ministers meeting, 3 May 1928.

60. *Ibid.,* unsigned note, 9 May 1928, W. Rep. 1109.

61. *Ibid.,* extract from the minutes of the Reich Ministers meeting, 3 May 1928.

62. BA R43I/657, pp. 106–107, letter Reich Labor Minister to SS in Reich Chancellery, 18 May 1928.

63. Protocols of the ministers discussions, 3 May and 24 May 1928, and letter RFM, 1 June 1928, in BA R43I/657.

64. Kuczynski, *Banker's Profits,* pp. 29–30.

65. These figures come up repeatedly in reports found in BA, NL Silverberg 362, pp. 156–166, 234–238, and 240–266.

66. Kuczynski, *Banker's Profits,* pp. 29–30.

67. Ritter to German Embassy Paris, WR 609, 24 December 1930. AA, Botschaft Washington, Fi3, 2:95.

68. "National Survey of Bond Market," results from a questionnaire sent out by Lawrence Stern and Company, September 1928. Copy in BA R2/2113.

69. Chandler, *Benjamin Strong, Central Banker,* p. 455.

70. See the memo by Grosvenor Jones to Hoover, 21 April 1928, commenting on Sprague's article, "Banker's Loans Dangerous—Reserve Bank Largely Responsible

for Inflation," *The Annalist,* 20 April 1928, in HHPL, Presidential Papers, Commerce Papers, OF Commerce, F. & D. C. Finance and Investment.

71. Chandler, p. 424.

72. *Berliner Tageblatt,* no. 358, 31 July 1928.

73. Kuczynski, *Deutsche Anleihen 1924-28,* pp. 36-37. The *Berliner Tageblatt* reported that in the first seven months of 1928, Germany borrowed 1,131 million RM abroad (no. 358, 31 July 1928). Chandler, p. 456, records that foreign loans taken in the United States in the last half of 1928 and first half of 1929 were only 65 percent of the volume taken in 1927 and this fell to one-third of the 1927 rate by the second half of 1929.

74. Clarke, *Central Bank Cooperation,* p. 149.

75. Clipping from *Financial News,* 25 October 1928, in BA R2/2142, p. 218, and Johannes Houwink Ten Cate, "Amsterdam als Finanzplatz Deutschlands 1919-1932."

76. Chandler, p. 456; Clarke, p. 148. In the year ending June 1928 $500 million in gold flowed out of the United States, while in the sixteen months ending in October 1929, $300 million flowed back into the United States.

77. *Berliner Tageblatt,* 31 July, 31 August, 30 September 1928.

78. BA R2/2130, minutes of the Advisory Board meeting, 13 November 1928; and BA R2/2002, p. 121, letter *Deutsche Städtetag* to RFM, 3 September 1928.

79. Letter Mainz Oberbürgermeister to Hessian Minister of Interior, 13 December 1929; remark by President Schröder of the Seehandlung, in minutes from the Advisory Board meeting, 7 January 1930. Also letter RFM to Hessian Minister of Interior, 13 January 1930. BA R2/2057.

80. *Berliner Tageblatt,* 31 January 1929.

81. The General Director of the State Bank of the Rhineland Province to members of the Board of Directors, 7 November 1928, in HA Köln, 902-91:3, p. 249.

82. Theodore Balderston, in "The Beginning of the Depression in Germany, 1927-30," notes that an inventory recession was made far more severe by capital shortages.

83. British Foreign Office officials also recognized that the interests of "Eastern bankers" were not necessarily the same as those of Morgan, the Federal Reserve Board, or the United States Treasury. DBFP, Series IA, 4:59.

84. DBFP, Series IA, 5:80.

85. AA, SS-Ggil, 1:43, memo of Schubert conversation with Schurman, 21 January 1928.

86. British Treasury Official Finlayson prepared a report pointing out the same German deficiencies as Gilbert. DBFP, Series IA, 4:121.

87. Hoesch (Paris) to AA, no. 1325, 22 December 1927, in AA, SS-C, vol. 13; and Schubert conversation with Gilbert, 18 August 1928, in AA, SS-Ggil, 1:174.

88. See the report from German Embassy Washington to AA no. 456, 3 April 1928, in AA, WR FV allg. 14 Am., vol. 12.

89. The plan is outlined in DBFP, Series IA, 5:358. It is commonly regarded as Gilbert's and the Americans' basic goal. See Link, *Stabilisierungspolitik,* pp. 416-433; Leffler, *The Elusive Quest,* p. 183; and Jacobson, *Locarno Diplomacy,* pp. 162-164. Leffler, unlike Link, believes that the plan was only tentative.

90. DBFP, Series IA, 5:196-200, and 362. Also Clarke, *Central Bank Cooperation,* p. 145.

91. The phrase is credited to Foreign Minister Austen Chamberlain. DBFP, Series IA, 4:354 and 350.

92. DBFP, Series IA, 5:79. Gilbert outlined his plans and at the same time admitted that the American market could not presently absorb large volumes of German bonds. See letter Gilbert to Mellon, 26 or 27 September 1928, in NA RG39, box 77, file G733C; also Leffingwell to Lamont, 22 October 1928, in Lamont Papers, 103-13.

93. FRBNY, Strong Papers 1012.2, Strong to Gilbert, 14 July 1928.

94. Link, *Stabilisierungspolitik*, pp. 448-449.

95. Schubert's analysis and uncertainty are reflected in his report and analysis of a conversation with Gilbert on 28 February 1928, and his recapitulation of events dated 12 November 1928, in AA, SS-Ggil., 1:95 and 220-235; see also memorandum dated 26 July 1928, pp. 150-152.

96. *Ibid.*, memorandum of Schubert's conversations with Gilbert, 27 July 1928, and 14 November 1928.

97. Ritter, "Aufzeichnung zu dem Bericht des Generalagenten, vom Juni 1928," W. Rep. 1840/28, in AA, Ritter-Rep., vol. 5.

98. BA NL Pünder no. 86, p. 2, memorandum by Dorn, April 1931. Also NL Pünder no. 68, p. 259, unsigned undated memorandum, probably by Pünder, in August 1928.

99. BA NL Pünder no. 86, pp. 44-46, memorandum, probably by Hans Schäffer, dated 9 April 1931.

100. AA, SS-C, vol. 13, note by Valletta, 27 December 1928.

101. Schäffer diary, vol. 4, 26 April 1928.

102. Memo by Rowe-Dutton of conversation with Schacht, 11 January 1928. PRO, FO-371/12875, Rowe-Dutton's underlining to show Schacht's emphasis.

103. Stresemann, in *His Diaries, Letters and Papers*, 3:413. Stresemann may have been referring to a report to President Coolidge by the American Bankers Association urging a low reparations settlement. Contents of the report are in German Foreign Ministry report, 22 October 1928, in AA, Ritter-Rep., vol. 6.

104. "Aktenvermerk über die Sitzung des R.P.A.," 14 January 1928, in AA, WR-2A, vol. 3.

105. Curtius remarks during "Bericht des Reichsbankpräsidenten . . . ," 7 February 1929, in *Akten der Reichskanzlei . . . Das Kabinett Müller II,* 1:426.

106. AA, SS-C, vol. 13, note by Valletta, 27 December 1928.

107. DBFP, Series IA, 4:219-220.

108. AA, SS-C, vol. 13, note by Valletta, 27 December 1928.

109. Strong had great respect for Leith-Ross and tried to mediate a growing feud between him and Gilbert as the differing views became more apparent. See Strong's letter to Gilbert, 3 March 1928, FRBNY, Strong Papers 1012.2. But, like Gilbert, he hoped (or wanted to believe) that a new, stable reparations agreement might avoid a crisis. See his letter to Gilbert, 27 March 1928. Gilbert's disagreement with the British view is expressed in his conversation with Schubert, 10 October 1928, in AA, Ritter-Rep., vol. 5.

110. PRO, T-188/273, Leith-Ross to Rowe-Dutton, 17 October 1928. In the same file, Leith-Ross to Dutton, 19 June 1928, reflects his anticipation of a crisis and the fatalistic assumption that reparations and war debts would be reduced only in the aftermath of a crisis.

111. Von Schubert conversations with Gilbert, 18 August, 1 October, and 14 November 1928, in AA, SS-Ggil, 1:174, 238, and 301. Lüke quite wrongly asserts that Gilbert attempted to play a double game of urging the French to reach a settlement before the German economy collapsed while urging the Germans to settle before their economy became so prosperous that higher demands would be made (*Von der Sta-*

bilisierung, p. 148). Link points out the error of Lüke's analysis (*Stabilisierungspolitik*, p. 431). Lüke's claim, however, is not entirely without foundation. In fact, Gilbert did argue in England that an arrangement should be made before the German economy became too prosperous. In this way, he tried to win British support for a settlement now on the grounds that it would be lower than a settlement later when Germany was even more prosperous. See the telegram from Dieckhoff (London) to AA no. 682, 19 October 1928, in AA RM5, vol. 22.

112. Stresemann conversation with Gilbert, 13 November 1928, AA, SS-Ggil, 1:249–250.

113. Schubert comments after a discussion with Gilbert, 14 November 1928, AA, SS-Ggil, 1:297; and Stresemann telegram to Berlin (AA), 30 November 1928, on p. 208.

114. In April 1928, Gilbert reportedly told a *Times* journalist that he had been offered a partnership in J. P. Morgan but wanted to finish up his job as Agent General before taking it. DBFP, Series IA, 4:348; Dieckhoff to AA, 19 October 1928, in AA, RM5, vol. 22; Frederick Leith-Ross, *Money Talks; Fifty Years of International Finance*, p. 102; and Leffler, *The Elusive Quest*, p. 183.

115. See Stresemann's comments on his discussion with Gilbert, 13 November 1928, *Stresemann, His Diaries, Letters and Papers*, 3:403–410.

116. Gilbert specifically informed Hilferding of these conditions on 25 October 1928, Aktenvermerk Ritter, 25 October 1928, in AA, Ritter-Rep., vol. 5. The basic terms of the agreement were reported to the German Foreign Ministry in Dieckhoff's telegram to the AA no. 697, 24 October 1928, in AA, RM5, vol. 21, and Gilbert's discussion with Müller is reported in telegram American Embassy Berlin to State Department, 26 October 1928, in NA RG 39, box 77, file G733C.

117. Besides the observation by Stresemann in his talk with Gilbert on 13 November 1928, Owen Young told Prittwitz that Germans should harbor no illusions about the size of payments and implied that he felt 2 billion RM was fair. Prittwitz telegram to AA, 14 November 1928, in AA, RM5, vol. 23. Morgan was rumored to favor a similar settlement. See Hoesch to AA, 3 April 1928, in AA, SS-C, vol. 14. Frederick Leith-Ross had also warned the Germans that the allies expected 2 billion marks, a sum which he felt could not be paid. He even warned them that once the experts began meeting, Germany would be trapped and forced to accept that sum. Leith-Ross discussion with Dieckhoff reported in Dieckhoff telegram to AA no. 682, 19 October 1928, in AA, Ritter-Rep., vol. 4.

118. AA, Ritter-Rep., vol. 6, table prepared by Ruppel given to Ritter and de Haas, 19 November 1928.

119. BA NL Pünder no. 86, p. 5, memorandum by Dorn written in April 1931. In the same file the memorandum probably by Hans Schäffer, 9 April 1931, reports Schacht's assurance that he could secure a low final settlement. Karl Ritter expressed German expectations that the end sum was still open to the expert's calculations in his telegram to German embassies, 3 November 1928, no. 373, in AA Botschaft Washington, Reparations (Dawes Plan V. 11).

120. PRO, FO-371/13592, memo by Thelwell, 12 January 1929.

121. AA, Ritter-Rep., vol. 6, unsigned, undated memo, probably by Ritter, written about 10 December 1928.

122. Telegram Herrick (France) to Kellogg, 3 March 1929. FRUS 1929, 2:1029–1034.

123. BA NL Pünder no. 86, p. 47, memorandum probably by Hans Schäffer, 9 April 1931.

124. Excellent and detailed discussions of Young Plan negotiations are contained in Jon Jacobson, *Locarno Diplomacy*, pp. 239–276; Leffler, *Elusive Quest;* and Link, *Stabilisierungspolitik.*

125. AA, RM5, vol. 24, Schacht letter to Stresemann, 16 February 1929.

126. *Akten der Reichskanzlei . . . Das Kabinett Müller II*, 1:555–556 and 585–586; telegram Stresemann to Washington embassy, no. 150, 25 April 1929, AA, Ritter-Rep., vol. 6; and Jacobson, *Locarno Diplomacy*, pp. 261–266.

127. NL Schäffer, Schäffer-Claussen correspondence, vol. 1, Claussen to Schäffer, 12 March 1929.

128. BA R431/277, p. 261.

129. *Akten der Reichskanzlei . . . Das Kabinett Müller II*, 1:588–589; and letter Müller to Schacht, 30 April 1928, pp. 606–607.

130. *Ibid.*, pp. 614–620, 627, 632–637.

131. Jacobson, *Locarno Diplomacy*, pp. 260 and 269–276.

132. *Akten der Reichskanzlei . . . Das Kabinett Müller II*, Reparations policy discussion, 18 May 1929, 1:660–661.

133. See Jacobson, *Locarno Diplomacy*, pp. 353–355.

134. Jacobson, *Locarno Diplomacy*, pp. 272–276; Link, *Stabilisierungspolitik*, pp. 469–477; and Leffler, *Elusive Quest*, p. 211.

135. *Akten der Reichskanzlei . . . Das Kabinett Müller II*, see statements by Stresemann, 1:616, Hilferding, pp. 621–622, and Curtius, p. 626.

136. Schäffer diary, 22 November 1929.

137. *Akten der Reichskanzlei . . . Das Kabinett Müller II*, 1:620.

138. Jacobson makes this point in *Locarno Diplomacy*, pp. 262–267.

139. *Akten der Reichskanzlei . . . Das Kabinett Müller II*, 1:570.

140. Jacobson, *Locarno Diplomacy*, conclusion.

8. The Loans, the State, and the Depression

1. Knut Borchardt, "Wachstum und Wechsellagen 1914–1970," pp. 704–705; and Carl Schmidt, *German Business Cycles*, pp. 47–50. The Reich Labor Ministry was fully aware that a crisis was brewing and that the cyclical downturn had begun in the spring of 1928 and was becoming worse. RAM to SS in the Reich Chancellery, 2 February 1929, in BA R431/2034, p. 20.

2. T. Balderston, "The Beginning of the Depression in Germany, 1927–30," pp. 395 and 402. Neither Balderston nor I would want to ignore the world-wide ramifications of the depression and the role that declining exports played after 1929. But in focusing on the origins of the depression in Germany and the ingredients that made the depression so severe in Germany, we both would argue that German domestic considerations are of primary importance. I, in contrast to Balderston, will argue that political considerations made the economic difficulties which he focuses on even more serious.

3. This is one of the major themes in Charles Kindleberger, *The World in Depression, 1929–1939*, see especially p. 292.

4. Harold James has recently argued that the Reichsbank was losing reserves even before Schacht's memorandum nearly ended the Reparations Conference. While it may be true that fear of a massive mobilization of the German debt lay behind the withdrawal of money from Germany, it is also apparently true that Schacht triggered the impending crisis with his memorandum. James cites Thomas Lamont to support

this view. See James, "The Reichsbank and Public Finance in Germany 1924–1933," pp. 72–76, especially p. 75, n. 68. The Reichsbank itself argued that its reserves were being drawn down as borrowers purchased foreign exchange rather than use the funds for business purposes. Reichsbank directors to RFM, 6 May 1929, and enclosed report of 4 May, in BA R2/2151.

    5. *Statistiches Jahrbuch für das Deutsche Reich,* 1929, pp. 334–335; 1930, pp. 378–379; and 1931, pp. 358–359. These data are for daily money rates. Monthly rates show the same trend, and it is clear that in this period as earlier, Reichsbank discount rates moved in response to market rates and did not lead market rates.

    6. Rudolf Stucken, *Deutsche Geld- und Kreditpolitik, 1914–1963,* pp. 82–83.

    7. See, for example, the remarks by Saxon Finance Minister Weber to the Cabinet in report of Reichsbank President Schacht to the Cabinet, 7 February 1929, AA, RM5, vol. 24.

    8. BA R2/2002, letter Board of Directors DST to RFM, 24 March 1928.

    9. *Ibid.,* letter Board of Directors Westphalian *Städtetag* to RFM, 31 October 1928. Also James, "The Reichsbank and Public Finance," pp. 99–100.

    10. Copy of speech prepared for either Konrad Adenauer or Cologne Treasurer Suth to be given 8 November 1932, HA Köln, 902-207-3, p. 999.

    11. Peter-Christian Witt, "Finanzpolitik als Verfassungs- und Gesellschaftspolitik." table 2, pp. 398 and 399.

    12. These statistics are taken from a report prepared by Reichsbank Director Hülse. Since the Reichsbank was particularly critical of municipal spending policies, there is every reason to assume that the report would not place the debt in any better light than necessary. Note by Hülse, "Zur Frage der Aufnahme von Krediten im In- und Auslande durch die öffentliche Hand." The report is undated but was probably prepared in January or February 1930, BA R2/4067, p. 27. At least one branch of the *Städtetag* asserted that municipal debt had risen more slowly since 1924 than prior to 1913. See the letter from the Board of Directors of the Westphalian *Städtetag* to the RFM, 13 October 1928, in BA R2/2002.

    13. Norden, head of the Advisory Board for Foreign Credit, expressed similar views in an interview in *Industrie- und Handelszeitung,* 15 October 1927. Reported in *European Economic and Political Survey* (Paris), 31 October 1927, pp. 90–93.

    14. Peter-Christian Witt, "Capitalist Resistance to the Economic Policies of the State in Germany 1918 to 1923," and "Finanzpolitik als Verfassungs- und Gesellschaftspolitik," p. 393 and table 2, p. 396; and Konrad Littman Speyer, "Der Staatsanteil am Sozialprodukt," p. 506.

    15. Balderston, "The Beginning of the Depression in Germany," pp. 401 and 409.

    16. J. D. Tomlinson, "Unemployment and Government Policy Between the Wars: A Note." Tomlinson's central argument is that this large share of national income gave the government an effective lever which it could have used to stimulate the British economy.

    17. BA R2/2128, report by O. R. R. Prause in minutes of the meeting of the Advisory Board, 18 January 1928. The Enquête-Ausschuss estimated the debt at only 468 million RM and agreed that this was mostly domestic. In notes on the meeting of the Reparations Policy Committee, 14 January 1928, AA, WR-2A, vol. 3. See also the letter from the Reich Finance Minister to Chairman of the Enquête-Ausschuss, 23 April 1929, which argues that city short-term debts were very small and a small share of all German short-term debt. Based on data from the *Städtetag* report of 1928 in BA R2/2002.

18. The report was carried in *Finanz- und Handelsblatt der Vossischen Zeitung,* 9 January 1928.

19. BA R2/2111, letter Norden to Saxon representative to the Reichsrat, 30 January 1928.

20. *New York Times* report dated 12 December 1931, sent to the German Foreign Ministry. In AA, Botschaft Washington Fi. 3, 2:23.

21. HA Köln, 902–207–2, letter Suth to Adenauer, 20 March 1928.

22. LA Berlin, DGT (Rep. 142) 2.8.5/2–2, letter Magistrat Landeshaupstadt Oldenburg to DST, 25 November 1927.

23. See the numerous meetings of the Advisory Board where this was a common practice, in BA R2/2128; and Rebentish, *Ludwig Landman,* pp. 195–197.

24. This and other facets of Advisory Board policy are discussed in Arthur Norden, "Die Beratungsstelle für Auslandskredite," and rejoinder by Robert Kuczynski, "Norden's Antwort," in *Finanzpolitische Korrespondenz,* 16 May 1928, and Oskar Mulert, *Die Bedeutung des Auslandskredites für die deutschen Gemeinden.*

25. BA R2/2128, minutes of the meeting of the Advisory Board, 9 December 1927.

26. Confidential "report on the extraordinary credits and spending approved by the Stadtverordnetenversammlung, but not yet definitely covered by loans as of 20 September 1928," HA Köln, 902–207–2, p. 297.

27. Speech by either Adenauer or City Treasurer Suth on 8 November 1932, HA Köln, 902–207–3, p. 999; see also telegram Adenauer to Minister Director Leyden of the Prussian Ministry of Interior, HA Köln, 902–207–2, p. 539.

28. F. H. Neuerbourg of the Commerz und Privat Bank Berlin to Bankers Trust Company, New York, 22 July 1929, in BA R111/209.

29. HA Köln, 902–207–2, p. 721, Adenauer to Dr. Brüning at the Deutsche Bank, 21 October 1929.

30. Letter Parker McComas (Paris) to Eric Archdeacon (Berlin), 12 September 1929, in BA R111/209.

31. McComas to Lippincott, 23 December 1929; and McComas to Eager (New York), 5 January 1930, in BA R111/209.

32. Telegram McComas to Eager, 5 January 1930 and McComas to Lippincott (New York), 23 December 1929, in BA R111/209.

33. HA Köln, 902–207–2, p. 777, letter August Adenauer to Konrad Adenauer, 22 November 1929; letter K. Adenauer to Wasserman (Deutsche Bank), 6 January 1930, p. 837; and memo to Adenauer, p. 857.

34. *Ibid.,* p. 949, "very confidential notes on the meeting of the Finance Committee on 28 February 1930."

35. HA Köln, 902–2–1, p. 15, letter Adenauer to Brüning, 22 December 1930.

36. HA Köln, 902–207–3, p. 489.

37. BA R111/209, *Berliner Börsencourier,* no. 281, 19 June 1931, and HA Köln, 902–207–3, p. 741, copy of letter Landesbank der Rheinprovinz to A. Schaaffhaus'schen Bankverein, 12 September 1931.

38. HA Köln, 902–207–3, p. 521. Of the city's 155.8 million RM short-term debt, 49 million RM was owed to publicly owned banks; 73 million RM to the "big banks"; 24.6 million RM to private banks; and 8.2 million RM to "others."

39. *Kölnische Volkszeitung,* 14 July 1929, no. 487, clipping in HA Köln, 902–207–2, p. 635.

40. The figures are from "minutes of the meeting of the Advisory Board, 11 December 1929," BA R2/2130. The city had long-term loans of 364 million RM,

communal businesses had borrowed another 246 million RM, and the city also had short-term domestic debts of 398 million RM. See the letter from the Oberpräsident der Provinz Brandenburg und von Berlin to the Minister in the Reich Finance Ministry, 7 December 1929, BA R2/2028. Also letters from Eric Archdeacon to McComas, 9 October 1929, and McComas to Stahle, 27 November 1929, in BA R111/200.

41. HA Köln, 902–207-2, p. 713, telegram Adenauer to Direktor Wassermann, Deutsche Bank, 17 October 1929, and letter Adenauer to Wassermann, 21 October 1929.

42. Circular Mülert to mayors dated 5 November 1929 and entitled "Kommunalkredit," BA R431/657, p. 312. Another note was sent a few weeks later also urging municipal frugality and warning mayors that short-term loans could no longer safely be taken in the expectation of later conversion into long-term loans. DST to member cities, 29 November 1929. BA R2/2002, p. 100.

43. See numerous newspaper clippings in BA R431/657, p. 304.

44. BA R431/657, pp. 302–303, unsigned note of comments by Adenauer, 1 November 1929; and BA R431/658, p. 77, unsigned note, 19 March 1930.

45. Both Balderston, "The Beginning of the Depression in Germany" and Witt, "Finanzpolitik als Verfassungs- und Gesellschaftspolitik," place heavy emphasis on the reduction of government spending on construction, but neither mentions the role of the savings and loans or explores the relationship between political and financial policies.

46. See unsigned note, 1 November 1929, BA R431/657, pp. 302–303, and "memo on the conversation between . . . Dr. Mülert and . . . Schacht," 25 November 1929, BA R2/4067, p. 49.

47. BA R2/2022, memorandum by Norden and Hosse, 24 July 1925.

48. Würtemberg representative in Munich to the state president et al., no. 153, 6 July 1925; Stuttgart, E130b–1340, "Vor allem um die drückenden kurzfristigen Verpflichtungen sich vom Halse zu schaffen."

49. BA R2/2022, notes on the meeting of the Advisory Board, 14 July 1926; letter Min. Rat. Sterner (Bavarian Finance Ministry) to Norden, 12 July 1926.

50. The Bavarian government's recognition that it had the responsibility to borrow funds to pay for make-work projects was also enthusiastically expressed by Ministerialrat Weigmann in late 1923 and supported by the Landstag members. See excerpt from the protocol of the Landstag committee, 29 November 1923, in BHsa/MA103743.

51. BA R2/2022, letter from Reich representative in Munich to Reich Chancellory, 21 July 1926.

52. Note by Norden, January 1927; letters from Reich representative in Munich to Reich Chancellery, 16 and 25 February 1927, in BA R2/2022.

53. Letter Bavarian Finance Minister to Advisory Board, 11 June 1927, letter Reich representative in Munich to Reich Chancellery, 4 June 1927; and Reich finance minister to Abteilung IV, 5 July 1927, in BA R2/2022.

54. Bavarian State Finance Minister to Advisory Board, 25 March 1928, BA R2/2022. The debt in the operating budget was RM 11.9 million in 1927 and RM 23.9 million in 1928. The capital budget debt was RM 86 million in 1927 and RM 30 million in 1928. The operating deficit continued at over 20 million RM in 1930. BHsa/MA101096, letter Bavarian state government to Reich Chancellor, 20 May 1930.

55. BA R2/2022, Aktenvermerk, Reich Finance Minister IC 1806, 20 February 1928; and Bavarian State Finance Ministry to Advisory Board, 25 March 1928.

56. Norden to State Secretary, 30 March 1928; letter President of Bavarian State Bank Wolf to Chairman of the Advisory Board, 3 April 1928; and notes on the meeting of the Advisory Board, 4 April 1928, BA R2/2022.

57. Note by Norden to State Secretary, 14 April 1928, BA R2/2022.

58. BA R43I/660, letter Lewinski to Reichskanzler, 9 December 1931, and Vermerk Pünder, 10 December 1931; BA R111/10, Bankers Trust Berlin to Bankers Trust New York, 1 September 1931; and telegram Stahl (Paris) to Bankers Trust New York, 5 September 1931. Also letter Stahl to Bankers Trust Vice President, E. S. Chappelear, 16 December 1931, in BA R111/214.

59. BA R43I/660 and 661. Robert Kuczynski wrote that no German bonds were in default as of 1932. This may have been true of German bond issues, but there were three borrowers unable to pay interest on short-term loans: Bavaria, Ruhrverband, and the Catholic Church. For Kuczynski's comment, see *Bankers' Profits*, p. 28.

60. BA R111/214, letter John A. Stahl to McComas (New York), 15 December 1931.

61. BA R43I/176, memo Reich Finance Minister to State Secretary in the Reich Chancellery, 1 November 1927.

62. BA, NL Koch-Weser 37, p. 127, Koch-Weser note, 15 March 1928.

63. BA R43I/878, pp. 361–365, RFM to SS in RK, 29 October 1928.

64. AA, RM5, vol. 24, Ritter (Berlin) to German Embassy Washington, no. 33, 21 January 1929.

65. Ministers' meeting of 22 April 1929. In *Akten . . . Müller II*, 1:578–580.

66. BA, NL Pünder 120, p. 88, memorandum, "Kassenlage des Reichs," 22 April 1929.

67. AA, SS-CF, vol. 16, app. 2, telegram Curtius (Berlin) to Prittwitz (Washington, D.C.), no. 398, 20 December 1929.

68. See the various discussions in *Akten . . . Müller II*, vol. 1; the issues were spelled out by Pünder in his note of 26 April 1929, on pp. 585–586; and the statement of RFM Hilferding to the Cabinet, in the minister's conference of 22 April 1929, p. 579.

69. *Ibid.*, "Vorlage einer Aufzeichnung des Staatssekretärs Popitz über die Kassenlage des Reichs durch Staatssekretär Pünder," 29 April 1929. Includes the report by Popitz dated 27 April, pp. 601–606.

70. Statistisches Reichsamt, Einzelschriften zur Statistik des Deutschen Reichs, no. 27, "Öffentlicher Kredit und Wirtschaftskrise," p. 18. This deficit is actually an underestimate since it does not include the debts of publicly owned corporations or guarantees of private loans for housing, agriculture, trade, and banking—a sum which from 1924 to 1929 may have totalled as much as 10 billion RM, p. 21.

71. *Akten . . . Müller II*, 1:585–586 and 601–606, see also the unsigned memo from the RFM dated 26 April 1929, "Vorschlag zur Regelung der Kassenlage," in BA Nachlass Pünder 120, p. 77.

72. *Akten . . . Müller II*, 1:578–579, comments by Hilferding in minister's conference of 22 April 1929.

73. BA R2/1997, letter Verband Deutscher öffentlichrechtlicher Kreditanstalten to RFM, 10 May 1929.

74. Negotiations are contained in BA R2/2151. See especially RFM to state representatives in the Reichsrat, 3 May 1929, and letters from the Reichsbank to RFM, 6 May and 8 May 1929.

75. Claussen to Schäffer, 15 April 1929, NL Schäffer, Schäffer-Claussen correspondence.

76. Letter Rudolf Breitscheid to Müller, 8 July 1929, in Ebert Stiftung—NL Müller-Mappe I.

77. BA R2/2450, contract dated 20 June 1929.

78. BA, NL Moldenhauer 3, pp. 7–8.

79. BA R2/2450, contract dated 20 June 1929.

80. AA, WR-2A, vol. 4, telegram Curtius to Prittwitz (Washington, D.C.), no. 398, 20 December 1929.

81. RFM to SS in RK, 27 August 1929, no. IB510 in Ebert Stiftung, NL Müller-Mappe II.

82. BA R431/2035, p. 104.

83. *Ibid.*, pp. 133–139, 190; p. 369; and pp. 219–220, party leaders meeting, 15 August 1929. Comment by Reich Minister of Agriculture.

84. Hilferding's apparent submissiveness to Popitz' expertise and leadership is asserted by Paul Moldenhauer, who became Economics Minister in November 1929 when Curtius moved to the Foreign Ministry upon Stresemann's death, and became Finance Minister when Hilferding was forced to resign in December. In BA, NL Moldenhauer 3, especially pp. 9 and 13. The continuing conflict between the two Social Democratic ministers can be traced in Reichskanzlei Vermerk, 22 August 1929, in BA R431/879, p. 438; RFM to SS in RK, 27 August 1929, in Ebert Stiftung, NL Müller-Mappe II; letter RFM to RAM, 31 August 1929, in BA R431/2036, p. 3; RFM letter to RAM, 4 November 1929, in BA R431/2037, p. 7.

85. AA, SS-CF, 16, app. 2, report of a conversation between Hilferding and Parker Gilbert, 25 October 1929.

86. *Ibid.*, report of conversation with Gilbert by (Schubert?), 29 October 1929.

87. AA, SS-Ggil, 3:10, secret telegram AA to Hoesch (Paris), no. 888, 19 November 1929.

88. Hoesch (Paris) to AA no. 1111, 14 November. AA, SS-CF, 16, app. 2.

89. AA, SS-Ggil, 3:10–19, secret telegram AA to Hoesch (Paris), no. 888, 19 November 1929; Schubert to Hoesch, 20 November 1929; AA, SS-CF, 16, app. 2, Schubert-Gilbert conversation, 23 November 1929; and Hoesch to AA, no. 1146, 21 November 1929.

90. PRO, FO-371/13631, Rumbold to FO, 27 December 1929.

91. See letter Rudolf Breitscheid to Müller, 8 July 1929, in Ebert Stiftung, NL Müller-Mappe I, in which Breitscheid reports Schacht's efforts to discredit SPD policies.

92. BA, NL Moldenhauer 3, pp. 7–9; the dinner meeting took place in late November 1929.

93. This story is recounted in BA, NL Koch-Weser 39, Vermerk, 28 November 1929, pp. 79–80. Bernhard Dernburg speculated that Schacht might have been drunk.

94. Vermerk SS. Pünder, 6 December 1929, in Ebert Stiftung, NL Müller-Mappe II.

95. BA, NL Moldenhauer 3, p. 9.

96. The discussion is in the Hans Schäffer diary, entry for 9 December 1929.

97. Party leaders conference, 14 December 1929, BA R431/2362, pp. 186–188.

98. Schäffer diary, entry for 12 December 1929. Most other German bankers also lined up to oppose Schacht and support the Reich government. See entry for 16 December. Hilferding remained more convinced of Schacht's passivity than he should have been. See his comment in the meeting of party leaders, 14 December 1929, in BA R431/2362, pp. 186–188.

99. *Akten . . . Müller II*, 2:1266–1267 and 1270–1272.

100. *Ibid.*, pp. 1270–1277.

101. *Ibid.,* p. 1275. "Wenn diese Hoffnung schwinde, sei es mit der Liquidität und der Wirtschaft dahin."

102. *Ibid.,* pp. 1274–1275.

103. *Ibid.*

104. *Ibid.,* p. 1276.

105. AA, SS-Ggil, 3:29, secret telegram AA to Botschaft Washington, D.C., no. 395, 17 December 1929.

106. *Ibid.,* telegram Hoesch to AA, no. 1260, 17 December 1929.

107. AA, SS-CF, 16, app. 2, Curtius telegram to Hoesch, no. 989, 18 December 1929.

108. BA, NL Moldenhauer 3, pp. 12–14.

109. BA R431/2362, Prittwitz to AA no. 588, 19 December 1929; AA, SS-Ggil, 3, Hoesch telegram to AA, no. 1260, 17 December 1929; and AA, SS-CF, 16, app. 2, Prittwitz (Washington, D.C.) to Schubert (AA), no. 572, 19 December 1929.

110. AA, SS-Ggil, 3:36–50, and 24–27.

111. AA, SS-Ggil, 3:50.

112. *Ibid.,* Prittwitz to AA, 19 December 1929, p. 55; and *Akten . . . Müller II,* 2:1283–1289.

113. BA R431/2362, p. 198.

114. *Akten . . . Müller II,* 2:1283–1289. Also BA, NL Moldenhauer 3.

115. *Akten . . . Müller II,* 2:1289–1291.

116. *Ibid.,* pp. 1292–1294, party leaders conference in the Reichstag, 19 December 1929, 3 P.M. and 5 P.M. Bruning (Center), Hass (DDP), and Leicht (BVP) immediately pledged their party's support while Breitscheid (SPD) and Zapf (DVP) had to consult their members.

117. AA, SS-CF, 16, app. 2, Schubert memo of telephone conversation with Hoesch (Paris), 19 December 1929, 2:15 P.M.; Curtius to Hoesch, no. 992, 19 December 1929. See also Erich Koch-Weser letter to Hamm, 24 December 1929, in which Koch-Weser notes that Schacht's action not only hurt Reich finances but also made any tax reduction in the foreseeable future very difficult. BA, NL Koch-Weser 39.

118. *Akten . . . Müller II,* 2:1297.

119. *Ibid.,* pp. 1297–1302, ministers conference, 21 December 1929, 15:00.

120. BA NL Moldenhauer 3, p. 19. Moldenhauer asserted that the two leading bureaucrats in the Economics Ministry, Trendelenburg and Schäffer, wanted to dump Popitz in order to renew relations with Schacht. In his diary, Schäffer writes that both he and Trendelenburg felt that Hilferding and Popitz had to be kept in office to help guide through the needed reforms. Schäffer asserts that Moldenhauer led the attack on Hilferding in order to win the job as Finance Minister for himself. Schäffer diary entry for 20 December 1929. See also *Akten . . . Müller II,* vol. 2, ministers conference, 21 December 1929, 15:00.

121. Memo on meeting of the leadership of the SPD Reichstag faction, 13 January 1930, probably by Müller, in Ebert Stiftung. NL, Müller-Mappe II, no. 329.

122. Harold James makes this point in "The Causes of the German Banking Crisis of 1931".

123. NL Müller-Mappe II, memo on meeting of 13 January 1930. These views are repeated in a memorandum by Müller dated 3 February 1930, in BA R431/962.

124. BA R431/962, p. 171. Notes on the party leaders conference of 27 January 1930. Comments by Zapf (DVP) and by Dernburg. See also the Economics Minister's disappointment when Schacht did not resign his post in January when the government forced the Reichsbank to participate in the new Bank for International Settlements

over Schacht's protest. Letter RWM to Reich Chancellor, 17 January 1930, in NL, Müller-Mappe II, no. 322.

125. Harold James, "The Reichsbank and Public Finance," pp. 113–115, makes this point very clearly. See also Schäffer diary entry for 11 December 1929.

126. See AA, SS-Ggil, 1:155. Gilbert's remarks to Schubert, 27 July 1928, and the discussion of Schacht's antics during the Hague negotiations, in notes on the party leaders conference, 27 January 1930, in BA R43I/637.

127. BA R43I/637, party leaders conference, 27 January 1930.

128. Schacht's claim of Morgan's support and Morgan's weak denial are contained in AA, SS-Ggil, vol. 4, telegram Curtius to Washington, 1 February 1930; Prittwitz (Washington) to Curtius, 4 February 1930, and von Schubert memorandum dated 15 February 1930, p. 44.

129. AA, SS-Ggil, 4:3.

130. *Ibid.*, p. 44.

131. Hardach, *Weltmarktorientierung*, pp. 106–107, and Wiesbrod, *Schwerindustrie*, pp. 273–298.

132. AA, SS-Ggil, 4:126.

133. BA R43I/637, minutes of a ministers' conference, 7 March 1930.

134. Helga Timm, *Die deutsche Sozialpolitik und der Bruch der Grossen Koalition im März 1930*, p. 190.

135. In view of the lessons learned from the crisis of December 1929, this position is not surprising. Studies that have noted this SPD support for deflationary policies, but have concentrated on the power of "orthodox" economic theory or reparations policy goals in shaping Brüning's policies include: Robert Gates, "German Socialism and the Crisis of 1929–33," pp. 335 and 342; George Garvy, "Keynes and the Economic Activists of Pre-Hitler Germany," p. 398; Wolfgang J. Helbich, "Between Stresemann and Hitler: The Foreign Policy of the Brüning Government," pp. 33 and 38–41; and Dietmar Petzina, "Elemente der Wirtschaftspolitik in der Spätphase der Weimarer Republik," pp. 128–129. Petzina and Knut Borchardt focus on structural weaknesses within the German economy as the source of the depression. Borchardt argues that the government did not foresee the seriousness of the depression in time to take preventative action and that it did not have the leverage to make a positive impact anyway. Knut Borchardt, "Zwangslagen und Handlungsspielräume."

136. Peter-Christian Witt has recently argued that the reduction in government spending in constant dollars was not very great from 1929–32. He emphasizes the disastrous effect of Brüning's policy of aiding agriculture and heavy industry while cutting funds for construction and finishing industry. Witt, "Finanzpolitik als Verfassung- und Gesellschaftspolitik," pp. 400–401.

Conclusion

1. See Gerald Feldman's discussion of Weimar's fatal weaknesses, "Weimar from Inflation to Depression, Experiment or Gamble?" especially p. 273 in Gerald Feldman, ed., *Nachwirkung des deutschen Inflation*.

2. This discussion draws on the literature examining corporatist social solutions in the Weimar period. I am inclined to think that the corporatist model implies more stability than one can find in Weimar. This is especially true in Charles Maier, *Recasting Bourgeois Europe*, pp. 513–515 and 592. Maier seems to back away from the assumption of stability in "The Two Postwar Eras and the Conditions for Stability in

20th Century Europe." Ulrich Nocken explores the conflicting corporatist solutions proposed in the Weimar period and tries to determine why they failed in the twenties and succeeded in the 1950s. Ulrich Nocken, "Interindustrial Conflicts and Alliances in the Weimar Republic: Experiments in Societal Corporatism", ch. 1; also available as "Corporatism and Pluralism in German History" in Dirk Stegmann et al., eds., *Industrielle Gesellschaft und politisches System.* David Abraham in *The Collapse of The Weimar Republic,* focuses on the conflict between heavy industry and the finishing industries but assumes greater coherence within groups and greater divisions between groups than that found by Bernd Weisbrod in *Schwerindustrie in der Weimarer Republik.*

3. The most comprehensive statement of this position with attacks on all aspects of government activity is the pamphlet by the RDI, "Aufstieg oder Neidergang?"

4. Stanley Hoffman, in his article "Paradoxes of the French Political Community," in Hoffman, et al., *In Search of France,* coined the term "stalemate society" referring to France in the interwar period. Hoffman emphasized France's rigid social structure which effectively preserved small business and an unproductive economy. This is, of course, almost a direct antithesis of German society in the 1920s when these same small businessmen were being ground up by the pressures of industrial concentration. Yet, in its own terms, the irresolution of Germany's social crisis can be, I think, most usefully described as a political stalemate, with no group being able to dominate all others and a general unwillingness to compromise with competitor groups.

Bibliography

I. Archival Sources in Germany
  A. Records from the German Foreign Ministry received by the Department of State (microfilm)
    1. Kabinettsprotokolle
    2. Records of the State Secretary for Foreign Affairs
  B. Bundesarchiv Koblenz (BA)
    1. Alte Reichskanzlei (R43I)
    2. Reichsfinanzministerium (R2)
    3. Deutscher Industrie- und Handelstag (R11)
    4. Verein Deutscher Eisen- und Stahlindustrieller (R131)
    5. Reichskanzlei (1933–1945) (R43II)
    6. Berliner Vertretung der Bankers Trust Company (R111)
    7. Liberale Partein (R45)
    8. Nachlässe
      a. Moritz J. Bonn
      b. Hermann Dietrich
      c. Ludwig Kastl
      d. Erich Koch-Weser
      e. Hans Luther
      f. Paul Moldenhauer
      g. Herman Pünder
      h. Friedrich Sämisch
      i. Paul Silverberg
  C. Politisches Archiv des Auswärtigen Amtes—Bonn (AA)

1. Büro Staatssekretär-von Schubert (SS)
   a. Aktenzeichen Ggil (Ggil)
   b. BaAllg-Allgemeine Wirtschaftsfragen (BaAllg)
   c. Die Reparationsfrage . . . C (C)
   d. Dillon Read Anleihe-Kassenkrise im Dez 1929 (CF)
2. Sonderreferat Wirtschaft (SW)
   a. Finanzwesen 2A (FW2A)
   b. Anleihen-Wertpapiere-Finanzwesen 2 (FW2)
3. Wirtschafts-Reparations (WR)
   a. Frage der Aufnahme deutscher Kredite im Auslande—2A (2A)
   b. Die 800 Mill-Anleihe und weitere deutsche Anleihen (14D)
   c. Friedensvertrag, Allg. 14 Amerika (FV Allg. 14 Am.)
4. Reichsminister (RM)
   a. Transfer Dawes-Young Anleihe 6.34
   b. Vereinigte Staaten von Nordamerika—27
   c. Finanzfragen—45
   d. Finanzen—RM16
   e. Reparation—5
5. Handakten K. Ritter
   a. Reparation—HaPol Ritter (Ritter-Rep)
   b. Reichsfinanzministerium und Reichsbank (Ritter-R.fin und Rbank)
   c. Amerika—The Chase National Bank (Ritter-Chase Nat. Bank)
6. Botschaft Washington
   a. Deutsche Anleihen 1922–23 (Fi3)
7. Geheimakten
   a. W6—Vereinigte Staaten. Wirtschaftliche Beziehungen zu Deutschland
D. Friedrich Ebert Stiftung—Bonn
   1. Nachlass Carl Severing
   2. Nachlass Hermann Müller
E. Institut der Deutschen Wirtschaft—Cologne
F. Institut für Zeitgeschichte—Munich
   1. Tagebuch Hans Schäffer
   2. Classen—Schäffer Schriftwechsel
G. Historisches Archiv der Stadt Köln (HA Köln)
   1. Büro des Oberbürgermeisters Konrad Adenauer (902)
   2. Beigeordneter Wilhelm Suth (901)
H. Landesarchiv Berlin (LA)
   1. Deutscher Städtetag (DST)
   2. Gruppe B—Sachakten der ehemaligen Kommunalen Spitzenver-bände
   3. D.G.T. (Rep. 142)
I. Hauptstaatsarchiv Stuttgart (Hsa Stuttgart)
   1. Staatsministerium (E130b)
   2. Ministeriums des Innern (E151dI)

   J. Archiv der August Thyssen-Hütte AG—Duisberg
1. Amerika Anleihe (A1)
2. Anleihen (CCa-54)
3. Abg. Finanzen II (CCa-138)
   K. Historisches Archiv der Gutehoffnungshütte AG, Oberhausen (HA GHH)
   L. Bayerisches Hauptstaatsarchiv—Munich (BHsa)
1. Min. Äussern (MA)
2. Finanz Ministerium (MF)
3. Min. Wirtschaft (MW)
   M. Siemens Archiv—Munich (SAA)
1. NL Max Haller

II. Archival Sources in the United States
   A. Federal Reserve Bank of New York (FRBNY)
1. C261
2. Germany 1924–28
3. Germany 1929–31
4. Benjamin Strong Papers
5. United States 1926
6. Directors A-P, 320.121
   B. Arthur N. Young Papers, Hoover Institution, Stanford University, Stanford, Calif.
   C. National Archives, Washington, D.C. (NA)
1. Bureau of Accounts (Treasury), Record Group 39
2. General Records of the Department of State, Record Group 59
3. Records of the Bureau of Foreign and Domestic Commerce, Record Group 151
   D. Herbert Hoover Papers, Herbert Hoover Presidential Library, West Branch, Iowa, (HHPL) (from photocopies provided by Professor Richard Abrams)
   E. Thomas Lamont Papers, Baker Library, Cambridge, Mass.

III. Archival Sources in Great Britain
   A. Public Records Office, Kew Gardens, London (PRO)
1. Foreign Office General Correspondence, Political (FO-371)
2. Treasury Papers
     a. Finance (T-160)
     b. Neimeyer papers (T-176)
     c. Leith-Ross papers (T-188)

IV. Published Government Documents
Akten der Reichskanzlei, Weimarer Republik, Die Kabinette Luther I und II.
   Boppard: 1977. Karl-Heinze Minuth, ed.
Akten der Reichskanzlei, Weimarer Republik, Die Kabinette Marx I und II.
   Boppard: 1973. Günter Abramowski, ed.
Akten der Reichskanzlei, Weimarer Republik, Das Kabinett Müller II. Boppard:
   1970. Martin Vogt, ed.

Akten zur deutschen auswärtigen Politik 1918–1945, aus dem Archiv des Deutschen Auswärtigen Amts. Series B. Göttingen: 1966.

Ausschuss zur Untersuchung der Erzeugungs- und Absatzbedingungen der deutschen Wirtschaft: Die Reichsbank (cited as Enquête-Ausschuss, *Die Reichsbank*). Berlin: 1929.

Allied Powers Reparations Committion, "Transfer Committee Economic Service Notes" (typescript). 1925–1929.

Documents on British Foreign Policy 1919–1939, Series I-A (cited as DBFP) *Documents on British Foreign Policy 1919–1939,* Second Series.

Kapitalbildung und Investitionen in Deutschland 1924–1928, Vierteljahreshefte zur Konjunkturforschung, Sonderheft 22. Berlin: 1931.

Papers relating to the Foreign Relations of the United States (FRUS) *Verwaltungsbericht,* Reichsbank. Berlin: 1927–1940.

The Economic Development of Germany, Reichskreditgesellschaft. Berlin: various dates.

Report of the Agent-General for Reparation Payments. London: 1925–1930.

Monatliche Nachweise über den auswärtigen Handel Deutschlands, Statistisches Reichsamt. Berlin: 1925–1932.

Offentlicher Kredit und Wirtschaftskrise, Einzelschriften zur Statistik des Deutschen Reichs Nr. 27, Statistisches Reichsamt. Berlin: 1933.

Die öffentliche Verschuldung im Deutschen Reich am 31 März 1928 und am 31 Dezember 1929, Einzelschriften zur Statistik des Deutschen Reichs Nr. 13, Statistisches Reichsamt. Berlin: 1930.

Statistisches Jahrbuch für das Deutsche Reich, Statistisches Reichsamt. Berlin: 1924–1932.

Wirtschaft und Statistik, Statistisches Reichsamt. Berlin.

United States Senate Committee on Finance: *Hearings pursuant to Senate Resolution 19 on the Sale of Foreign Bonds and Securities in the United States,* Parts 1–4. Washington, D.C.: 1931 and 1932.

Ursachen und Folgen. Vom deutschen Zusammenbruch 1918 und 1945 bis zur staatlichen Neuordnung Deutschlands in der Gegenwart, Vol. 6. Berlin.

Verhandlungen des Reichstags, III Wahlperiode. 1924.

Vierteljahreshefte zur Statistik des Deutschen Reichs.

V. Newspapers and Journals

Berliner Tageblatt.

The Chase Economic Bulletin, 1925–1931. Issued by Chase National Bank of New York.

The Commercial and Financial Chronicle.

Deutsche Bergwerks-Zeitung.

Deutsche Tageszeitung.

Der Deutsche Volkswirt.

The Economist.

European Economic and Political Survey. Paris.

Kuczynski, Robert, ed. *Finanzpolitische Korrespondenz.*

Frankfurter Zeitung.

Journal of Commerce.

Kreuz-Zeitung.

The New York Times.

Vossische Zeitung.

VI. **Books and Articles**

Abraham, David. *The Collapse of the Weimar Republic: Political Economy and Crisis.* Princeton: Princeton University Press, 1981.

Abrams, Richard. "United States Intervention Abroad: The First Quarter Century." *American Historical Review* (1974), vol. 79.

Adler, Selig. *The Uncertain Giant: 1921–1941, American Foreign Policy between the Wars.* New York: Macmillan, 1965.

Angell, James W. *The Recovery of Germany.* New Haven: Yale University Press, 1929.

Balderston, Theodore. "The Beginning of the Depression in Germany, 1927–30: Investment and the Capital Market." *Economic History Review* (August 1983), 2d Series, vol. 36, no. 3.

—— "The Origins of Economic Instability in Germany 1924–1930. Market Forces versus Economic Policy." *Vierteljahrschrift für Sozial- und Wirtschaftsgeschichte* (1982), 69 Band, Heft 4.

Barber, Clarence L. "On the Origins of the Great Depression." *Southern Economic Journal* (1978), vol. 44.

Barkin, K. D. "Organized Capitalism. A Review Article." *Journal of Modern History* (1975), vol. 47.

Bell, Laird. "Report of Laird Bell to the Foreign Bondholders' Protective Council on the German Dollar Bond Situation and German Debt Conference of January, 1934." Typescript.

Bennett, Edward W. *Germany and the Diplomacy of the Financial Crisis, 1931.* Cambridge: Harvard University Press, 1962.

Bergmann, Carl. *The History of Reparations.* Boston and New York: Houghton Mifflin, 1927.

Best, Gary Dean. *The Politics of American Individualism: Herbert Hoover in Transition, 1918–1921.* Westport, Conn.: Greenwood, 1975.

Blaich, Fritz. "Garantierter Kapitalismus: Subventionspolitik und Wirtschaftsordnung in Deutschland zwischen 1925 und 1932." *Zeitschrift für Unternehmensgeschichte* (1977). 22 Jahrgang, Heft 1.

—— *Die Wirtschaftskrise 1925/26 und die Reichsregierung: Von der Erwerbslosenfürsorge zur Konjunkturpolitik.* Kallmünz: Michael Lassleben, 1977.

Bloomfield, Arthur I. *Short-Term Capital Movements Under the Pre-1914 Gold Standard.* Princeton Studies in International Finance No. 11. Princeton: Princeton University Press, 1963.

Böhret, Carl. *Aktionen gegen die "Kalte Sozialisierung," 1926–1930: ein Beitrag zum Wirken ökonomischer Einflussverbände in der Weimarer Republik.* Berlin: Duncker and Humblot, 1966.

Böse, Dr. Franz, ed. *Wandlungen des Kapitalismus: Auslandsanleihen. Kredit und Konjunktur.* Verhandlungen des Vereins für Sozialpolitik in Zürich

13 bis 15 September 1928. Schriften des Vereins für Sozialpolitik Band 175. Munich and Leipzig: Dunker and Humblot, 1929.

Borchardt, Knut. "Wachstum und Wechsellagen, 1914–1970." *Handbuch der deutschen Wirtschafts- und Sozialgeschichte.* Hermann Aubin and Wolfgang Zorn, eds. Stuttgart: Union Verlag, 1976.

—— "Zwangslagen und Handlungsspielräume in der grossen Wirtschaftskrise der frühen dreissiger Jahre: zur Revision des überlieferten Geschichtsbildes." *Jahrbuch der Bayerischen Akademie der Wissenschaften,* 1979.

Born, Karl Erich. *Die deutsche Bankenkrise, 1931: Finanzen und Politik.* Munich: Piper, 1967.

Brady, Robert A. *The Rationalization Movement in German Industry: A Study in the Evolution of Economic Planning.* New York: Fertig, 1933.

Brandes, Joseph. *Herbert Hoover and Economic Diplomacy: Department of Commerce Policy, 1921–1928.* Pittsburgh: University of Pittsburgh Press, 1962.

Braun, Otto. *Von Weimar zu Hitler.* New York: Europe Verlag, 1940.

Bresciani-Turroni, Constantino. *The Economics of Inflation: A Study of Currency Depreciation in Post-War Germany, 1914–1923.* London: Allen and Unwin, 1937.

Brooks, John. *Once in Galconda: A True Drama of Wall Street, 1920–1938.* New York: Harper and Row, 1969.

Büttner, Ursula. *Hamburg in der Staats- und Wirtschaftskrise, 1928–1931.* Hamburg: Hans Christians Verlag, 1982.

Carosso, Vincent P. *Investment Banking in America: A History.* Cambridge, Mass.: Harvard University Press, 1970.

Cassel, Gustav. "Deutschlands Kapitalwirtschaft." Wirtschaftbericht der Commerz - und Privat - Bank A.G. Hamburg and Berlin: 1928.

Chandler, Lester V. *Benjamin Strong Central Banker.* Washington, D.C.: Brookings Institution, 1958.

Childers, Thomas. *The Nazi Voter: The Social Foundations of Fascism in Germany, 1919–1933.* Chapel Hill and London: University of North Carolina Press, 1983.

Clarke, Stephen V. O. *Central Bank Cooperation, 1924–1931.* New York: Federal Reserve Bank of New York, 1967.

Cooper, R. N., ed. *International Finance.* Baltimore: Penguin, 1969.

Costigliola, Frank. "The United States and the Reconstruction of Germany in the 1920's." *Business History Review* (Winter 1976).

Curtius, Julius. *Sechs Jahre Minister der deutschen Republik.* Heidelberg: Carl Winter Universitäts Verlag, 1948.

Dawes, Rufus C. *The Dawes Plan in the Making.* Indianapolis: Bobbs-Merrill, 1925.

Deutschen Industrie- und Handelstages, Die Verantwortung des Unternehmers in der Selbstverwaltung. Frankfurt am Main: 1961.

Diehl, James M. *Paramilitary Politics in Weimar Germany.* Bloomington and London: Indiana University Press, 1977.

Dietrich-Tröltsch, Hermann. "Kommunalkredit, Reparationen und Föderalistisches Prinzip: Ein Beitrag zur Geschichte der Weimarer Zeit." Dissertation, Mainz, 1970.

Eckes, Alfred E. "Open Door Expansionism Reconsidered: The World War II Experience." *Journal of American History* (March 1973).

Edwards, George W. "Government Control of Foreign Investments." *American Economic Review* (December 1928).

Engeli, Christian. *Gustav Böss Oberbürgermeister von Berlin, 1921 bis 1930.* Schriftenreihe des Vereins für Kommunalwissenschaften e.v. Berlin, Band 31. Stuttgart: W. Kohlhammer, 1971.

Falkus, M. E. "The German Business Cycle in the 1920's." *Economic History Review* (August 1975).

Feis, Herbert. *The Diplomacy of the Dollar: First Era, 1919–1932.* Baltimore: Johns Hopkins University Press, 1950.

Feldman, Gerald D. *Iron and Steel in the German Inflation, 1916–1923.* Princeton: Princeton University Press, 1977.

——— "The Large Firm in the German Industrial System: The M.A.N., 1900–1925." In Dirk Stegmann, Bernd-Jürgen Wendt, and Peter-Christian Witt, eds., *Industrielle Gesellschaft und politisches System.* Bonn: 1978.

——— "The Social and Economic Policies of German Big Business, 1918–1929." *American Historical Review* (1969), vol. 75.

Feldman, Gerald D., ed. *Nachwirkung des deutschen Inflation.* forthcoming.

Feldman, Gerald D., Carl-Ludwig Holtfrerich, Gerhard A. Ritter, and Peter-Christian Witt, eds., *Die deutsche Inflation: The German Inflation.* Berlin: de Gruyter, 1982.

Felix, David. "Reparations Reconsidered with a Vengeance." *Central European History* (June 1971).

——— *Walter Rathenau and the Weimar Republic: The Politics of Reparations.* Baltimore: Johns Hopkins University Press, 1971.

Fischer, Wolfram. *Deutsche Wirtschaftspolitik 1918–1945.* Opladen: Leske, 1968.

Fleisig, Heywood. "War-Related Debts and the Great Depression." *American Economic Review* (1976), vol. 66.

Ford, A. G. *The Gold Standard 1880–1914: Britain and Argentina.* Oxford: Clarendon Press, 1962.

Friedman, Milton and Anna Jacobson Schwartz. *A Monetary History of the United States, 1867–1960.* Princeton: Princeton University Press, 1963.

Galbraith, John Kenneth. *The Great Crash.* Boston: Houghton Mifflin, 1961.

Garvy, George. "Keynes and the Economic Activists of Pre-Hitler Germany." *Journal of Political Economy* (1975), vol. 83.

Gates, Robert A. "German Socialism and the Crisis of 1929–33." *Central European History* (December 1974).

Gerschenkron, Alexander. *Bread and Democracy in Germany.* Berkeley: University of California Press, 1943.

Gessner, Dieter. *Agrarverbände in der Weimarer Republik: Wirtschaftliche und soziale Voraussetzungen agrarkonservativer Politik vor 1933.* Düsseldorf: Droste, 1976.

Grathwol, Robert. *Stresemann and the DNVP: Reconciliation or Revenge in German Foreign Policy, 1924–1928.* Lawrence: University of Kansas Press, 1980.

Haas, Rudolf, Ernst Knacke, and Knut Borchardt. *100 Jahre Rheinische Hypothekenbank.* Frankfurt am Main: Fritz Knapp, 1971.

Habedank, Heinz. *Die Reichsbank in der Weimarer Republic.* Berlin: Akademie Verlag, 1981.

Hahn, L. Albert. *Aufgaben und Grenzen der Währungspolitik: Eine Kritik der deutschen Währungspolitik seit der Stabilisierung.* Jena: Gustav Fischer, 1928.

Hansmeyer, Karl-Heinrich, ed. *Kommunale Finanzpolitik in der Weimarer Republik.* Stuttgart: Kohlhammer, 1973.

Hardach, Gerd. "Reichsbankpolitik und Wirtschaftliche Entwicklung, 1924–1931." *Schmollers Jahrbuch für Wirtschafts und Sozialwissenschaften* (1970).

—— *Weltmarktorientierung und relative Stagnation: Währungspolitik in Deutschland, 1924–1931.* Berlin: Dunker and Humblot, 1976.

Harris, C. R. S. *Germany's Foreign Indebtedness.* London: Oxford University Press, 1935.

Hawley, Ellis W. *The Great War and the Search for a Modern Order: A History of the American People and Their Institutions, 1917–1933.* New York: St. Martin, 1979.

Helbich, Wolfgang J. "Between Stresemann and Hitler: The Foreign Policy of the Brüning Government." *World Politics* (1959), vol. 12.

Hertz-Eichenrode, Dieter. *Wirtschaftskrise und Arbeitsbeschaffung Konjunkturpolitik 1925/26 und die Grundlagen der Krisenpolitik Brünings.* Frankfurt am Main: Campus Verlag, 1982.

Hildebrand, Klaus. *The Foreign Policy of the Third Reich.* Berkeley: University of California Press, 1974.

Hochdörfer, Karl. "Die staatlichen Subventionen der Nachkriegszeit in Deutschland." Dissertation, Köln, 1929.

Hoffmann, Stanley. "Paradoxes of the French Political Community." In Stanley Hoffmann et al., *In Search of France.* Cambridge: Harvard University Press, 1963.

Hoffmann, Walther. *Das Wachstum der deutschen Wirtschaft seit der Mitte des 19. Jahrhunderts.* Berlin: Springer Verlag, 1965.

Hofmann, Wolfgang. *Zwischen Rathaus und Reichskanzlei.* Stuttgart: Kohlhammer, 1974.

Hogan, Michael J. *Informal Entente: The Private Structure of Cooperation in Anglo-American Economic Diplomacy, 1918–1928.* Columbia: University of Missouri Press, 1977.

Holtfrerich, Carl-Ludwig. "Amerikanischer Kapitalexport und Wiederaufbau der deutschen Wirtschaft 1919–23 im Vergleich zu 1924–29." *Viertel-*

Jahrschrift für Sozial- und Wirtschaftsgeschichte (1977). 64. Band, Heft 4.

—— *Die deutsche Inflation 1914–23: Ursachen und Folgen in internationaler Perspektive.* Berlin: de Gruyter, 1980.

—— "Internationale Verteilungsfolgen der deutschen Inflation 1918–1923." *Kyklos* (1977), Fasc. 4.

Hoover, Herbert. *The Memoirs of Herbert Hoover.* 3 vols. New York: Macmillan, 1952.

Huthmacher, J. Joseph and Warren I. Susman, eds. *Herbert Hoover and the Crisis of American Capitalism.* Cambridge, Mass.: Schenkman, 1973.

Institute of International Finance. "Credit Position of Germany." Bulletin No. 19 (1928).

Iverson, Carl. *Aspects of the Theory of International Capital Movements.* Copenhagen: Levin and Munksgaard, 1935.

Jacobson, Jon. *Locarno Diplomacy, Germany and the West 1925–1929.* Princeton: Princeton University Press, 1972.

—— "Is there a New International History of the 1920's?" *American Historical Review* (June 1983), vol. 88, no. 3.

James, Harold. "The Causes of the German Banking Crisis of 1931." *Economic History Review* (February 1984), 2d series, vol. 37, no. 1.

—— "Did the Reichsbank Draw the Right Conclusions from the Great Inflation?" Paper presented at Kolloquim des Historischen Kollegs, München 1983, *Die Nachwirkungen der Inflation auf die deutsche Geschichte, 1924–1933.*

—— "The Reichsbank and Public Finance in Germany, 1924–1933." Dissertation, Cambridge University, 1982.

Johnson, Harry G. *The Problem of International Monetary Reform.* London: Athlone Press, 1974.

Jones, Kenneth Paul. "Discord and Collaboration: Choosing an Agent General for Reparations." *Diplomatic History* (Spring 1977).

Keynes, J. M. *The Economic Consequences of the Peace.* London: Macmillan, 1919.

—— "The German Transfer Problem." *The Economic Journal* (1929), vol. 39.

Kindleberger, Charles. *The World in Depression, 1929–1939.* Berkeley and Los Angeles: University of California Press, 1973.

Klein, Julius. "When Germany Pays in Kind—What Does it Mean to Your Profits." *The Magazine of Business* (December 1927).

Klöter, Heidegret. "Der Anteil der Länder an der Wirtschaftspolitik der Weimarer Republik 1919–1933." Dissertation, Bonn, 1967.

Kocka, Jürgen. "Theoretical Approaches to the Social and Economic History of Modern Germany: Some Recent Trends, Concepts and Problems in Western and Eastern Germany." *Journal of Modern History* (March 1975).

Köhler, Heinrich. *Lebenserinnerungen des Politikers und Staatsmannes 1878–1949.* Stuttgart: Kohlhammer, 1964.

Krohn, Claus-Dieter. *Stabilisierung und ökonomische Interessen: Die Finanzpolitik des Deutschen Reiches 1923–1927*. Düsseldorf: Bertelsmann, 1974.

Krüger, Peter. *Deutschland und die Reparationen 1918/19*. Stuttgart: Deutsche Verlags-Anstalt, 1973.

—— "Das Reparationsproblem der Weimarer Republik in Fragwürdiger Sicht." *Vierteljahrshefte für Zeitgeschichte* (January 1981), 29, 1 Heft.

Kuczynski, Robert. *American Loans to Germany*. New York: Macmillan, 1927.

—— "American Loans to Germany." Harris Foundation Lectures, 1928. *Foreign Investments*. Chicago: 1928.

—— *Bankers Profits from German Loans*. Washington, D.C.: Brookings Institution, 1932.

—— *Deutsche Anleihen in Ausland, 1924–1928*. Washington, D. C., and Berlin: Institute of Economics, 1929.

League of Nations, (Ragner Nurkse). *International Currency Experience— Lessons of the Inter-War Period*. Geneva: 1944.

Leffler, Melvyn. *The Elusive Quest: America's Pursuit of European Stability and French Security, 1919–1933*. Chapel Hill: University of North Carolina Press, 1979.

—— "The Origins of Republican War Debt Policy, 1921–1923: A Case Study in the Applicability of the Open Door Interpretation." *Journal of American History* (1972), vol. 59.

—— "Political Isolationism, Economic Expansionism, or Diplomatic Realism: American Policy toward Western Europe, 1921–1933." *Perspectives in American History* (1974).

Leith-Ross, Frederick. *Money Talks: Fifty Years of International Finance*. London: Hutchinson, 1968.

Leuchtenberg, William E. *The Perils of Prosperity, 1914–1932*. Chicago: University of Chicago Press, 1958.

Lewis, Cleona. *America's Stake in International Investments*. Washington, D.C.: Brookings Institution, 1938.

—— *The United States and Foreign Investment Problems*. Washington, D.C.: Brookings Institution, 1948.

Link, Werner. *Die amerikanische Stabilisierungspolitik in Deutschland, 1921–1932*. Düsseldorf: Droste, 1970.

Lüke, Rolf. *Von der Stabilisierung zur Krise*. Zurich: Polygraphischer Verlag A. G., 1958.

Luther, Hans. *Politiker ohne Partei*. Stuttgart: Deutsche Verlag-Anstalt, 1960.

Machlup, Fritz. *International Payments, Debt, and Gold: Collected Essays by Fritz Machlup*. New York: Scribner's, 1964.

—— *The Stock Market, Credit, and Capital Formation*. New York: Macmillan, 1940.

Madden, John, Marcus Nadler, and Harry C. Sauvain. *America's Experience as a Creditor Nation*. New York: Prentice-Hall, 1937.

Maier, Charles S. "Between Taylorism and Technocracy: European Ideologies and the Vision of Industrial Productivity in the 1920's." *Journal of Contemporary History* (April 1970).

—— *Recasting Bourgeois Europe: Stabilization in France, Germany, and Italy in the Decade After World War I.* Princeton: Princeton University Press, 1975.

—— "The Truth About the Treaties." *Journal of Modern History* (1979), vol. 51.

—— "The Two Postwar Eras and the Conditions for Stability in 20th Century Europe." *American Historical Review* (1981).

—— "The Vulnerabilities of Inter-War Germany." *Journal of Modern History* (March 1984).

Mantoux, Etienne. *The Carthaginian Peace or the Economic Consequences of Mr. Keynes.* New York: Scribner's, 1952.

Marks, Sally. "Reparations Reconsidered: A reminder." *Central European History* (December 1969).

—— "The Myths of Reparations." *Central European History* (September 1978).

McDougall, Walter A. *France's Rhineland Diplomacy, 1914–1924: The Last Bid for a Balance of Power in Europe.* Princeton: Princeton University Press, 1978.

McKinnon, Ronald I. *Money and Capital in Economic Development.* Washington, D.C.: Brookings Institution, 1973.

Meier, Gerald M. *International Trade and Development.* New York: Harper and Row, 1963.

Menderhausen, Horst. *Two Postwar Recoveries of the German Economy.* Amsterdam: North-Holland, 1955.

Metcalf, Evan B. "Secretary Hoover and the Emergence of Macroeconomic Management." *Business History Review* (1975), vol. 69.

Mikesell, Raymond. *United States Economic Policy and International Relations.* New York: McGraw-Hill, 1952.

Mikesell, Raymond, ed. *U. S. Private and Government Investment Abroad.* Eugene: University of Oregon Books, 1962.

Mintz, Ilse. *Deterioration in the Quality of Foreign Bonds Issued in the United States, 1920–1930.* New York: National Bureau of Economic Research, 1951.

Moggridge, D. E. *The Return to Gold, 1925: The Formulation of Economic Policy and its Critics.* Cambridge: Cambridge University Press, 1969.

Mommsen, Hans, Dietmar Petzina, and Bernd Weisbrod, eds. *Industrielles System und politische Entwicklung in der Weimarer Republik.* Düsseldorf: Droste Verlag, 1974.

Moulton, H. G. and C. E. McGuire. *Germany's Capacity to Pay.* New York and London: McGraw-Hill, 1923.

Müller, Helmut. *Die Zentralbank—eine Nebenregierung: Reichsbankpräsident Hjalmar Schacht als Politiker der Weimarer Republik.* Schriften zur politischen Wirtschafts- und Gesellschaftslehre, Band 5. Opladen: Westdeutscher Verlag, 1973.

Mulert, Oskar. *Die Bedeutung des Auslandskredites für die deutschen Gemeinden.* Munich: Duncker and Humblot, 1928.

Netzband, Karl-Bernhard and Hans Peter Widmaier. *Währungs- und Finanzpolitik der Ära Luther, 1923–1925.* Basel: Kyklos Verlag, 1964.

Newman, William J. *The Balance of Power in the Interwar Years, 1919–1939.* New York: Random House, 1968.

Nochen, Ulrich. "Interindustrial Conflicts and Alliances in the Weimar Republic: Experiments in Societal Corporatism." Dissertation, University of California, Berkeley, 1979.

Norden, Arthur. "Die Beratungsstelle für Auslandskredite." *Wirtschaftsdienst* (April 1928).

Northrop, Mildred. *Control Policies of the Reichsbank, 1924–1933.* New York: Columbia University Press, 1938.

Ohlin, Bertil. "The Reparations Problem: A Discussion." *The Economic Journal* (1929), vol. 154.

Parrini, Carl. *Heir to Empire: United States Economic Diplomacy, 1916–1923.* Pittsburgh: University of Pittsburgh Press, 1969.

Pedersen, Jørgen. "Some Notes on the Economic Policy of the United States during the Period 1919–1932." In Hugo Hegeland, ed., *Money, Growth, and Methodology, and Other Essays in Economics.* Lund: Gleerup (Lund Social Science Studies 20), 1961.

Pentzlin, Heinz. *Hjalmar Schacht: Leben und Wirken einer umstrittenen Personlichkeit.* Berlin: Ullstein Verlag, 1980.

Petzina, Dietmar. "Elemente der Wirtschaftspolitik in der Spätphase der Weimarer Republik." *Vierteljahrshefte für Zeitgeschichte* (1973), Heft 21.

Pfitzner, Johannes. *Deutschlands Auslandsanleihen.* Berlin: Carl Heymanns Verlag, 1928.

Pohl, Karl Heinrich. "Die Finanzkrise bei Krupp and die Sicherheitspolitik Stresemanns—Ein Beitrag zum Verhältnis von Wirtschaft und Aussenpolitik in der Weimarer Republik." *Vierteljahrschrift für Sozial und Wirtschaftsgeschichte* (1974), Heft 61.

Pollard, Sidney, ed. *The Gold Standard and Employment Policies between the Wars.* London: Methuen, 1970.

Rebentisch, Dieter. *Ludwig Landmann: Frankfurter Oberbürgermeister der Weimarer Republik.* Wiesbaden: Steiner Verlag, 1975.

Reichsverband der deutschen Industrie (RDI). *Aufstieg oder Niedergang?* Ein Denkschrift des Präsidiums (1929), No. 49.

—— *Deutsche Wirtschafts- und Finanzpolitik.* Berlin: 1925.

—— *Geschäftliche Mitteilungen.* Available in Institut der deutschen Wirtschaft-Köln.

Rhodes, Benjamin D. "Reassessing Uncle Shylock: The United States and the French War Debt." *Journal of American History* (1969) vol. 55.

Rupieper, Hermann J. *The Cuno Government and Reparations, 1922–1923: Politics and Economics.* The Hague: Martinus Nijhoff, 1979.

Salin, Edgar. *Das Reparationsproblem:* Teil I. *Verhandlungen und Gutachten der Konferenz von Pyrmont.* Berlin: Reimar Hobbing, 1929.

Sanmann, Horst. "Daten und Alternativen der deutschen Wirtschafts- und Finanzpolitik in der Ara Brüning." *Hamburger Jahrbuch fur Wirtschafts- und Gesellschaftspolitik* (1965).

Sayers, R.S. *The Bank of England, 1891–1944.* 3 vols. Cambridge, London, New York: Cambridge University Press, 1976.

Schacht, Hjalmar. *Account Settled.* London: Weidenfeld and Nicolson, 1949.

—— Confessions of "The Old Wizard." Boston: Houghton-Mifflin, 1956.

—— *The End of Reparations.* New York: Cape and Smith, 1931.

—— *The Magic of Money.* London: Oldsbourne, 1967.

—— *The Stabilization of the Mark.* London: Ayer, 1927.

Schmidt, Carl T. *German Business Cycles 1924–1933.* New York: National Bureau of Economic Research, 1934.

Schmitter, Philippe C. "Still the Century of Corporatism?" In Fredrik B. Pike and Thomas Stritch, eds., *The New Corporatism.* Notre Dame, Ind., and London: University of Notre Dame Press, 1974.

Schön, Lother. *Studien zur Entwicklung hydroelektrischer Energienützung: Die Elektrifizierung Irlands.* Düsseldorf: VDI-Verlag, 1979.

Schröder, Hans-Jurgen. *Deutschland und die Vereinigten Staaten 1933–1939.* Wiesbaden: Franz-Steiner Verlag, 1970.

Schuker, Stephen A. *The End of French Predominance in Europe: The Financial Crisis of 1924 and the Adoption of the Dawes Plan.* Chapel Hill: University of North Carolina Press, 1976.

Schulze, Hagen. *Otto Braun: oder, Preussens demokratische Sendung: Eine Biographie.* Frankfurt am Main, Berlin, Vienna: Propylaen, 1977.

Schumpeter, Joseph. *Business Cycles.* 2 vols. New York and London: McGraw-Hill, 1939.

Seidenzahl, Fritz. *100 Jahre Deutsche Bank, 1870–1970.* Frankfurt am Main: Deutsche Bank Aktiengesellschaft, 1970.

Schackle, G. L. S. *The Years of High Theory: Invention and Tradition in Economic Thought, 1926–1939.* Cambridge: Cambridge University Press, 1967.

Silverberg, Paul. *Reden und Schriften,* Franz Mariaux, ed. Cologne: Kölner Universitäts Verlag, 1951.

Simpson, Amos E. *Hjalmar Schacht in Perspective.* The Hague: Mouton, 1969.

Skaupy, W. "Die Bereinigung deutscher Dollarbonds in den Vereinigten Staaten." *Der Betriebs Berater* (1954), Heft 15.

Smith, Robert Freeman. *The United States and Revolutionary Nationalism in Mexico, 1916–1932.* Chicago: University of Chicago Press, 1974.

Sobel, Robert. *Herbert Hoover at the Onset of the Great Depression 1929–1930.* Philadelphia: Lippincott, 1975.

Speyer, Konrad Littman. "Der Staatsanteil am Sozialprodukt." In Carl Christian von Weizsacher, ed., *Staat und Wirtschaft*. Berlin: Schriften des Vereins für Sozialpolitik, NF 102, 1979.

Stambrook, F. G. " 'Das Kind'—Lord D'Abernon and the Origins of the Locarno Pact." *Central European History* (1968), vol. 1.

Stegmann, Dirk, Bernd-Jürgen Wendt, and Peter-Christian Witt, eds. *Industrielle Gesellschaft und politisches System*. Bonn: Verlag Neue Gesellschaft, 1978.

Stegmann, Dirk. "Zum Verhältnis von Grossindustrie und Nationalsozialismus 1930–1933. Ein Beitrag zur Geschichte der sog. Machtergreifung." *Archiv für Sozialgeschichte* (1973), Heft 13.

Steinborn, Peter. *Grundlagen und Grundzüge: Münchener Kommunalpolitik in den Jahren der Weimarer Republik*. Munich: Neue Schriftenreihe des Stadtarchivs München, Bd. 21, 1968.

Stigler, George J. *Essays in the History of Economics*. Chicago: University of Chicago Press, 1965.

Stolper, Gustav. *German Economy, 1870–1940: Issues and Trends*. New York: Reynal and Hitchcock, 1940.

Stoneman, William E. *A History of the Economic Analysis of the Great Depression in America*. New York: Garland Publishing, 1979.

Stresemann, Gustav. *Gustav Stresemann: His Diaries, Letters and Papers*. Eric Sutton, ed. and trans. New York: Macmillan, 1940.

Stucken, Rudolf. *Deutsche Geld- und Kreditpolitik, 1914–1963*. Tübingen: Mohr, 1964.

Stürmer, Michael. *Koalition und Opposition in der Weimarer Republik, 1924–1928*. Düsseldorf: Droste, 1967.

Svennilson, Ingvar. *Growth and Stagnation in the European Economy*. Geneva: United Nations Economic Commission for Europe, 1954.

Temin, Peter. "The Beginning of the Depression in Germany." *Economic History Review* (1971), vol. 24.

—— *Did Monetary Forces Cause the Great Depression?* New York: Norton, 1976.

Ten Cate, Johannes Houwink. "Amsterdam als Finanzplatz Deutschlands 1919–1932." Paper delivered at the Volkswagen Conference on the Interwar Economy, Berlin, December, 1983.

Timm, Helga. *Die deutsche Sozialpolitik und der Bruch der Grossen Koalition im März 1930*. Düsseldorf: Droste, 1952.

Tomlinson, J.D. "Unemployment and Government Policy between the Wars: A Note." *Journal of Contemporary History* (1978), vol. 13.

Trachtenberg, Marc. *Reparation in World Politics: France and European Economic Diplomacy, 1916–1923*. New York: Columbia University Press, 1980.

Tretheway, Richard J. "International Economics and Politics: A Theoretical Framework." In Robert A. Bauer, ed., *The Interaction of Economics and Foreign Policy*. Charlottesville: University Press of Virginia, 1975.

Treviranis, Gottfried R. *Das Ende von Weimar, Heinrich Brüning und seine Zeit.* Düsseldorf: Econ-Verlag, 1968.

Triffin, Robert. *Our International Monetary System.* New York: Random House, 1968.

Turner, Henry Ashby, Jr. "Big Business and the Rise of Hitler." *American Historical Review* (1969), vol. 75.

—— *Stresemann and the Politics of the Weimar Republic.* Princeton: Princeton University Press, 1963.

Waller, Ernst. *Studien zur Finanzgeschichte des Hauses Siemens, 5 Teil, 1918-1945.* In Siemens Archiv, Munich, 1960.

Wandel, Eckard. *Die Bedeutung der Vereinigten Staaten von Amerika für das deutsche Reparationsproblem 1924-1929.* Tübingen: Mohr, 1971.

Warburg, Max M. *Aus Meinen Aufzeichnungen.* New York: 1952.

Weber, Alfred. *Hat Schacht Recht? Die Abhängigkeit der deutschen Volkswirtschaft vom Ausland.* Munich and Leipzig: Duncker and Humblot, 1928.

Weill-Raynal, Etienne. *Les Réparations allemandes et la France.* 3 vols. Paris: Nouvelles Editions Latines, 1947.

Weisbrod, Bernd. *Schwerindustrie in der Weimarer Republik: Interessenpolitik zwischen Stabilisierung und Krise.* Wuppertal: Peter Hammer Verlag, 1978.

Welter, Erich. *Die Ursachen des Kapitalmangels in Deutschland.* Tübingen: Mohr, 1931.

Williams, William Appleman. *The Roots of the Modern American Empire.* New York: Random House, 1969.

—— *The Tragedy of American Diplomacy.* New York: Dell, 1962.

Williamson, John G. *Karl Helfferich 1872-1924: Economist, Financier, Politician.* Princeton: Princeton University Press, 1971.

Wilson, Joan Hoff. *American Business and Foreign Policy 1920-1933.* Lexington: University Press of Kentucky, 1971.

Winch, Donald. *Economics and Policy, a Historical Study.* London: Hodder and Stoughton, 1969.

Winkler, Heinrich A. "German Society, Hitler and the Illusion of Restoration 1930-1933." *Jouranal of Contemporary History* (1976), vol. 11.

Winkler, Heinrich A., ed. *Organisierter Kapitalismus.* Göttingen: Vandenhoeck and Ruprecht, 1974.

Witt, Peter-Christian. "Capitalist Resistance to the Economic Policies of the State in Germany 1918-1923. Paper presented at the American Historical Association meetings, December 1979, New York.

—— "Finanzpolitik als Verfassungs- und Gesellschaftspolitik. Überlegungen zur Finanzpolitik des deutschen Reiches 1929-32." *Geschichte und Gesellschaft* (1982), 9 Jahrgang, Heft 2.

—— "Konservatismus als 'Überparteilichkeit.' Die Beamten der Reichskanzlei zwischen Kaiserreich und Weimarer Republik 1900-1933." In Dirk Stegmann et al., eds., *Deutscher Konservatismus im 19. und 20. Jahrhundert.* Bonn: Neue Gesellschaft, 1983.

—— "Reichsfinanzminister und Reichsfinanzverwaltung, 1918–1924." *Vierteljahrshefte für Zeitgeschichte* (1975), 23 Jahrgang.

Würm, Clemens A. "Interalliierte Schulden, Reparationen—Sicherheit/Abrüstung: Die Kriegsschuldenfrage in den britisch-französichen Beziehungen 1924–1929." In Gustav Schmidt ed., *Konstellationen Internationaler Politik 1924–1932.* Bochum: Brokmeyer, 1983.

Yeager, Leland B. *International Monetary Relations: Theory, History, and Policy.* New York: Harper and Row, 1966.

Ziebill, Otto. *Geschichte des deutschen Städtetages: Fünfzig Jahre deutsche Kommunalpolitik.* Stuttgart: Kohlhammer Verlag, 1955.

Index